Management for Professionals

For further volumes:
http://www.springer.com/series/10101

Douglas M. Walker

Casinonomics

The Socioeconomic Impacts
of the Casino Industry

 Springer

Douglas M. Walker
Department of Economics & Finance
College of Charleston
Charleston, SC, USA

ISSN 2192-8096　　　　　　　　ISSN 2192-810X (electronic)
ISBN 978-1-4614-7122-6　　　　ISBN 978-1-4614-7123-3 (eBook)
DOI 10.1007/978-1-4614-7123-3
Springer New York Heidelberg Dordrecht London

Library of Congress Control Number: 2013936718

© Springer Science+Business Media New York 2013
This work is subject to copyright. All rights are reserved by the Publisher, whether the whole or part of the material is concerned, specifically the rights of translation, reprinting, reuse of illustrations, recitation, broadcasting, reproduction on microfilms or in any other physical way, and transmission or information storage and retrieval, electronic adaptation, computer software, or by similar or dissimilar methodology now known or hereafter developed. Exempted from this legal reservation are brief excerpts in connection with reviews or scholarly analysis or material supplied specifically for the purpose of being entered and executed on a computer system, for exclusive use by the purchaser of the work. Duplication of this publication or parts thereof is permitted only under the provisions of the Copyright Law of the Publisher's location, in its current version, and permission for use must always be obtained from Springer. Permissions for use may be obtained through RightsLink at the Copyright Clearance Center. Violations are liable to prosecution under the respective Copyright Law.
The use of general descriptive names, registered names, trademarks, service marks, etc. in this publication does not imply, even in the absence of a specific statement, that such names are exempt from the relevant protective laws and regulations and therefore free for general use.
While the advice and information in this book are believed to be true and accurate at the date of publication, neither the authors nor the editors nor the publisher can accept any legal responsibility for any errors or omissions that may be made. The publisher makes no warranty, express or implied, with respect to the material contained herein.

Printed on acid-free paper

Springer is part of Springer Science+Business Media (www.springer.com)

For Keegan. Don't be afraid to take risks. "You can't win if you don't play."

Preface

The casino industry has seen dramatic expansion over the past two decades. But this expansion is not without controversy and debate. There has been an increase in the frequency of articles on the casino industry appearing in economics journals, and there is now even a journal dedicated to economic and business issues surrounding gambling. There continues to be, however, few economists who consistently do research on the economic and social impacts of gambling.

Despite the increased research attention given to the casino industry, there still seems to be few comprehensive resources for economists, other researchers, and the general public interested in the casino industry. I hope that this book provides such a resource. This volume contains much more material than my 2007 book, yet the focus is narrower. While the 2007 book examined concepts and theories with some supporting empirical evidence, this book puts substantially more emphasis on empirical studies, and the conceptual and theoretical issues are more engrained in those empirical discussions.

Importantly, almost all of the analysis contained in this book focuses on commercial casinos. Although tribal casinos and racetrack casinos are important components of the overall U.S. casino industry, tribal casino data are not publicly available, and racetrack casinos are relatively small in many states. For these reasons, I focus almost entirely on the commercial casino industry.

Legalized casinos are still a controversial public policy. Therefore, I make a sincere attempt to acknowledge other perspectives and to alert the reader to specific areas of debate. To be sure, there is disagreement even among economists about the effects of casino gambling. These areas of debate receive a significant amount of attention throughout the book. It is left to the reader to decide which perspectives seem most reasonable and convincing based on the available empirical evidence. My hope is that this volume will provide an informative, interesting, and even controversial discussion of the economic impacts of the casino industry.

This is an economics book but the fundamental concepts needed to understand much of the analysis in the book are outlined in the Appendix. I recommend that non-economists read the appendix first.

The book is organized into four parts. Part I examines some of the alleged economic benefits of casinos. These include economic growth, tax revenues, and consumer benefits. The first several chapters provide a general discussion of these benefits. This is followed by empirical evidence on the relationship between the casino industry and economic growth. In Chap. 7 we examine the effects of legalized gambling on state tax revenues. The analysis suggests that casinos tend to have a positive impact on economic growth, at least at a state level. Interestingly, however, the empirical evidence indicates that casinos have a slightly negative or no effect on state tax revenues, on net.

Part II focuses on behaviors typically associated with "disordered" gambling. In Chap. 9 we perform a county-level analysis of the effect of casinos on drunk driving fatalities. In Chaps. 10 and 11 we utilize a nationally representative survey of adolescents to analyze the relationship between gambling behavior and a variety of other behaviors, including crime, binge drinking, drug use, and hiring prostitutes. While some of these same issues have been addressed by psychologists and other social scientists, what makes these chapters unique is that they address the issues using a standard economic empirical framework. Even still, we find results similar to psychologists and medical researchers.

Part III is on the negative social and economic impacts of gambling. Part III arguably includes the most important material in the book, with respect to political and academic debate over casinos. We begin by addressing a key problem in the literature and political debate over casinos: the definition and measurement of "social cost." After addressing the definitional and measurement issues of social costs in general, the next several chapters focus on specific impacts typically associated with casinos: crime, whether gambling is an unproductive activity, and how it affects other businesses.

Part IV includes only one chapter. In Chap. 20 I first describe my perception of how the "economics of gambling" field has developed over the past two decades. Then I discuss topics that I believe will be increasingly important for research attention in the near future.

The first three parts of the book cover benefits (Part I) and costs (Parts II and III). The chapters are placed into a particular part of the book based on the common perception about the costs and benefits of the casino industry. For example, Chap. 7 discusses the impact of legalized gambling on state tax receipts. Although the empirical analysis finds that casinos have a negative impact on state tax revenues, the chapter is in Part I because most people expect casino taxes to be a benefit from the industry. Likewise, most observers are concerned with the "substitution effect" of casinos (i.e., the increased competition for other businesses). Chapter 17, which examines the effect of casinos on commercial property values—and finds that casinos have a positive impact on commercial property values—is in Part III because people consider this substitution effect to be a significant cost of casino legalization. So the chapters in Part I cover topics which people will expect to be benefits of casinos. Parts II and III include chapters on topics which people expect to be costs of casinos.

Preface   ix

Some of the material in the book is rather technical. However, I have edited the material in a way that should be accessible to most readers. Readers can usually skip econometric discussions without much loss in understanding, as I make an effort to explain and interpret technical material for the reader. The most technical material is probably in Chaps. 7 and 18. Readers who wish to completely avoid technical discussions can focus on the introductions and conclusions of those chapters.

The empirical work included in the book is based on data from the United States. Obviously other markets are also interesting and important. Although these other markets are not examined in this book, the analyses included here could be applied to other countries and markets. It is my hope that other researchers can find the work in this volume helpful in adapting similar research to other casino markets.

Much of the content of this book is based on my coauthored articles published in academic journals. As a result, the reader will notice that I often write "we" instead of "I" in describing the analysis. So, although the book is published under a single author's name, it is the product of working with several other people over the years. In particular, I wish to thank John Jackson and Andy Barnett for their contributions. Our collaborations when I was in graduate school are what really launched my career in research on gambling economics. John Jackson and I have been writing on casino economics for 15 years now. Other coauthors whose contributions are included in this book are Chris Clark, Chad Cotti, Lia Nower, and Jon Wiley. I am grateful to all of these people for their contributions to this book, and I alone am responsible for any errors in this volume.

My editor at Springer is Jon Gurstelle. I am grateful to Jon for his advice, guidance, and patience during this project. Clancy Bryant provided good feedback on an early draft of the book, and I am thankful to Wes Akers and Russell Sobel, who took time to proofread the manuscript and provided many good suggestions for improving it.

I would like to express my deepest gratitude to my friend and mentor, Bill Eadington, who passed away early in 2013. Bill was the pioneer of the gambling studies field. Despite his absence, his contributions to the field will live on through his influence on the work of others.

Finally, this book would not be possible without the permission to use research previously published in academic journals. I acknowledge the following publishers for their permission to use material included in this book: De Gruyter and Company (*Journal of Business Valuation and Economic Loss Analysis*); Digital Scholarship@ UNLV (*UNLV Gaming Research & Review Journal*); Elsevier (*Journal of Health Economics*); Emerald (*International Journal of Social Economics*); Sage (*Public Finance Review*); Springer (*Public Choice, Journal of Gambling Studies, Journal of Real Estate Finance and Economics*); Taylor & Francis (*International Gambling Studies*); and John Wiley & Sons (*American Journal of Economics and Sociology, Contemporary Economic Policy*).

Douglas M. Walker

Contents

1 Introduction 1
   1.1 Overview of the Commercial Casino Industry 2

Part I Economic Benefits from Commercial Casinos

2 Casinos and Economic Growth 9
   2.1 A Simple Model of Economic Growth 11
   2.2 Increased Employment and Wages 12
   2.3 Capital Inflow 13
   2.4 Increased Tax Revenues 14
   2.5 Import Substitution 15
   2.6 Increased "Trade" 15
   2.7 Conclusion 16

3 Gambling, Consumer Behavior, and Welfare 19
   3.1 Mutually Beneficial Transactions 19
   3.2 Consumer Surplus and Variety Benefits 22
   3.3 Potential for Immiserizing Growth 23
   3.4 Conclusion 24

4 Misconceptions About Casinos and Economic Growth 25
   4.1 Industry Cannibalization 26
   4.2 The Factory–Restaurant Dichotomy 28
   4.3 The Export Base Theory of Growth 30
   4.4 Money Inflow (Mercantilism) 32
   4.5 Conclusion 35

5 Analysis of the Relationship Between Casinos and Economic Growth 37
   5.1 The Empirical Question 38
   5.2 Nontechnical Explanation of Granger Causality 40

	5.3	Granger Causality with Panel Data	41
		5.3.1 Synopsis of Granger's Procedure	42
		5.3.2. Modifying the Procedure for Panel Data	43
	5.4	Empirical Results	46
		5.4.1 Casino Gambling	47
		5.4.2 Greyhound Racing	49
	5.5	Summary and Conclusion	51
6	**Recent Evidence on Casinos and Economic Growth**		53
	6.1	Casino Gambling and Economic Growth: An Update	53
	6.2	Recent Evidence	54
	6.3	Hurricane Katrina and the Gulf States Casino Industry	56
		6.3.1 Background on the Gulf Coast Casino Industry	57
		6.3.2 Data and Model	60
		6.3.3 Results	63
	6.4	Conclusion	65
7	**The Impact of Casinos on State Tax Revenues**		67
	7.1	Introduction	67
	7.2	Literature Review	69
	7.3	Data and Model	73
		7.3.1 Data	73
		7.3.2 Model	75
	7.4	Results	80
		7.4.1 Discussion	85
		7.4.2 Robustness Check of Casino Results	85
	7.5	Summary and Conclusion	87
8	**Overview of Part I**		89
	8.1	A Look Ahead	90

Part II Disordered Gambling and Related Behaviors

9	**Casinos and Drunk Driving Fatalities**		93
	9.1	Introduction	93
	9.2	Background and Theoretical Considerations	94
	9.3	Data and Methods	97
		9.3.1 Casino and Fatal Accident Data	98
		9.3.2 Methodology	99
	9.4	Results	103
		9.4.1 Basic Results	103
		9.4.2 Robustness Checks	105
		9.4.3 Border County Analysis	108
	9.5	Conclusion	109

10	**Gambling, Crime, Binge Drinking, Drug Use, and Hiring Prostitutes**	111
	10.1 Introduction	111
	10.2 Background on Gambling Behavior and Crime	113
	10.3 Background on Gambling, Drinking, Drug Use, and Risky Sex	115
	10.4 Data and Models	116
	10.4.1 Data	117
	10.4.2 Models	125
	10.5 Results	126
	10.5.1 Results for Gambling and Crime	126
	10.5.2 Results for Gambling and Binge Drinking, Drug Use, and Hiring Prostitutes	131
	10.6 Conclusion	135
11	**Gambling and Attention Deficit Hyperactivity Disorder**	137
	11.1 Introduction	137
	11.2 Data	139
	11.2.1 Gambling Behavior Variables	139
	11.2.2 ADHD Symptom Variables	143
	11.3 Model	144
	11.4 Results	145
	11.5 Discussion and Conclusion	146
12	**Overview of Part II**	149

Part III Negative Socioeconomic Impacts of Gambling

13	**The Social Costs of Gambling**	153
	13.1 Chapter Outline	154
	13.2 The Economic Definition of "Social Cost"	154
	13.3 Modeling Social Costs	157
	13.3.1 The Definition Applied	157
	13.3.2 Theft as an Illustration of Social Cost	158
	13.3.3 Externalities and Social Costs	159
	13.3.4 Alleged Social Costs of Gambling	161
	13.4 Legitimate Social Costs	163
	13.4.1 Legal Costs	163
	13.4.2 Treatment Costs	165
	13.4.3 Psychic Costs	165
	13.5 Items Improperly Defined as Social Costs	167
	13.5.1 Wealth Transfers	167
	13.5.2 Bad Debts	168
	13.5.3 Bailout Costs	169
	13.5.4 Government Welfare Expenditures	170
	13.5.5 Modeling Transfers	171
	13.5.6 Industry Cannibalization	173

		13.5.7	Money Outflow	173
		13.5.8	Productivity Losses	173
		13.5.9	Theft	174
	13.6	Conclusion		174
14	**Issues in Social Cost Analysis**			**177**
	14.1	Introduction		177
	14.2	Problems Estimating Social Cost Values		178
		14.2.1	Counterfactual Scenario	178
		14.2.2	Comorbidity	179
		14.2.3	Surveys on Gambling Losses	181
	14.3	Different Approaches to Social Costs		183
		14.3.1	Cost-of-Illness Approach	184
		14.3.2	Economic Approach	185
		14.3.3	Public Health Perspective	185
		14.3.4	Can a Consensus Be Reached?	186
	14.4	Unidentified and Unmeasured Social Costs		189
		14.4.1	Restriction Effects	189
		14.4.2	Lobbying	192
		14.4.3	Summary of Political Costs	194
	14.5	Conclusion		195
15	**Is Gambling an "Unproductive" Activity?**			**197**
	15.1	Introduction		197
	15.2	The Claims		197
	15.3	Samuelson's *Economics* Text		198
	15.4	Why Gambling Is Not a DUP Activity		200
	15.5	DUP and Rent Seeking		201
	15.6	Conclusion		202
16	**Casinos and Crime: A Review of the Literature**			**203**
	16.1	Introduction		203
	16.2	Theoretical Background		204
		16.2.1	Economic Theory of Crime	204
		16.2.2	Routine Activities Theory	204
		16.2.3	Hot Spot Theory	205
		16.2.4	Economic Development	205
	16.3	Measurement Issues		206
	16.4	Empirical Evidence		208
		16.4.1	"Early" Studies	208
		16.4.2	"Recent" Studies	209
	16.5	Two Key Studies		210
		16.5.1	Grinols and Mustard (2006)	210
		16.5.2	Reece (2010)	212
	16.6	Unresolved Issues		213
	16.7	Conclusion		214

17 Casinos and Commercial Real Estate Values: A Case Study of Detroit ... 217
17.1 Background ... 218
17.2 Casino Activity and Real Estate Property Values ... 219
17.3 Data and Methodology ... 220
17.4 Results ... 226
17.5 Conclusion ... 230

18 Relationships Among Gambling Industries ... 233
18.1 Introduction ... 233
18.2 Literature Review ... 234
18.3 Data ... 236
  18.3.1 Gambling Volume Variables ... 237
  18.3.2 Adjacent-State Variables ... 240
  18.3.3 Demographic Variables ... 242
18.4 Model and Results ... 243
  18.4.1 Discussion of Results ... 246
  18.4.2 Effects of Cross-Equation Constraints ... 249
18.5 Policy Issues ... 250
  18.5.1 Tax Revenues ... 251
18.6 Conclusion ... 252

19 Overview of Part III ... 253

Part IV Conclusion

20 Past and Future ... 257
20.1 Introduction ... 257
20.2 Development of the Gambling Research Field ... 257
20.3 The Future of Research on the Economics of Gambling ... 258
20.4 Conclusion ... 260

Appendix: Primer on Microeconomics ... 263

References ... 275

Index ... 291

Chapter 1
Introduction

In a recent survey, professional economists were asked about their opinions on a variety of current economic issues (Whaples 2009). One of the questions was "A casino typically generates more benefits to society than costs" (p. 341). Among the 129 respondents, 68 % of whom were academic economists, only 17.1 % agreed; 30.2 % were neutral; and 52.8 % disagreed.[1] Being neutral on the issue is reasonable, since most economists have probably never performed or read research on the economic and social impacts of casinos and may therefore not have an informed opinion on the issue. But one must wonder why a majority of economists disagree that the benefits of casinos are greater than the costs. Why do these economists view casinos differently from other types of businesses?

Some of the literature on casino gambling economics, particularly in the mid-1990s, may offer some explanation. The early literature in this field propagated a number of myths about casinos. I use the word "myth" because many of the alleged social and economic impacts were described in studies that offered no empirical evidence whatsoever. There were a few academic articles in the 1990s that suggested that casinos had a positive impact on the host economy. But could a few articles and books on casinos really have much of an impact on the economics profession? Probably not. Most economists do not read journals that are outside their fields of expertise (and many do not even read journals within their fields). Most of the economists who responded to Whaples' survey probably developed their opinion about the economic impact of casinos based on their economic intuition or perhaps their biases about gambling and casinos. Or perhaps they read a famous economist who briefly mentioned gambling or casinos.

Some very important economists, including Nobel Laureates, have discussed the impacts of casinos and gambling. Paul Samuelson's principles textbook is often quoted (selectively) by casino opponents. Gary Becker has also written about

---

[1] Respondents who agreed chose responses "agree" or "strongly agree." Those who disagreed chose either "disagree" or "strongly disagree."

gambling, arguing that it should be more available to consumers, not less.[2] Still, unless ordinary economists are interested in casinos or gambling economics, they would have no reason to seek out authority figures' opinions on the economic impacts of gambling. For this reason, I suspect most economists simply relied on their economic intuition in responding to Whaples' survey question on the economic impacts of casinos.

I think the 52.8 % of economists who disagree with Whaples' survey question are wrong on this issue. In this book I present much of the research I have done during my career thus far. Although I haven't studied each aspect or effect of casino gambling, I have examined a number of the effects, both costs and benefits, and I am familiar with most of the academic literature on the industry. The economic and social impacts of casinos are not easily measured in money terms. However, to me it is clear that many of the costs and benefits associated with commercial casinos have been misdiagnosed in typical debates over casino legalization or expansion. The ideas and empirical evidence provided in this book can hopefully be interesting and informative to readers on both sides of the issue.

1.1 Overview of the Commercial Casino Industry

Prior to 1989 commercial casino gambling was legal only in Nevada and New Jersey. Nevada legalized casinos in 1931, and casinos opened in Atlantic City, NJ, in 1978. With the US Supreme Court's 1987 decision in *California v. Cabazon Band of Mission Indians* and the subsequent passage of the Indian Gaming Regulatory Act (IGRA) in 1988, the stage was set for a new wave of casino legalization.

In *California v. Cabazon*, the Court ruled that states lacked the authority to regulate tribal gambling, but with the IGRA the federal government effectively delegated regulatory powers over Indian casinos to state governments. Furthermore, the IGRA laid out conditions under which tribal gaming could be offered. In practice, the legislation has meant that federally recognized Indian tribes can offer a particular form of gambling on their reservations, so long as that type of gambling is not banned under state law. However, because the IGRA delegated regulatory powers to the states, tribes wishing to offer gambling must negotiate the terms under which gambling will be offered in a tribal-state compact. The IGRA outlines the general terms of such agreements, and the states are expected to negotiate with the tribes in good faith in developing compacts.[3]

---

[2] The material from Samuelson's principles book (Samuelson 1976) is discussed later in the book. Becker's discussion was in a *Business Week* article (Becker and Becker 1997).
[3] See Light and Rand (2005) for a detailed discussion of tribal gambling law.

1.1 Overview of the Commercial Casino Industry

Table 1.1 State commercial casino legalization and 2010 data

State	Year legalized	Date casino(s) opened	# Casinos operating in 2010	Commercial casino employees in 2010	2010 Revenues ($ million)	2010 Taxes paid ($ million)
Colorado	1990	October 1991	37	9,589	759	107
Illinois	1990	September 1991	9	6,892	1,374	466
Indiana	1993	December 1995	11	14,144	2,794	874
Iowa	1989	April 1991	14	8,915	1,368	305
Louisiana	1991	October 1993	14	16,873	2,374	572
Michigan	1996	July 1999	3	8,067	1,378	311
Mississippi	1990	August 1992	30	24,707	2,390	285
Missouri	1993	May 1994	12	11,071	1,788	486
Nevada	1931	1931	256	175,024	10,405	835
New Jersey	1976	1978	11	34,145	3,565	305
Pennsylvania	2004	October 2007	4	12,664	2,486	1,328
South Dakota	1989	November 1989	34	1,512	106	16
Totals			435	323,603	30,787	5,890

Data source: American Gaming Association (2010)

As the states negotiated compacts with Indian tribes, some state governments also began considering the legalization of commercial casinos, often with a stated goal of attracting tourism and new tax revenue, and stimulating economic development. Beginning in 1989 with Iowa and South Dakota, a new wave of commercial casino legalization spread across the United States through the mid-1990s.

The United States saw relatively slow casino industry growth, in terms of legalization in new states, from 1995 to 2005. However, a new wave of legalization (or serious consideration of it) began taking shape during the recession of 2007–2009. Several states have recently legalized commercial casinos (e.g., Ohio and Massachusetts), and several others are considering it. Some states that previously had machine gaming only have recently added table games (e.g., Pennsylvania, Maine, and Maryland).

As of December 2010, there were 939 commercial, tribal, and racetrack casinos operating in 38 states (American Gaming Association 2011). By the end of 2010, no fewer than 435 *commercial* casinos were operating in 12 states, with revenues of over $30 billion. Taxes paid to state governments in that year were $5.9 billion. Table 1.1 shows the dates commercial casino gambling was legalized in different states, as well as revenue and tax data for 2010. As demonstrated by these data, the US commercial casino industry is a significant one. In some other regions of the world, the commercial casino industry is expanding at an even greater pace.

The commercial casino industry is still one of the fastest growing entertainment industries and tourism sectors in the world. Recent growth has been largest in Asian countries, and by 2015 many industry observers expect the casino industry in Asia Pacific to be much larger than the industry in the United States. Macau now earns five times more revenue than Las Vegas (Siu and Lo 2012). Singapore's Marina Bay Sands casino has been a great success thus far, and other Asian countries (e.g., Japan, Taiwan, and Thailand) may try to emulate Singapore's successful casino market.

Table 1.2 Casino revenues and projected revenues (million US$)[a], select countries

Country	2006 Revenue	2008 Revenue	2010 Revenue	2012 Projected revenue	2014 Projected revenue
Asia Pacific					
Australia	2,801	3,316	3,429	3,439	3,698
Macau	7,049	13,541	34,608	44,862	57,680
Malaysia	847	993	948	942	1,012
New Zealand	383	373	365	353	388
Philippines	515	602	558	719	1,102
Singapore	–	–	2,827	5,090	6,516
South Korea	2,044	2,639	2,637	2,770	2,706
Vietnam	48	59	69	102	122
Europe					
Austria	581	629	608	606	656
Belgium	365	401	392	399	433
The Czech Republic	573	534	488	465	498
Denmark	245	262	254	255	272
Finland	838	885	876	879	939
Germany	1,953	2,014	2,027	2,082	2,217
Greece	933	1,000	710	608	629
Italy	118	115	108	107	104
The Netherlands	877	852	665	662	696
Poland	379	428	417	416	438
Spain	646	588	478	453	493
Sweden	186	214	205	205	218
Switzerland	1,056	1,097	961	964	1,111
UK	1,245	1,160	1,209	1,198	1,291
Americas					
Argentina	1,796	2,105	2,322	2,632	3,179
Canada	5,354	5,694	5,704	5,621	5,986
Colombia	481	532	526	529	574
Mexico	284	605	639	624	701
The United States	57,470	59,433	57,488	62,315	69,110
Totals	*83,768*	*94,431*	*115,855*	*133,714*	*156,825*

[a]Revenues in millions of nominal US$ calculated by PwC using the exchange rate on September 26, 2011
Source: PricewaterhouseCoopers (2011)

As discussed by Eadington (2011), the United States and countries in Europe can expect continued development of casino markets. However, revenues in these regions are not expected to grow as much as in the Asian Pacific region. Table 1.2 provides data on total casino revenues for selected countries.[4] Casino revenues in the countries shown in Table 1.2 totaled US $83.7 billion, and are expected to rise

---

[4]Revenue data include all types of casinos. For example, data for the United States include commercial and tribal casinos.

1.1 Overview of the Commercial Casino Industry

to almost $157 billion by 2014. The region that is likely to see the largest growth is surely the Asian countries. Macau, in particular, is likely just beginning to see the rate of growth that is going to continue for the next several years. The United States may see modest growth as new states legalize commercial casinos. In Europe there is unlikely to be significant growth unless more destination resort casinos are introduced.

As the industry continues to expand in the largest markets, it becomes a more important component of country and regional economies, providing key tax revenues and employment opportunities. The point at which casino markets become saturated is unclear, but we are quickly moving toward a situation where many people in the world will be a short distance from a casino.

Understanding of the economic and social impacts of casinos has developed dramatically during the past two decades. Since the 1990s there has been substantial interest in this subject, but most of the academic research has focused on psychology and physiology related to problem gambling. Relatively few economists have focused on the casino industry, but still we are beginning to see some consensus on key issues that are typically heard in policy debates.

There have been significant changes in the availability of online gambling over the past decade. The availability of online gambling expanded dramatically in the 2000s. However, the Unlawful Internet Gambling Enforcement Act (UIGEA) of 2006 was an attempt by the federal government to restrict online gambling in the United States. Although the UIGEA made online gambling more difficult, the industry has steadily expanded around the world. On December 22, 2011, Nevada became the first state to adopt regulations for online gambling. Just a day later the Office of Legal Counsel at the Department of Justice released an opinion on the Wire Act (Seitz 2011) that implies that states will have the right to regulate intrastate online gambling. Several states aside from Nevada have been working on legislation to allow online gambling. The casino industry itself is now lobbying for a federal regulatory framework to allow online poker but ban all other forms of Internet gambling in the United States (Sieroty 2012). However the online gambling landscape develops, the bricks-and-mortar casino market is sure to change. The developments in online gambling are the most significant changes in the US casino industry since the 1990s.

As technology changes quickly, it is impossible to predict exactly how the gaming industry will change, even in the very near future. However, it is pretty clear that the industry will continue to expand, both within existing casino jurisdictions and into new ones. A solid analysis of the economic and social impacts of the casino industry can be of critical importance for policymakers and voters in deciding how best to regulate the industry.

Part I
Economic Benefits from Commercial Casinos

Chapter 2
Casinos and Economic Growth

One of the primary reasons for governments legalizing casino gambling is the purported economic benefits from casino development. Among these benefits is economic growth. Over the last half-century, policies that promote economic growth have become an integral part of public sector economic activity. In the United States, state government attempts to attract industry via tax breaks and financial incentives have been the object of considerable research attention. But the apparent inability of either of these sets of policies to sustain successful outcomes over time has led state policy makers to explore alternative avenues. Writing in the 1930s, Joseph Schumpeter noted that one method of spurring economic growth is to provide a new good to the consuming public. Since legalization of a previously illegal activity is tantamount to introducing a "new good" to the public menu of consumption possibilities, there should be no surprise that a growth policy that has seen increasing popularity is legalized gambling.

The last two decades have witnessed an explosion of the US state legalization of betting on horse racing, dog racing, lotteries, casino games, and so on. Even now, states are considering legalizing additional types of gambling. Since gambling (locally provided, at least) is sometimes considered a "bad" by the electoral majority, some offsetting benefit to its provision must be offered to justify legalization. That benefit, politicians argue, is economic growth resulting from increased (export or local) spending, tax revenues, and employment. Eadington (1993) writes, "The fact that there is a strong latent demand for gambling—that, given the option, many people will choose to gamble—has not by itself been a sufficient reason for moving from prohibition to legalization." He explains,

> In order to be politically acceptable, the legalization of casino gaming—as well as other forms of commercial gaming—are usually linked to one or more "higher purposes" that can benefit from an allocation of a portion of the created economic rents and overcome the arguments against gambling. Such higher purposes may be tax benefits, investment stimuli, job creation, regional economic development or redevelopment, and revenue enhancement for deserving interests. (Eadington 1993, 7)

Because the availability of casino gambling, in particular, has been strictly limited, regions that were early to legalize casinos could expect highly profitable industries and increased tax earnings and employment. Most of the literature deals with the US experience, and that is the focus here.

There are numerous success stories of legalized casino gambling in the United States. Las Vegas is certainly the most famous. Tunica County, Mississippi, provides another interesting example. It had been known as the "poorest county in the nation" and was the focus of many poverty studies. Webster Franklin, director of the Chamber of Commerce of Tunica, testified to the effects of the casinos at a 1994 Congressional hearing. He explained how most of the studies on his county suggested government aid as the remedy for most problems. Yet government aid did not help lower the 26 % unemployment rate. Franklin (1994, 18–20) explains the effects of casinos:

> In January 1992, per capita income in the county was $11,865; ... 53 % of residents received food stamps ... Since casinos have been legalized, however, land once valued at $250/acre now sells for $25,000/acre ... The county's planning commission has issued more than $1 billion worth of building permits ... Because of the increased government revenues, property taxes have been lowered by 32 % in recent years ... Unemployment has dropped to 4.9 % ... The number of welfare recipients has decreased 42 %; the number of food stamp recipients has decreased by 13 % ... In 1994 the county recorded the highest percent increase in retail sales of all Mississippi counties: 299 %.[1]

Other studies tend to confirm the phenomenal growth that has occurred in Mississippi. The November 1993 issue of *U.S. News & World Report* ranked the state #1 for economic recovery due to gaming (Olivier 1995). In the wake of Hurricane Katrina in 2005 that devastated the Gulf Coast, the Mississippi casino industry made an extraordinary recovery.[2]

There are also states and cities that have had less successful experiences with casinos. Many researchers believe the casinos in Atlantic City, for example, have largely failed to revitalize that economy. In some countries, the casinos are so small and few that they could hardly have an effect on local economies. An example of this would be casino gambling in Belgium and in some other European countries. Yet, the industry expands despite little understanding among voters and policymakers about the economic and social impacts of casinos.

Quality academic treatments of the economic effects of legalized gambling are still rare. Proponents of the industry—usually the industry itself and some politicians—argue that legalizing gambling will create new employment and boost tax revenues in a region, state, or country. Although they have obvious conflicts of interest, the claims have some merit although the magnitude of the benefits is debatable. But there are

---

[1] This is a summary of the main points raised by Franklin.

[2] The extent to which the industry received federal aid is unclear. Certainly the casinos held insurance. In any case, most of the casinos were rebuilt and have been doing well. The Mississippi State Tax Commission reported that in July 2005, the month prior to Hurricane Katrina, the state's gross gaming revenue was $237.6 million (including $101.7 million from Gulf Coast casinos). The July 2006 gross gaming revenue was $222.7 million (including $74.4 million from the Gulf Coast). The effects of the casino industry on disaster recovery are examined later in the book.

other potentially more important arguments for legalizing casino (or other forms of) gambling. These are often ignored, even by gambling proponents.

This chapter provides an outline of some of the potential sources of growth from casinos. Along with Chap. 3, this discussion should provide the reader with a solid understanding of economic growth as it relates to legalized casinos. Subsequent chapters examine relevant empirical evidence.

2.1 A Simple Model of Economic Growth

The production possibilities frontier (PPF) is a simple model of an economy. It illustrates the maximum quantities of goods that can be produced, given the input resources available in society, and assuming full employment of those inputs. The negative slope of the PPF demonstrates that there is an opportunity cost of producing more of one type of good, namely, less of another good must be produced.[3] Economic growth in an economy can be represented as an expansion of the PPF, or a movement away from the origin. This is shown in Fig. 2.1. For a given population, the expansion of the PPF means a higher standard of living because there are now more goods and services available for consumption.

The introduction of casinos to a local economy represents a new good available to consumers. The building and operation of casinos generate new economic activity in the local economy. This economic activity can be seen as generating economic growth. However, whether growth is created depends on what would have otherwise happened. If casinos were not introduced into the local economy, would some other industry have developed instead? If so, then any net growth effect of casinos would be the difference between that of the casinos and that of the alternative industry. Alternatively, for the particular region, its primary concern may be only with its

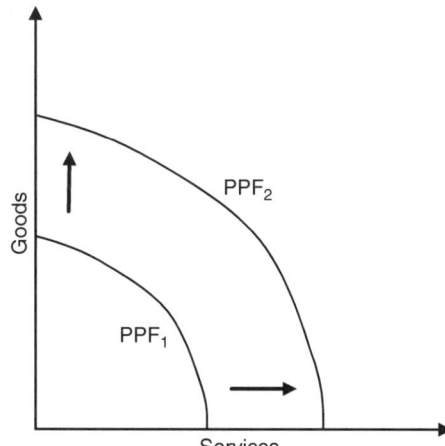

Fig. 2.1 Economic growth represented by an expansion of the PPF

---

[3]The PPF is explained in more detail in the Appendix.

own economy. To the extent that the casino industry draws resources from outside the region, the casinos may generate growth. However, on a macro level, the benefits in one region may be coming at the expense of other regions from which the resources are drawn.

The key question is whether the economic growth that would theoretically be created by casinos is so in reality. Empirical testing is required, and is presented in later chapters.

2.2 Increased Employment and Wages

When a community is considering legalizing casino gambling, one of the major benefits expected is an increase in local employment and the average wage rate. Yet, analyzing the effect of a new industry to a community can be tricky. Does the new industry create new jobs on net, or are jobs merely shifted among industries? This is an important issue that is commonly raised by researchers (e.g., Grinols 2004). Is the community better or worse off if the gambling industry "cannibalizes" existing industries? It is possible that a community would benefit through increased wages or increased competition among employers for qualified employees. This would occur, for example, because the casino industry is more labor intensive than many other tourist or service industries. Even if other industries are harmed by the presence of casinos, employment and average wages may increase as a result of the introduction of casinos. The effects of gambling on local labor markets have not received adequate attention in the economics literature. Clearly, the effect of casinos could be different in different economies.

Overall, there are probably significant employment benefits from the expansion of gambling industries at least in small economies. Often a new industry will attract an inflow of labor from neighboring areas. This inflow of labor effectively shifts the PPF for the region outward, as shown in Fig. 2.2, increasing productive capacity in the area. Note that the inflow of labor to the local area implies that there is decreasing productive capacity outside the local region. Thus, it is important to note that, while the introduction of casinos may benefit a region, those benefits may come at the expense of other regions.

In the event no new labor is attracted to the area, some researchers have argued, "there is no net gain to the economy from shifting a job from one location to another, unless it increases profits to the economy" (Grinols and Mustard 2001, 147). This view ignores the effects the expanding industry has on consumer welfare. If the new job creates more value for consumers than the old job, consumers certainly benefit. Furthermore, Grinols and Mustard (2001) ignore the fact that workers who switch jobs to work at casinos must benefit from the new job; otherwise they would not have accepted it. Indeed, casino jobs must be the best employment opportunity available for all casino employees or they would work somewhere else. This benefit is certainly difficult to estimate in monetary terms, but its abstract nature does not mean it is irrelevant.

Fig. 2.2 Economic growth from the inflow of productive resources

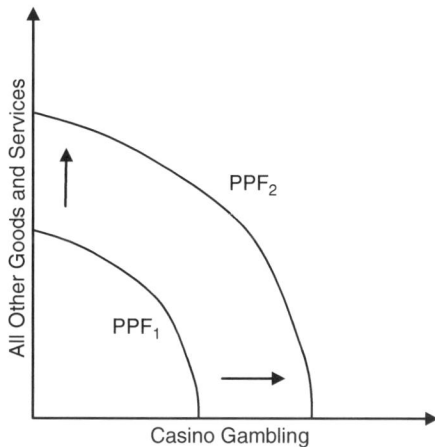

It is possible that casinos could enter an area, cannibalize all other industries, and then lower wages and benefits so that the new jobs are worse than the old jobs. But there is simply no empirical evidence to support this case. The extent of the positive employment effects from casinos depends on the circumstances of the case in question. But like any other industry, we would expect that increased competition for labor should benefit workers. If employers wish to hire capable and productive workers, they must offer wages competitive enough to attract them from other industries.

The best empirical evidence on the employment and wage effect of casinos in the United States is provided by Cotti (2008), who examines the county-level data used in the study by Grinols and Mustard (2006). Cotti finds that counties with casinos see an increase in employment after casinos open. He concludes that casinos create mild benefits to both employment and wages in the communities surrounding casinos, and that the employment growth effect is inversely related to county population. These findings are all consistent with economic intuition, and would be expected with the expansion of any new industry to a county or a region.

2.3 Capital Inflow

Another effect of legalized gambling is the potential inflow of capital to the local region. The building of casino resort is an example of this capital inflow. This capital expansion in effect expands the PPF, as illustrated in Fig. 2.2. Once casinos are established, the potential for other firms to enter the market and succeed may rise or fall. It would depend, to an extent, on local market conditions.

Less capital-intensive industries (e.g., racetracks) may have the same effects, but to a lesser extent than casinos. Empirical research on the effects of capital inflow due to legalized gambling is scarce, but conceptually, its effect would be similar to that of labor inflow.

The alternative view, of course, is that the expansion of casinos simply reduces capital dedicated to expanding other industries in the local economy. Still, one could argue that the industry that best pleases consumers will be the most likely to expand and succeed in the long run.

2.4 Increased Tax Revenues

Most researchers, politicians, media reporters, and citizens believe that the tax revenues from gambling are the primary benefits of legalized casinos. Indeed, this is one of the major selling points of casinos.[4] However, from a purely economic perspective, tax revenue should not be considered a net benefit of any policy. The reason is that the taxes gained by government come at the expense of the taxpayer. In other words, the benefits to one group are offset by costs to another group (Landsburg 1993, 96).

Even so, voters or politicians in a state/province/country may decide that certain types of taxes are preferable to others. For example, if there is the choice between an "avoidable" tax like a tax on lotteries or casino owners where taxes fall on the consumers or sellers of specific "sin" goods, and an "unavoidable" tax like a sales tax, then many people may prefer the lottery tax or taxes on casino revenues over a general sales tax.[5] The popularity of casinos as a fiscal policy tool has something to do with politicians wanting to generate tax revenue in a relatively painless way. Taxes on casinos may face less opposition than increasing a general sales tax. Overall, taxpayers would prefer avoidable rather than unavoidable taxes, so in this sense gambling taxes could be considered a benefit. In cases where casinos are located on state or country borders, much of the tax revenue may accrue from outsiders. In this case, the "tax exporting" can be counted as a benefit to the local population who may see their own tax burdens decrease as a result of casino expansion.

Obviously, good records exist for tax revenue making it relatively easy to measure. In determining the net tax benefits from casinos, as with other purported benefits from casino expansion, it is necessary to consider the *net* change in tax revenue, not simply the absolute taxes paid by casinos. This issue is addressed in Chap. 7. Our empirical evidence suggests that, all things considered, casinos may have a slightly *negative* impact on state government revenues.

---

[4]In the 1990s the casino industry hired accounting firms such as Arthur Andersen to perform "economic analyses" of casino expansion. These studies often speculate on the employment, wage, and tax effects of casino expansion. However, the validity of these studies is questionable. Such studies are less common now.

[5]From the consumer perspective, a sales tax *is* avoidable, but not easily, and much less so than a casino tax.

2.5 Import Substitution

Another argument for legalizing casinos in a particular state, region, or country is that the citizens enjoy gambling and they are currently going outside to gamble. If instead they had the opportunity to gamble at a casino in their home area, the local benefits would be greater. So instead of "importing" gambling services (e.g., going to another state to visit a casino) they substitute the imports with locally provided gambling services. This may result in positive economic effects from casino expansion, including capital development, increased demand in labor markets, and increased tax revenue. The tax revenue "kept home" is one of the arguments used by supporters of legalized casinos and is perhaps the primary motivation for the recent casino legalization in Massachusetts and Ohio, as well as the consideration in other states, such as New Hampshire.[6]

The basic issue here is that the economic benefits will be kept at home rather than going to "foreign" casino markets. But as casinos become more widespread, the touristic economic benefits would be expected to decline. In the extreme case with casinos prevalent everywhere, the amount of tourist casino gambling would be minimal. In this case, casino opponents argue that little or no economic benefits will result from adding new casinos. Whether "local" gambling creates economic benefits is discussed below.

2.6 Increased "Trade"

Trade, either interregional or international, can serve an important role in fostering economic growth. In one sense, trade with outsiders is no fundamentally different than any other mutually beneficial voluntary transaction. However, trade often receives special attention from policymakers, especially in tourism-based economies. Tourism can be thought of as an export. Still, as Tiebout (1975, 349) explains, there are other important factors that determine economic growth:

> There is no reason to assume that exports are the sole or even the most important autonomous variable determining regional income. Such other items as business investment, government expenditures, and the volume of residential construction may be just as autonomous with respect to regional income as are exports.

Nourse (1968, 186–192) gives another account of exports and their role in economic growth.[7] He explains that increases in the demand for an exported product lead to increases in demands for inputs to that industry. The increased factor

---

[6] A current international example can be seen in Taiwan, which has been considering developing casinos for several years. One argument used by supporters is that the casinos will raise tax revenue from those Taiwanese who currently travel to Macau, South Korea, or elsewhere to gamble.

[7] Also see Hoover and Giarratani (1984) and Emerson and Lamphear (1975, 161).

demand pushes factor prices up, attracting additional resources to the industry from other regions and industries. As resources move in, factor prices drop back in line and migration stops. As a result of this process, the region now has more capital and labor resources. In effect, the PPF for the region has shifted outwards—economic growth. This growth is consistent with North's concession that, although "the fortunes of regions have been closely tied to their export base ... it is conceivable that a region with a large influx of population and capital might simply 'feed upon itself' and thereby account for a substantial share of its growth" (North 1975, 339, note 334).

In analyzing how economic growth occurs, we must consider not only exports and demand but also imports and supply-side issues. We could alternatively base our casino analysis, as Hoover and Giarratani (1984, 329–330) note, on a "*supply-driven model* of regional growth [which] takes *demand* for granted ... and thus makes regional activity depend on the availability of resources put into production." They stress that the sole focus on either exports or a supply-driven model "is one-sided and can be seriously misleading; for full insight into real processes, both need to be combined."

When considering the economic effects of casinos, it is imperative to have an understanding of growth theory. Exports *and* imports can be important in a region's growth. However, an industry need not export to have a positive effect on economic growth. A region—like a firm or an individual—may experience economic growth from numerous sources, including imports, capital inflows, and, more generally, increased transactions or spending. At the most basic level, economic growth comes from mutually beneficial voluntary transactions between consumers and producers. Economic growth and consumer theory are examined in more detail in Chap. 3.

2.7 Conclusion

Economic growth is not solely dependent on exports or monetary inflows to a region. Rather, it depends fundamentally on mutually beneficial exchange. *Any* industry that increases consumer options will increase social welfare as long as the consumption is not harmful to others. And even in the case that the consumption does harm third parties, overall welfare may still increase.

It is true that some industries may suffer as a result of introducing a new industry (gambling or other) into an economy. This effect can be represented by a movement along the PPF for the economy, as shown in Fig. 2.3. Jobs will be lost in some industries, but are made up in others. The movement toward the "casino gambling" axis and away from "all other goods" represents a loss in employment in "other" markets, but this is offset by job increases in the casino industry. This transition—a reallocation of productive resources in the economy—is a normal occurrence in market economies; as new industries and firms enter markets, others will leave. Transition is a necessary component of the process of economic development, and this requires that as some industries expand, others contract.

2.7 Conclusion

Fig. 2.3 Movement along the PPF, showing an increase in casino employment and a decrease in employment in other industries

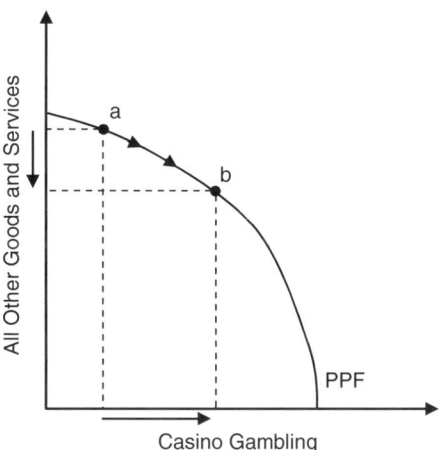

A key concept that is tied to the benefits of casinos is the welfare impact on consumers. This issue is discussed in Chap. 3. The economic growth effects of casino gambling are not without controversy, of course, or costs. Chapter 4 is an analysis of the arguments that suggest that casino gambling does *not* provide economic benefits. In some cases, these arguments are valid, but in other cases there are serious flaws.

The net effects of introducing a new good such as casino gambling are examined through the empirical evidence presented in Chap. 5. The idea that casinos must "export" in order to have any positive effect on economic growth is commonly held, but empirical evidence suggests that exports are not necessary for growth. When jurisdictions consider the legalization of gambling, they should look at more than how many tourists they expect to draw. What effect will the capital and labor inflow have on the local or the regional economy? How will local consumers benefit from the introduction of a good previously unavailable in the area? These questions must be addressed if policymakers and the voting public are to be better informed.

Once the data are analyzed, we will be better equipped to determine whether the introduction of casinos to an economy should be represented as in Fig. 2.3, where there appears to be little, if any, economic growth, or as in Fig. 2.2, where we see an expansion of the productive capacity in the economy.

At the outset, however, I believe it is important to emphasize that there is no fundamental reason from an economic growth perspective why the casino industry should be viewed differently from how any other industry would be viewed. Yes, casino gambling is a service, and not a manufactured product. Those who focus solely on the production of tangible goods as the key to economic well-being are seriously flawed. Yet, in the gambling literature one can find frequent allusions to the idea that the activity of gambling is not "productive." I address this issue in Chap. 15.

Chapter 3
Gambling, Consumer Behavior, and Welfare

Chapter 2 examined several basic explanations for how the introduction of casinos to a state or a region could have a positive impact on economic growth or the overall output (or income) of the economy. In this chapter I discuss the role of consumer welfare in the economic growth equation. We wish to move beyond a simple tallying of the spending on the building of casinos, of the wages paid to casino employees, or of the taxes paid by casinos to state governments. How does the proliferation of casinos affect people's *well-being*?

3.1 Mutually Beneficial Transactions

Economists view consumers as "utility maximizers." That is, given their budget and prices for the array of products available, individuals try to spend their money in a way that maximizes their benefits from consumption. Of course in real life, there are important details that affect consumers' behavior, including product quality, concerns about the environmental impacts of producing the goods, and any number of others.

The fundamental aspect of consumer behavior that is relevant for helping to understand the economic impacts of the casino industry is that market transactions—for cars, clothing, food, haircuts, and yes, gambling services—are mutually beneficial. That is, both parties enter into the transaction with the expectation of benefitting. For the buyer, he or she expects the benefits of consumption to be of greater value than the money he or she is paying to obtain the good or the service. For the seller, they value the money they are receiving at more than the value of the good or the service they are offering. Put differently, the consumer receives more benefit than they have to pay for, and the seller receives more money than the cost of production. These amounts are, respectively, consumer and producer surplus.[1]

---

[1] Consumer and producer surplus are discussed in more detail in the Appendix.

For most people, these concepts are fairly easy to understand, especially in the context of manufactured goods, such as a toaster oven or a car. These issues are covered in any introductory college course on economics. Yet, some people have a difficult time conceptualizing the consumer's benefit, in particular, when "services" rather than "goods" are considered.[2] If we consider a simple example such as tickets to a football game, it is clear that, for an individual to be willing to spend $50 on a ticket, they must expect to get entertainment worth at least $50 from going to the game. They do not receive anything tangible from attending the game, but it gives them benefits nevertheless. Other types of entertainment are analogous.

Casino gambling is a form of entertainment. Many casino customers likely budget a certain amount of money that they are willing to lose in a trip to the casino. Of course, not everyone loses each time they go to a casino, but most patrons surely know there is a negative expected value associated with almost every bet at a casino.[3] This means that casino patrons are willing to lose some money for the entertainment value of playing the games. This is no different from paying money for a movie ticket. Theater patrons pay money for the experience of watching the movie. As with a casino, theater patrons do not leave with anything tangible.

How to conceptualize the "price" of casino gambling is not straightforward. See, for example, the discussion by Siu (2011). Considering the amount of money lost to be the price of casino gambling, however, does not seem appropriate. This is because the negative expected value of each bet is relatively small, maybe about 5 % on average. Siu (2011) argues that a correct conception of the price of casino games should consider the house advantage (i.e., the player's negative expected value from playing the game), which typically is from 1 to 5 %, depending on the game, times the minimum bet allowed by the casino. This is typically $5 or $10 at many table games, and can be as low as 1¢ on slot machines. However one conceives of the price of casino gambling, a rational consumer—one who weighs expected costs and expected benefits—expects the fun, uncertainty, or social interaction from gambling—to outweigh the expected loss from making the casino bet.

Critics of casino gambling can argue that it is very unlikely that an individual can get, say, $1,000 of benefit from a single hand of blackjack that was lost. This may be true, but it assumes that the price of the hand of blackjack was the amount lost. This is an incorrect conception of price. Nevertheless, one can argue that problem gamblers do not actually benefit from playing casino games. For them, it

---

[2] For example, consider Thompson and Schwer (2005, 65), who write, "Some economists will argue that there is no economic gain from gambling activity as it represents only a neutral exercise in exchanging money from one set of hands to another. Indeed, as no product is created to add wealth to society, the costs of the exchange (time and energy of players, dealers, and other casino employees) represent a net economic loss for society." This idea comes up more formally in Chap. 15.

[3] One exception is the odds bet behind the pass/don't pass line in craps, which is a fair bet. But the player must make an unfair bet to be able to make an odds bet.

3.1 Mutually Beneficial Transactions

is more of a compulsion or an addiction. But such behaviors are still the result of actions within the "rational behavior" framework of economics, as discussed in Sect. 14.3.4.[4]

If we can agree that most casino patrons enjoy the activity and view it as a form of entertainment, then we can move on to the more general point, that casino bets, like transactions for football game and movie theater tickets, represent mutually beneficial (and voluntary) transactions. The "mutual benefits," as introduced above, are called consumer and producer surplus. These represent real wealth to the consumer and producer that come as a result of trading with others.

When the availability of gambling is increased, the number of potential mutually beneficial, voluntary transactions increases. This a fundamental source of economic growth. After all, each additional transaction increases the wealth of the two individuals involved while typically harming no one. Note that I am saying that the wealth of the gambler increases, even though he is (on average) losing money with each transaction (bet) at a casino. His overall well-being increases because he makes the rational decision to place a bet, aware of the negative expected value of the bet. He must therefore be receiving satisfaction or "utility" from the activity of gambling (Marfels 2001).

One may argue that the introduction of gambling simply enables the consumer to, say, spend $100 at a casino rather than at a department store. While the total amount of spending may not change as the result of increased gambling, presumably the value to the consumer increases since the choice was made to switch from spending at the department store to spending at the casino. This change in consumption can be represented as in Fig. 3.1. The movement from consumption point *a* to point *b* improves the consumer's well-being since they move to a higher indifference curve. (See Appendix for an explanation of indifference curves.)

Schumpeter ([1934] 1993, 66) lists five primary sources of economic development:

(1) The introduction of a new good—that is one with which consumers are not yet familiar—or of a new quality of a good. [New casinos are examples of this.] (2) The introduction of a new method of production, that is one not yet tested by experience in the branch of manufacture concerned, which need by no means be founded upon a discovery scientifically new, and can also exist in a new way of handling a commodity commercially. (3) The opening of a new market, that is a market into which the particular branch of manufacture of the country in question has not previously entered, whether or not this market has existed before. [This applies to casino gambling in many markets.] (4) The conquest of a new source of supply of raw materials or half-manufactured goods, again irrespective of whether this source already exists or whether it has first to be created. (5) The carrying out of the new organisation of any industry, like the creation of a monopoly position (for example through trustification) or the breaking up of a monopoly position.

A common feature of each of these paths to growth is that each implies an increase in the number of mutually beneficial, voluntary transactions.

---

[4]Even if one concedes the point that for some patrons, casino gambling is not "enjoyable," the vast majority of them are not problem gamblers. Yet, some researcher suggests that a large proportion of casino revenues do come from problem gamblers.

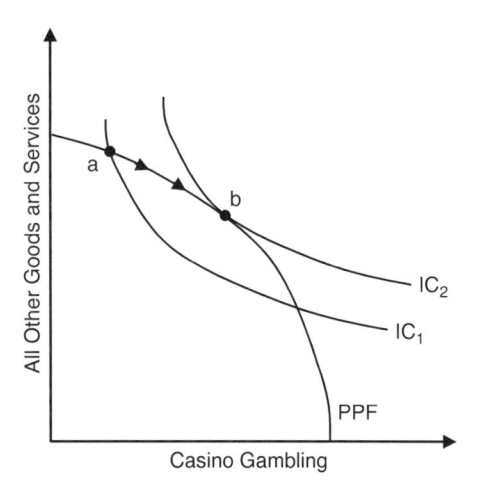

Fig. 3.1 Welfare impact of increased spending at casinos

3.2 Consumer Surplus and Variety Benefits

Each voluntary transaction involves consumer and producer surplus (CS and PS) as described in the Appendix. There may be no greater benefit from legalized casino gambling than the enjoyment consumers receive from the activity. After all, consumers vote on their favorite goods and services with their spending. The consumer benefits from gambling are likely to be much greater than tax revenue or employment growth benefits from casinos. Several authors have acknowledged this, including Eadington (1996), Australian Productivity Commission (1999), Walker and Barnett (1999), and Collins (2003); but most researchers discount or ignore it, e.g., Grinols and Mustard (2001) and Grinols (2004). Yet, consumer benefits are critical to understanding how the availability of legal gambling can benefit society.

There are at least two potential sources of consumer benefits from casino gambling. Normally, consumers benefit when increased competition in markets leads to lower prices. This is one source of consumer surplus, illustrated in two examples. First, sometimes casinos advertise particular games and offer better odds than competing casinos. If the effective price of playing the casino games falls, then CS rises. Second, casinos are often bundled with other products like hotels and restaurants. To the extent casino competition increases competition in the local restaurant and hotel markets, whether through price decreases or quality increases, the casinos provide more benefits to consumers in the form of CS. These benefits have been ignored in most cost–benefit of gambling studies.[5]

There have been some recent empirical studies on the issue. For example, in studying the UK horse racing industry, Johnson, O'Brien, and Shin (1999) test for a utility component to gambling. When betting on a horse, a person has the choice of paying a 10 % tax on the wager or on the return (if his or her horse wins). The authors show that the first choice is always best from an expected wealth perspective. However, as the size of

---

[5] In the case of casinos, many researchers have instead focused only on the "cannibalization" effects.

3.3 Potential for Immiserizing Growth

Fig. 3.2 Immiserizing growth

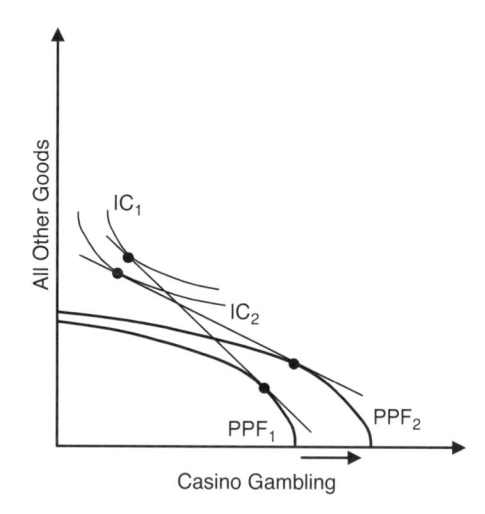

wagers rises, the tendency to choose a tax on the return rises. This suggests a "consumption value" of gambling that rises as the size of the wager rises.

The other consumer benefit that has been ignored by most researchers relates to product variety. When casino gambling is first introduced to a state, it has the effect of increasing the product choices for consumers. This "variety benefit" could be significant but it is difficult to measure.[6] In his book, Grinols (2004) ignores both of these potential benefits from gambling and instead focuses on "distance consumer surplus." He argues that one of the few benefits of the spread of casinos in the United States is that gamblers do not have to travel as far to reach a casino. But this benefit seems trivial compared to the other potential benefits of casino expansion.

Some of the largest benefits of gambling defy measurement. As a result, many researchers focus on more obvious benefits of gambling, like employment and tax revenues. If research is to improve in quality, these consumer benefits must be considered.

3.3 Potential for Immiserizing Growth

The above discussion suggests that the introduction of a new firm or industry—including casino gambling—that caters to consumer demands tends to increase economic well-being. However, it is conceptually possible that economic growth can cause a *decrease* in welfare—the so-called immiserizing growth. This would be graphically represented as in Fig. 3.2, by an expansion of the PPF.[7] Yet, through a process of trade and price adjustments, the society ends up on a lower indifference curve (IC) than it was originally.

---

[6] Some economists have examined this effect. For examples, see Hausman (1998), Hausman and Leonard (2002), Lancaster (1990), and Scherer (1979).

[7] Figure 3.2 is based on a similar figure from Carbaugh (2004, 74).

This potential was first identified by Bhagwati (1958). The context is that of international trade when a country specializes in the production of a particular good. If specialization in oil increases the world supply to such an extent that it places significant downward pressure on the world price, overall welfare in the country may decrease as a result of specialization and trade. The same could apply to a regional or a state economy that specializes in the production of gambling services.[8] Although this is technically possible, examples of immiserizing growth are very rare, since very specific criteria must be met.[9] For a general discussion, see Bhagwati (1958) and Carbaugh (2004, 73–74). For an application to gambling, see Li, Gu, and Siu (2010).

3.4 Conclusion

In Chap. 2 we described the principles of economic growth in the context of a simple PPF model. In this chapter we have examined the role of benefits to the consumer in economic growth. This is done by incorporating preferences, through the indifference curve, into the model of growth. What we find is that, like any other industry whose output consumers value, the gambling industry can contribute to economic growth.

It is important to be cognizant of the benefits that consumers receive from gambling, even though the expected monetary value of the activity is negative. The vast majority of consumers consider gambling to be a form of entertainment for which they are willing to pay. In this respect, the casino industry is conceptually identical to other entertainment venues, such as movie theaters and football stadiums.

Although there is little empirical evidence on the consumer benefits of introducing casinos, and the issue seems to rarely arise in political debates over casinos, my view is that this is probably the most important net impact of legalizing casinos—even greater than tax or employment benefits.

---

[8] This possibility requires trade. As a result of trade, the region or the country is able to consume on an IC beyond the PPF. This is the reason that trade is beneficial to individuals and countries. As the casino industry expands the region attracts more tourists (Fig. 3.2). The region develops a stronger comparative advantage in casino gambling and the opportunity cost of production in that industry falls relative to the other industry. This explains why the slope of the line tangent to PPF_2 is lower than the slope of the tangency to PPF_1.

[9] To fully understand the implications of the immiserizing growth theory, one must have an understanding of international trade theory. Carbaugh (2004, 73) explains, "The case of immiserizing growth is most likely to occur when (a) the nation's economic growth is biased toward its export sector; (b) the country is large relative to the world market, so that its export price falls when domestic output expands; (c) the foreign demand for the nation's export product is highly price-inelastic, which implies a large decrease in price in response to an increase in export supply; and (d) the nation is heavily engaged in international trade, so that the negative effects of the terms-of-trade deterioration more than offset the positive effects of increased production."

Chapter 4
Misconceptions About Casinos and Economic Growth

The economic effects of the casino industry have been examined in a number of US states and regions, and in other countries, by a number of authors. Despite the volume of studies on the effects of gambling, there is no consensus among researchers. Indeed, the economic impacts of casinos are to some extent market specific and vary by the type of casino (e.g., destination resort, riverboat). This chapter focuses on different arguments related to the economic growth effects of casino gambling, with a specific focus on some fallacious arguments that continue to arise in the literature and in political debate. The goal of the discussion in this chapter is to set these arguments in the context of a mainstream economic perspective on exchange and economic growth.

A number of adamant and vocal critics of casinos (e.g., Grinols and Kindt) have published numerous papers during the past 20 years arguing that the expansion in the gambling industry has led to decreases in other industries—"cannibalization"—resulting in little overall economic stimulus for the host state or region. Yet, there is little evidence to support such contentions. It appears that these authors simply dislike casinos and were trying to influence policymaking accordingly. Nevertheless, the argument has been relatively influential among politicians and voters.

There are four varieties of the argument that casino expansion comes mostly at the expense of other industries, resulting in no or little net positive economic effect:

1. "Industry cannibalization"
2. The "factory–restaurant" dichotomy
3. Export base theory of growth
4. Money inflow (mercantilism)

The reader will notice that the four ideas are close relatives, so the presentations of the different arguments and the responses overlap somewhat.

4.1 Industry Cannibalization

One of the most common arguments about legalized gambling is that any additional economic activity spurred by gambling comes at the expense of activity in other industries. That is, the introduction of casinos merely shuffles spending among industries, so any positive employment or income from gambling are offset by losses in existing industries that see less business and therefore decreased employment. This idea is typically referred to as "industry cannibalization" or the "substitution effect," and was commonly heard throughout the 1990s and early 2000s.[1] Some examples include Gazel and Thompson (1996), Goodman (1994a, 1995b), Grinols (1994a, 1995), Grinols and Mustard (2001), Grinols and Omorov (1996), and Kindt (1994). As casinos have become more widespread across the United States, without the economic devastation predicted by some of these authors, the argument has lost some of its influence in political and academic debate. For other perspectives on the issue, see Eadington (1993, 1995, 1996), Evart (1995), and Walker and Jackson (1998).

It is clear that legalized gambling may replace other businesses. This is always the case when one producer offers a product or a service that consumers prefer to those previously available. "Cannibalization"—the result of *market competition*—is the normal and healthy part of the market process that helps ensure consumers get the products they most desire. From a social welfare perspective, the significant issue is not whether some firms are replaced by others but whether the introduction of the new product increases total societal wealth. Detlefsen (1996, 14–15) explains,

> Invocation of the substitution effect [argument] in this context not only presumes a static, zero-sum economy in which no business can grow except at the expense of other firms.[2] It mistakenly implies that certain types of commercial activities, such as casino gambling, create no new "real" wealth and provide no "tangible" products of value. That view overlooks the key point that all voluntary economic exchanges presumably are intended to improve the positions and advance the preferences of *both* parties (in other words, improve their social welfare). That the gains from such exchanges (particularly in a wealthier, service-oriented economy in which a greater portion of disposable income is consumed for recreational activities) are not easily quantifiable in every case is beside the point. After all, the only true measure of the value of entertainment-oriented goods and services in the diverse U.S. economy ultimately remains in the spending preferences expressed by individual consumers.

This issue can be analyzed in the context of the PPF model introduced in the Appendix and discussed in previous chapters. The model sheds light both on the employment and welfare effects of increased gambling activity within an economy.

---

[1] I am uncertain of the origin of the term "cannibalization effect." However, it does not seem appropriate if it describes casinos negatively impacting *non-casino* businesses. Nevertheless, the term is commonly used, and I have used it and continue to.

[2] The "zero-sum economy" is unrealistic because it ignores the fact that there are always more and different things that consumers would like. When a particular industry fails, productive resources (land, labor, capital, managerial skills) are freed up to produce in other industries.

4.1 Industry Cannibalization

Fig. 4.1 Movement along the PPF, with an increase in welfare

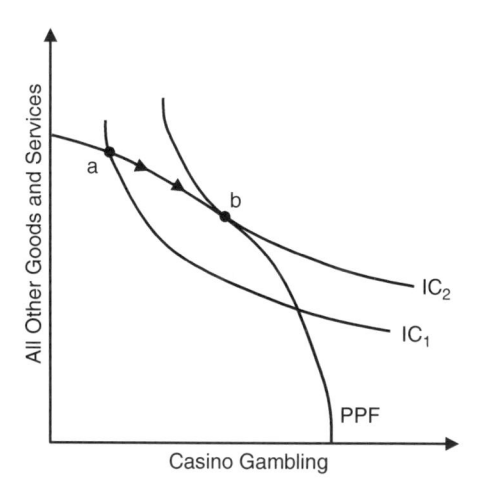

With existing unemployment, it is possible that there would be no significant "cannibalization" if currently unemployed individuals are hired by the new industries. If there is near-full employment initially, and we assume that no increase in productive capacity occurs, then the situation would appear as in Fig. 4.1. In this case, it is true that there will be a reallocation of productive resources among industries.

The consumers' choice to consume more gambling and fewer other goods implies movement along the PPF toward more gambling (from *a* to *b*). Employment in casinos increases, while it falls in other industries. Generally, the effects of this movement along the PPF are about neutral with respect to overall employment.[3] Of course, there are two other possibilities. Overall employment could increase or decrease, depending on whether the expanding or the contracting industry is more labor intensive. Empirical evidence suggests that casinos tend to modestly increase local employment (Cotti 2008).

Perhaps more importantly, the industry cannibalization argument ignores the fact that pure shifts in employment due to consumer preferences increase welfare. Production is shifted from less to more preferred goods and services. This is illustrated by the movement of consumers to a higher indifference curve (Fig. 4.1). This adjustment makes some displaced workers unhappy, but it is a necessary part of economic development in capitalist societies. Eventually displaced workers find employment in other industries (Roberts 2001).

The PPF model can be more enlightening if we incorporate the government restrictions of the casino industry. Consider Fig. 4.2 that represents the production of casino gambling and all other goods and services in the United States. The PPF for 1978 represents the situation in which casinos are legal only in Nevada and New Jersey. By 1993, some economic growth has occurred, both in terms of casino and non-casino industries (PPF_{1993}). PPF_{2012} shows moderate non-gambling industry

---

[3] Obviously, this statement depends on several assumptions, and is not always true. In the context of international trade, however, empirical studies suggest that it is generally true (Krugman 1996, 36).

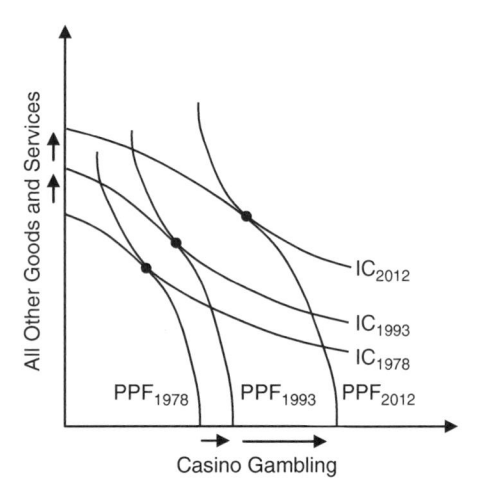

Fig. 4.2 Economic growth in the casino and other sectors over time

growth and a massive expansion of legalized casino gambling due to the changing legal status of casinos across the United States.

Depending on the relative preference for casino gambling, it is likely that expansion of the activity has increased social welfare as illustrated. In a case with extremely flat ICs this would not occur. (It would also not occur if gambling was a "bad" to consumers.) But evidence of significant increases in gambling volume suggests that the US social ICs are not very flat. If the ICs were flat, which would suggest a very weak preference for gambling relative to other goods and services, the tangencies in Fig. 4.2 would be nearly vertically aligned. But the substantial increase in gambling industry revenues from 1978 to 2012 implies no such vertical alignment.[4] The expansion of gambling *is* due, at least in part, to consumer preferences for the activity despite the arguments of many antigambling advocates, e.g., Gross (1998) and Goodman (1994a, 1995b).

4.2 The Factory–Restaurant Dichotomy

Advocates of the cannibalization argument suggest that economic growth from legalized gambling is unlikely under any circumstances. A less strict form of the argument is the factory–restaurant dichotomy because it allows economic growth when "outsiders" or tourists are the gambling customers (when goods/services are exported). The terms "factory" and "restaurant" have been used to describe the effects of "export" casinos and "local" casinos, respectively:

> A factory, when it locates in an area, sells to the rest of the country. Its payroll, materials purchases, and profits spent locally are new money to the area that represents tangible goods produced. On the other hand, adding a new restaurant that caters to local population

---

[4] We are ignoring social costs created by gambling, but these are not relevant for understanding whether the industry expansion alone causes an increase in welfare.

4.2 The Factory–Restaurant Dichotomy

in an area simply takes business from local firms [i.e., industry cannibalization]. The question for a particular region therefore is: Is a casino more like a factory or a restaurant? In Las Vegas, casinos are more like factories because they sell gambling services to the rest of the Nation. In most other parts of the country, gambling is like a restaurant, however, drawing money away from other businesses, creating no economic development, but leaving social costs in its wake. (Grinols 1994b)[5]

Also consider these quotations supporting this view:

> Providing gambling to residents transfers money from one local pocket to another and from one local sector to another, but does not lead to a net increase in regional demand. (Grinols and Omorov 1996, 80)

> But only *new* spending associated with a gambling venture, like spending by tourists who come into a region to gamble or new jobs, actually brings new money into the local economy. [This has a positive spending multiplier effect.] But when local people substitute spending on gambling for their other expenditures, this *induced* impact has a negative multiplier effect of decreasing spending on other forms of recreation and businesses in the area. (Goodman 1994a, 50)

> A casino acts like a black hole sucking money out of a local economy. No one cares if you suck money out of tourists, but large-scale casinos that do not bring in more new tourist dollars than they take away from local players and local businesses soon find themselves outlawed. (Rose 1995, 3)

Goodman (1995b, 25) admits that

> in those rare instances where a casino was located in an area with a negligible economic base and few jobs to begin with—an impoverished rural area ... or a severely depressed area ... there could be a significant positive economic transformation ... since there are almost no preexisting local businesses to be negatively affected.

It is probably true that the more tourists a casino resort can attract to a locality, the greater the economic benefits. This is simply because there is more economic activity than there would otherwise be. In addition, the tax revenues generated from the casino could be seen as coming more from tourists than locals. This would have the effect of lowering local citizens' tax burden, *ceteris paribus*. It is true that most people who gamble in Nevada are from other states. Indeed, many casinos worldwide are designed to be resort attractions. However, this is not always the case, so perhaps the restaurant–factory analogy is appropriate to some extent.

But even if we accept that the dichotomy may have theoretical legitimacy, the conclusions are certainly debatable. Do Grinols, Goodman, and the others believe that a new restaurant opening in town is a bad thing? If consumers like the new restaurant better than existing ones they should be allowed to "vote with their money." If spending is unregulated, the producers who best please consumers will be rewarded with profitable futures. These researchers suggest that more choice in entertainment, by itself, is a *bad* thing simply because it means more competition for existing entertainment firms, and the competing entertainment firms will be cannibalized. Of course casinos will attract dollars that otherwise would have been spent elsewhere, but so does Target and the neighborhood hardware store. Aside from

---

[5] Also see Grinols (2004, Chapter 4).

this, when a new restaurant opens in a market, for example, it does not necessarily mean that other restaurants will fail. When economic growth occurs, more businesses can succeed. Incumbent firms can survive even when new firms enter a market.

Just because some industries are harmed, the introduction of casinos cannot be described as "bad" for society. In the unlikely case that casino revenues do represent consumer spending that is solely "reshuffled" from other local businesses in a zero-sum game, Evart (1995) asks, "So what? Why is the redistribution of expenditure caused by casinos any worse or any better than the redistribution that was caused when the Falcons [football team] moved into [Atlanta]?" She argues that opposing casinos on this basis "is in contrast to other consumer products which meet consumer demand or expand consumer choice, even though they put existing businesses out of business." She cites the introduction of VCRs and movie rentals and asks why their effect on movie theaters and other entertainment firms was not met with alarm. Harrah's Entertainment argues a similar point: if it was true that "casinos have positive local economic impacts only to the extent that 'non-local', out-of-state players ... are attracted by opportunities to gamble," then "it would be true for other forms of spending. That is, spending on movies could only help a local economy if moviegoers are 'non-local, out-of-state'." (Harrah's Entertainment 1996, 1).

The factory–restaurant argument begs the following question: Was society harmed when the horse-drawn buggy industry was cannibalized by the automobile industry or when cell phones began replacing landline phones? With countless other examples, we could show that it is often in society's interest for particular industries to decline. This is what Schumpeter (1950, Chapter 7) referred to as "the process of creative destruction."

4.3 The Export Base Theory of Growth

Much of the doubt about legalized gambling fostering economic growth is based on the idea that a good or a service must be "exported" for it to be beneficial to the regional economy. The factory–restaurant dichotomy is a simpler version of this idea. This argument is formally referred to as the export base theory of economic growth. On the surface the theory may seem applicable to the case of legalized gambling. But on closer examination, the fit of this theory to casino gambling is not so straightforward.

Exports do play a large role in the development of some economies, to be sure. For example, on many Caribbean islands tourism is the primary industry. Tourism can be considered an export because most of the consumers are not locals. Obviously a large influx of tourists means an increase in consumer spending. This would also apply to Nevada and Macau as casino economies. This type of activity is beneficial for the economy because it will lead to increases in local income. Common sense suggests that tourism means more money coming into the local economy, and economic growth. For some countries, regions, or cities, exports may seem to be the only significant source of economic activity.

4.3 The Export Base Theory of Growth

The export base theory of economic growth is supported by many researchers for a variety of circumstances outside of legalized gambling. For example, Riedel argues, "The case for an export promotion strategy rests not so much on principles of theory as on what works in practice. Of all the stylized facts about development, by far the most robust is the empirical relation between overall economic growth and export growth" (Riedel 1994, 51–52).

It is worth noting that Riedel believes that "most of what constitutes an export promotion policy is removing, or offsetting, obstacles that government itself put in the way of exporting" (Riedel 1994, 55). This certainly applies to the case of legalized gambling since it faces significant government restrictions.

Although this idea makes some intuitive sense, the typical application to gambling is flawed.[6] Contrary to what one reads in the casino industry research, few (if any) growth theorists believe that exports are *solely* responsible for growth. Tiebout (1975, 352) explains,

> Formally speaking, it is the ability to develop an export base which determines regional growth. Yet in terms of causation, the nature of the residentiary [restaurant-type] industries will be a key factor in any possible development. Without the ability to develop residentiary activities, the cost of development of export activities will be prohibitive.

Even if one does accept the general idea that exports are critical for regional economic growth, there are difficulties with the theory. For example, how does one differentiate an export ("basic") industry from a local ("residentiary") industry? This distinction can be rather difficult; some industries perform both basic and residentiary functions (Thompson 1968, 44–45). What is the requisite range of export goods?[7]

Upon closer examination, the export base theory of growth alone cannot explain the economic effects of casino gambling. In their growth theory text, Hoover and Giarratani (1984, 319) use a simple example to discredit the theory's simplest form:

> Consider ... a large area, such as a whole country, that comprises several economic regions. Let us assume that these regions trade with one another, but the country as a whole is self-sufficient. We might explain the growth of each of these regions on the basis of its exports to the others and the resulting multiplier effects upon activities serving the internal demand of the region. But if all the regions grow, then the whole country or "superregion" must also be growing, despite the fact that it does not export at all. The world economy has been growing for a long time, though our exports to outer space have just begun and we have yet to locate a paying customer for them. It appears, then, that *internal* trade and demand can generate regional growth...

Tiebout (1975, 349) gives a similar explanation:

> A further consideration will help to point up the error of identifying exports as the sole source of regional income change. In an exchange economy one person considered in a spatial context may be entirely dependent on his ability to export his services. Probably this is true of a

---

[6] For explanations of the theory's flaws, see Vaughan (1988), Hoover and Giarratani (1984), and Walker (1998a, 1998b, 1999).

[7] Range is defined as "the farthest distance a dispersed population is willing to go in order to buy a good offered at a place. This range will take on a lower limit if there is competition from another center" Berry and Horton (1970, 172).

neighborhood area, except for the corner grocer. For the community as a whole, the income originating in non-exports increases. In the United States economy, exports account for only a small part of national income. Obviously, for the world as a whole, there are no exports.

Yet, Grinols (1995, 11) illustrates an example of the misconception that we live in a zero-sum society where exchanges are win–lose and not mutually beneficial: "It is a logical impossibility for every area to win at the others' expense when gambling is present in every region. For the nation as a whole there will be no net economic development from the spread of gambling." Grinols is mistaken because he apparently either views exports as the only source of economic growth or believes voluntary exchanges are at their core zero sum rather than mutually beneficial.

If exports are not solely responsible for economic growth, then casinos may promote economic growth even if their customers are not tourists. Many of the conclusions in the casino literature of the 1990s and early 2000s must be reconsidered.

4.4 Money Inflow (Mercantilism)

Another, very simplistic, form of the export base theory can be seen in researchers who have wrongly emphasized the importance of money inflow to a region and its impact on economic development. Examples of this fallacy are found in Grinols and Omorov (1996), Ryan and Speyrer (1999), Thompson (1996, 2001), Thompson and Gazel (1996), and Thompson and Quinn (1999). An example is provided by Grinols (1995, 11):

> Whether any business adds to the economic base or diminishes it depends on whether the business draws more new dollars to the area that are then spent on goods and services in that area. To benefit the local economy these new dollars must exceed the number of dollars the business causes to be removed from the area. Because casinos have artificially high profit margins, are often owned by out-of-area investors, and frequently take dollars from the area's existing tourist base rather than attracting new tourists, the effect of gambling in many cases is to diminish the economic base and cost jobs. The possibility, dependent on the net export multiplier theory and regional input–output multiplier analysis is not in dispute among responsible economists.

The argument that an inflow of money to a region leads to economic growth seems to make intuitive sense, like the alleged unemployment created by importing goods. For example, it would seem that an American purchasing a Japanese-manufactured car would cause a loss in Detroit jobs. But this perspective ignores half of the trade equation. As Williams (1992) and Krugman (1996, 76) show quite clearly, a deficit in the trade of goods is offset by a surplus in the trade of capital or assets.

As another example, consider Thompson and Gazel (1996, 1), examining the effect of casinos in Illinois:

> We wished to identify monetary flows to and from the local areas around the casinos ... and also the monetary flows to and from the state as a whole. Quite simply, we were asking from where the money comes and where the money goes .... The money gambled was a positive factor for the state and local economies, if the players were from out-of-state.

4.4 Money Inflow (Mercantilism)

They conclude, "Casinos have drawn monetary resources away from depressed communities and away from individuals who are economically poor ...." (p. 10).

Thompson (1996, 2001) and Thompson and Quinn (1999) argue that an economy can be modeled similar to a "bathtub." The model is used to analyze the economic effects of video gaming machines in South Carolina:

> The model portrays gambling enterprise as a bathtub for the economy with money running into and out of the bathtub as if it were water ... A local or regional economy attracts money. A local or regional economy discards money. If as a result of the presence of gambling enterprise more money comes into an economy than leaves the economy, there is a net positive impact. However, if more money leaves than comes in, then there is a net negative impact. (Thompson and Quinn 1999, 3–4)[8]

The obvious response to this is that market transactions are mutually beneficial, as discussed previously. So money is only spent on something when the buyer expects to receive something of greater value in return. But according to Thompson and Quinn, any transaction in which "money leaves" (i.e., *any* purchase of goods or services paid for with money) is bad. This flies in the face of economic sense.

The argument about monetary inflows also ignores nonmonetary benefits of casino legalization. Specifically, consumers receive benefits from goods and services. In addition, the focus on monetary flows ignores the effects of increased production on labor and capital markets.

The "money inflow" argument seems to be an example of mercantilist thought.[9] Blaug (1978, 10–11) explains,

> The leading features of the mercantilist outlook are well known: bullion and treasure as the essence of wealth; regulation of foreign trade to produce an inflow of specie; promotion of industry by inducing cheap raw-material imports; protective duties on imported manufactured goods; encouragement of exports, particularly finished goods; and an emphasis on population growth, keeping wages low. The core of mercantilism, of course, is the doctrine that a favourable balance of trade is desirable because it is somehow productive of national prosperity.

Carbaugh (2004, 27–28) explains mercantilist thought as well as the arguments that discredited it. Because the mercantilists focused on having a positive trade balance (exports > imports) they supported government restrictions in imports and the promotion of exports when possible. This policy would have the effect of increasing the inflow of money into an economy. Because money was viewed as wealth by the mercantilists, these trade policies naturally followed. Blaug (1978, 12) explains, "the idea that an export surplus is the index of economic welfare may be described as the basic fallacy that runs through the whole of the mercantilist literature." Put differently, the mercantilists wrongly equated money with capital (Blaug 1978, 11).

Another major problem with mercantilism, identified by Carbaugh (2004, 28), is that it represents a static view of the world. Thompson, Quinn, and Grinols view the economic pie as constant in size. In the context of the bathtub model, money coming

---

[8] One must wonder about their understanding of mutually beneficial transactions. Consider their statement that "a local economy *discards* money" (emphasis added).

[9] See Ekelund and Hébert (1997).

into the tub is a benefit to the economy in question and harms the region from where the money came. This implies that all transactions are zero sum. Clearly this is a flawed view of market transactions, as economists have long shown that specialization and trade benefit society (Ricardo [1817] 1992; Smith [1776] 1981). The same is generally true of all transactions that are voluntary. Participants expect the transactions to be mutually beneficial or they would not be willing participants.

Perhaps some simple everyday examples can be useful in pinpointing the problems with the money inflow perspective. Consider the argument by Thompson and Quinn (1999, 4). They write, "Gaming establishments need many supplies. Many of these are purchased from sources outside of the area. This is money lost. So too are profits that go to outside owners. Some gaming owners may reinvest monies in the local economy, but few have incentives to do so."

They offer a specific example, South Carolina video gaming machines purchased from out of state:

> There are 31,000 machines [in South Carolina]. Each costs $7,500. They have a life of from three to five years. Assuming a five year life, they carry a value of $1,500 per year each, or collectively $46,500,000. The machines are for all intents and purposes manufactured out of state. We can assume that $46,500,000 leaves the state each year because of the machines. (Thompson and Quinn 1999, 10)

This is only one component of the cash outflow from South Carolina due to gaming machines. When they total all of the estimated outflows, they conclude:

> The money leaving the state—from direct transactions—equals $133.3 million compared to $122 million coming into the state. In direct transactions, the state's economy loses. For the state as a whole, we can see that each dollar ($1.00) brought into the state as a result of the machines leads to a direct loss of one dollar and nine cents ($1.09). (Thompson and Quinn 1999, 11–12)

This argument should raise red flags with readers. Consider that a person in South Carolina purchases a car. Few cars are manufactured in the state. Most are produced in Detroit and Japan, let us say. Each car purchased then results in an outflow of money from the state. According to Thompson and Quinn's theory, then, each car purchase has a negative impact on the state's economy. Even in the case where a BMW car factory locates in South Carolina, according to Thompson and Quinn, there would not be economic benefits unless BMW reinvested all the "money" earned by the factory back into the state. Aside from these problems, this view also ignores capital inflows and the effects of the factory on the labor market, not to mention the utility from driving new cars.

The Thompson and Quinn argument seems quite similar to an argument made by antigambling advocate Robert Goodman. In his book *The Last Entrepreneurs* (1979) Goodman, who is a professor of architecture, explains what he believes to be the ideal economic structure. He argues that economies should strive to be self-sufficient. He explains the plight of a region that specializes too much:

> Since [a] booming manufacturing region has few incentives to develop its agricultural or energy technology, it falls progressively farther behind the agricultural or energy-specialized regions in its ability to do so. It is trapped in its own production specialization in order to generate the dollars it needs to buy the food and other resources for its survival. (Goodman 1979, 183)

Goodman's argument, taken to the extreme case of an individual, suggests that self-sufficiency is the ideal situation. This conclusion is in direct conflict with modern economics. Self-sufficiency implies poverty. We are much wealthier by specializing and trading, compared to the alternative of producing our own food, sewing our own clothing, building our own homes, developing our own pharmaceuticals, and so on. This was one of the fundamental insights of early economists like Adam Smith and David Ricardo.

If we are supposed to be concerned with the cash outflow that results from transactions with outsiders, should we be concerned with cash outflows from a particular individual? If cash leaving a state is harmful to that economy, is cash leaving a particular household harmful to it? This would appear to be a logical argument based on the Thompson and Quinn model. Obviously it leads to problems, since any purchase of goods or services increases the welfare of the individuals who undertake the transaction. Indeed, the money inflow model proponents (mercantilists?) appear to have it exactly backwards. Any voluntary cash transaction must lead to an increase in welfare for the involved parties. This would imply that cash outflows lead to increased welfare. Many of the monetary flow models that purport to measure the economic effects of gambling fail to recognize this basic point. Any conclusions based on these models should be viewed with extreme skepticism.

4.5 Conclusion

This chapter has examined some of the most common arguments given in opposition of casino development. Basically, the argument is that the casino industry simply cannibalizes other industries leaving no net positive economic effect of casino gambling. The different versions of the argument have unique twists. However, overall, these perspectives represent a very narrow view of casino gambling as beneficial only to the extent it can attract tourism to a region.

There have been very few studies that have empirically examined the economic growth impacts from the casino industry, be they consistent with the discussion in Chaps. 2 and 3 or neutral to negative, as suggested by the "industry cannibalization" theory discussed in this chapter. Next we examine an empirical analysis of the growth effects of the commercial casino industry in the United States.

Chapter 5
Analysis of the Relationship Between Casinos and Economic Growth

It should be clear that there is uncertainty and disagreement in the literature regarding the economic effects of legalized gambling. While some argue that gambling cannibalizes other industries, gambling advocates disagree. Some papers in the literature analyze particular states during specific years (mostly the early 1990s) but still relatively few studies have attempted a comprehensive analysis of the economic effects of gambling in the United States or in other countries. For an overview, see Eadington (1999) and Clement (2003).

Grinols (2004, Chapter 4) offers a general discussion of economic development as it relates to casinos and job growth, but no empirical evidence. He argues that researchers who have written export multiplier or cost–benefit analyses of the casino industry have often been confused. Grinols' critique is mostly on-target; he correctly argues that economic development occurs when welfare or utility increases. Development may or may not be associated with employment growth. They key for development is that individuals are better off.

The purpose of this chapter is to develop an empirical model of the economic growth effects of gambling, with a focus on the initial expansion of casinos outside of Nevada and New Jersey, in the early 1990s.[1] In addition, by comparing the effects of two different industries (casinos and greyhound racing), we can gain some information on the extent to which exports are necessary to promote economic growth. The results will provide information that can be useful to researchers, politicians, and concerned citizens. The analytical framework developed here could be applied to other industries or countries.

The material in this chapter is based on Walker DM, and JD Jackson. 1998. New goods and economic growth: Evidence from legalized gambling. *Review of Regional Studies* 28(2): 47–69. Used with permission from the Southern Regional Science Association.

[1]The data used in this chapter are relatively old, going from the mid-1970s through 1996. In Chap. 6, I provide additional analysis using more current data, in order to see if the longer term impacts appear any different.

Section 5.1 fleshes out the empirical question and provides background for its application to two of the major types of gambling, casinos and greyhound racing. Section 5.2 presents a nontechnical chapter summary for readers who may not be familiar with Granger causality or methods of time series analysis. The description in this section should enable readers to skim or skip the mathematical notation in the remainder of the chapter without loss. For readers who would like a technical description of the methodology, Sect. 5.3 provides it. Specifically, Granger causality techniques are used to test whether casino gambling causes growth or vice versa. The same methodology is used in an analogous set of tests for gambling at greyhound racetracks. The empirical results for all industries are presented in Sect. 5.4.

5.1 The Empirical Question

Many researchers, politicians, and advocacy groups argue that the expansion of legalized gambling cannibalizes other industries. Basically, the argument is that spending on newly legalized gambling completely crowds out spending on alternative locally produced goods, leading to no increase in total spending. If this theory were correct, then legalized gambling would be at best a zero-sum game. On the other hand, there are numerous factors, aside from exports, which contribute to economic growth. This debate over legalized gambling and economic growth, discussed in previous chapters, can be examined in the context of two testable hypotheses: (1) "Does the introduction of legalized gambling lead to economic growth?", and given an affirmative answer, (2) "Is it necessary to export gambling to obtain growth?"

The factory–restaurant dichotomy (Sect. 4.2) is related to the first question above. If the dichotomy is valid, if casinos can be factories in a few states but only restaurants in most others, then we should expect no consistent results. The issues of "import substitution" and "defensive legalization" are closely related to the factory–restaurant dichotomy. It is legitimate to expect state governments to consider the legalization of gambling simply to try to keep consumer dollars in the state. Eadington explains, "if the presence of casinos in the region allows regional residents to gamble at local casinos rather than becoming tourists to casinos in other regions, the economic impact from spending so generated is the same as it would be for tourists"[2] (Eadington 1995, 52). Indeed, such defensive legalization has been seen recently in Massachusetts and Ohio, and is being considered in a variety of other states. We attempt to develop an empirical model to determine whether casino "exports" are necessary for growth.

---

[2] This view is supported by growth theorists Hoover and Giarratani (1984, 319): "If a region can develop local production to meet a demand previously satisfied by imports, this 'import substitution' will have precisely the same impact on the regional economy as an equivalent increase in exports. In either case, there is an increase in sales by producers within a region."

5.1 The Empirical Question

The casino and greyhound racing industries have different market thresholds and ranges. (Threshold is the minimum number of consumers required to support the industries; range refers to the area over which the industry draws customers.[3]) This allows us to address the second question above, regarding the export base theory of growth. The casino industry likely has a much larger threshold and range than the greyhound racing industry does. Consider that casinos keep a much lower percentage of consumers' bets, typically 5 % or less. Racetracks, on the other hand, keep about 18–20 % of each dollar bet. The fact that casinos keep much less of each dollar bet indicates that it has a much higher threshold compared to greyhound racing. Coupled with the fact that casino net revenues are many times larger than racetrack revenues (industry averages), this suggests that casinos draw from a much larger range. For a given export range, even if casinos draw substantially more local customers than greyhound tracks, the casinos draw higher revenue, and most likely export in greater magnitude. Advertising and "clustering" patterns support this conclusion. There are many nationwide advertisements by Las Vegas, Atlantic City, and Mississippi casinos. Casinos hope to attract tourists from afar. National advertisements for greyhound racing are virtually nonexistent, although racing is often advertised locally. In addition, casinos often cluster together. Such agglomeration economies are not to be expected unless the producers are selling in national markets. This provides anecdotal evidence that the industries themselves view the range of casino gambling as much greater (national) than that for greyhound racing (regional at most).

This is not to suggest that casinos export but greyhound racing does not. Even the smallest crossroad gasoline station exports when an out-of-state car stops for gas. Rather, the suggestion is that a consistent finding that both activities "cause" growth indicates that exports may not be a fundamental factor in generating that growth due to the starkly different thresholds and ranges of the two goods. Specifically, a comparison of the empirical results for the two industries will help to answer the second question posed above. If the casino industry causes growth but the greyhound industry does not, we may conclude that exports have a significant impact on economic growth since the industry with the smaller range does not show evidence of driving economic growth. On the other hand, if both industries have a similar positive impact on growth, then we may conclude that exports *may not* be crucial since even with little or no export base, greyhound racing is found to be an engine for growth. The third possible finding is that greyhound racing causes growth but casinos do not—a result that would frankly be difficult to explain. Of course there is a fourth possibility, that neither industry has a significant impact on growth. This would be the finding, if proponents of the cannibalization theory are correct, that gambling industries merely replace other industries.

---

[3]For more discussion, see Berry and Horton (1970).

5.2 Nontechnical Explanation of Granger Causality

There is no statistical way to prove "causality" in the common sense of the word. However, there are statistical analyses that can test for what would appear to be a causal relationship. One of the more common analyses is called Granger causality, named for Clive Granger, recipient of the 2003 Nobel Prize in economics, who developed his causality analysis in the late 1960s (Granger 1969). We adapt Granger's methodology to examine the relationship between state-level gambling activity and economic growth.

The analysis in this chapter takes data from various US states with legalized casinos and greyhound racing. Economic growth is commonly measured by increases in per capita income (PCI), and we collect this data for states and years in which casino gambling and greyhound racing are available. Gambling activity is measured by the revenues from the respective industries. Casino activity is measured by casino revenues (money retained by the casino after paying winning bets to customers), while greyhound racing volume is measured by "handle," or the total amount of bets placed at racetracks. These are the standard measures of gambling volume in the respective industries, as reported to the various state gaming agencies, which are the source of our gambling volume data.

The goal of "Granger causality" analysis is to determine the relationship between the series of data. There are two different analyses performed: (1) casino revenue and PCI (in 10 states; 1978–1996; quarterly data), and (2) greyhound racing handle and PCI (in 18 states; 1975–1995; annual data). Note that some of the states are dropped from the analysis when they are determined not to have enough observations to yield information. Although the data analyzed run only through 1995 or 1996 and the models cover relatively short time periods, this analysis provides a foundation for subsequent researchers to further investigate these relationships in the United States or elsewhere.[4]

In order to analyze the effect of the legalized gambling on state-level PCI, several adjustments must be made to the data. First, the effect of variation due to state-specific factors must be removed so that odd differences among the states do not cause the appearance of a systematic relationship between the gambling and economic growth variables. These are the state dummies discussed in the subsequent sections. The effect of time must also be removed. Otherwise, for example, we might expect both casino revenues and PCI within a state to be rising as time passes in a time trend. Without adjusting for this tendency, the increase in both revenue and income might appear to be a causal relationship between the two, when in fact it is due solely to other factors affecting both variables through time.

Once adjustments to remove time- and state-specific effects have been made, we are left with "pure" data on the processes that explain PCI and gambling volume.

---

[4]This empirical analysis is from Walker and Jackson (1998). At the time of that writing, data were only available through 1996. It is presented here because I think this is useful information on the short-term impacts of casino gambling, in particular. More recent data are analyzed in the next chapter.

Next we test for a Granger causal relationship. Granger causality looks at time series data through numerous time periods and isolates the relationship between variations in the series of data. So if the time trend and state-specific effects have been removed from the data series, and the two variables still seem to move together, there may be a causal relationship between the two. One way of saying this is that changes in one of the series (x) precede changes in the other (y) in some systematic way. Then x "Granger causes" y.

The Granger causality test has four potential outcomes. For the example just given above,

1. x Granger causes y
2. y Granger causes x
3. Both 1 and 2 or
4. None of the above

Whatever the results of the Granger test, it does not give any information on *why* there is a relationship. As a preview, the statistically significant results of the analyses are that casino gambling Granger causes PCI and that greyhound racing Granger causes PCI. This combination of results suggests that legalized gambling does indeed promote economic growth, and that "exports" are not necessary for economic growth to occur.

5.3 Granger Causality with Panel Data[5]

Granger causality has proved a useful means of evaluating the potential sources of aggregate economic growth in recent empirical work. Balassa (1978), Jung and Marshall (1985), and Xu (1998) consider the relationship between exports and growth; Joerding (1986) and Kusi (1994) analyze the relationship between military spending and economic growth; Conte and Darrat (1988) look at the size of the government sector and economic growth; and Ramirez (1994) has shown that real government investment Granger causes real private investment in Mexico. This wide applicability makes Granger causality a natural technique to employ in causal inquiry.

Granger's methods, however, are not directly applicable to the problems at hand. These techniques were originally intended to apply to a set of linear covariance-stationary time series processes. This suggests that we should test for Granger causality on gambling revenue and PCI on a state-by-state basis. Unfortunately (for this study, at least), only two of the ten states with legal non-reservation casino gambling

---

[5]Readers who are not interested in the underlying econometric theory may wish to skip to Sect. 5.4.1.

had casinos prior to 1990, and fully two-thirds of the states having legal greyhound racing adopted post 1985. Establishing the requisite stationarity on a state-by-state basis and appealing to the asymptotic properties of a number of the associated estimators and tests cannot be justified due to the brevity of the time series. For this reason the data are pooled for each gaming industry, creating a panel consisting of a time series of observations for each of a cross section of states.

The statistical analysis of panel data using time series methods is still in its infancy. The paper by Holtz-Eakin, Newey, and Rosen (1988) relates directly to the estimation and testing of vector autoregressive models such as those needed to apply Granger's procedure to panel data. There have been several studies that look at the related problem of unit roots in panel data. Works by Breitung and Meyer (1994), Frances and Hobijn (1997), MacDonald (1996), Strazicich (1995), and Wu (1996) fall into this category.

5.3.1 Synopsis of Granger's Procedure

The application of Granger causality to panel data is not straightforward. A brief review of the general methodology of Granger causality here is followed by a detailed discussion of the modifications imposed in order to apply it to panel data.

According to Granger, a variable (X_t) causes another variable (Y_t) if, with information on all factors affecting both X_t and Y_t, the current value of Y_t can be predicted more accurately using past values of X (i.e., $X_{t-j}, j=1,\ldots,J$) than by not using them. More precisely, define (A_t) as the set containing all possible information affecting Y_t except information on X_t. Also define the mean square (prediction) error of Y_t given A_t as $\sigma^2(Y_t|A_t)$. "Granger causality" states that X causes Y if

$$\sigma^2(Y_t|A_t, X_t) < \sigma^2(Y_t|A_t) \tag{5.1}$$

Since adding a statistically significant set of variables reduces the error variance in least square regression, traditional t- and F-tests are available to test for Granger causality.

The testing procedure is straightforward. Assuming that X_t and Y_t are a pair of linear covariance stationary processes, they can be written as

$$X_t = \sum_{j=1}^{k} \beta_j X_{t-j} + \sum_{j=1}^{m} \delta_j Y_{t-j} + \varepsilon_{1,t} \tag{5.2}$$

$$Y_t = \sum_{j=1}^{m} \gamma_j Y_{t-j} + \sum_{j=1}^{k} \theta_j X_{t-j} + \varepsilon_{2,t} \tag{5.3}$$

where β_j, δ_j, γ_j, and θ_j are unknown parameters to be estimated, and $\varepsilon_{1,t}$ and $\varepsilon_{2,t}$ are white noise. Applying least square regression techniques to estimate these two models yields four types of Granger causality tests: (1) X causes Y if we can reject H_0:

$\theta_1 = \theta_2 = \ldots = \theta_k = 0$; (2) Y causes X if H_0: $\delta_1 = \delta_2 = \ldots = \delta_m = 0$ can be rejected; (3) if both null hypotheses can be rejected, feedback (simultaneous determination of X and Y) is indicated; and (4) if neither null hypothesis is rejected, X and Y are independent.

Typical caveats for the procedure relate to the structure of the hypothesis tests (one actually rejects Granger non-causality rather than accepting Granger causality) and to whether variables other than lagged values of Y_t should be included in A_t.[6] The most important caveat, however, relates to stationarity of the two series. Without stationarity, common trends could result in spurious regressions having perverse causality implications, such as business cycles causing sunspots.[7] Wold's theorem tells us that a stationary time series process can always be written as the sum of a self-deterministic component and a moving average component of possibly infinite order (Granger 1980, 60). If Y_t is stationary, it is possible for A_t to include only its past values, thereby eliminating the ambiguity in specifying A_t noted above.

5.3.2 Modifying the Procedure for Panel Data

As suggested earlier, the extension of these procedures to pooled time series cross section data is not straightforward, but our data paucity problem necessitates this type of model. Walker and Jackson (1998) first developed this methodology, which has subsequently been used elsewhere, e.g., Granderson and Linvill (2002). A three-stage procedure is used: (1) "filtering" trend and state-specific effects from the data, and (2) selecting the appropriate time series process that generates each variable. After making these adjustments, we (3) conduct the Granger causality tests.

5.3.2.1 Stage One

Perhaps the best way to visualize the problems involved and to understand the attempted solutions is to consider the way that we array the data on each variable. Consider a general gambling revenue variable REV_{it}. Later we examine the specific variables, e.g., casino revenue, CR. We have i states ($i = 1, \ldots, I$) with legalized gambling and t time periods ($t = 1, \ldots, T$) on a particular state. In all of the subsequent analyses, we "stack" these data by state, and within each state we organize the data in ascending order of time. Thus, it is routine to find the last observation on revenue for state i, REV_{iT}, followed by the first observation for state $(i+1)$,

---

[6] It is perfectly legitimate to include variables other than lagged values of X_t and Y_t in the two regressions. For example, see Conte and Darrat (1988). But including such variables "muddies the causality waters" since X could cause Y through affecting some other included variables, rather than directly.

[7] See Sheehan and Grieves (1982) and Noble and Fields (1983).

$REV_{i+1,1}$. The following discussion of filtering the data should make it clear that the order in which the states are stacked is not a matter of concern, but the obvious discontinuities involved in proceeding from the last period's observations in one state to the first period's observation in the next require some adjustment in the ordinary time series methodology.

The most obvious adjustment is filtering out state-specific and trend effects from the vector of observations on REV_{it}. We pursue this requirement by regressing REV_{it} on (1) a constant term; (2) a set of $(I-1)$ state dummy variables, to account for state-specific effects; (3) a time trend ($t=1$ is the beginning observation for each state) to account for a common trend in the data; and (4) interaction variables computed by multiplying each state dummy by the trend variable, to allow for different trends for each state. If the data are quarterly, seasonal adjustment (via a set of quarterly dummies) is also appropriate. Finally, a dummy variable equal to unity for the first observation of a new state is included to promote continuity of the pooled variable. The residual from this regression $REVr_{it}$ should be free of state-specific, trend, and other idiosyncratic anomalies. We refer to this residual as the "filtered series."

At this stage, it is appropriate to test the filtered series for stationarity. Recall the primacy of stationarity as a condition for the legitimate application of Granger's causality tests.[8] Several procedures are available to test for the presence of stationarity or lack thereof, as denoted by the presence of a unit root in the series: Dickey–Fuller, augmented Dickey–Fuller, and Phillips–Perron are three popular unit root tests. Since the filtered revenue series is a detrended, zero-mean series, the choice among these alternative tests is not likely to be crucial. Nevertheless, the Phillips–Perron test is chosen since it is robust with respect to the number of lagged differenced variables included in the test equation. If the unit root tests allow us to reject non-stationarity, we proceed to the next step in the analysis; otherwise we continue to respecify the filtering equation until we are able to reject non-stationarity.

The modifications so far serve three purposes. First, filtering out unspecified state-specific effects and state-specific trend effects should eliminate any concern about the order in which the state data are stacked, particularly since the filtered measure is stationary. Second, filtering out trend effects should eliminate any concern that the results are attributable to a common trend between the revenue and income variables. Third, stationarity of the filtered series guarantees that any innovation in the series, whether state specific or attributable to another time-independent factor, is of temporary duration. Thus, ruling out (or reducing the likelihood of) permanent shocks, common trend, and common factor problems, gives us reason to believe that any causality found between gambling revenue and PCI is not caused by exogenous forces.

---

[8] This may be an overstatement. Holtz-Eakin, Newey, and Rosen (1988, 1373) suggest that a large number of cross sections make it possible for lag coefficients to vary over time. Of course, there is always the question of how large is "large." It is unlikely that the 8 to 14 cross sections here are "large" numbers.

5.3.2.2 Stage Two

With filtered revenue and income series, the next step is to determine as precisely as possible what autoregressive process generates each series.[9] This stage amounts to an application of Box–Jenkins procedures to each filtered variable. The intent is to continue to add lags in the variables to the specification of the generating process until we obtain a white noise residual. We employ correlograms and partial correlograms to aid in specifying the generating process, along with Box–Pierce Q-statistics to detect white noise residuals. Here parsimony is our guide, choosing the shortest possible set of lags such that no significant (10 % level) autocorrelations exist among the residuals as judged by Q-statistics for the first 36 lags.

While this step is not traditional, it is done with a purpose. If we can identify the process generating a filtered series so that residuals of the estimated process are white noise, we can be reasonably certain that we have extracted all possible information on the current value of the variable from its past values. There is no temporally systematic effect left to explain. Then, if lagged values of another new variable are added to the model and if it provides a statistically significant improvement in explaining filtered income, it is legitimate to claim that revenue "causes" income. This stage introduces a problem concerning lagging the data that comes to fruition in the third stage of the analysis.

5.3.2.3 Stage Three

The second stage of the analysis provided all of the information needed to accurately specify the regression equations. The final stage of the analysis is to estimate the vector autoregressions implied by Granger causality testing and to perform the requisite hypothesis tests. Assuming that the second stage indicated that filtered per capita income (PCIr$_{it}$) was generated by an AR(k) process and filtered gambling revenue (REVr$_{it}$) was generated by an AR(m) process, the sequels to (5.2) and (5.3) are

$$\text{PCIr}_{i,t} = \sum_{j=1}^{k} \beta_j \text{PCIr}_{i,t-j} + \sum_{j=1}^{m} \delta_j \text{REVr}_{i,t-j} + \varepsilon_{1,t} \tag{5.4}$$

$$\text{REVr}_{i,t} = \sum_{j=1}^{m} \gamma_j \text{REVr}_{i,t-j} + \sum_{j=1}^{k} \theta_j \text{PCIr}_{i,t-j} + \varepsilon_{2,t} \tag{5.5}$$

The corresponding hypothesis tests are H_0: $\delta_1 = \delta_2 = \ldots = \delta_m = 0$ to test whether REVr Granger causes PCIr, and H_0: $\theta_1 = \theta_2 = \ldots = \theta_k = 0$ to test whether PCIr Granger

---

[9] Technically, all Wold's theorem guarantees is that a stationary series can be specified by an ARMA process. While a moving average error process cannot be ruled out a priori, it turns out for our problem that adding enough lagged terms will yield a white noise residual in all cases.

causes REVr. The models are estimated by ordinary least square regression[10] and the tests are standard F-tests of the joint hypotheses.

We conclude the discussion of the modifications of traditional Granger causality analysis deriving from the use of panel data with consideration of a point mentioned earlier. Lagging variables use up considerably more degrees of freedom than one might first expect because of the stacked panel data. If we lag the data, say, three periods to estimate the appropriate autoregressive process in stage two, we lose $3I$ (not 3) degrees of freedom when employing panel data on I states since *each state's* data must be lagged three periods. The reason for these extra lags is not statistical. Recall that we establish at stage one that the process is stationary. Rather, the extra lags are economically motivated: it makes no economic sense to allege that the early period observations (say $t=1, 2, 3$) in state $i+1$ are explained by the later period observations (say $T-2, T-1, T$) in state i. But that is precisely what we assume does happen if we do not drop the first three observations for state $i+1$ and similarly for all other states. The gain in degrees of freedom from pooling time series and cross-sectional data may not be nearly as much as one might expect at first blush.

This problem is even more exaggerated at stage three of the analysis. If REVr is found to be AR(m) and PCIr is found to be AR(k) from stage two where $k>m$, then we must drop the first k observations from *each state* after lagging to avoid an economically meaningless set of parameter estimates for (5.4) and (5.5). This means that, *inter alia*, for a state to remain in the model after the filtering stage, it must have at least $k+1$ observations. (A state would be dropped from the model in the filtering state if $n<v$, where v is the number of explanatory variables, excluding other states' dummy and interaction variables.) This, in turn, implies an iterative procedure between the three stages of analysis until a useable sample of data can be determined.

Clearly, the application of Granger causality techniques to panel data is not altogether straightforward. Nevertheless, a careful analysis along the lines outlined above can provide reliable and useful information concerning causal relationships between state gaming revenues and economic growth. We now turn to our empirical analysis of these questions.

5.4 Empirical Results

Certainly consumer welfare is enhanced by the availability of new goods and services. But do these new opportunities have a measurable effect on economic growth? Legalized gambling provides a unique opportunity to test this. If industries with different ranges are tested and compared, we can evaluate the importance of exports on economic growth. Using the methodology developed in the previous section, the empirical results are presented for casino gambling and greyhound racing.

---

[10] Since the explanatory variables are the same for both models, there is no difference between OLS and seemingly unrelated regression estimates whether or not $\varepsilon_{1,t}$ is correlated with $\varepsilon_{2,t}$.

5.4 Empirical Results 47

As noted above, the analysis in this chapter uses data through the mid-1990s. This analysis will help to give us a picture of how the casino industry and economic growth were related when the casino industry first started expanding outside of Nevada and New Jersey, in the early 1990s.

5.4.1 Casino Gambling

Quarterly real casino revenue and real PCI data are collected on ten states, listed with beginning year and quarter[11]: Colorado (1991.4), Illinois (1992.3), Indiana (1995.4), Iowa (1992.4), Louisiana (1993.4), Mississippi (1992.3), Missouri (1994.3), Nevada (1985.1), New Jersey (1978.2), and South Dakota (1991.3). Data for the analysis run through the fourth quarter of 1996 (i.e., 1996.4). A total of 248 observations are available. A first pass through the testing procedure indicates that estimating the Granger causality equations would require a ten quarter lag, i.e., dropping ten observations per state. Since Indiana had only five observations and Missouri 11, both states are dropped from the model. There are 232 observations on the other eight states' casino revenue and PCI.

The first step in our application is to filter the series, as illustrated:

$$\text{PCI}_t = \text{constant} + \text{trend} + \text{first-year dummy} + \text{pre-1990} + \text{quarterly dummies} \\ + \text{state dummies} + \text{state-trend interaction terms} + \text{error} \quad (5.6)$$

$$\text{CR}_t = \text{constant} + \text{trend} + \text{first-year dummy} + \text{quarterly dummies} \\ + \text{state dummies} + \text{error} \quad (5.7)$$

A state dummy for all but one of the states should remove any effects from stacking the data and from fixed effect state-specific differences in measurement. A time trend and quarterly dummy variables are included to remove any time-dependent trends or seasonal components that might be included in the processes. Seven state–trend interaction terms are used to remove any state-specific trends in the data. South Dakota is the state lacking the dummy and interaction variables, the base state. Because stacking the data for the states results in a "spike" at the first observation of a new state, we add a "first year dummy" variable (the first observation for each state is 1, 0 for all other observations). Since PCI data come from two different sources, we add a dummy variable "pre-1990" for observations in the PCI_t equation prior to 1990 in order to distinguish the sources and to account for any recording differences from those sources. This dummy affects only Nevada and New Jersey in the PCI filtering equation. Finally, there are stochastic disturbances in the "error."

The testing process begins with the filtering regressions. Then, testing the filtered variables, PCIr and CRr, for unit roots, the Phillips–Perron (PP) test indicates that the hypothesis of a unit root can be rejected. Both series are stationary at the 1 % level

---
[11] Quarterly PCI data are calculated using personal income data (Department of Commerce) and linearly interpolated annual census population estimates.

Table 5.1 Casino model Granger causality results

Hypothesis	F-statistic (F*)	Probability (F>F*)
$\pi_1=\pi_2=\ldots=\pi_9=0$ (CRr does not cause PCIr)	2.577	0.009
$\lambda_1=\lambda_2=\ldots=\lambda_7=0$ (PCIr does not cause CRr)	0.404	0.898

($PP_{CRr}=-8.324$; $PP_{PCIr}=-4.594$; critical value$=-2.575$). The next step is to determine the time series process that generates each of the filtered variables. Box–Jenkins methods indicate that PCIr can legitimately be viewed as being generated by an AR(7) process and CRr by an AR(9). Note that for the remainder of the procedure, we must drop the higher lag-number of observations (i.e., 9) from each state. This leaves us with 160 total observations, compared to 232 in the original model specification.

Finally, we alternately regress the stationary filtered series, PCIr and CRr, on their own respective lagged values and on past values of the other variable, and then test whether the coefficients on the other lags are jointly significantly different from zero. Defining C as the constant term, we estimate

$$\text{PCIr}_{i,t} = C + \sum_{j=1}^{7} \psi_j \text{PCIr}_{i,t-j} + \sum_{j=1}^{9} \pi_j \text{CRr}_{i,t-j} + \mu_{1,t} \qquad (5.8)$$

$$\text{CRr}_{i,t} = C + \sum_{j=1}^{9} \phi_j \text{CRr}_{i,t-j} + \sum_{j=1}^{7} \lambda_j \text{PCIr}_{i,t-j} + \mu_{2,t} \qquad (5.9)$$

In the case of (5.8), we test H_0: $\pi_1=\pi_2=\ldots=\pi_9=0$. If the null hypothesis is rejected, then casino revenue Granger causes economic growth. Failure to reject the null means there is no evidence of a causal relationship in this direction. For (5.9), we test H_0: $\lambda_1=\lambda_2=\ldots=\lambda_7=0$. Analogous to the case above, rejection of the null implies that economic growth Granger causes casino gambling. Failure to reject would imply that increases in PCI do not cause increases in casino revenues. Since we can reject the former null hypothesis but not the latter, the results in Table 5.1 indicate that casino revenue Granger causes economic growth (significant at the 1 % level) and not conversely.

Several points concerning these results are worthy of note. As many politicians and the casino industry suggest, the product does have a positive effect on growth. We have taken precautions to ensure that Nevada does not dominate the empirical results. Recall that data on Nevada are included only back until 1985, while New Jersey goes back to its beginning, 1978, and all other states to theirs, the early 1990s. When the model is split and component models are tested, the results are consistent with those presented in Table 5.1. For example, New Jersey and Mississippi were tested together, yielding results similar to those here.[12]

---

[12] A complete discussion can be found in Walker (1998b).

5.4 Empirical Results 49

Second, with regard to the factory–restaurant dichotomy, the entire industry appears to be a factory—not just Nevada, as Grinols (1994b) has suggested. If a few states were the only factories, we would not expect such significant results in the overall model, since other alleged restaurant states comprise about half of the observations in the model. If there did not exist a causal relationship in these states, one would expect this to add sufficient variation to the model to prevent rejection of non-causality hypothesis.

The results in this section should not be expected merely because gambling revenues are theoretically a component of PCI. If that reasoning were valid, we should have found Granger causality in the other direction as well. Simply because two variables may be expected to move in the same direction over time does not imply that one detrended variable is causing the other.

Overall, these results suggest that there is a positive causal relationship from the introduction of legalized casino gambling (a new good) to economic growth. Comparing this to the results of similar tests on greyhound racing will give us better information on the validity of the export base theory of economic growth.

5.4.2 Greyhound Racing

The legalization of greyhound racing was not as explosive as that of casino gambling. In some states racing has been legal since the 1930s while others have legalized it as recently as the 1980s. Annual data are collected on PCI and gross handle (HAN, dollar amount of bets placed at the tracks) for greyhound racing in 18 states.[13] In most cases, the greyhound data were supplied by the individual state racing commissions. For those states whose commissions were uncooperative, data were found in the *Annual Statistical Summary of Pari-Mutuel Racing* published by the Association of Racing Commissioners International.

The procedure from casino gambling is repeated to analyze the greyhound racing industry. Variables included in the filtering equations were a constant, trend, the "new state" variable, and the state dummy and trend-dummy interaction terms, all described earlier. Of course, no quarterly dummies are needed since the data are annual. Initially, there were 222 observations on the 18 states. Preliminary tests for proper lag length yielded a number which required four states dropping from the model for lack of sufficient observations: Kansas, Texas, Vermont, and Wisconsin. Each of these states had only five to seven observations. The end result is a pooled data set covering 14 states, consisting of 195 observations. The states included are listed below, using data through 1995. The first year of data for each state is indicated: Alabama (Mobile and Birmingham counties only; 1975), Arizona (1984), Arkansas (1975), Colorado (1985), Connecticut (1985), Florida (1985), Idaho

---

[13] Annual data are used here primarily because quarterly are not available. This does not cause complications because greyhound racing has been legal much longer (generally) than casino gambling.

Table 5.2 Greyhound model Granger causality results

Hypothesis	F-statistic (F^*)	Probability ($F > F^*$)
$\pi_1 = \pi_2 = \pi_3 = 0$ (HANr does not cause PCIr)	3.657	0.014
$\lambda_1 = \lambda_2 = \lambda_3 = \lambda_4 = 0$ (PCIr does not cause HANr)	0.841	0.501

(1985), Iowa (1985), Kansas (1989), Massachusetts (1985), New Hampshire (1975), Oregon (1975), Rhode Island (1985), South Dakota (1982), Texas (1990), Vermont (1985–1992), West Virginia (1985), and Wisconsin (1990). As in the casino tests, the data used in this model are adjusted for inflation.

After filtering the variables, we test for unit roots. The Phillips–Perron test statistic on HANr is −7.97, and on PCIr, the statistic is −6.35. With a critical value at the 1 % level of −2.58, the hypothesis of a unit root can be rejected for both series.

A Box–Jenkins analysis of the filtered residuals indicates that PCIr was generated by an AR(4) process and HANr by an AR(3). The final step is to conduct the Granger causality test. This involves estimating the following models and conducting the requisite F-tests:

$$\text{PCIr}_{i,t} = C + \sum_{j=1}^{4} \psi_j \text{PCIr}_{i,t-j} + \sum_{j=1}^{3} \pi_j \text{HANr}_{i,t-j} + \mu_{1,t} \tag{5.10}$$

$$\text{HANr}_{i,t} = C + \sum_{j=1}^{3} \phi_j \text{HANr}_{i,t-j} + \sum_{j=1}^{4} \lambda_j \text{PCIr}_{i,t-j} + \mu_{2,t} \tag{5.11}$$

The F-test results are presented in Table 5.2. The result that greyhound handle Granger causes PCI is significant at standard levels. There is no evidence of bilateral causality.

As with the casino gambling model, we attempt to investigate whether a single state or a small group of states is responsible for the results. This is done by splitting the sample into two component parts, one with states that have had greyhound racing for a relatively long period of time back through 1975, and the other with states that have more recently legalized the activity. Both sets of analyses exhibited results highly consistent with those of Table 5.2. For the long series states, the F-statistic for testing the null hypothesis that HANr does not cause PCIr is 4.77 and the F-statistic for testing the null that PCIr does not cause HANr is 0.70. For the short series, the respective F-values are 7.30 and 0.93.[14]

The results indicate that greyhound racing, like casinos, Granger causes PCI at the state level. Because of the different thresholds and ranges of the industries, these results taken with the casino results suggest that exports are *not* necessary for economic growth.

---

[14] The interested reader may see Walker (1998b) for the full analysis and results.

5.5 Summary and Conclusion

Effusive rhetoric surrounds attempts by state governments to legalize various gaming activities. Those in favor of legalization argue that, among other potential advantages, the new gambling activity will promote state economic growth. Opponents argue that the economic growth argument is without merit. Typically neither side offers any empirical evidence.

In the first part of this chapter, two questions were posed related to the economic growth effects of legalizing gambling: (1) Does legalized gambling contribute to state economic growth? (2) If so, is it necessary for gambling to be exported for economic growth? These questions were addressed with Granger causality analysis of panel data on casino gambling, greyhound racing, and PCI at a state level.

We can conclude that casino gambling and greyhound racing Granger cause state PCI. (The hypotheses that casino and greyhound gambling do not Granger cause state PCI are rejected.) There is no evidence that causality also runs in the other direction. These results suggest that the answer to question (1) is "yes." Our results imply that adding a new good to a state's consumption menu does indeed spur state economic growth. Certainly, we have no evidence to the contrary in this analysis.

Regarding question (2) on the export base theory, recall that the two gambling activities have disparate thresholds and ranges. Based on our results, it does not appear that exports play the crucial role that they often are sometimes alleged to play in the state growth process. This latter inference is not intended to suggest that exporting goods and services does not result in state economic growth. After all, casino gambling has both a threshold and range exceeding the size of the states where casinos are offered, and we found that it causes state economic growth. On the other hand we found the same results for greyhound racing with a much smaller threshold and range. We may conclude that exports of the newly legalized gambling activity may be sufficient but not necessary for the gambling industry to result in state economic growth.

As discussed in previous chapters, there are a variety of channels through which the legalization of a gambling activity may translate into economic growth. It could be that the construction of casinos and racetracks expands a state's capital stock. Or it could be the immigration attendant to the higher wages attributable to this expanded state infrastructure. Alternatively, the velocity of spending may increase because consumers have an additional product to purchase. Or it could be the result of a Keynesian-type government spending multiplier effect attributable to what the state does with its additional revenue. Exactly how does legalized gambling spur economic growth? This question warrants more empirical attention now that there is evidence of a relationship between the variables.

This chapter provides some early empirical evidence that, indeed, legalized gambling does have a positive impact on state-level economic growth. These results are much more general than other investigations that tend to analyze the experience of just a single state or for a very short time period. Still there are many issues that demand further empirical analysis, especially considering the fact that the empirical analysis here relies on data through only 1995 and 1996.

In the next chapter more recent evidence on the relationship between casino gambling and economic growth is presented.

Chapter 6
Recent Evidence on Casinos and Economic Growth

The results from the previous chapter are interesting because they capture the economic effects of casinos at a state level, right as the industry began its spread outside of Nevada and Atlantic City. However, the results do not provide any evidence on whether the economic growth effects persist beyond a few years. In this chapter I provide additional empirical evidence on the impact of casinos on state-level economic growth. First, I repeat the casino analysis from the previous chapter, using updated data. Then I present an analysis of how the casino industry impacted the recovery from Hurricane Katrina in 2005 in the Gulf States. This newer evidence is consistent with the previous evidence we found.

6.1 Casino Gambling and Economic Growth: An Update

Since the commercial casino industry has seen such enormous growth since the early 1990s, it seemed appropriate to reanalyze the relationship between casinos and economic growth, using the most current data available. To date, we have performed two additional analyses to determine whether the results we initially found using the 1978–1996 data (discussed in Chap. 5) were robust.

Jackson and I published an update to the analysis in Chap. 5, and we present those results here. The 2007 analysis used annual data from 1991 to 2005 (Walker and Jackson 2007). We used the starting data of 1991 (for all states that already had casinos by then) so that the panel would be more balanced, and so that Nevada and

---

The material in this chapter is based on Walker DM, and JD Jackson. 2007. Do casinos cause economic growth? *American Journal of Economics and Sociology* 66(3): 593–607. Used with permission from John Wiley & Sons. Walker DM, and JD Jackson. 2008. Market-based "disaster relief": Katrina and the casino industry. *International Journal of Social Economics* 35(7): 521–530. Used with permission from Emerald. Walker DM, and JD Jackson. 2009. Katrina and the Gulf States casino industry. *Journal of Business Valuation and Economic Loss Analysis* 4(1). Used with permission from De Gruyter and Company.

Table 6.1 Casino model Granger causality results, 1991–2005

Hypothesis	F-statistic (F^*)	Probability ($F>F^*$)
$\pi_1=\pi_2=0$ (CRr does not cause PCIr)	0.195	0.824
$\lambda_1=\lambda_2=\lambda_3=\lambda_4=0$ (PCIr does not cause CRr)	0.433	0.785

New Jersey would not dominate the model. The 11 states included are listed with the initial year for which their data was included: Colorado (1991), Illinois (1991), Indiana (1996), Iowa (1991), Louisiana (1993), Michigan (1999), Mississippi (1992), Missouri (1994), Nevada (1991), New Jersey (1991), and South Dakota (1991). This yields an initial 165 observations.

For brevity, I do not provide all of the details of the analysis here. Rather, I simply present the results (using the same notation as in Chap. 5) and discuss them.[1] As Table 6.1 shows, there appears to be no Granger causal relationship between casino revenues and per capita income using the 1991–2005 annual data. Obviously these results are a contrast to the results presented in Chap. 5. In the 2007 paper we attempted to explain why we found significant results using the 1978–1996 quarterly data but not the 1991–2005 annual data.

Of course, it could simply be that using the newer data set, the relationship between casino revenues and economic growth disappeared. Perhaps there is an initial short-term positive stimulus effect from casinos, which dies out over time as the casinos become an integral part of the regional economy. Alternatively, as casinos have become more widespread, perhaps any positive stimulus effects they have are competed away. Alternatively, perhaps the use of quarterly data in the earlier study, but annual data in the more recent one, is the explanation for the contradictory results. Given these results, we decided to rerun the analysis in 2012, using data through 2010. This analysis is discussed in the next section.

6.2 Recent Evidence

Many observers considered the casino industry to be "recession proof." Yet, the industry did see a modest reduction in revenues during the 2007–2009 recession. Commercial casino revenues declined from a peak of $37.5 billion in 2007 to a low of $34.3 billion in 2009. By 2011, revenues had increased to $35.6 billion, and 2012 revenues will likely be a new record high. The casino industry was perhaps not as negatively affected by the recession as many other industries. In any case, state governments have shown an increased interest in legalizing casinos or expanding

---

[1] The analysis indicates that two lag periods are required for casino revenue and four lag periods are required for per capita income, for the residuals to be white noise.

6.2 Recent Evidence

Table 6.2 Casino model Granger causality results, 1990–2010

Hypothesis[a]	Lag periods	Obs.	F-statistic (F^*)	Probability ($F>F^*$)
CRr does not Granger cause PCIr	2	228	4.784	0.009
PCIr does not Granger cause CRr			1.808	0.166
CRr does not Granger cause PCIr	3	216	3.339	0.020
PCIr does not Granger cause CRr			1.283	0.281
CRr does not Granger cause PCIr	4	204	3.009	0.019
PCIr does not Granger cause CRr			1.231	0.299
CRr does not Granger cause PCIr	5	192	3.438	0.005
PCIr does not Granger cause CRr			1.369	0.238

[a]The hypothesis "CRr does not Granger cause PCIr" relates to (5.8): $H_0: \pi_j=0$, for all j. The hypothesis "PCIr does not Granger cause CRr" relates to (5.9): $H_0: \lambda_j=0$, for all j

existing casino industries in states where they are already legal. Relatively recent legalizations have occurred in Massachusetts, Kansas, and Ohio, and a variety of other states are currently considering it. Therefore, it is informative to again visit the question of casinos and economic growth.

The most recent iteration of the model includes the 12 states shown in Table 1.1 (CO, IL, IN, IA, LA, MI, MS, MO, NV, NJ, PA, and SD). In this model we use real commercial casino revenues and real personal per capita income, for 1990–2010. Thus, we have 21 years' data on 12 states, or 252 observations.

In considering the optimal lag structure, we examined the literature and found some different perspectives on how this should be done. For example, it has been suggested that a 4-period lag structure is traditionally used in Granger causality applications (Thornton and Batten 1985). To be inclusive of the various perspectives on this issue, we run the model using different lag structures, from 2-year through 5-year.

The results are presented in Table 6.2. In each model, we find that casino revenues (CRr) Granger cause economic growth, i.e., personal per capita income (PCIr), at either the 5 or 1 % level. In none of the models did we find that economic growth (PCIr) Granger causes casino revenues (CRr).

The results from this most recent analysis suggest that there is, in fact, a positive impact of casino revenues on state-level per capita personal income, using data from 1990 to 2010. These results are robust to different lag lengths. As the casino industry has grown in existing casino states, and has spread to new states during our sample period, our strong results suggest that the industry has a long-term positive impact on state-level economic growth. These results are consistent with the positive labor-market impacts found by Cotti (2008). Perhaps any new industry may be expected to have a similar simulative impact on the state economy, as explained by Schumpeter ([1934] 1993, 66).

More interesting, perhaps, is the comparison of the current results with our results from previous studies. The current results are consistent with our initial results using 1978–1996 data. However, in the 2007 study we found no relationship between growth and casino revenues; that study used 1991–2005 annual data.

One possible interpretation of these different results is that casinos have a countercyclical effect on the state economy. Consider that the sample periods in the original analysis and these most recent results—both of which found a positive economic growth effect from casinos—include a large number of periods during which the United States was in recession, relative to the 2007 study, in which a smaller proportion of its sample period was recessionary.[2] These different findings, in light of the recessions included in the different analyses, suggest that casinos might be acting as a countercyclical stimulus. The casino industry has continued to grow rather dramatically, except during the 2007–2009 recession. Perhaps the casino industry was more "recession-proof" than many other industries, and in this way the industry was helpful in mitigating some of the negative effects of the recession in host states.[3]

6.3 Hurricane Katrina and the Gulf States Casino Industry

Hurricane Katrina was one of the most devastating natural disasters affecting the United States in recent history. The storm made landfall near the Louisiana–Mississippi border. The media coverage of Katrina focused on the devastation and humanitarian trauma of New Orleans. Although the Mississippi Gulf Coast was almost completely destroyed, it did not receive as much attention. Of course, the overall impact of Katrina outweighs the effect on any particular segment of the economy. But among the most seriously impacted industries, the casino industry suffered staggering losses from Katrina. Then in September 2005, Rita made landfall near the Louisiana–Texas border, wreaking additional damage to Louisiana and further crippling the casino industry there.[4]

When Hurricane Katrina hit the Gulf Coast in 2005, the casino industry in Mississippi represented the third largest commercial casino market in the United States, behind Las Vegas and Atlantic City. The Louisiana casino market is also significant. According to the American Gaming Association (American Gaming Association 2005), total gaming revenues in 2004 were $2.16 billion in Louisiana and $2.78 billion in Mississippi. The states raise a significant amount of tax revenue from the casinos: in 2004, $436 million in Louisiana and $333 million in Mississippi. The industry employs a sizable workforce: in 2004, over 20,000 employees in Louisiana, and almost 29,000 in Mississippi. Hurricanes Katrina (August 2005) and Rita (September 2005) devastated the casinos located on the Gulf Coast of Mississippi, in the New Orleans area, and in Lake Charles, Louisiana.

---

[2] In the 2007 study, 8.9 % of the sample periods were during a recession, while approximately 13 % of the sample periods in the 1998 and current study were during a recession.

[3] It is not unusual to find results indicating that entertainment industries are "recession proof," for example, movie theaters during the Great Depression. Skinner, Ekelund, and Jackson (2009) also find museum attendance to be countercyclical.

[4] For maps of Louisiana and Mississippi casino locations, and other information, see American Gaming Association (2006b, 13–14).

6.3 Hurricane Katrina and the Gulf States Casino Industry

The Gulf Coast casinos immediately began rebuilding in the wake of Katrina (and Rita). Aside from its focus on capital reinvestment, the industry has also publicized its efforts to help its employees in the wake of the hurricanes.[5] By October 2007, casino revenues on the Mississippi Gulf Coast and New Orleans' land-based casino had surpassed pre-Katrina levels, and Louisiana riverboat casino revenues were nearly up to pre-Katrina/Rita levels,[6] even though some properties had not been rebuilt. In perhaps no other industry was the recovery effort so immediate, intense, and noticeable.

In this section we describe how the Gulf Coast casino industry was affected and how it reacted to Hurricane Katrina.[7] Using the available data we also perform a simple empirical analysis of the casino industry's impact on the economic recovery of Louisiana and Mississippi after Katrina. Did the casino industry have a measurable positive impact on the states' recoveries? This is an interesting empirical question, considering how many people view the casino industry as parasitic and gambling as a zero-sum game. The results support the earlier analysis which suggests that casinos Granger cause economic growth.

6.3.1 Background on the Gulf Coast Casino Industry

Since casinos were legalized in the early 1990s the casino industry in Louisiana and Mississippi has expanded significantly. At the end of 2006 there were 14 large casinos in Louisiana and 28 in Mississippi, many of which are located near or on the Gulf coast and along the Mississippi River.[8] The casinos in these two states enjoy some measure of isolation. Commercial casinos are not legal in any surrounding states (Alabama, Arkansas, Tennessee, Texas), suggesting that casinos in these states are able to attract tourists from around the Southeast United States and beyond.

Katrina was one of the most devastating hurricanes in history. Certainly, no other storm has damaged the casino industry as significantly. Nine casinos in Louisiana and thirteen in Mississippi were seriously damaged and shut down, or destroyed, by Hurricanes Katrina and Rita in late summer 2005 (Table 6.3). Six of the casinos—three in Louisiana and three in Mississippi—never reopened.

Specific data on damages are not available by casino property. However, pictures of some of the damaged properties illustrate just how devastating Katrina was,

---

[5]For example, see the press release by the American Gaming Association (2006b), documenting the charity funds that had been established to help the affected Gulf Coast casino employees.

[6]August 2005 Mississippi Gulf Coast revenues were $105 million; in September 2007 they were over $111 million. The New Orleans land based casino revenue was $29 million in July 2005, and $32 million in October 2007. Riverboat casino revenues in Louisiana were $157 million in July 2005 and $137 million in October 2007.

[7]We include information on Hurricane Rita, too, to the extent it impacted the casino industry.

[8]The sizes of these casinos range from 14,000 to 180,000 square feet. In addition to these there are a variety of smaller casinos. Information on specific casinos can be found at casinocity.com.

Table 6.3 Casinos damaged by Hurricanes Katrina and Rita

Damaged by Katrina (August 2005)			Damaged by Rita (September 2005)
New Orleans area	*Mississippi Gulf Coast*		*Lake Charles, LA*
Bally's	Beau Rivage	Grand Casino (Gulfport)	Grand Palais
Boomtown	Boomtown	Hard Rock	Isle Lake Charles
Harrah's	Casino Magic (Bay St. Louis)	Imperial Palace	Harrah's Pride
Treasure Chest	Casino Magic (Biloxi)	Isle of Capri	Harrah's Star
	Copa Casino	Silver Slipper	L'Auberge du Lac
	Grand Casino (Biloxi)	The New Palace	
		Treasure Bay	

Source: Walker and Jackson (2009). Used with permission from De Gruyter and Company

particularly in Biloxi and Gulfport, MS. Of course, New Orleans received most of the media attention after Katrina because of the large number of people affected by the storm and the subsequent flooding, but the casino industry in Mississippi was damaged more seriously than that in Louisiana. This is mainly because of the high concentration of casinos along the Mississippi Gulf Coast.

To get a picture of the casino damage caused by the hurricanes, we can piece together data provided by each state's casino regulatory agency.[9] Unfortunately, the states do not publish the same type of data on their casinos. Louisiana publishes monthly revenue data by property, but Mississippi does not. Mississippi publishes the number of slot machines operating at each property each month; Louisiana does not. Revenue by property is the ideal measure of gambling volume, but the number of slot machines is an adequate substitute, since the industry relies on a basic formula in allocating slot machines to floor space, and this is directly related to total revenue. By examining the revenue data (LA) and slot count (MS) we can get a picture of the impact of Katrina on the industry's revenues.[10]

Figure 6.1 illustrates the monthly (nominal) revenue from New Orleans area casinos. Katrina forced the closing of all of the casinos through the end of September 2005. Boomtown and Treasure Chest reopened in October 2005, and Harrah's reopened in February 2006. Bally's never reopened.

Table 6.4 lists the slot count at Mississippi Gulf Coast casinos the month before Katrina (July 2005), several months after (December 2005), and in October 2006, over 1 year after Katrina. After Katrina many casinos rebuilt and, in some cases, expanded. By looking at the total number of slots operating on the Gulf Coast during each month (last row, Table 6.4) we get an idea of the extent to which the casino industry in Mississippi had recovered from Katrina, over a year after.[11]

---

[9] The agencies are the Louisiana Gaming Control Board, lgcb.dps.louisiana.gov/; and the Mississippi Gaming Commission, msgamingcommission.com/.

[10] The state agencies do track aggregate state monthly casino revenue, but these data do not reveal the extent to which Katrina affected Gulf Coast casinos since not all casinos in the state are on the coast.

[11] Occasional snap-shots of slot positions provide a better picture than a monthly listing would. This is because casino expansion and remodeling may affect slot count and revenue in different ways.

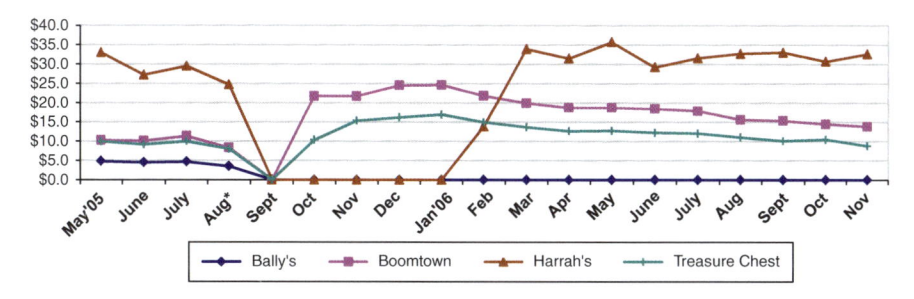

6.3 Hurricane Katrina and the Gulf States Casino Industry

Fig. 6.1 Nominal casino revenue, New Orleans area casinos affected by Katrina (millions of $), 2005–2006. *Data source*: Louisiana Gaming Control Board. *Source*: Walker and Jackson (2009). Used with permission from De Gruyter and Company

Table 6.4 Mississippi Gulf Coast casino slot machine positions, casinos affected by Katrina

Casino	Slot positions July 2005	December 2005	October 2006
Beau Rivage (Biloxi)	2,217	–	2,017
Boomtown (Biloxi)	1,052	–	1,388
Casino Magic (Biloxi)	1,177	–	–
Copa Casino (Gulfport)	1,354	–	–
Grand Casino (Biloxi)	2,610	–	838
Hard Rock Casino[a] (Biloxi)	1,500	–	–
Hollywood[b] (Bay St. Louis)	1,206	–	915
Imperial Palace (Biloxi)	1,484	1,885	1,999
Island View Casino[c] (Gulfport)	2,060	–	1,032
Isle of Capri (Biloxi)	1,184	728	1,333
New Palace (Biloxi)	1,189	827	849
Silver Slipper (Biloxi)	860	–	–
Treasure Bay (Biloxi)	973	–	228
Total slot positions	17,366	3,440	10,599

Data source: Mississippi Gaming Commission
Source: Walker and Jackson (2009). Used with permission from De Gruyter and Company
[a]The Hard Rock Casino was set to open the week Katrina hit. The rebuilt hotel/casino opened in July 2007, with 1,445 slot machines
[b]Prior to Katrina the Hollywood was named Casino Magic
[c]Prior to Katrina the Island View was named Grand Casino

Hurricane Rita affected the casino industry in Lake Charles, LA, less than a month after Katrina. Figure 6.2 illustrates revenues at the affected casino properties. The area's largest casino, L'Auberge du Lac, opened in May 2005, the first month for which data are shown. This casino's opening probably accounts for the decline in revenues at the other casinos leading up to Hurricane Rita. After Rita this market appeared to have stabilized.

The repair and rebuilding of the casinos on the Mississippi Gulf Coast and, to a lesser extent, in New Orleans and Lake Charles, LA, raise the question of whether the casino industry has an impact on the overall recovery of the region. The question

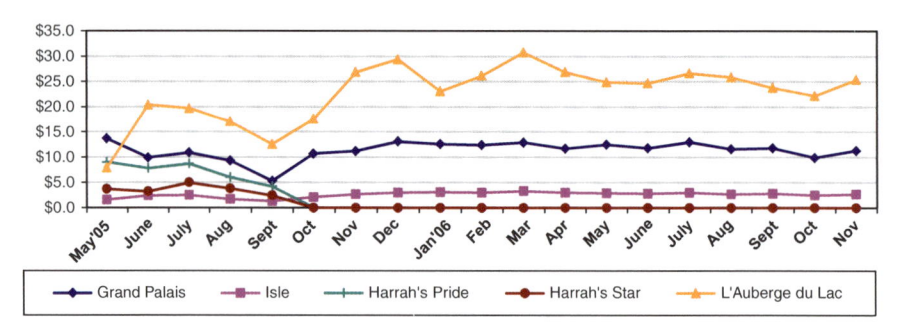

Fig. 6.2 Nominal casino revenue, Lake Charles area casinos affected by Rita (millions of $), 2005–2006. *Data source*: Louisiana Gaming Control Board. *Source*: Walker and Jackson (2009). Used with permission from De Gruyter and Company

is more relevant for Mississippi, as the casino industry is the dominant industry in Biloxi and Gulfport, and is significant relative to the state economy. However, the industry is also a noteworthy component of the New Orleans, Lake Charles, and Louisiana economies.

6.3.2 Data and Model

We wish to test whether there has been any positive impact of rebuilding the casino industry on the post-Katrina economies of Louisiana and Mississippi. Our hypothesis is that the immediate, large scale rebuilding efforts after Katrina might have an effect similar to the stimulus effect found in Chap. 5 and in the analysis earlier in this chapter.

In order to have a control for the model, we include the two states with casinos (Louisiana and Mississippi)[12], as well as two states without commercial casinos (Alabama and Texas).[13] We collected quarterly data on state-level personal income and casino revenues, to measure economic growth and casino activity, respectively.

Although some of our previous analyses have used per capita income as the variable measuring economic growth, we instead use personal income in this analysis. There was a significant amount of migration caused by Katrina. It is unclear exactly how effectively per capita income would reflect such migration. For example, if

---

[12] Slot revenues at racetracks ("racinos") are omitted from this analysis. Indian casinos are not included because their revenue data are not publicly disclosed. However, based on our empirical results, we would expect Indian casinos to amplify the effects we find for commercial casinos.

[13] We initially included Florida in the study because it was affected by Katrina. However, after weighting the data, as described below, Florida drops out of the model because it did not sustain significant damage. Another possible model would be to have four groups of states, two with casinos and two without, with one group of each type being affected by Katrina, and the other having not been affected.

6.3 Hurricane Katrina and the Gulf States Casino Industry

Table 6.5 Data weights: proportion of counties affected by Hurricane Katrina and/or Rita

State	# Affected counties	# Total counties	% Counties affected
Alabama	11	67	16.4
Florida	0	67	0
Louisiana	37	64	57.8
Mississippi	49	82	59.8
Texas	22	254	8.7

Source: Walker and Jackson (2008b). Used with permission from Emerald

there is a significant amount of migration out of Louisiana and Mississippi then per capita income measures may actually *rise* as a result of Katrina, if the loss in income is relatively less than the population decrease. Other possible anomalies led us to avoid using per capita income. The personal income data are from the Bureau of Economic Analysis, and are seasonally adjusted.

Casino revenues are the best measure of the volume of gambling activity. These data are net of payments to players for winning bets. Not only do these revenues represent consumer spending and tourism, but also the capital reinvestment, labor demand, etc., associated with rebuilding the casinos. Casino revenue data are provided by the respective state gaming regulatory agencies.

Both data sets (personal income and casino revenues) are quarterly, and are adjusted for inflation. The data set runs from 1997.1 through 2007.2, the most recent period for which data were available at the time of the analysis (in 2008).[14] Since we are using quarterly data, Hurricanes Karina and Rita occur in the same period (2005.3). Since both storms affected the Louisiana and Mississippi casino industries, we examine their effects jointly. Katrina had the most serious impact on Louisiana and Mississippi, and to a lesser extent, Alabama and Florida; Rita affected mostly Louisiana and Texas.

We want the emphasis in the model to be on the most seriously affected states by the hurricanes, so we weighted the personal income and casino revenue data. Our primary goal was to keep Texas from dominating the model, as it has a significantly larger personal income than the other states in the model, but was not as seriously affected by the storms.

In order to weight the data, we obtained a list of counties (or parishes, for Louisiana) declared by FEMA to be most seriously damaged by Katrina and Rita. FEMA offers aid in the form of public assistance or individual assistance. The most seriously affected counties (parishes) qualify for both public and individual assistance. We weight the personal income and casino revenue data by the percentage of the state's counties (parishes) that qualified for both public and individual assistance as a result of the hurricanes. The weights are shown in the right-most column of Table 6.5.

---

[14] We chose 1997.1 as the beginning period of the sample so that any "newness" effect of the casinos, which were introduced in the early 1990s, would not be driving the results.

Florida drops out of the model because none of its counties was classified in the most serious FEMA category. Obviously these weightings do not perfectly reflect the relative damage caused to the states, but we view this as the best available weighting strategy.[15]

In order to test whether the casino industry has had a significant effect on the recovery from Katrina, we posit a simple OLS model to explain personal income at the state level. Obviously there are many components of personal income. However, such series are explained, to an extent, by their own past values. After an analysis of the series' correlograms and unit root tests, we conclude that personal income and casino revenues are generated by AR(2) and AR(1) processes, respectively. We choose to model these time dependencies directly, rather than simply adding a time trend in the model. Therefore, the model includes *Casino Revenue* $(t-1)$, *Personal Income* $(t-1)$, and *Personal Income* $(t-2)$ as explanatory variables.

The model includes a series of dummy variables for the affected states: Alabama, Louisiana, and Mississippi. Texas and Florida were also affected by Katrina/Rita. Texas is the omitted dummy. Florida was omitted from the analysis entirely, as explained above.

We include a series of interaction terms: state dummies with a Katrina dummy (value of 1 in 2005.3, 0 otherwise) to allow the state personal income intercepts to adjust as a result of Katrina/Rita. By interacting the Katrina dummy with the various state dummies, we are able to gauge the differential (before and after) effect of Katrina/Rita on the various states' personal incomes. Including the Katrina dummy directly as well would muddy the waters considerably, so the dummy is not included alone.[16]

Finally, we include two variables to account for the effect of the commercial casino industry on the states' personal incomes. *Casino Revenue* measures current period net casino revenues, and is a measure of the economic activity in the industry. The second variable is an interaction term between *Casino Revenue* and the *Post-Katrina Dummy*.[17] This variable measures the contribution of the casino industry to state personal income after Katrina. This important effect is above and beyond the "normal" effect found in the *Casino Revenue* variable, and is the primary focus of the model.

---

[15] Weighting by the affected population would be difficult and imprecise, especially considering migration after Katrina. Weighting by the amount of aid received is problematic because such measures are not available quarterly. It is also questionable whether the monetary aid accurately reflects the severity of damage, as much of disaster relief may be motivated politically rather than by need (Sobel and Leeson 2006, 61). The FEMA designation for affected counties is probably the best available indicator of damage sustained.

[16] The Katrina dummy by itself would measure the Katrina/Rita impact on Texas, the base state, and the one least affected by the storms. The presence of this variable in our model would change the interpretation of the other state/Katrina interactions so that they would then measure how each state's differential impact differs from the differential impact on Texas personal income. This "difference in differences" interpretation is an unnecessary convolution as well as a rather meaningless distinction, and hence one which we eschew.

[17] The post-Katrina dummy takes a value of 0 prior to 2005.3, and 1 for 2005.3 and after.

6.3 Hurricane Katrina and the Gulf States Casino Industry

Table 6.6 Regression results

Variable[a]	Coefficient	t-Statistic
Constant	2757.38***	7.89
Personal Income $(t-1)$	0.28***	7.02
Personal Income $(t-2)$	0.39***	9.85
Casino Revenue	3.31 e–6*	1.69
Casino Revenue $(t-1)$	4.89 e–7	0.25
Post-Katrina × Casino Revenue	3.08 e–6***	6.12
Alabama Dummy[b]	−1831.56***	−7.70
Alabama Dummy × Katrina Dummy	19.60	0.07
Louisiana Dummy	−75.80	−0.27
Louisiana Dummy × Katrina Dummy	−6264.69***	−20.44
Mississippi Dummy	−1805.47***	−3.93
Mississippi Dummy × Katrina Dummy	−693.22**	−2.20
$N=160$ (4 states, 40 obs. each)		
$R^2=0.98$		

Dependent variable: weighted real quarterly personal income, 1997.1–2007.2
Source: Walker and Jackson (2008b). Used with permission from Emerald
[a]All monetary variables are inflation-adjusted
[b]Texas is the omitted state
*Significant at the 10 % level; **significant at the 5 % level; ***significant at the 1 % level

Admittedly, this is a very simple model of state personal income; we are estimating current period personal income by using its own past values, as well as data on casino revenue, and a series of dummy and interaction terms. But such a model should highlight the extent to which Katrina and the casino industry have affected the states' economies.

6.3.3 Results

The full model uses data from Alabama, Louisiana, Mississippi, and Texas, for 1997.1 through 2007.2. Hence, we have 42 observations on four cross-sections. Since there is a two-period lag for the *Personal Income* variable, the first two observations get dropped from each state. This leaves 160 observations in the model. The results of the model are shown in Table 6.6.[18]

First notice that the state dummies reflect the different levels of personal income, as Texas (the base state) has the largest weighted personal income, followed closely by Louisiana; the personal incomes of Alabama and Mississippi are significantly

---

[18]The Durbin-Watson statistic is 0.953. However, the statistic does not have the standard interpretation since we are using panel data. Any autocorrelation present would likely be due to the fact that the data for the different cross-sections are "stacked." Restacking the data in an alternative order would alter the Durbin-Watson statistic. The unit root test rejects the hypothesis of the presence of a unit root in the residuals. For brevity, summary statistics are not presented.

lower. Keeping in mind that Katrina and Rita damaged Louisiana the most seriously, followed closely by Mississippi, and Alabama and Texas to a much less extent, the state dummy and Katrina interaction terms exhibit the expected signs and relative values. These variables confirm that Louisiana suffered the most serious damage, followed by Mississippi. Alabama's personal income was not significantly affected by Katrina.

Unfortunately, good state-level *quarterly* data on federal aid and charities are not available, even for Katrina. However, one would expect a large inflow of aid accruing to Louisiana and Mississippi to have a direct or indirect impact on personal income. The Bureau of Economic Analysis (2005) notes that personal income data do include insurance settlements, but it does not explicitly explain how federal aid to individuals is reflected in personal income data. Presumably, any effects of such aid would be manifest in the personal income data. All lagged-period variables (personal income and casino revenue) are statistically significant, a reflection of the general economic growth and casino industry growth that was experienced during the sample period.

Finally, consider the *Casino Revenue* and *Post-Katrina × Casino Revenue* variables. Since the personal income and casino revenue data are weighted by the states' proportion of hurricane-affected counties, the interpretation of the casino revenue estimated coefficients is not straightforward. Rather than analyzing the monetary effects of these variables, we instead focus on the signs and statistical significance of the estimated coefficients.

The casino revenue variable indicates that, during the sample period the casino industry has had a positive impact on the states' personal income. This obviously applies only to Louisiana and Mississippi, as they are the only two states in the sample with commercial casinos. The interaction term between the post-Katrina dummy and the casino revenue variable is a measure of the impact casino gambling had on personal incomes in the wake of Katrina. Thus, it shows the impact of the industry *above and beyond* its "regular" effect. The strongly positive coefficient on this variable suggests that the casino industry has been effective "disaster relief," in terms of spurring personal income in Louisiana and Mississippi after Katrina/Rita. Indeed, this effect is stronger than the "regular" effect found in the model. Perhaps this should not be surprising, considering the industry's extraordinary amount of capital investment, its strong labor demand, and its demand for other input resources, especially after Katrina/Rita. This result stands in stark contrast to the rather poorly rated response from FEMA and other government agencies.[19]

---

[19] Alternatively, one could argue that because the states receive significant tax benefits from casinos, the governments had a strong incentive to get the casino industry back in operation. This might explain Mississippi's law change which allowed for Gulf Coast casinos to be built on land.

6.4 Conclusion

Our empirical results suggest that the commercial casino industry has had a significantly positive impact on state-level personal income in the Katrina-affected states of Louisiana and Mississippi. Our model does not tell us exactly *how* the casino industry rebuilding has led to economic development, but it is likely an amalgamation of capital and labor effects, and the attraction of tourism. In any case, the model does provide additional evidence that the industry helps to create growth, and does not simply "cannibalize" other industries.

What seems clear, based on the recent empirical evidence in this chapter, as well as Chap. 5, is that casinos do represent a net contributor to state economic growth. I am unaware of empirical analysis such as this applied to other industries, so a direct comparison with other industries is not currently possible. But it seems as though the industry has certainly had a positive impact to the economy up to now.

Chapter 7
The Impact of Casinos on State Tax Revenues

7.1 Introduction

A primary reason for legalizing gambling—especially recently in the cases of lotteries and casinos—is to provide alternative revenue sources to those which states typically employ. Arguably, the intended effect of these new revenue sources is to increase state revenues and reduce fiscal pressure. Oddly, few researchers have attempted to analyze whether this intended effect has, in fact, been realized. This neglect raises the important empirical question: What is the relationship actually observed between legalized gambling and state government revenues? This is a critical question, especially as many states struggle to deal with increasingly serious fiscal shortfalls. The issue also has significant international importance, as casinos spread worldwide.

The proponents of legalized gambling point to total taxes paid by gambling industries as an indication of the benefits of gambling to the states. Table 7.1 lists government revenue by state from commercial casino taxes, lotteries, and pari-mutuel taxes for 2004.

Although the tax revenue from legalized gambling is sizable in many states, this does not necessarily mean that legalized gambling has contributed to a *net increase* in overall state revenues. As people spend more of their income on gambling activities, their spending on other goods and services is likely to decline. Thus, the net effect of legalized gambling on state receipts depends on complicated relationships among spending on gambling industries, spending on non-gambling industries, and the tax rates imposed on the various forms of spending. Furthermore, politicians could substitute revenues from these new gambling sources for those from existing sources, leading to an ambiguous net effect on total state revenue. Clearly, the introduction of a new good does not necessarily imply increases in government revenue will follow.

The material in this chapter is based on Walker DM, and JD Jackson. 2011. The effect of legalized gambling on state government revenue. *Contemporary Economic Policy* 29(1): 101–114. Used with permission from John Wiley & Sons.

Table 7.1 Gambling-related State Government Revenue, 2004 (millions $)[a]

	(1) Commercial casino taxes	(2) Net lottery receipts[b]	(3) Pari-mutuel taxes	(4) Total gambling tax revenue (=1+2+3)	(5) Net state revenue[c]	(6) % of state revenue from gambling (=4/5)
Alabama			3.2	3.2	15,290.8	0.0
Alaska				0.0	6,659.0	0.0
Arizona		108.0	0.6	108.6	17,171.2	0.6
Arkansas			4.6	4.6	10,206.4	0.0
California		1,045.8	42.1	1,087.9	18,3736.7	0.6
Colorado	99.5	113.7	4.5	217.7	18,550.8	1.2
Connecticut		283.9	10.7	294.6	15,396.0	1.9
Delaware		283.9	0.2	284.1	4,675.6	6.1
Florida		1,042.3	26.7	1,069.0	58,567.5	1.8
Georgia		783.6		783.6	25,774.2	3.0
Hawaii				0.0	6,596.7	0.0
Idaho		25.9		25.9	5,376.4	0.5
Illinois	801.7	542.1	12.0	1,355.8	48,605.4	2.8
Indiana	760.5	200.8	4.8	966.1	20,005.8	4.8
Iowa	250.6	53.5	3.2	307.3	11,379.6	2.7
Kansas		70.0	3.5	73.5	8,077.7	0.9
Kentucky		196.3	15.5	211.8	14,286.5	1.5
Louisiana	448.2	121.8	20.4	590.4	16,830.2	3.5
Maine		42.6	4.5	47.1	5,749.7	0.8
Maryland		466.2	3.0	469.2	22,168.1	2.1
Massachusetts		1,153.9	5.7	1,159.6	32,989.3	3.5
Michigan	279.4	684.9	11.8	976.1	43,978.8	2.2
Minnesota		82.6	1.5	84.1	23,501.1	0.4
Mississippi	333.0			333.0	10,122.3	3.3
Missouri	403.1	219.3		622.4	19,082.9	3.3
Montana		9.2	0.1	9.3	3,758.2	0.2
Nebraska		19.4	0.3	19.7	5,954.8	0.3
Nevada	887.0			887.0	8,567.2	10.4
New Hampshire		73.7	4.1	77.8	4,718.2	1.6
New Jersey	470.6	795.9		1,266.5	41,582.2	3.0
New Mexico		36.0	1.2	37.2	8,375.6	0.4
New York		1,959.2	36.1	1,995.3	95,301.4	2.1
North Carolina				0.0	33,326.6	0.0
North Dakota			2.6	2.6	4,037.1	0.1
Ohio		600.9	15.9	616.8	61,963.2	1.0
Oklahoma			2.8	2.8	13,037.6	0.0
Oregon		195.9	2.9	198.8	20,341.0	1.0
Pennsylvania		837.3	26.6	863.9	54,037.2	1.6
Rhode Island		278.4	4.7	283.1	5,279.2	5.4
South Carolina		290.9		290.9	15,420.3	1.9
South Dakota	11.9	116.6	0.9	129.4	2,644.1	4.9

(continued)

7.2 Literature Review

Table 7.1 (continued)

	(1) Commercial casino taxes	(2) Net lottery receipts[b]	(3) Pari-mutuel taxes	(4) Total gambling tax revenue (=1+2+3)	(5) Net state revenue[c]	(6) % of state revenue from gambling (=4/5)
Tennessee				0.0	15,148.6	0.0
Texas		1,063.1	11.8	1,074.9	65,706.8	1.6
Utah				0.0	10,357.4	0.0
Vermont		20.1		20.1	2,988.5	0.7
Virginia		422.2		422.2	29,648.8	1.4
Washington		120.3	1.8	122.1	28,416.7	0.4
West Virginia		520.5	9.5	530.0	8,374.9	6.3
Wisconsin		140.6	1.8	142.4	28,157.6	0.5
Wyoming			0.2	0.2	3,240.1	0.0

Note: Indian casino revenues are not included because reliable data are not available
Data sources: Casino taxes from American Gaming Association (2006); other data from Statistical Abstract of the United States.
Source: Walker and Jackson (2011). Used with permission from John Wiley & Sons
[a]Data in this table are in nominal terms
[b]This figure is total lottery ticket sales minus jackpots and administrative costs
[c]This is total state government receipts minus funding from the federal government

In this paper we perform a relatively comprehensive analysis of the relationship between legalized gambling and state government revenues. We perform a panel data analysis on all 50 states for the 1985–2000 period, using annual data. We utilize data on gambling volume at casinos, Indian casinos, greyhound racing, horse racing, and lotteries; and total state government revenues net of transfers from the federal government. Our findings indicate mixed results. Lotteries and horse racing appear to have a positive impact on total state government receipts, but casinos and greyhound racing appear to have a negative effect on state revenues. Therefore, we argue that there is not a unique monotonic relationship between generic legalized gambling activity and overall state revenues. Of course, the effect of legalized gambling in a particular state or states may differ from the general effects we find.

This chapter is organized as follows. Section 7.2 is a literature review. In Sect. 7.3 we describe the data used and develop our model. The results are presented and discussed in Sect. 7.4. Section 7.5 summarizes and concludes.

7.2 Literature Review

There is a long-established literature on "optimal taxes," which focuses on setting tax rates in an effort to minimize distortions or maximize welfare (i.e., efficiency). Such papers include Ramsey (1927), Mirrlees (1971) and Slemrod (1990). Several studies have focused on the goal of revenue maximization from excise taxes, e.g., Lott and

Miller (1973, 1974), and Caputo and Ostrom (1996). With respect to legalized gambling and government revenues, there have been several theoretical treatments, notably Clotfelter and Cook (1991, appendix to Chapter 11) and Mason and Stranahan (1996). Empirical studies of gambling industries and their effects on state budgets are still rather scarce, but there has been a substantial amount of work on lotteries. For example, Garrett (2001) examines revenue maximization from lotteries; Tosun and Skidmore (2004) analyze the effects of new lottery adoptions in nearby states on West Virginia lottery revenue. Much of the lottery research has focused on the decision to adopt the lottery; Alm, McKee, and Skidmore (1993) and Jackson, Saurman, and Shughart (1994) are representative of such studies. Comprehensive lottery analyses include Clotfelter and Cook (1991) and Borg, Mason, and Shapiro (1991).

Whether legalized gambling affects overall state government revenue depends on several factors. First, in many states there is more than one type of legal gambling. The extent to which the different gambling industries are substitutes (or complements) to each other will have an impact on the state revenues from gambling. The relationships between gambling industries and *non*-gambling industries are also important, for example, to the extent that consumers substitute gambling for other types of expenditure. The tax rates applied to the various types of spending are among a number of other important factors.

Here we provide a brief summary of some of the empirical papers that are relevant to our analysis of gambling and state government revenue. There are two basic types of study discussed below. The first type includes papers that primarily analyze the relationships among gambling industries, whether or not state tax revenue is explicitly considered. The second type includes papers that focus specifically on the relationship between gambling industries and state tax revenues.

Some of the papers that address interindustry relationships are Elliott and Navin (2002), Fink and Rork (2003), Grote and Matheson (2006), Gulley and Scott (1989), Kearney (2005), Mobilia (1992a), Ray (2001), Siegel and Anders (2001), Thalheimer and Ali (1995), and Walker and Jackson (2008a).

Elliott and Navin (2002) run a probit model to test the factors that affect the probability of lottery adoption, then model the determinants of lottery sales in 48 states, from 1989 to 1995. In analyzing how other gambling industries affect lottery sales, they use the number of Indian casinos in the state and the highest gross revenues per capita for a lottery and gaming in any neighboring state. They find that casinos and pari-mutuels harm the lottery, and that adjacent state lotteries have a small negative effect on in-state lottery sales. The number of Indian casinos in a state and riverboat casinos in neighboring states do not significantly affect lottery sales. The note by Fink and Rork (2003) extends the work by Elliott and Navin (2002) by taking into account the fact that states self-select when legalizing casinos. They argue that low-revenue lottery states are more likely to legalize casinos, and treat casino legalization as endogenous. This partly explains the negative relationship between casinos and lotteries.

Grote and Matheson (2006) consider the effect of large, multi-state lotteries (e.g., Powerball) on smaller in-state lotteries. Although the introduction of the multi-state lotteries may have a negative impact on the smaller in-state games, the overall effect on state lottery revenue tends to be positive.

7.2 Literature Review

Gulley and Scott (1989) examine the relationship between lotteries and pari-mutuels prior to the explosion of casino gambling. They used a sample of 61 racetracks from 1978 to 1980. They found that $1 in lottery ticket purchases leads to 18¢ less in racing handle. However, these results are not statistically significant. The states still benefit because, despite the potential cannibalization, overall tax revenues would increase because of the relatively high lottery tax.

Kearney (2005) examines household expenditure data from 1982 to 1998, a period during which 21 states implemented a state lottery. Among other issues, she studies the source of lottery ticket expenditures. Kearney finds that spending on lottery tickets is financed completely by a reduction in non-gambling expenditures. This implies that other forms of gambling are not harmed by a lottery, but that non-gambling industries are. One might expect, as noted above, that the lottery would therefore increase overall state revenues since the lottery tax is significantly higher than taxes on most other types of expenditure.

Mobilia (1992a) analyzes the impact of lotteries on greyhound and horse racing attendance and total bets (handle) from 1972 to 1986. She notes that a lottery dummy is negative and significant for pari-mutuel attendance, but not for per attendee handle. Ray (2001) finds that horse racing and casino dummies have significantly negative effects on total state greyhound handle, from 1991 to 1998. Both Mobilia (1992a) and Ray (2001) analyze all relevant racing states.

Siegel and Anders (2001) test the effect of Arizona Indian casinos on the state's lottery sales from 1993 to 1998. Independent variables include the number of Indian casino slot machines, horse and greyhound handle, plus a trend. They find the number of slots to have a significantly negative effect on lottery sales, but horse and dog racing have no effect.

Thalheimer and Ali (1995) model attendance and handle at three horse racetracks in the Ohio-Kentucky border market from 1960 to 1987. They find that the lottery (measured by payout rate) reduces the handle at racetracks. However, the state that has both lotteries and racetracks benefits in terms of overall tax revenue. The other state (without lottery) loses, as do all the racetracks. This suggests that lotteries harm horse racing. Major sporting events are also found to have a negative effect on horse racing.

Walker and Jackson (2008a) examine state-level relationships among gambling industries. We utilize annual revenue or handle data on the various industries and estimated a seemingly unrelated regression (SUR) model. Our results indicate that casinos and lotteries have a negative effect on each other; lotteries and dog racing are complementary; and horse racing and casinos are complementary. Our results do not paint a simple, consistent relationship among the different gaming industries. This suggests that the relationships among gambling industries and net state revenues may also be inconsistent.[1]

Although many of these studies do not directly address the effect of the gambling industries on state revenues, their results are informative, since knowing

---

[1] This analysis is presented in Chap. 18.

whether the different industries act as complements or substitutes has obvious implications for their effects on tax revenues. It is noteworthy that the interindustry results are not all consistent.

Papers that directly examine the effect of gambling industries on state revenues include Anders, Siegel, and Yacoub (1998), Borg, Mason, and Shapiro (1993), Davis, Filer, and Moak (1992), Fink, Marco, and Rork (2004), Mason and Stranahan (1996), Popp and Stehwien (2002), and Siegel and Anders (1999).

Anders, Siegel, and Yacoub (1998) examine the effect of Indian casinos on transactions tax revenue of one Arizona county. Since Indian casino revenues are not taxed by the state, politicians may be concerned that increases in casino expenditures will result in less spending on taxable goods and services. In their model estimating state tax revenues from 1990 to 1996, the authors include a dummy for the introduction of casinos. The coefficient is negative and significant, which suggests that tax losses from the retail, restaurant, bar, hotel, and amusement sectors were significant. Popp and Stehwien (2002) can be seen as a complement to Anders, Siegel, and Yacoub (1998), but applied to New Mexico county-level tax revenue, from 1990 to 1997. The explanatory variables in their model include employment, unemployment rate, wages, and dummies for Indian reservation, the first and second casino present, and the first and second adjacent county casino present. They find that the casinos have a negative effect on tax revenues within the county. But the effect of neighboring county casinos is somewhat odd: the first has a negative effect, while the second one has a positive effect on county tax revenue.

Borg, Mason, and Shapiro (1993) use a time series analysis and find that $1 in net lottery revenue has a cost of 15–23¢ in other types of government revenue, particularly sales and excise taxes, but that the lottery leads to an overall increase in revenues. Fink, Marco, and Rork (2004) also study the overall revenue effect of lotteries. Their results are partially consistent with those of Borg, Mason, and Shapiro (1993). However, Fink, Marco, and Rork (2004) find that overall state tax revenue *decreases* when lottery revenues increase. Both of these papers consider lotteries, but do not account for other types of gambling in their models.

Davis, Filer, and Moak (1992) test the factors that determine whether or not a state will adopt a lottery, the timing of adoption, and the level of revenue a state can expect if it adopts a lottery. Among other things, the authors find that state lottery revenue is higher the smaller the state government's revenue from the pari-mutuel industry and the smaller the percentage of bordering states that have lotteries.

Finally, Siegel and Anders (1999) examine Missouri sales tax revenues at the county level (1994–1996) as a result of introducing riverboat casinos. Like Anders, Siegel, and Yacoub (1998), they find taxes from certain amusement industries are negatively impacted. Siegel and Anders (1999) estimate that a 10 % increase in gambling tax revenue leads to about a 4 % decline in tax revenues from other amusement and recreation sources. However, there is no clear and consistent negative effect on other types of tax revenues.

These various studies have certainly enhanced understanding of the economic effects of gambling and the relationships among gambling industries. For the most part, however, the literature does not provide information on the *overall effect of all types of legalized gambling* on other industries or on state revenues. That is, most of the analyses are (1) on the impact of a single industry on one other industry, and not vice versa; (2) on the impact of a single industry on state tax revenue; (3) for relatively short time periods; or (4) on a single state or a small number of states. None of the studies reviewed attempts to jointly consider multiple forms of legalized gambling and their overall impact on state total revenue. As a result, one is left with an incomplete picture of how legalized gambling, all types considered, affects state government revenues in the longer term. The purpose in this chapter is to supplement the literature by providing a more comprehensive analysis. We examine the relationship between legalized gambling and total state government revenues, net of federal transfers, for all states from 1985 to 2000.

7.3 Data and Model

Whether legalized gambling affects state tax receipts depends on the tax rate applied to gambling industry revenues and/or profits, the size of the particular gambling industry, and its relationship to other gambling and non-gambling industries, among other factors. We focus on the existence and volume of each type of gambling in each state as the explanatory variables of primary interest. We measure the volume of gambling rather than the actual taxes paid by each industry in each state, for example, because we are more interested in whether there is a *general relationship* between the volume of gambling and overall state revenues than in the effect of a particular tax regime. Obviously gambling tax rates and revenues are very important, as are the taxes applied to non-gambling goods and services. However, we view an examination of optimal tax rates as an extension to this analysis. Consider, for example, that Pennsylvania taxes gross casino revenues at 55 % while Nevada's rate is around 7 %. Many states have very intricate tax rules, including various tax brackets, slot machine fees, etc., which would be very difficult to model using our state-level panel data. However, such issues would be interesting subjects for subsequent research.

7.3.1 Data

We posit a panel model for all 50 US states during the 1985–2000 period. (Washington, DC, is excluded because it is not a state, and its fiscal decisions are handled primarily by the federal government.) We utilize annual data and, consequently, we have 800 observations on each variable. Our dependent variable is total state government revenue from all sources, minus funding from the federal government. It is important to note that federal government contributions to state governments are sizeable. "Federal contributions" is also used as an explanatory variable in order to determine the extent to which state government revenues are driven by federal government monies. We use aggregated state government revenue rather than only gambling-related tax revenue, for example, because we wish to pick up any "substitution" effects that may be occurring with other gambling and non-gambling industries.

Our primary explanatory variables measure the *volume* of gambling for five industries: commercial casinos, greyhound racing, horse racing, lotteries, and Indian casinos. Volume is reported as "handle," or the total dollar amount of bets placed, for greyhound racing, horse racing, and lotteries.[2] For casinos, reported volume is in net gambling revenue, or the revenue kept by the casino after paying winning bets to customers.[3] While it would be preferable to have the same volume measure for all industries, it is difficult to convert casino revenue into casino handle. Although casinos measure handle for slot machines, they only track the "drop" (i.e., the money used by customers to buy casino chips) for table games. Casino revenues are regularly reported at the state level, but handle is not. In any case, having a different measure for casinos is not problematic since revenue is still a good measure of volume.

Since Indian casinos are not required to report revenues and because there are no reliable sources for Indian casino volume data, we use square footage of Indian casinos as proxy of their volume.[4] This square footage measure is used in estimating the volume of other gambling industries; see the structural equation system (7.1) below. Indian casinos are thus used to indirectly explain state revenues. We opt for this strategy since most gambling policy discussions deal with the legalization or expansion of non-tribal gambling—since tribal gambling policy is largely outside the discretion of state governments.

To account for potential border crossings by consumers, we created a measure of the availability of the various forms of gambling in adjacent states. We follow Davis, Filer, and Moak (1992) and Walker and Jackson (2008a) in using the percentage of adjacent states with each type of gambling. Using these variables will help to account for cross-border spending on each of the gambling industries.

We collected a variety of demographic data by state that may help explain government revenues. These include state population, population density (population/square miles), percentage of the population over 25 years old holding bachelor degrees, per capita income, percentage of population estimated to be living below poverty level, and percentage of state population over 65 years old. Because tourism and legalized gambling may be complementary, at least for casino gambling, we include the estimated level of hotel employment in each state (the number of

---

[2] Slot machines and video lottery terminals (VLTs) were available at some racetracks during our sample period. However, this is a relatively recent phenomenon, and these revenues are not included in our data.

[3] Casino revenue data are from the American Gaming Association and various states' gaming commissions. Data on lottery ticket sales come from LaFleur's 2001 World Lottery Almanac, 9th edition. Greyhound and horse racing handle are from the 1985–2000 issues of *Pari-Mutuel Racing*, published by the Association of Racing Commissioners International, Inc. State government revenue data are from the Statistical Abstract of the United States, various editions. All of the data are adjusted for inflation using the CPI from the Bureau of Labor Statistics.

[4] Indian casino square footage is calculated by the author using the casino listing and square footage data at CasinoCity.com, along with phone calls to the casinos to determine opening dates.

employees in the industry).[5] We expect that each of these, except "poverty" and possibly "older" (over 65 years old) would have a positive impact on state government revenues. Finally, the explanatory variables include a series of regional dummy variables (following Ekelund et al. 2006)[6] and a time trend.

We provide a list of the variables included in the final stage of our empirical analysis; these variables are defined and their summary statistics are listed in Table 7.2. Not all of the variables discussed above are included in the table, because the final stage of the analysis does not provide coefficient estimates on them.

7.3.2 Model[7]

A number of theoretical and empirical questions must be addressed before we begin our estimation process. We posit a naïve theoretical model in which the representative state's government revenue is jointly determined with the volume of (up to) four types of state sanctioned gambling activities. The volume of each gaming activity (V_i, $i=1,\ldots,4$) is assumed to be determined by the volume of other gambling activities conducted in the state[8] (to allow for substitution and complementarity among games), the presence of gambling activities in adjacent states (A_m, $m=1,\ldots,M$; to allow for competition among states for gaming revenue), demographic factors (D_p, $p=1,\ldots,P$; to allow for exogenous effects on the demand for the gambling activity), and some other variables (Z_k, $k=1,\ldots,K$) related to the idiosyncratic nature of the data, such as regional dummies and a time trend.

Then state government revenue net of federal transfers (GR), our variable of primary interest, is determined by the presence of the gaming activity as indicated by a set of dummy variables ($G_{ijt}=1$ if gaming activity i is available in state j at time t ($i=1,\ldots,4$, $j=1,\ldots,50$, and $t=1,\ldots,16$)), the volume of the gaming activities offered in that state (V_i, $i=1,\ldots,4$), federal government transfers (FT) to that state, demographic factors (D_p, $p=1,\ldots,P$), and other variables, such as regional dummies and a time trend (Z_k, $k=1,\ldots,K$), related to the idiosyncratic nature of the data.

---

[5] Hotel employee and per capita income data are from the Bureau of Economic Analysis. Annual estimates for some demographic data are not available, so we created annual estimates by linear interpolation. The years used to derive our annual estimates vary due to availability: *Education* (1990 and 2001), *Older* (1990 and 2001), and *Poverty* (1992 and 2001). These data are from the Census Bureau.

[6] We use regional, rather than state, dummies because we already include state-specific dummies to indicate whether a particular type of gambling is legal. An additional advantage of using the regional dummies is that previous evidence suggests that neighboring states influence a particular state's decision to adopt gambling (Calcagno, Walker, and Jackson 2010). Nevertheless, in one specification we did include state dummies and the results proved insignificant, perhaps due to the sizable reduction in the degrees of freedom.

[7] Readers who wish to avoid the technical details may wish to skip to Sect. 7.4.1.

[8] As noted earlier, Indian casino square footage is used to estimate the volume in each of the other four industries (V_i, $i=1,\ldots,4$), which are then used as explanatory variables in the model of state revenue.

Table 7.2 Variable names, descriptions, and summary statistics[a]

Variable	Description	Mean	Standard deviation	Minimum	Maximum
Net State Revenue (dependent variable)	Total state government receipts minus funds received from the federal government[b]	8,985,908,280	10,850,052,900	432,055,749	80,469,221,800
Casino Revenue	State total casino revenues after paying winning bets[b,c]	172,766,208	702,694,559	0	5,576,596,980
Greyhound Handle	State total bets placed on greyhound racing[b,c]	42,362,920	109,092,150	0	893,013,613
Horse Handle	State total bets placed on horse racing[b,c]	204,719,413	431,310,956	0	3,072,320,730
Lottery Sales	State total lottery ticket sales[b,c]	337,022,012	511,046,906	0	2,487,414,330
Casino Dummy	Dummy variable to indicate the presence of commercial casino gambling in the state	0.13	0.34	0	1
Greyhound Dummy	Dummy variable to indicate the presence of legal greyhound (pari-mutuel) racing in the state	0.33	0.47	0	1
Horse Dummy	Dummy variable to indicate the presence of legal horse (pari-mutuel) racing in the state	0.73	0.44	0	1
Lottery Dummy	Dummy Variable to indicate the presence of a state-run lottery	0.63	0.48	0	1

7.3 Data and Model

Federal Transfers (to the given State)	The amount of state government revenue that is from the federal government[b]	2,353,906,530	2,907,911,340	238,847,584	20,739,256,700
Education	Percentage of the state population aged 25 or higher with a bachelor degree	15.42	5.38	4.01	31.69
Hotel Employees	Estimated number of hotel workers in the state	36,052	41,372	2,660	232,206
Income Per Capita	State level per capita income[b]	14,506.75	2,331.07	9,221.19	24,068.53
Older	Percentage of state population over 65 years old	12.54	2.07	3.37	18.62
Population	Estimated population of the state	5,161,101	5,608,851	453,690	33,871,648
Pop Density	State population divided by square mileage of the state	170.73	236.94	0.931	1,134.47
Poverty	Estimated percentage of state population living below the poverty level	13.85	4.12	6.73	28.08
Year	Time trend	1992.5	4.61	1985	2000
Regional Dummies	Dummy variables for Great Lakes, Mid-East, New England, Plains, Rocky Mountain, Southeast, and Southwest regions (The Pacific region is the base region)				

Summary statistics are shown for variables included in the net state revenue model, but not for variables included only in the reduced-form equations. Summary statistics for the regional dummies are omitted for brevity

Source: Walker and Jackson (2011). Used with permission from John Wiley & Sons

[a]The summary statistics should be interpreted with care, as they are for panel data (50 states, 16 years)

[b]These variables are adjusted for inflation using the CPI from the Bureau of Labor Statistics

[c]Industry revenue/handle summary statistics are calculated using only states and years in which the gambling industry was present (i.e., zero observations were not included when calculating the summary statistics)

The gambling volume variables V_i and the demographic variables D_p are defined and discussed earlier in this section. The Ps are indexed in equation system (7.1), below, because not all demographic variables enter each structural equation. The adjacent state variables (A_m) include the percent of adjacent states offering legalized casino gambling (A_1), the percent of adjacent states offering legalized lotteries (A_2), the percent of adjacent states offering legalized horse racing (A_3), the percent of adjacent states offering legalized dog racing (A_4), the percent of adjacent states having Indian casinos (A_5), and adjacent state Indian casino square footage (A_6). The Z_k variables include dummy variables for seven of the eight census regions and a time trend. Ekelund et al. (2006) found this approach to defining cross section and time series units of observation useful; we adopt their approach for essentially the reasons they offer. Finally, the dummies $G_{i(jt)}$ are included to indicate the presence of the ith gaming activity (in the jth state in the tth period) because not all states offer all gaming activities. In essence, the gaming volume measures are observationally equivalent to interaction variables arising as the product of the various gaming revenues with corresponding dummy variables indicating the presence of the relevant activity. As such, the state revenue equation specification would be incomplete without including the indicator dummies.

The structural equations for the implied system can be written in linear form, with an appended stochastic disturbance term ($\varepsilon_j, j=1,\ldots,5$) as

$$V_1 = \beta_0 + \sum_{i=2}^{4}\beta_i V_i + \sum_{m=1}^{M}\gamma_m A_m + \sum_{p=1}^{P_1}\delta_p D_p + \sum_{k=1}^{K}\eta_k Z_k + \varepsilon_1$$

$$V_2 = \beta_0 + \beta_1 V_1 + \sum_{i=3}^{4}\beta_i V_i + \sum_{m=1}^{M}\gamma_m A_m + \sum_{p=1}^{P_2}\delta_p D_p + \sum_{k=1}^{K}\eta_k Z_k + \varepsilon_2$$

$$V_3 = \beta_0 + \beta_4 V_4 + \sum_{i=1}^{2}\beta_i V_i + \sum_{m=1}^{M}\gamma_m A_m + \sum_{p=1}^{P_3}\delta_p D_p + \sum_{k=1}^{K}\eta_k Z_k + \varepsilon_3$$

$$V_4 = \beta_0 + \sum_{i=1}^{3}\beta_i V_i + \sum_{m=1}^{M}\gamma_m A_m + \sum_{p=1}^{P_4}\delta_p D_p + \sum_{k=1}^{K}\eta_k Z_k + \varepsilon_4$$

$$\text{GR} = \beta_0 + \sum_{i=1}^{4}\lambda_i G_i + \sum_{i=1}^{4}\beta_i V_i + \lambda \text{FT} + \sum_{p=1}^{P_5}\delta_p D_p + \sum_{k=1}^{K}\eta_k Z_k + \varepsilon_5 \qquad (7.1)$$

While this system forms the framework for our empirical analysis, it is only the last equation in the system that is of interest for our analysis to come. Indeed, the identification properties of the parameters in the first four equations in the system are of no concern to the present inquiry. The system does, however, provide us with a rationale for estimating specific reduced form equations for the various gambling activities in order to correct for their simultaneous determination with government revenue.

Confining our attention to the government revenue (GR) equation for the moment, there are a number of empirical difficulties that arise in its estimation. We have 16 years of data on each of 50 states. Traditional ways of dealing with panel data are to estimate either a fixed-effects or a random-effects model.

7.3 Data and Model

The fixed-effects model simply assumes common slope coefficients but different intercepts across cross sectional units and/or over time, and accomplishes this correction by including dummy variables for different cross sectional units and/or time periods. Alternatively, the random effects model assumes common intercepts and slope coefficients; the cross sectional and intertemporal differences arise in the disturbance term. That is, the disturbance variance of this model can be partitioned into a model specific component, a cross sectional specific component, and/or a time specific component. The typical question that arises is whether the fixed- or random-effects approach to panel data estimation is correct for the problem at hand.

Ekelund et al. (2006) address this question by arguing that the answer need not be a mutually exclusive choice. They suggest employing the multiplicative heteroscedasticity model discussed in Greene (2000, 518–520). Specifically, that model involves using maximum likelihood techniques to jointly estimate a regression function and a variance function. By incorporating cross sectional dummies and a time trend into both the regression and variance function specifications, this procedure allows us to account for both the differential intercept aspect of a traditional fixed-effects model concurrently with the cross-region variation in the disturbance variance aspect of a traditional random-effects model. See Ekelund et al. (2006, 530, notes 518 and 519) for a thorough explanation of this statistical model. We adopt this procedure to address problems arising from the "panel" nature of our data.

A second estimation problem arises due to the possible simultaneous determination of the volumes of the various gambling activities and net government revenue. We employ a "brute force" two stage procedure to address this problem. That is, we obtain two stage least squares (2SLS) estimates of the net revenue equation, literally in two stages. In stage I, we estimate reduced form equations for each of the gambling volume variables by regressing each in turn on all of the exogenous variables (i.e., all of the right hand side variables except the V_i's) in equation system (7.1). In stage II, we estimate the net revenue equation with each of the gambling volume measures replaced by its corresponding estimated value derived from the reduced form estimates of stage I. This procedure allows us to correct for simultaneity while retaining our multiplicative heteroscedasticity estimation framework.

This two stage procedure highlights a final empirical difficulty that we must address. The problem arises in stage I. The instrumental variables we derive from the reduced form estimates in the first stage are only as reliable as the parameter estimates used to calculate them. A potential problem with these parameter estimates arises due to the left censored nature of the gambling volume measures, the dependent variables in the stage I regressions. Specifically, the dependent variables in each reduced form regression will have observed values of zero for each state and in each time period for which the state did not allow that type of gambling. Ignoring this type of left censoring in a dependent variable can lead to inconsistent parameter estimates.

We use Heckman's (1976, 1979) two step approach to address this problem. For each particular gaming activity, we estimate a probit equation explaining the probability of adoption. If state i legally offered gaming activity j in time period t, the dependent variable in the relevant probit equation receives a value of one; zero, otherwise. The explanatory variables in the probit equations are the same as those in the reduced forms. The estimated probit index values from these models are then used to compute inverse Mills ratios (IMRs) for the various gambling activities, which in turn, are included in the relevant reduced form models as additional explanatory variables. This procedure corrects for biases in coefficient estimates due to censoring, so that gambling volume estimates derived from estimating these augmented reduced form equations can be viewed as appropriate instruments for stage II estimation.

While this "tobit" correction assures more reliable coefficient estimates in our reduced form equations and hence better instruments for gambling volumes in the state revenue equation, the zero observations in these measures still do not address completely the fact that some states do not offer some of the gambling activities. To measure the *ceteris paribus* difference between state revenue averaged across states offering the ith gaming activity and states that do not, we include the dummy variable G_i for the $i=1,\ldots,4$ gaming activities. As an interpretive note, the coefficient on the dummy tells us this difference while the coefficient on the corresponding volume measure tells us the marginal effect on state revenue from an additional dollar of handle or revenue for that activity; the *ceteris paribus* total effect of that gambling activity is the sum of these two effects.

In light of all of these issues, we estimate the net government revenue (GR) equation in equation system (7.1). Our model accounts for both fixed and random effects by including the trend and regional dummies. And our use of the Heckman two-step approach in the multiplicative heteroscedasticity framework corrects for left-censoring in the reduced form equations prior to using the "brute force" two stage procedure outlined above. We further address the left-censoring through the introduction of industry dummies. Thus, we correct for simultaneity between tax revenues and gambling industry volumes within a partially left censored, panel data framework.

7.4 Results

The results are presented in Table 7.3. Our discussion of the results focuses on the gambling industry variables in the regression function. We partition the effect of the gambling industries on net state revenue into two components. The dummy variables indicate the average impact on net state revenue from having a particular type of gambling in the state. The industry volume variables measure the marginal impact of an additional dollar of handle (for lottery and racing) or revenue (for casinos). The interpretation of the coefficients is not straightforward, however, as the gambling industries are not present in each state, have different histories, regulations, tax schemes, etc. It should be emphasized that the coefficient estimates represent effects on the "average state" (i.e., the hypothetical state taking on the average values for the explanatory variables—not necessarily any of the actual states in the sample) in the average year (same *caveat*); coefficients can be interpreted as applying to a particular state only to the extent that the state exhibits the mean state characteristics and behavior.

We discuss each industry, in turn, focusing on the overall impact from the dummy and volume variables. The *Lottery Dummy* variable is statistically significant and positive suggesting that states with a lottery will have state revenue that is on

7.4 Results

Table 7.3 Effect of legalized gambling on state government revenue (Dep. variable: *Net State Revenue*)

Variable	Regression function[a]	Variable	Variance function[a]
Constant	9.49e10*	Sigma	0.00
	(2.96)		(0.09)
Casino Revenue[b]	−1.44*	Great Lakes	−2.49e5
	(−5.81)		(−1.17)
Casino Dummy	−9.02e7	Mid-East	−1.49e5
	(−0.76)		(−0.70)
Greyhound Handle[b]	−7.61*	New England	−3.49e6*
	(−4.94)		(−17.08)
Greyhound Dummy	−1.57e8*	Plains	−1.97e6*
	(−2.77)		(−10.04)
Horse Handle[b]	−1.46*	Rocky Mountain	−4.68e6*
	(−3.12)		(−21.86)
Horse Dummy	6.71e8*	Southeast	−1.44e6*
	(6.72)		(−8.17)
Lottery Sales[b]	−0.30	Southwest	2.80e5
	(−0.77)		(1.23)
Lottery Dummy	3.15e8*	Year	1.34e5*
	(2.96)		(12.41)
Federal Transfers	2.32e6*	$\chi^2(8)$[c]	621.58*
	(22.59)		
Education	−2.66e7	Log Likelihood	−6,703.4
	(−1.49)		
Hotel Employees	3.59e4*		
	(5.01)		
Income Per Capita	2.02e5*		
	(7.30)		
Older	4.37e7		
	(1.06)		
Population	566.35*		
	(8.74)		
Pop Density	2.18e6*		
	(7.36)		
Poverty	−5.04e6		
	(−0.26)		
Year	−4.89e7*		
	(−2.99)		
Great Lakes	−6.23e8		
	(−1.63)		
Mid-East	−5.93e8		
	(−1.40)		
New England	−1.91e9*		
	(7.62)		
Plains	−1.37e9*		
	(−5.14)		
Rocky Mountain	−1.06e9*		
	(−3.87)		

(continued)

Table 7.3 (continued)

Variable	Regression function[a]	Variable	Variance function[a]
Southeast	−1.58e9* (−4.81)		
Southwest	−1.97e9* (−4.52)		

Source: Walker and Jackson (2011). Used with permission from John Wiley & Sons
[a]The coefficients are reported with *t*-statistics in parntheses beneath
[b]The gambling variables are estimated values from a reduced form regression which has also been corrected for their left censoring (see the discussion concerning left censoring in stage I above)
[c]The hypothesis is that the slope coefficients in both the regression function and the variance function are jointly zero
*Indicates significance at the 0.01 level

average $315 million greater than non-lottery states, *ceteris paribus*. However, each additional $1 of ticket sales is associated with a statistically insignificant $0.30 *decline* in net state revenues. This point estimate conflicts with the fact that the average state's effective tax on lottery tickets is about 30 %, but this estimated effect could as easily be zero. The insignificance of the marginal impact may be the result of "revenue substitution," i.e., the increase in revenues from lottery sales comes at the expense of expenditures on non-lottery expenditures. As Kearney (2005) found, lottery expenditures come at the expense of reduction in non-gambling expenditures, which may be the reason we find no significant marginal revenue effect from lottery ticket sales. Recall that we are partitioning the full effect into two components. The existence of lotteries together with the insignificant marginal impacts, nevertheless, shows that the lottery has an overall economically and statistically positive effect on state revenues.

The *Casino Dummy* variable indicates that the existence of casinos in a state is associated with a decrease of net state revenue of $90 million. This effect is not statistically significant, that is, the average state revenue for states having casinos is roughly the same as for those not having casinos. However, *Casino Revenue* suggests that each additional dollar of casino revenue causes a $1.44 decline in state revenue. This is a statistically significant impact. It is useful at this point to interpret the casino result in terms of estimated handle—to be consistent with the other industries' volume measures (i.e., handle). Suppose the relationship between casino revenues and handle is such that revenue equals around 5 % of handle.[9] Then the coefficient on *Casino Revenue* implies that for each additional dollar of casino *handle*, net state

---

[9]This estimate is somewhat arbitrary. Determining the exact relationship between casino revenue and handle is complicated by table games. (Handle *is* tracked by slot machines, however, and a generally accepted industry average is that revenue is 5 % of handle.) Although the casino "edge" is well known for table most games to be less than 5 % of each dollar bet, players typically bet winnings from previous plays. Thus, handle may vary greatly. For example, a player who buys $100 in chips and bets it all on a single hand of blackjack and loses would create $100 revenue for the casino. The handle for this player would also be $100. But if the player instead bet $25 on blackjack hands until he lost all his money, and he was able to play 50 hands on his original $100 chip purchase, then casino revenue from that player is $100, but handle is $1,250. For a general explanation of casino revenue and handle, see Hannum and Cabot (2005, Chapter 3).

7.4 Results

revenues will fall by only $0.07. Although it is statistically significant, the negative marginal impact of casinos is fairly minor, suggesting only a mild "substitution" effect away from other consumer expenditures and ultimately, a decline in state tax revenues that may or may not be economically significant. Obviously, this effect need not hold in each casino jurisdiction. Nevada, for example, derives a significant proportion of its state revenue from casinos, and we would be very surprised if the negative marginal impact we estimate applies to Nevada. But for the average state, it appears that casinos have a small but negative net impact on state revenues.

Our results on horse racing indicate a large positive and statistically significant impact from the existence of horse racing ($671 million). This large effect is perhaps due to a cumulative economic development effect in states with horse racing. The industry is rather mature, and it plays a significant role in some local economies. The effect of the industry, compounded over time, may explain the large existence effect on net state revenues. (Such an effect is unlikely to occur in lottery states, for example, since lotteries require little capital investment.) However, for each additional dollar of horse racing handle, there is a statistically significant –$1.46 effect on net state revenue. As with the other types of gambling discussed above, this represents a significant tax substitution effect. This negative impact of horse racing may be due, in part, to the recent strongly negative trend in horse racing handle that is attributable in part to the spread of casinos. Consideration of the total effect of horse racing on state revenue for the average state offering it is revealing. The total effect on state revenue will be positive so long as less than about $460 million is spent playing the horses. Since only about $277 million is spent in the average state allowing horse racing ($204 million considering all states; see Table 7.2), there is an average positive impact on state revenues of about $266 million for the average state.

Finally, we present the greyhound racing results. The existence of greyhound racing in a state is estimated to have a significant and negative impact on average net state revenue for those states offering it of about $157 million. Furthermore, each additional dollar of greyhound handle is estimated to reduce net state revenue by a whopping and statistically significant $7.61. Even if we adopt an extremely conservative point estimate that is two standard deviations below $7.61, the marginal effect on state revenue of an extra dollar bet on the dogs is still a decrease of $4.50. Frankly, this marginal effect is very difficult to explain, especially considering the greyhound industry is relatively small in most states. We note that the greyhound industry produces questionable results of similar (negative) magnitude no matter what specification we have attempted in this analysis.

The large constant term is statistically significant. As expected, the *Federal Transfers* variable has a statistically positive effect on state revenues, even after these funds have been subtracted from total state government receipts. (Recall that the dependent variable in each model is net state revenue.) This suggests that federal funding drives other forms of state revenues, or at least that the formulae used to allocate these federal transfers are tied closely to the respective state's revenue efforts from its own sources.

The *Income Per Capita* variable shows that net tax revenues are significantly larger in states with higher per capita incomes. *Poverty* has a negative coefficient, but the effect is not statistically significant. These results are consistent with a priori expectations. The *Hotel Employee* variable is positive and strongly significant, which suggests that tourism has a strong positive impact on state revenues. This makes sense, as tourist expenditures are often heavily taxed (e.g., hotels and car rentals).

One important observation should be made regarding our casino findings with respect to the per capita income and hotel employee variables mentioned above. One could argue that economic growth (i.e., increases in per capita income) and tourism are channels through which casinos generate tax revenues for a state. That is, there is a direct tax effect, which our *Casino Revenue* and *Casino Dummy* variables pick up, as well as indirect tax effects, or the effect casinos have on other industries which then affect state tax receipts. Then although the direct casino effects are mildly negative, the indirect effects considering *Hotel Employees* and *Income Per Capita* are positive, so that casinos may still have a net positive impact on state tax receipts. This consideration would likely apply less to the other forms of gambling, as they draw fewer tourists than casinos do and have an uncertain economic growth impact.

Population is positive and significant, as would be expected since we analyze total, rather than per capita, net revenues. *Population Density* is positive. Large urban areas would be expected to generate more revenues and monitoring tax collections is less costly than in less populated regions. *Education* and the percentage of the population aged 65 or higher (*Older*) are both insignificant.

Most of the regional dummies in the regression equations are negative and significant. The Pacific region was the base region to which the others were compared. The time trend appears to be negative and significant. These results on the regional dummies and the time trend taken together suggest that a two-way fixed-effects model of the regression function is reasonable.

The results of the variance function are also displayed in Table 7.3. The estimates for the variable *sigma* are estimates of that part of the variance not affected by the other variables in the variance function. In other words, if all of the other variables in the variance function were insignificant, the antilog of the estimate for *sigma* would be the constant variance estimate for the homoscedastic regression function. To the degree that other variables are significant in the variance function, the regression function is heteroscedastic and its disturbance variance depends on these measures. Clearly, the latter case is the relevant one here, as four of the regions are significant in the variance function estimate and the time trend is positive and highly significant. This means that the variance of the regression function varies significantly across regions and over time, indicating a two-way random effects specification of the net revenue equation also to be appropriate.

Finally, it is worth noting that our results here, i.e., that the regression function exhibits different constant terms across regions while the variance of the model varies both across regions and over time, demonstrates that the multiplicative heteroscedasticity approach allows a level of generality not available in the typical fixed/random-effects approach to analyzing panel data. These results further suggest that the usual approach may be overly restrictive, and in turn, by imposing inappropriate restrictions, could have generated a possibly vast set of inappropriate parameter estimates.

7.4.1 Discussion

When we consider the overall impact of each industry—both the "existence" effect measured by the industry dummy variables and the "marginal effect" as measured by the industry volume variables—we can summarize the estimated impacts of each industry on net state revenues. According to our analysis, casinos and greyhound racing have a negative impact on net state revenues, while lotteries and horse racing have a positive impact. While our results can be compared with other studies in the literature (such as those discussed in Sect. 7.2), keep in mind that our results are more comprehensive, in the sense that our models consider the simultaneous effect of all of the gambling industries in all states. Most of the previous studies have considered only one industry and often only within a single state.

The positive effect from lotteries is not surprising, since the average tax rate from lotteries is significantly higher than taxes on most other goods and services. The positive horse racing finding is also consistent with other studies in the literature. The casino and greyhound racing results indicate substitution away from other, revenue productive forms of spending which, ultimately, leads to a reduction in state revenues.

The discrepancy between horse and greyhound racing—that the two forms of racing do not have the same direction of effect on net state revenues—is an unexpected result. Previous evidence has indicated that these industries are substitutes, and one would expect that they would then have a similar effect on state revenues. Perhaps horse racing has a positive effect because there are more major events in horse racing (e.g., the Triple Crown) than there are for greyhound racing. These events draw a significant amount of tourism that is not seen with the typical greyhound race.

We are surprised by the casino results. Although the magnitude of the marginal effect is small, it is statistically significant and negative. Policymakers and voters seem quite certain that casino gambling is an effective type of "voluntary" taxation, perhaps because of the licensing fees and relatively high taxes on gross gambling revenues. In most states' policy debates over casinos, the question has been whether the tax benefits (along with other potential economic growth effects) were worth the potential social costs imposed by pathological gamblers. Our results here indicate that the benefits side of the casino question is less of a certainty than is suggested in much of the public debate or literature.

7.4.2 Robustness Check of Casino Results

As noted at the beginning of the chapter, one of the major reasons politicians and voters legalize casinos is for the tax revenues. Since the major focus of the book is the casino industry, we now examine the casino results in more depth. The negative casino tax effect is a bit surprising, considering the taxes on adjusted gross casino revenues range from 7 to 55 %. Casinos are generally taxed at rates much higher

Table 7.4 Granger causality results, 1991–2010 (change in casino revenues and change in tax revenues)

Hypothesis	Lag periods	Obs.	F-statistic (F^*)	Probability ($F>F^*$)
ΔTR does not cause ΔCR	4	192	0.404	0.806
ΔCR does not cause ΔTR	4	192	0.114	0.978

than other goods and services. At the same time, as shown in Table. 7.1, casino and other gaming taxes are not very significant in the big picture of state tax receipts, so we might have reasonably expected no significant casino effect at all. In order to check the robustness of our previous casino results, I posit a different model of the relationship between casinos and state tax revenues.

The Granger causality analysis described and performed in Chaps. 5 and 6 provides an ideal framework for a robustness check of the tax revenue results. Since casinos are found to Granger cause economic growth, we might also expect that there would be a Granger causal relationship with tax revenues. In order to test this, I use the same casino revenue data used in Sect. 6.2. Recall that it includes annual inflation-adjusted casino revenues for the 12 states with commercial casinos (CO, IL, IN, IA, LA, MI, MS, MO, NV, NJ, PA, and SD), from 1990 to 2010. The data are filtered in the same way described in Chap. 5. The unit root test indicates no unit root.

For state-level tax revenues I use a different data set than was used in the analysis in this chapter. I use annual state tax revenues (net of amusement taxes) from the Census Bureau's Annual Survey of State Government Tax Collections.[10] As above, these data are from 1990 to 2010. The unit root test indicates that this series does have a unit root, so it cannot be used for the Granger causality analysis.

Instead of using the level data (casino revenues and tax revenues net of casino taxes), I use the annual change in casino revenues (ΔCR) and change in tax revenues (ΔTR). Neither of these series has a unit root. However, it does reduce the number of observations, as the sample period changes to 1991–2010.

In testing for the appropriate lag length for each filtered series to result in white noise, four lag periods are required for both series. When I run the Granger causality test, I find no causality, in either direction. These results are presented in Table 7.4.

As a robustness check of the previous casino and tax revenue results, the model represented in Table 7.4 presents a conflict. If casinos have a negative impact on state tax revenues, as we found earlier, then we might expect there to be a Granger causal relationship as well. It is important to remember that the model presented in Table 7.3 included data on all 50 states, for the years 1985–2000. The Granger causality analysis here runs from 1991 to 2010, and only includes the 12 states with commercial casinos.

Nevertheless, in neither analysis can we find any positive impact of casinos on state tax revenues. It appears that casinos either have no effect, or a slightly negative one, on state tax revenues. Again considering the data in Table 7.1, casino taxes in

---

[10] See census.gov/govs/statetax/historical_data.html.

particular simply do not amount to a large proportion of tax revenues in most states. The "no result" here is certainly consistent with that.

This begs the question: Why are some politicians so strongly in favor of introducing casinos? The answer may be purely political in nature. Even if casinos do not provide a large tax benefit to the states, they may provide a large *political* benefit to politicians. Consider, for example, the fact that casino legalization becomes more popular during recessions.[11] Politicians want to appear to be "doing something" to help the state of the economy, and want to avoid unpopular acts, such as raising taxes or cutting spending. The legalization of casinos fits the bill because there is an obvious positive employment impact of building and then operating casinos. (Indeed these employment effects may be the most commonly touted benefits of introducing casinos.) The permit process can yield a large amount of revenues, as do the taxes on gross gaming revenues. Politicians can quote tax revenue projections as a benefit of legalization. This may enable them to avoid raising taxes or cutting spending (either as soon or as much as might otherwise be required). Thus, even if casinos do not have a large tax effect, they may have a large and important political effect.

7.5 Summary and Conclusion

In this chapter we have tested the effects of gambling volume on total state government receipts net of federal government transfer funding. We use a multiplicative heteroscedastic maximum likelihood estimation procedure with data for all 50 states over the 1985–2000 period. We find that lotteries and horse racing tend to supplement net state government revenue on average, while casinos and greyhound racing tend to have a negative impact. Of course, the effects of a particular industry in a particular state, or during a particular time period, may vary from our results. For example, we would be very surprised if casino gambling did not have a positive impact on revenues in Nevada and Mississippi, since these markets generate a significant amount of tourism.

The casino industry is of particular interest, both as a political matter in the United States and in the context of this book. A Granger causality test on changes in casino revenues and changes in state tax revenues finds no Granger causal relationship, which may be in conflict with the earlier finding of a negative impact of casinos on state tax revenues. In any case, we find no empirical evidence to suggest that casinos have a positive impact on state tax revenues.

Overall, our results make it clear that voters and policymakers cannot simply assume that the introduction or expansion of legalized gambling will have a positive effect on net state revenues. Indeed, one of the most popular policy proposals during

---

[11] This may also help explain our negative casino effect on tax revenues. If casinos are often introduced during a recession, then casino revenues are increasing during a period in which tax receipts are falling.

recent fiscal crises is casino legalization. Our results show that casinos may be ineffective or counterproductive in the long run in terms of tax revenue generation.

We certainly acknowledge that there are other possible ways of modeling state revenues. We have attempted several different specifications of the model. However, more serious complications were encountered with the alternatives we tested. Ultimately, we believe the model we present here to be the best one, given our data. Obviously there are several possible extensions to this work. For example, it would be useful for states to understand the optimal mix of gambling, in terms of tax revenue maximization. Our results do not address that issue. Another important issue is how the gambling tax structure impacts net revenues. Such issues could be analyzed at the individual state level.

The analysis in this chapter provides new information on the general relationships between legalized gambling industries and state government revenue. It is the first study to consider the effects of the different forms of legalized gambling simultaneously and in all states. To our knowledge, this is the first study of its type in any country. The analysis could be replicated in other countries, as there is no a priori reason to believe that the US results would hold worldwide. Such information would be valuable to other countries' governments that may be considering casino legalization, lotteries, or pari-mutuels, as well as to governments of countries with already flourishing gambling industries (e.g., Australia and Canada). For the United States, our results provide new and important information for policymakers and voters. States or localities that are searching for ways to raise revenue should carefully research their particular situation before introducing new forms of gambling, as the effect on total state revenues is not necessarily positive. Legalized gambling may not always be the "golden egg" that it is sometimes promoted to be.

Chapter 8
Overview of Part I

This first part of the book comprises three chapters (2–4) that provide a basic theoretical discussion of the relationship between casino gambling and economic growth. The remaining chapters review the empirical literature and provide empirical analyses of various casino impacts. As a group, these chapters provide a fairly comprehensive examination of the potential economic benefits of casinos.

My view of the casino industry is that it generally functions the same as any other entertainment industry. It provides a service that people are willing to pay for, similar to movie theaters, professional sports teams, and amusement parks. Admittedly, many observers have a bias against casinos and gambling in general, because they view the activity as being immoral. Objections are also raised on economic grounds, for example, the claim that the industry merely "cannibalizes" other industries, so that there is no net economic benefit from casinos. I view such arguments as being remarkably naïve at best, and at worst intentionally myopic.

In the first few chapters I discuss how the casino industry can lead to economic growth, simply because it represents economic activity. Building a casino requires a capital investment and labor. Such transactions benefit the parties to the transactions, of course. The operation of a casino also requires labor. Presumably workers who take a job at a casino see that as their best option in the labor market—otherwise they would work somewhere else. Empirical evidence (Cotti 2008) suggests that casinos have a positive impact on the labor market, although the net impact is probably not as large as is claimed by the casino industry.

Perhaps the most important economic benefit of casinos is one that has rarely been mentioned in public debate. It is the benefit that consumers receive from having the casinos as an option for them to spend their money. Since people "vote with their dollars," casino revenues indicate that the product pleases people. As simple as this is, this benefit is often ignored in debate, even by the casino companies themselves. Although I provide a conceptual discussion of the issue, I do not provide original empirical estimates of these benefits. Others have, however.

Casino critics are correct in arguing that what matters is the *net impact* on the economy. The industry reports employment, wages paid, and taxes paid as if those amounts represent the real benefits the industry contributes to the economy. What is important, instead, are the net effects. How much more employment is there in a region with a casino than there would otherwise have been? Some other industry may have expanded if the casino industry did not. Such net effects are difficult to study empirically because it is not known "what would otherwise have been" (the counterfactual). Nevertheless, since casinos provide a service for which people willingly pay, it generates economic benefits.

In the remaining chapters of Part I, empirical evidence was presented. I believe that our work on economic growth to be some of the only empirical work that attempts to statistically test for such casino effects. Finally, we provide the most comprehensive analysis to date on the tax impacts of casinos at a state-level. The empirical work in this first part of the book use data from 1985 to 2010, mainly.

Overall, I believe that the empirical evidence shows that casinos are net contributors to their host economies. There is fairly convincing evidence that casinos have a positive effect on economic growth at the state level, that they have a positive impact on employment and wages at a county-level. Finally, although tax revenues are touted as one of the major benefits of legalizing casinos, we find no evidence that casinos actually cause a net increase in tax revenues at the state level. Of course, this does not mean that host cities or counties do not benefit from casino taxes. That issue has not been tested yet. But it is somewhat surprising that we are unable to find any tax benefits from the introduction of casinos. Nevertheless, there are certainly political benefits from legalizing casinos, since it enables policymakers to perhaps delay other unpopular decisions, such as raising other taxes or cutting spending.

8.1 A Look Ahead

Now that we have outlined some of the major economic benefits from the casino industry, in Parts II and III we turn to some of the negative consequences of problem gambling behavior and of the casino industry. Part II examines individual behaviors associated with gambling behaviors. In particular, we examine crime, drunk driving, binge drinking, drug use, and hiring prostitutes, as these behaviors relate to gambling behavior. We also look at gambling and ADHD symptoms.

Part III looks at the "social costs of gambling," including crime, gambling as an unproductive activity, and the "substitution effect" of casinos on other businesses (commercial businesses and other gambling industries).

Part II
Disordered Gambling and Related Behaviors

Chapter 9
Casinos and Drunk Driving Fatalities

9.1 Introduction

Although there are certainly economic benefits of casinos in many jurisdictions, the growth of the industry is not without controversy. Casino opponents argue that casinos bring a variety of social problems, including increases in crime, bankruptcy, and divorce. Recently claims of casinos leading to higher drunk driving prevalence have also been noted. For example, newspaper reports often link DUI arrests and/or alcohol-related traffic fatalities to casinos that serve alcohol (e.g., Cornfield 2009; Smith 2010). Many casinos follow a "destination resort" model; they include restaurants, bars, shows, shops, and a hotel. Other casinos cater more to a local clientele. At a minimum, both types of casino typically include a bar service and casino customers often enjoy drinking alcohol while they socialize and play casino games. The fact that alcohol is readily available at many casinos suggests that casinos may, in fact, be a catalyst for increased drunk driving and hence, increased alcohol-related traffic fatalities. However, a more detailed look at the possible impact of casinos on drunken driving behavior demonstrates that there could be an inverse relationship between casinos and drunk driving under the right circumstances. Regardless, we are aware of no previous study that rigorously examines the possibility of such a link.

The purpose of this study is to test whether there is, in fact, a relationship between the spread of casinos and the number of alcohol-related fatal traffic accidents. Our analysis utilizes US county-level data from 1990 to 2000, a period of time that saw the overwhelming majority of casino openings in the last 30 years. Overall, this presents a natural laboratory to test the effects of casino entry on accident risk.

The material in this chapter is based on Cotti CD, and DM Walker. 2010. The impact of casinos on fatal alcohol-related traffic accidents in the United States. *Journal of Health Economics* 29(6): 788–796. Used with permission from Elsevier.

In the next section we provide background information and discuss various theoretical issues and predictions surrounding possible effects.

In general, our estimates reveal that casino entry does significantly impact the danger posed by drunk drivers, but that the direction and size of this effect is related to the size of the population where the casino opens. Specifically, our best estimate indicates that alcohol-related fatal accidents increase by about 9.2 % for casino counties with the mean log population, yet this estimated effect declines as population increases. Although this is a striking result, we demonstrate below that our estimates are robust to the inclusion of controls for area and time fixed effects, changes in population, changes in other policies that may impact drunk driving behavior (e.g., beer taxes, blood alcohol content regulations), as well as changes in factors that may influence overall driving risk separate from drinking behavior (e.g., road construction, weather). Furthermore, these estimates are also robust to several alternative definitions of the control group, the dependent variable, and to the estimation method selected (e.g., weighted least squares, Poisson, probit).

9.2 Background and Theoretical Considerations

The principle motivation by governments to allow casinos to open in their jurisdictions is the hope that casinos will create economic growth and increase tax revenues at the state level. The casino expansion of the early 1990s had mostly died off until the 2007–2009 recession compounded state-level fiscal crises. Consequently, much of the existing research focuses on the pre-2000 period of time that saw the vast majority of casino openings in the United States. Given the typical motivation for casinos, research has often focused on evaluating the impacts of casino introduction on economic development or government revenue generation (e.g., Elliott and Navin 2002; Mason and Stranahan 1996; Siegel and Anders 2001). While less numerous, other studies have looked at how casino introduction has impacted consumers' behavior with respect to related sectors of the local economy, such as hotels, restaurants, bars, and property values (Anders, Siegel, and Yacoub 1998; Popp and Stehwien 2002; Siegel and Anders 1999; Wenz 2007). Of course, other researchers have also recognized that this large increase in the presence of casinos and gambling could have important impacts on crime, bankruptcy, divorce, and other social ills (Barron, Staten, and Wilshusen 2002; Curran and Scarpitti 1991; Garrett and Nichols 2008; Grinols and Mustard 2006; Stitt, Nichols, and Giacopassi 2003; Thalheimer and Ali 2004). However, little attention has been paid to how the introduction of casinos into a community or region impacts drinking and driving habits and their effects. This lack of research is surprising, given the degree to which alcohol use often accompanies casino gambling.

There is an extensive literature that estimates the impacts of changes in public policies, such as minimum legal drinking age laws, beer taxes, and zero tolerance policies, on drunk driving behavior (e.g., Carpenter 2004; Chaloupka, Grossman,

9.2 Background and Theoretical Considerations

and Saffer 2002; Dee 1999; Ruhm 1996). The motivation behind these policy changes is that they will impact individual behavior and reduce drunk driving. Of course, any factor that changes drinking behavior or the location of drinking activities can impact drunk driving outcomes, whether intended or not. The introduction of casinos into an area may be one such factor.

One can imagine a variety of ways by which casinos might impact drunk driving behavior. For example, there are several reasons to suspect that casino presence may lead to an increase in drunk driving. First, the location of a casino could promote an increase in the total number of miles driven after drinking, which could lead to an increase in automobile accidents in an area following the opening of a casino. Existing literature on consumer behavior supports the contention that small differences in consumer utility can prompt changes in driving habits. For example, the cross border shopping literature indicates that people will consume what they desire in an alternate location when their own jurisdiction has limits or restrictions on consumption, or relatively high costs (Asplund, Friberg, and Wilander 2007; Ferris 2000). Some Canadians, for example, drive great distances to consume health services in the United States. In the case of casinos, their presence may draw people from a large surrounding area to gamble. However, this effect on drunk driving fatalities would depend on the extent to which the introduction of casinos actually does lead to a net increase in the number of people driving and the average distance to casinos. The distance to casinos is likely to decrease as casinos become more widespread, but the introduction of casinos could increase the number of people driving in the area immediately surrounding the casino. If this is the case, we would expect that the introduction of a casino will likely increase the number of miles driven in a county, which could also increase the amount of drunk driving accidents, *ceteris paribus*, as drinking and gambling often go together.

Similarly, a product differentiation effect could also lead to greater distances driven after drinking. Specifically, Lee (1997) applies a Löschian location model (Lösch 1954) to describe the hexagonal market areas created by bar service differentiation. He posits that bar differentiation leads to more drunk driving. As casinos can act as a substitute for bars in many ways, yet allow for extensive gambling activities while drinking, the introduction of a casino may increase the degree of product differentiation among drinking options in an area. So, one can assume that consumers will drive to the casino if their additional transportation and time costs do not cause their total costs to exceed their benefits from being able to gamble and drink. Therefore, the casino represents a new option for some consumers and may be likely to increase the proportional miles driven drunk as a result.

Of course, the impact of casinos on drunk driving could be negative, and this alternative possibility must be considered. The attraction of a nearby casino may cause a substitution effect, as many individuals substitute away from other discretionary pursuits, such as a night out at the local bar or club, to spend an evening gambling at a casino. As a result, if the ability to gamble at a casino creates a sufficient substitute to drinking at a bar, or if casino patrons drink less at the casino than they would have without the casino option, then we may see a decrease in alcohol-related accident risk in an area after the introduction of a casino. Moreover, while many casinos must follow local "bar time" laws when it comes to serving alcohol, the casinos themselves are typically open 24 h. This could give intoxicated individuals the opportunity to sober up before driving home.[1] We should also point out that, unlike casinos in Las Vegas or Atlantic City, which give complementary alcoholic beverages to those gambling, many casinos charge for alcoholic beverages, so a gambler would have to "sacrifice" some of their gambling dollars in order to purchase a drink. This might lead patrons to drink less at the casino than they might have otherwise at some bar or nightclub.[2] Lastly, if we assume that some drinkers choose to frequent the closest drinking establishment to their residence, by increasing the number of drinking options in a county, the casino could reduce the distance driven after drinking among some intoxicated drivers.

Regardless of the economic theory, the literature discussed above would support the idea that the relatively dispersed nature of casino locations across the country could lead to an increased accident-risk due to greater distances traveled by drunk driving gamblers. Indeed, some casinos have acknowledged such problems. For example, the Connecticut-based Mohegan Sun Casino admitted that there is a problem with drunk drivers leaving their casino (WFSB Radio 2009). A few studies have indirectly examined the link between casinos or gambling and DUI arrests (e.g., Reuter 1997; Stitt, Nichols, and Giacopassi 2003; Stokowski 1996; Wilson 2001), but drunk driving is not their primary focus. Furthermore, none of these studies addresses the potential link between casinos and *alcohol-related fatal accidents*. We can find no study that has previously tested for such a link.

In addition to the economic literature on drinking and driving, the gambling and psychology literatures provide an anecdotal link between casinos and drunk driving. In particular, a large proportion of problem gamblers[3] have coexisting disorders ("comorbidity"), including alcohol abuse, which may affect the relationship between casinos and drunk driving. For example, Welte et al. (2001) finds that problem drinkers (alcoholics) are 23 times more likely to have a

---

[1] We see professional sporting events actively facilitating this behavior as they frequently stop alcohol sales after the third quarter of a football game or after the seventh inning in a baseball game, for example.

[2] Casinos' policies with respect to alcohol vary by market; some states have a law that prohibits casinos providing free alcohol to patrons. That said, there is extensive complexity involved in identifying the casino specific treatment of these policies, which prohibited us from being able to specifically control for casino alcohol policies in our model. This exclusion would only impact our findings significantly if there was correlation between the county population and the likelihood of offering free drinks, and our anecdotal research suggests this is not the case. We do, however, recognize this limitation of our analysis.

[3] A "problem gambler" is defined as a person that gambles to such an extent that it disrupts their professional or personal life. Psychologists have estimated that between 0.4 and 2.0 % of the general adult public is afflicted (Petry, Stinson, and Grant 2005). Problem or "disordered" gambling is discussed in more detail in Chap. 10.

gambling problem than individuals who do not have a drinking problem. Petry, Stinson, and Grant (2005) have estimated that over 70 % of pathological gamblers in the United States also have an alcohol use disorder. Since gamblers are the individuals we would most expect to increase their driving after the introduction of a casino, and since a disproportionate number of alcoholics are gamblers, then it is plausible to expect a casino to encourage travel disproportionately by the individuals who are most likely to drive while intoxicated. Of course, casino patrons are not all problem gamblers and alcoholics, but there is a small proportion of the population that has drinking and gambling problems, and this may have an impact on any relationship between casinos and drunk driving and therefore, on alcohol-related fatal accidents.

Given the discussion above about the potential impacts of casino introduction on drinking and driving behavior, we must consider what factors we anticipate will impact the strength of a particular effect on drunk driving. Specifically, we believe that the largest factor is likely to be population of the area where the casino locates. In large cities, casino patrons will disproportionately be locals, who do not need to travel great distances, or who may have public transportation options. Indeed, the opening of a casino in an urban area may not be expected to have any impact on miles driven, since the casino represents one new entertainment option out of many existing ones. Yet, in the case of rurally located casinos, with small local populations, a large proportion of the casino's customers are likely to have driven longer distances, relative to patrons at urban casinos. Therefore, we might expect miles driven and the number of alcohol-related fatal accidents following the introduction of a casino to be greater in rural than in urban areas. To the extent that casinos—either rural or urban—attract new tourists to a particular area, then we would expect an increase in miles driven. Overall, we believe that the *net* impact of casino introduction on alcohol-related traffic risk will depend on the population or "urbanicity" of the area where the casino locates, and this hypothesis is reflected in our empirical specification.

In the remainder of the chapter, we investigate whether these theoretical predictions are verified by observing the how local alcohol-related fatal accidents were impacted by casino entry. We find substantial evidence that the number of fatal accidents involving alcohol is impacted by casino entry, but the magnitude and direction of the effect is indeed dependent on the size of the local population.

9.3 Data and Methods

In order to analyze any relationship that might exist between casinos and alcohol-related fatal accidents (ARFAs, hereafter), we must choose appropriate data. Although data are readily available at a state-level, such aggregation would likely not foster a good analysis since many states with casinos have few of them, which means the locations of the casinos would be a necessary control for the analysis. County-level data are available on casinos and on ARFAs, and we view this to be the ideal level for our analysis.

9.3.1 Casino and Fatal Accident Data

The vast majority of the expansion in the US casino industry occurred during the 1990–2000 period. Between 2000 and 2008, only one state (Pennsylvania) legalized commercial casinos. We are interested in analyzing whether and how the spread of casinos has affected ARFAs, so like most casino-focused studies we choose the 1990–2000 period of time for our analysis. A set of 131 counties saw casinos open within their borders between 1990 and 2000. These casino counties represent the treatment group for our primary estimates.[4] We link these data on casino location to data on fatal vehicle crashes obtained through the National Highway Traffic Safety Administration's (NHTSA) Fatality Analysis Reporting System (FARS).[5] Our primary variable of interest is the annual number of fatal accidents in a county for which a driver's imputed blood alcohol content (BAC) exceeds 0.08. The legal maximum BAC is set by state government and every state currently has a maximum legal BAC of 0.08.

Although Federal law requires that BAC levels be obtained from every fatal crash, this is frequently not done and can lead to substantial bias in any estimation. The NHTSA is aware of this issue and provides imputed measures of the BAC for all drivers who were not tested. The NHTSA creates the imputed values using a multitude of characteristics in each case, including factors such as time of day, day of week, contents of the police report, position of car in the road, etc. (National Highway Traffic Safety Administration 2002).[6] While previous studies using counts generated from older FARS data used imputed values based on discriminant analysis, or relied on counts generated from accidents that were more likely to be alcohol-related (e.g., crashes on weekend evenings), more recent studies use data generated by this new NHTSA procedure (e.g., Cummings et al. 2006; Hingson et al. 2005; Villaveces et al. 2003).

We aggregate NHTSA counts of fatal accidents involving a driver with a BAC content exceeding 0.08 by county and year. We can link annual fatal accident counts to other available county-level annual data (i.e., population data from the Census Bureau). Moreover, annual counts provide us with a sufficient number of accidents for each county upon which to base the analyses.

Unfortunately, county authorities sometimes fail to report any accident data for a particular year, leaving us with an unbalanced panel. For our main estimates we include only counties for which FARS data were available for all 11 years of our analysis (1990–2000). We do, however, test the robustness of this restriction.

---

[4] For clarity, Atlantic County, NJ and all counties in Nevada were excluded from the analysis due to the unique nature of the casino industry in these areas. Results are robust to this restriction.

[5] To be clear, the NHTSA reports fatal accidents on all roadways, not just "highways."

[6] This follows suggestions from Rubin, Shafer, and Subramanian (1998) and improves on the former procedure based on discriminant analysis (Klein 1986; National Highway Traffic Safety Administration 2002).

9.3 Data and Methods

Table 9.1 County-year means and proportions of key variables in balanced-sample analysis

	All counties	Casino counties	Non-casino counties
Number of annual fatal accidents involving a driver with a blood alcohol content (BAC) above 0.08	31.83	39.29	30.51
Number of fatal accidents involving a driver with a positive blood alcohol level	37.71	46.54	36.15
Number of fatal accidents involving no alcohol	63.89	78.52	61.30
Population (unweighted, from US Census Bureau)	150,471	270,803	139,501
County unemployment rate (from Local Area Unemployment Statistics)	5.68 %	5.98 %	5.63 %
Prevailing beer tax per gallon (in 2000 dollars)	$0.24	$0.23	$0.24
BAC law specifying minimum of 0.08	29.1 %	36.03 %	27.84 %
Zero tolerance laws	56.23 %	59.48 %	55.66 %
Number of observations (county-years)	17,248	1,441	15,807
(Number of counties)	(1,568)	(131)	(1,437)

Notes: (1) As the primary estimation is weighted by county population, the above means and proportions are weighted similarly, unless noted. (2) To maintain consistency with the primary sample utilized in the analysis, the above values are from a balanced sample of counties, and they exclude data from the state of Nevada and from Atlantic County, NJ
Source: Cotti and Walker (2010). Used with permission from Elsevier

Table 9.1 reports means and proportions of variables included in the analysis for both the treatment counties and counties without a casino. The second column in the table, casino counties, includes all county-year observations for counties that have a casino present within their borders for at least one year in the sample time period. In many cases there are small differences between the treatment and control counties, although some variables, such as county population and the prevailing beer tax, are very similar. There are two notable differences between the casino and non-casino counties. First, higher unemployment rates are observed in the treatment counties. This is consistent with the idea that some municipalities or states attempt to utilize casinos as a form of economic development in depressed areas. The second difference is that there is a larger number of fatal automobile accidents (alcohol-related and non-alcohol-related) in the casino counties.

9.3.2 Methodology

We first pool a balanced sample of all of the counties in which a casino was open (the treatment group) and the remaining counties in the United States that did not have a casino present during the sample period (the control group). We experiment later with alternative samples and the results prove robust. Our basic analysis begins with the following fixed effects regression model:

$$\text{ARFA}_{ct} = \alpha_c + \tau_t + \beta_1 C_{ct} + \beta_2 P_{ct} + \beta_3 CP_{ct} + \gamma' X_{ct} + \varepsilon_{ct} \quad (9.1)$$

where subscript c denotes counties and t denotes years. ARFA is the number of alcohol-related fatal accidents; α_c and τ_t are county and time fixed effects, respectively; C is a dichotomous variable indicating the presence of a casino; P is the log of county population; CP is an interaction term between the casino variable and the log of the county population; X is a vector of additional variables, explained in more detail along with the other variables, below; and ε is the error term.

ARFA is defined in most estimates as the log of the number of fatal accidents involving a driver whose measured BAC exceeded 0.08 in a given county-year cell. Specifically, in constructing ARFA we add one to the number of ARFAs in each county-year to prevent losing the very small counties that may have zero accidents when the values are logged. Results prove robust to this approach. We judge logs to be the most appropriate scale for the dependent variable because the median estimated number of fatal accidents for the county-years in the sample is less than the mean.

Given that the number of accidents may be highly variable in smaller counties and that we use data aggregated to the county-year level, we weight the OLS estimates by county-year population size obtained from the Census Bureau. Estimation of (9.1) therefore uses weighted least squares (WLS). We also correct all standard errors to allow for non-independence of observations from the same state through clustering. This follows Arellano (1987) and Bertrand, Duflo, and Mullainathan (2004). We show later that redefining the dependent variable or using a different estimation model yields qualitatively identical results.[7]

Variable C is a county indicator that is set to one if the county has a casino present in a given year.[8] Variable CP is the interaction of the casino dummy and the log of the county population. To allow for a more meaningful interpretation, we also estimate CP as the interaction of the casino dummy and the demeaned log of the county population. Thus, the estimate of β_3 can be read as an estimate of the percent

---

[7] For example, a Poisson regression (Hausman, Hall, and Griliches 1984) could be used given the discrete measurement of the dependent variable (before logging). Given the potential over-dispersion of the dependent variable, however, the Poisson might be inappropriate. Therefore, a negative binomial model might be more appealing, but the conditional negative binomial model correcting for over-dispersion has recently been criticized on the grounds of failing to be a true fixed effects estimator (Allison and Waterman 2002). We settle on weighted least squares as the least problematic and most easily interpretable measure to use in presenting the basic results. We conducted a multitude of robustness checks to ensure our choice of model is not driving the result, many of which are reported below in Table 9.4.

[8] We recognize that utilizing a dichotomous variable to indicate whether there is a casino present in a county or not ignores any differences in the size of the casino environment across counties and over time. Unfortunately we were unable to obtain any reliable or comprehensive measure of casino size at the county level or for individual casinos. This is a limitation of our analysis.

9.3 Data and Methods

increase in ARFAs after a casino opens in a county with an average log population, relative to a control group of counties that did not have a casino open at any point during the sample period. As mentioned earlier in the chapter, we believe that drinking and driving outcomes are likely to be affected by the population of the counties impacted, hence variable *CP*, capturing the casino population interaction, will help to identify whether such a relationship does exist.[9]

The inclusion of county fixed effects (α_c) and time fixed effects (τ_t) are imperative to proper identification when utilizing this empirical research design. Specifically, the inclusion of county fixed effects captures differences in accident prevalence across counties that are time-invariant. Therefore, the inclusion of fixed effects allows us to compare counties with persistent differences in accident prevalence, without concern that these differences will impact our estimates. On the other hand, time fixed effects capture changes in accident prevalence over time that is common in all counties.

We recognize the recent empirically rigorous studies that evaluate the determinants of drunk driving (e.g., Baughman et al. 2001; Dee 1999; Eisenberg 2003) and understand that our empirical strategy should isolate the impact of casinos from the other determinants of ARFAs. We know that population growth will likely increase the number of accidents, so one control is the log of the county's population (*P*), obtained from the Census Bureau. Although we think casino openings are likely exogenous in the context of our study, there may exist some correlation between casino presence and some other factors. Our empirical approach addresses this in a number of ways. First, the county fixed effects capture differences in counties that might affect accidents and are constant over time. We also add various covariates that capture county-specific changes in a county's ARFAs over time and include them in the *X* vector.

Second, Ruhm and Black (2002) showed that downturns in the economy have a small negative net impact on drinking behavior. So, county unemployment rates collected from the Local Area Unemployment Statistics (LAUS) program are included in *X*.

Third, we are concerned that there may be an underlying propensity for *all* traffic accidents to change in a county (or state) over time because of differences in speed limits, gas prices, general economic activity, highway construction, weather patterns, insurance rates, or other factors that might confound the interpretation of our estimates of ARFAs. To capture these, we employ an approach employed by Adams and Cotti (2008), which utilizes the log number of accidents per county that were *not* alcohol-related (also measured in the FARS data). This control isolates the effect of the independent variables (including the casino variables) apart from the many potentially omitted factors that make it more dangerous to drive in any

---

[9] It is important to note that the inclusion of the log of population is equivalent to the inclusion of the log of population per square mile, given that county fixed effects are included and that the area size of counties does not vary over time.

particular locality. Given that this captures underlying traffic trends in the data, it would capture any differences in general accident risk that may arise between the treatment and control groups during the sample period analyzed, and as such is a very powerful control.

Another issue that must be addressed in this analysis is the concern that the opening of a casino in a county is correlated with other government policies that are meant to deter drunk drivers. We use data from 1990 to 2000, however, which is a time period beyond the point that most states had engaged in most of their legislative activity aimed at deterring drunk driving. For example, since 1988 the minimum legal drinking age has been 21 in all states. This alleviates the concern that casino passage tended to coincide with legislation aimed to deter intoxicated drivers. The fact that our sample includes casinos from every region of the United States further supports the experimental nature of our study.

Nevertheless, during our sample period, there were three state-level variables that changed enough to raise concern that they might confound the interpretation of the estimated casino effect. First, a number of states lowered the minimum BAC used to determine whether a driver was legally intoxicated, from 0.10 to 0.08. Table 9.1 shows that more counties in our treatment group than the control group were affected by this reduction. Dee (2001) and Eisenberg (2003) use somewhat older data to show that stricter BAC requirements reduce drunk driving accidents. For this reason, we include controls for whether the county is located in a state that had a 0.08 statute for a given year; the remainder of the counties had 0.10 BAC laws during this time period. Second, many states passed zero-tolerance laws on teen drivers during our sample time frame. Carpenter (2004) shows that these laws play an important role in reducing drinking and driving among young drivers, so we include a dummy variable indicating if a state had a zero tolerance alcohol policy in place. Third, alcohol excise taxes varied over our sample period, as some states increased or decreased their rates. Ruhm (1996) finds beer taxes to be effective in deterring drunk driving for at least a subset of the population. Eisenberg (2003), however, finds limited evidence of such an effect from beer taxes. We include controls for the log of beer taxes (in 2000 dollars) to capture any tax effect. However, a look at Table 9.1 shows little differential variation in beer taxes between the treatment and control states.

There are obviously other minor state and local laws and regulations aimed at deterring drunk driving, many of which might be effective in certain areas. We find that adding control variables for BAC laws, zero tolerance policies, and beer taxes does not substantially change our estimated casino effect. So, if these much more visible and effective policies are not correlated with the introduction of casinos, it is unlikely our results would be affected by less visible policies.[10]

---

[10] We also included interaction terms of the casino variable and the policy variables. However, none of these interaction terms was significant and they did not affect the overall results.

9.4 Results

9.4.1 Basic Results

We begin by estimating (9.1) for a balanced sample of all the treatment and control counties. Results are shown in column (1) of Table 9.2 and indicate that, for counties of near the mean logged population, the opening of a casino increases alcohol-related fatal accidents (ARFAs) by a statistically significant 9.2 %. Consistent with our expectations, the casino population interaction shows that this effect declines as population size increases. Recall, we estimate the casino effect where the casino population interaction is defined as the interaction of the casino dummy and the demeaned log of the county population.[11] So, the estimates on the casino and casino-population interaction variables

Table 9.2 Effects of casino entry on ARFAs, 1990–2000

	Dep. variable: Nat. log alcohol-related fatal accidents (ARFAs)	
	WLS	
Explanatory variables	(1)	(2)
Casino dummy (C)	0.092** (0.041)	0.117*** (0.041)
Casino-population interaction (CP)[a]	−0.058** (0.023)	−0.081*** (0.028)
Border county dummy (B)	–	0.107*** (0.033)
Border county-population interaction (BP)[b]	–	−0.069*** (0.017)
Nat. log county population (P)	0.488*** (0.171)	0.449*** (0.175)
Nat. log non-alcohol-related fatal accidents	0.148*** (0.031)	0.135*** (0.024)
Zero tolerance law dummy	−0.052** (0.021)	−0.056*** (0.020)
0.08 blood alcohol content (BAC) dummy	0.034 (0.044)	0.029 (0.038)
Nat. log beer tax (in 2000 dollars)	−0.087 (0.074)	−0.069 (0.069)
Nat. log county unemployment rate	−0.085* (0.051)	−0.095* (0.054)
Observations	17,248	17,248
Counties	1,568	1,568
States	50	50
R-squared	0.940	0.941

Notes: (1) Robust standard errors are in parentheses. (2) Estimates are clustered at the state level to allow for non-independence of observations from the same state. (3) Estimates are weighted by county population. (4) Nevada and Atlantic County, NJ have been excluded. (5) Only counties where observations were available for all 11 years are included
Source: Cotti and Walker (2010). Used with permission from Elsevier
[a]The casino-population interaction is demeaned for interpretation at a meaningful population and is defined as (casino dummy) × [ln(population) − ln(mean population)]
[b]The border county-population interaction is demeaned for interpretation at a meaningful population and is defined as (border county dummy) × [ln(population) − ln(mean population)]
*p < 0.1, **p < 0.05, ***p < 0.01

---

[11] Average (unweighted) log population in the sample is 11.095.

provide evidence that casino presence does impact ARFAs, but the population of a county determines the magnitude and the direction of the effect. For example, the estimates in Table 9.2, column (1) suggest that smaller/rural counties with casinos, such as Sauk County, WI (average sample population=17,339; log population=9.76) would see a statistically significant increase in ARFAs of 16.9 % (p-value=0.014), while much larger/urban counties with casinos, such as Milwaukee County, WI (average sample population=936,589; log population=13.75) would see a statistically significant *decline* in ARFAs of 6.1 % from the introduction of a casino (p-value=0.064). In light of our earlier theoretical discussion of the possible effects of casinos on ARFAs, our results may indicate that in rural counties, casinos tend to increase miles driven by intoxicated drivers (potentially from residents of the county and by out-of-county visitors), and therefore make ARFAs more likely. In urban settings, however, it appears that this effect may be more than offset by a substitution of casino patronage for other drinking establishments, coupled with other aspects of urban living, such as a much greater availability of public transportation.

With regard to the other variables in the regression, as expected, all else equal, population growth increases the number of accidents. Also as expected, the number of fatal accidents involving no alcohol is also positive and highly significant. We believe that this captures the general accident trend in a county, which is driven by factors that impact the relative driving danger of an area separate from alcohol, such as road construction or weather. It is important to note that, although changes in non-alcohol-related accidents are highly correlated with ARFAs, the effect of the casino and casino-population interaction is still significant.[12] Estimates on the remaining controls are as anticipated or are insignificant.

The identification strategy utilized to this point is predicated on the assumption that after the inclusion of fixed effects and time-varying controls, the casino counties are comparable to the non-casino counties. Yet, even though we have controlled for changes in non-alcohol-related trends, there is always the concern that casino openings are somehow correlated with some unobserved trend in ARFAs. Although we view this to be unlikely, in light of the aforementioned controls and the exogenous nature of casinos with regard to drunk driving, we do test for the presence of such a correlation in two ways. First, we fail to reject the null hypothesis that the pre-casino trends of ARFAs in the treatment and control groups are identical, thus providing no evidence to indicate that there is a difference in accident trends between the control group and treatment group in the years prior to casino entry (p-value=0.562). Second, we look at the effect of casinos over time by introducing lead and lagged effects, as well as a contemporaneous effect of the casino entry. The lead effects are informative in that we can determine whether the estimates of the casino dummy variable (C) are indeed stemming from the opening of a

---

[12]One could envision a falsification exercise where the log of non-alcohol-related accidents is the dependent variable. However, we find no evidence of a casino effect on accidents with no alcohol involved (Coef.=0.019, SE=0.035). Likewise, the estimated effect of the casino-population interaction is both statistically and absolutely insignificant (Coef.=−0.001, SE=0.018). It is only the *alcohol*-related crashes that are impacted by casino entry.

9.4 Results

Table 9.3 Effects of casino entry on ARFAs, leads and lags

	Dep. variable: Nat. log alcohol-related fatal accidents (ARFAs)
	WLS
	Casino year effects
Lead 3 years +	0.049 (0.070)
Lead 2 years	−0.074 (0.063)
Lead 1 year	−0.036 (0.078)
Year of casino opening	0.057 (0.052)
Lag 1 year	0.126** (0.046)
Lag 2 years	0.090 (0.060)
Lag 3 years +	0.126** (0.059)
p-Value: Test joint significance of leads	0.5506
p-Value: Test joint significance of lags	0.0636*
Observations	17,248
Counties	1,568
States	50
R-squared	0.940

Notes: (1) Results are analogous to those presented in the first column of Table 9.2. Hence, all control variables from Table 9.2, column (1), as well as interactions between the lead/lag dummies and log of demeaned population were included in this regression. (2) Robust standard errors are in parentheses. (3) Estimates are clustered at the state level to allow for non-independence of observations from the same state. (4) Estimates are weighted by county population. (5) Nevada and Atlantic County, NJ have been excluded. (6) Only counties where observations were available for all 11 years are included
Source: Cotti and Walker (2010). Used with permission from Elsevier
*$p<0.1$, **$p<0.05$

casino, as opposed to the effect of a previously existing trend. The results, presented in Table 9.3, indicate the expected pattern as the lead effects are not significant and have opposing signs, while estimates only become statistically significant and consistently positive after the casino opens.[13] Overall, these results provide no evidence to suggest that the estimates in Table 9.2, column (1) are the result of trending differences between the treatment and control counties; instead they appear to be real effects of casinos.

9.4.2 Robustness Checks

Although we view our empirical decisions thus far as reasonable, we recognize there are several alternative definitions of the sample, the dependent variable, the policy variables, and estimation methods that we could have employed. In order to

---
[13] A test of the joint significance of leads fails to reject the null hypothesis that leads jointly equal zero (p-value = 0.5506). Test of the joint significance of lags successfully rejects the null hypothesis that lags jointly equal zero (p-value = 0.0636).

Table 9.4 Robustness checks of the basic results

	Model	Casino dummy (C)	Casino population interaction (CP)[a]
(1)	Basic specification (repeated from Table 9.2, column 1)	0.092** (0.041)	−0.058** (0.023)
	Alternative estimation method		
(2)	Unweighted Poisson fixed effects	0.088*** (0.029)	−0.068*** (0.015)
(3)	Fixed effects probit (dep. variable is ARFA rate) (marginal effects shown)	0.069** (0.029)	−0.049** (0.020)
(4)	State fixed effects (instead of county)	0.097** (0.046)	−0.048* (0.028)
	Alternative specifications		
(5)	Casino dummy given half-weight during year casino opened, one thereafter	0.107** (0.050)	−0.061** (0.024)
(6)	Casino dummy given zero-weight during year casino opened, one thereafter	0.099** (0.050)	−0.053** (0.021)
(7)	Dep. variable is log of number of accidents involving any alcohol	0.096** (0.042)	−0.054** (0.023)
	Alternative samples		
(8)	Only counties from a state with a casino (1,002 total counties)	0.099** (0.047)	−0.055** (0.022)
(9)	Propensity score analysis (701 counties)	0.133* (0.072)	−0.109** (0.048)
(10)	Unbalanced panel (3,114 total counties)	0.120** (0.048)	−0.054** (0.021)

Notes: (1) Each row represents a separate regression on the dependent variable ARFAs. County and year fixed effects, as well as controls for accidents not involving alcohol, population, beer tax, a zero tolerance dummy, the local area unemployment rate, and minimum BAC levels are included in all regressions. For the sake of brevity, these other variables are not shown here. Unless otherwise noted, the number of counties in consistent: 1,568. (2) Coefficient estimates and robust standard errors (corrected to allow for non-independence of observations within a state through clustering) are reported
Source: Cotti and Walker (2010). Used with permission from Elsevier
[a](casino dummy) × [ln(population) − ln(mean population)]
*p < 0.1, **p < 0.05, ***p < 0.01

verify that the results are not sensitive to our choices, we next engage in a series of robustness checks, which we summarize in Table 9.4. For comparison, row (1) repeats the primary results from Table 9.2, column (1), a 9.2 % increase in ARFAs after casino entry, with a −0.058 estimated coefficient on the demeaned casino-population interaction.

Our first set of robustness checks tests the robustness of our chosen estimation model. We have been using weighted least squares estimation with a log transformed dependent variable. However, several alternative estimation methods are also potentially good options. For example, given the discrete count-nature of the accident data, a Poisson approach may be appropriate. Row (2) of Table 9.4 provides estimates using a fixed-effects Poisson estimation approach and shows similar

9.4 Results

inference to the WLS estimates.[14] Next we note that frequently in the accident literature the dependent variable will be divided by a measure of population to generate an accident rate and a logit or probit approach will be utilized. In row (3) we have taken this approach, using a probit model to estimate the effects of casino entry. Again results prove robust as the estimated marginal effects are very similar to the WLS estimates. The last alternative estimation approach tests the sensitivity of the basic results to the use of county fixed effects. We recognize that three of the control variables we use are measured at the state level: beer tax, zero tolerance laws, and lower BAC requirements. In row (4) we employ state rather than county fixed effects; the estimates remain very similar to our original estimates.

Next, we checked the robustness of our chosen specification. First, to this point, we have considered a county to be a "casino county," with the casino dummy variable equal to one if a casino was open within a county's borders at any point during a calendar year. We could have weighted the casino dummy differently for the first year a casino is present in a county, because the impact may be lessened if the casino was not operating for the entire year. Alternatively, we could have considered a county as only having been affected by the casino's presence for a given year if the casino was present before the beginning of that year. So, in order to test our results to the sensitivity of the first year weighting we generate estimates where the year the casino opens is given half weight ($C=0.5$) or no weight ($C=0$). As detailed in rows (5) and (6) of Table 9.4, the overall impact of casinos remains both quantitatively and qualitatively the same regardless of how we treat the casino dummy variable and the corresponding casino-population interaction during the first year of a casino presence. Next we consider the robustness of our dependent variable definition. Instead of using the log of ARFAs where driver BAC exceeded 0.08, we could have chosen the log number of fatal accidents involving any alcohol. When we do this the outcome is nearly the same, as shown in row (7).

In our final set of robustness tests, we test whether the sample group we have been using is unduly influencing the results. We test three alternative samples. In the first alternative, we restrict the control group to only those states with a casino present at some point during the sample time-frame (1990–2000). From the perspective of cultural or regional driving norms, the non-casino counties from states with some casino presence may provide a better control group.[15] The results of this test are reported in row (8); the story remains virtually unchanged. Next, on a similar theme, we used a logistic regression to calculate propensity scores for each county as a means of matching the treatment counties to the most similar control counties in the sample. Results of this examination are presented in row (9) and also prove robust, albeit less precisely measured. Finally, thus far we have been using a balanced sample of counties, which has imposed a strong restriction on the data. So, in our last robustness check we replicate the analysis from Table 9.2, column (1), utilizing the

---

[14] Due to a limitation in the Stata programming, the estimation is not weighted and the standard errors from these estimates were clustered at the county, rather than the state level.

[15] For these estimates, we exclude counties from states such as Maine and South Carolina, which do not have any casinos present between the years 1990 and 2000.

much larger unbalanced sample. Although the estimated effect of casino entry on the mean population is larger, the inclusion of these additional counties does not alter our qualitative findings.

Overall, the results detailed in Table 9.4 provide us with a broad and comprehensive picture of the nature of the measured effects. Under most of the alternatives, we estimate an effect that is slightly stronger than the basic estimates. Under a few of the alternatives, the precision is smaller, but, regardless of empirical assumptions, the qualitative conclusions of the primary model remain intact. We therefore regard our results presented in Table 9.2, column (1) as being robust and fairly conservative estimates for the impact of casinos on ARFAs.

9.4.3 Border County Analysis

In Sect. 9.2 we advanced several potential mechanisms that might explain how opening a casino might impact alcohol-related fatal accidents. One such mechanism for an increase in drunk driving rates comes from the existing literature on consumer behavior which suggests that small differences in consumer utility can prompt changes in driving habits. In particular, if casinos act as a destination and attract people from a wide area, we could see an increase in accident deaths in counties near a casino county, as well as in the county in which the casino is located. Returning to Table 9.2, we address this possibility by testing for casino effects on fatal accidents in counties adjoining the casino counties. If there are increases in ARFAs in the adjoining counties after casinos open, this is suggestive that people are driving greater distances in response to this change in their incentives.

Our specification of this analysis, presented in (9.2) below, is nearly identical to that presented in (9.1), except we now include variable B, which is a dummy variable that is equal to one if a county borders a county with a casino, and variable BP, which is an interaction between the border county indicator and county population.

$$\text{ARFA}_{ct} = \alpha_c + \tau_t + \beta_1 C_{ct} + \beta_2 P_{ct} + \beta_3 CP_{ct} + \beta_4 B_{ct} + \beta_5 BP_{ct} + \gamma' X_{ct} + \varepsilon_{ct} \quad (9.2)$$

This specification allows for two distinct treatment groups, counties with a casino and counties that border counties with a casino, and a control group that consists of all remaining counties. This approach provides us not only the ability to estimate if any potential spillover effects of casinos exist in bordering counties, but, in the event spillovers are present, to also reestimate the impact of casinos on drunk driving accidents in the casino counties against a potentially more appropriate control group.

Results presented in the second column of Table 9.2 indicate that, for counties of near the mean logged population, the opening of a casino increases ARFAs in border counties by a statistically significant 10.7 % and in the casino county itself by 11.7 %. Moreover, both the county population interaction variables are negative and significant, indicating that again the size of the county plays an important role in outcomes. We should point out that, while the estimated border county interaction suggests that highly populated border counties could see a decline in ARFAs, given on the actual border county populations, these estimates would predict an *increase* in ARFAs in nearly 90 % of the border counties in the sample. With this in mind, these results suggest that there are generally relevant spillover costs onto neighboring counties, as residents seem to drive to and from casinos.

Overall, findings from this border county analysis seem to indicate that increases in visitors from nearby areas are at least partially responsible for any net increases in ARFAs observed in the casino counties. And, from a policy perspective, this result suggests that jurisdictions that border casino counties should be aware of a heightened risk of drunk drivers returning along major highways from the locations which have operating casinos.

9.5 Conclusion

This study is the first of which we are aware to show that casinos impact the fatal accident risk posed by drunk drivers. Specifically, we find that the magnitude and direction of the effect is dependent on the size of the population where the casino is opened. Thus, on average, rural or moderately sized counties will likely see an increase in alcohol-related fatal traffic accidents when casinos are present, but urban or greater-than-average populous counties may be expected to see a decrease in alcohol-related fatal traffic accidents when casinos are present. Among other factors, we believe that the net effect lies in the tradeoff between increases in the total number of miles driven while intoxicated in a county (increasing risk), and the potential that casinos may act as a substitute to other venues at which alcohol may be served (decreasing risk), with the former being stronger in all but the most urban areas.

We have shown that this result is robust to the inclusion of controls for area and time fixed effects, changes in population, changes in other policies that may impact drunk driving behavior (e.g., beer taxes, BAC laws), as well as changes in factors that may influence overall driving risk separate from drinking behavior (e.g., construction, weather). Furthermore, these estimates are also robust to several alternative definitions of the control group, the dependent variable, and to the estimation method selected (e.g., weighted least squares, Poisson, probit). Lastly, evidence from an analysis of border counties is consistent with the idea that the dispersed nature of casinos creates a destination effect—particularly in less urban areas—that attracts people from surrounding jurisdictions to drink and gamble, which leads to an increase in ARFAs in the casino county, as well as in the bordering counties.

Overall, this study provides an important new piece of information on the effects of casinos on local communities. This information can be helpful to jurisdictions currently weighing the casino option, as well as existing casino jurisdictions attempting to address the social impacts from casinos. In particular, we hope that this study will provide increased awareness about the potential problems that casino introduction can create, especially on rural highways, and that local communities will take the appropriate steps necessary to increase the private costs associated with the decision to drink and drive.

Chapter 10
Gambling, Crime, Binge Drinking, Drug Use, and Hiring Prostitutes

10.1 Introduction

Psychologists and medical researchers publish an enormous amount of research on the diagnosis and treatment of "pathological" gambling. This term is used to describe gambling that is far beyond recreational gambling. It represents gambling, for the person involved, to such an extent that it causes problems in their personal and/or professional life. Pathological gambling is a specific condition included in the *Diagnostic and Statistical Manual of Mental Disorders* (DSM-IV)[1], which is the "primary classification system for diagnosing mental disorders in the United States" (Petry 2010).

The diagnostic criteria from the DSM-IV (2000) are listed below. A person may be diagnosed as being a pathological gambler if described by five or more of the following conditions, and if the gambling "is not better accounted for by a Manic Episode" (American Psychiatric Association 2000): The person

1. Is preoccupied with gambling (e.g., preoccupied with reliving past gambling experiences, handicapping or planning the next venture, or thinking of ways to get money with which to gamble)

The material in this chapter is based on Clark C, and DM Walker. 2009. Are gamblers more likely to commit crimes? Evidence from a nationally representative survey of U.S. young adults. *International Gambling Studies* 9(2): 119–134. Used with permission from Taylor & Francis. Walker DM, C Clark, and J Folk. 2010. The relationship between gambling behavior and binge drinking, hard drug use, and paying for sex. *UNLV Gaming Research & Review Journal* 14(1): 15–26. Used with permission from the International Gaming Institute at UNLV.

[1] The DSM-IV was published in 1994. There was a text revision published in 2000. This is referred to as DSM-IV-TR in the literature, but I refer to it just as DSM-IV since the revision did not affect the diagnostic criteria for problem gambling. Ross et al. (2008) provide a review of how pathological gambling has changed in the evolution of the DSM through the DSM-IV.

2. Needs to gamble with increasing amounts of money in order to achieve the desired excitement
3. Has repeated unsuccessful efforts to control, cut back, or stop gambling
4. Is restless or irritable when attempting to cut down or stop gambling
5. Gambles as a way of escaping from problems or of relieving a dysphoric mood (e.g., feelings of helplessness, guilt, anxiety, depression)
6. After losing money gambling often returns another day to get even ("chasing" one's losses)
7. Lies to family members, therapist, or others to conceal the extent of involvement with gambling
8. Has committed illegal acts such as forgery, fraud, theft, or embezzlement to finance gambling
9. Has jeopardized or lost a significant relationship, job, or educational or career opportunity because of gambling
10. Relies on others to provide money to relieve a desperate financial situation caused by gambling

A new edition of the DSM, the DSM-V, is due to be published in May 2013. The editorial by Petry (2010) indicates that the terminology in the DSM-V is likely to be changed from pathological gambling to "disordered gambling," and that it will include nine criteria (rather than 10), of which a person must identify with four to be diagnosed. The criterion "has committed illegal acts ... to finance gambling" (number 8 in the list above) is "rarely endorsed and appears to add little diagnostic classification accuracy" (Petry 2010, 113). The prevalence rate of disordered gambling is somewhere around 0.4–2.0 % of the general public (Petry, Stinson, and Grant 2005), and is surprisingly independent of the region/country studied.[2]

One key concern about the spread of legal casinos in the United States is the problems associated with disordered gambling. As we will discuss in Part III of the book, there are potentially large social costs caused by disordered gamblers.

In this chapter we utilize survey data from a large, representative sample of the US young adults to analyze the relationship between gambling behavior, criminal behavior, and other "vices"—hard drug use, binge drinking, and hiring prostitutes. This study complements the existing body of research because it utilizes a previously unused data source, has a very large sample size, and is based on many unique survey questions. The chapter is organized as follows: In Sects. 10.2 and 10.3 we provide a brief overview of the relevant literatures. Our data and models are

---

[2] Other terms that have been used in the past include "problem," "pathological," and "compulsive" gambling, or gambling addiction. It is beyond the scope of this book to go into detail about the different severities of the problem, diagnosis, prevalence, or treatment. In this book I use the terms "problem gambling," "pathological gambling," and "disordered gambling" interchangeably, without attempting to differentiate between different severities of the affliction. Psychologists may be offended by this, but my focus is not on the severity of the problem; it is more on the costs associated with gambling problems. Interested readers can consult the enormous amount of psychological research on the topic if they want more detailed information on gambling problems and classifications.

explained in Sect. 10.4. In Sect. 10.5 the results are presented and discussed, and Sect. 10.6 concludes. In Chap. 11 we use the same data set to analyze the relationship between gambling behavior and ADHD symptoms.

10.2 Background on Gambling Behavior and Crime

Economic studies have examined the relationships among the levels of gambling activity and the amount of reported crime, while psychological studies have examined micro-level data from problem/pathological gamblers, to understand how problem gambling may be a catalyst of criminal behavior.

There are several explanations for why individuals who develop gambling problems may exhibit criminal behavior. For example, a person who has difficulty controlling his gambling behavior may exhaust his or her financial resources and turn to crime as a means to get money to continue gambling. Typically, studies of problem gambling and crime entail survey data from problem gamblers currently in treatment, Gamblers Anonymous members, or others who have been identified (or who have self-identified) as having a gambling problem to some degree. Empirical analyses usually entail the presentation of summary statistics from the survey or interview, correlation statistics, and a variety of other analytical components. Yet, few rigorous studies have been published on the gambling–crime relationship. See Lesieur (1987) for an early discussion of gambling and crime. Importantly, the factors affecting adolescents' and adults' gambling behavior may be significantly different, and separate adolescent and adult literatures exist. In our study we are examining the behavior of young adults, 75 % of which are 21 or older, with an average age of about 22. Here we wish to give a general overview, rather than a detailed review of the literature.[3]

Meyer and Stadler (1999) study pathological gamblers in treatment along with individuals from the general population, and find a significant relationship between pathological gambling and criminal behavior. Specifically, 89.3 % of their sample of pathological gamblers admitted having committed at least one crime in their lifetime. The rate was around 50 % for "high and low frequency gamblers" (p. 34). During their last year of regular gambling, almost 60 % of pathological gamblers and 22 % of the other group admitted having committed at least one criminal offense (pp. 34–35). Among the pathological gamblers who committed crimes, about 35 % indicated that the crimes were committed in order to help finance their gambling habits (p. 35).

Williams, Royston, and Hagen (2005) examine the gambling behavior by criminal offenders in particular. They review the literature and, although studies in different countries provide differing results, Williams et al. conclude that roughly

---

[3] Readers interested in a more detailed review should see Campbell and Marshall (2007) or Derevensky and Gupta (2004).

one-third of criminal offenders are problem or pathological gamblers (p. 679). They note, "This is the highest rate found in any population studied," comparable only to substance abusers being comorbid for problem gambling. One might expect offenders to have a higher than average likelihood of being problem gamblers, since clinicians have found that a significant number of problem gamblers commit crimes to support their gambling (p. 680).

In perhaps the largest study to date on gambling in the United States, the National Gambling Impact Study Commission (NGISC 1999) reported significantly higher arrest rates for problem and pathological gamblers than for non-gamblers. While non-gamblers reported a 4 % lifetime arrest rate, the reported lifetime arrest rates for gamblers were at least twice as high: low-risk gamblers, 10 %; at-risk gamblers, 21.1 %; problem gamblers, 36.3 %; and pathological gamblers, 32.3 %. Overall, the literature is consistent with the findings of the NGISC: there is a strong correlation between problem gambling and criminal behavior. Of course, factors other than gambling may explain this too; as much as 75 % of problem gamblers have other behavioral disorders (Petry, Stinson, and Grant 2005; Westphal and Johnson 2007). Several other studies address the gambling–crime relationship using surveys of problem gamblers (e.g., Blaszczynski and McConaghy 1994).

A number of "macro" studies—studies that examine aggregate rather than individual-level data—have questioned whether increases in casino gambling activity in the United States are associated with increases in crime rates. Of course, any relationship between pathological gambling and crime may not necessarily be due solely to casino gambling. Nevertheless, it is useful to briefly discuss these studies. The paper by Campbell and Marshall (2007) gives a detailed description of the types of crimes that are sometimes associated with gambling. However, they do not provide an empirical analysis. Several empirical studies have found that the spread of casino gambling has led to increases in crime rates (Giacopassi and Stitt 1993; Grinols and Mustard 2006; Stitt, Nichols, and Giacopassi 2003). However, such findings usually hold only when the crime rate measure is based on the casino jurisdiction's home population, i.e., when the population measure omits the tourists from the population measure. Critics have argued that this measure necessarily overstates the crime effect attributable to casinos (Albanese 1985; Curran and Scarpitti 1991; Walker 2008c). Empirical studies that adjust the population for tourism generally find a weak or no relationship between casinos and crime (e.g., Reece 2010). This issue is examined at length in Chap. 17.

It is obvious from the literature—both in psychology "micro" and economics "macro" studies—that the relationship between gambling and crime is an important one. Indeed, this is perhaps one of the most important issues raised in debates over the further expansion of legal gambling. Yet, the issue is not resolved empirically. There does seem to be a general consensus that problem gamblers may have higher propensities to commit crimes, but what about the majority of people who do not have a gambling problem? The best evidence on these individuals may be from the economic studies on casino gambling and crime, since the focus of those studies is on overall crime rates associated with the spread of casinos, not just on problem gamblers, which are so often the focus of studies in the gambling literature.

10.3 Background on Gambling, Drinking, Drug Use, and Risky Sex

Evidence on problem gambling risk factors and comorbid behaviors in the literature is based on a variety of sources, including studies of members from the general public, individuals who have been diagnosed as problem gamblers with one of various screening instruments, clinical studies of individuals in treatment, and Gamblers Anonymous members. Many studies rely on small sample sizes or limited empirical rigor, as noted above. Yet, the link between problem gambling and other problematic behaviors is well established.

Research further confirms that problem gamblers often have comorbid behaviors, such as alcohol use disorders, drug abuse, compulsive shopping, etc. The comorbidity issue has been a very important one, as numerous articles have been published on the topic. For example, an entire issue of *Journal of Gambling Studies* was dedicated to comorbidity in 2003 (vol. 19, no. 3, 257–337). Another issue of the *Journal* examined only gambling and alcohol use (vol. 21, no. 3, 223–361). Several recent studies illustrate just how widespread comorbid behaviors are among problem gamblers. Petry, Stinson, and Grant (2005) estimate that 73 % of pathological gamblers have other behavior problems. Westphal and Johnson (2007) estimate a similar comorbidity prevalence rate of 77 %. There have been many studies on the comorbidity issue, and researchers' understanding of it continues to develop.

The different risk factors for problem gambling have received significant attention in the literature. Johansson et al. (2009) summarize the research in this area. Among the risk factors that they classify as well established are alcohol and drug use, two issues which we examine in this chapter. The study by Ladouceur et al. (1999) confirms the association between problem gambling and drug and alcohol use, and shows that poor grades and delinquency may also be associated with problem gambling. The relationship between problem gambling and alcohol use disorders is examined by Grant, Kushner, and Kim (2002), Stewart and Kushner (2005), and many others. Welte et al. (2004) provide further evidence of a relationship between alcohol and drug use, and other risk factors for problem gambling, using a large sample in the United States. Vitaro et al. (2001) take a more general look at the risk factors of problem gambling, delinquency, and drug use among adolescents. Huang et al. (2007) focus on problem gambling and related disorders among the US college student-athletes. Other papers in the literature look at gambling behavior and mood/anxiety disorders (e.g., el-Guebaly et al. 2006). Still others look at the relationship between gambling and other problems, such as binge eating (Fischer and Smith 2008) and impulsivity (Nower, Derevensky, and Gupta 2004).

The relationship between sexual behavior and gambling has not been addressed to the extent of many other behaviors typically associated with problem gambling, such as drinking and drug use (Petry 2000, 1090). However, the evidence that does exist suggests that problem gamblers are more likely to engage in risky sexual behaviors (Huang et al. 2007; Petry 2000). Grant and Steinberg (2005) examine the incidence of compulsive sexual behavior among problem gamblers, and find a strong link.

As mentioned above, many studies focus on samples of known problem gamblers or individuals in treatment for problem gambling or other problem behaviors. For example, Feigelman et al. (1995) study problem gambling among methadone patients. Other studies focus on how different comorbid behaviors affect the treatment of problem gambling. Stinchfield, Kushner, and Winters (2005), for example, find that alcohol and substance abuse are associated with more serious gambling problems, but they do not affect the effectiveness of problem gambling treatment. Rush, Veldhuizen, and Adlaf (2007) focus on proximity to gambling venues and access to treatment as factors affecting problem gambling prevalence.

As is clear from even this overview of the literature, gambling researchers have undertaken study of many facets of problem gambling behavior. Recently published work varies by sample source (general public, diagnosed problem gamblers, and those in treatment; children, adolescents, and adults), sample size (under 50 to several thousand subjects), comorbid disorders and other behavioral issues examined (alcohol, drugs, binge eating, impulsivity, delinquency/criminal behavior, risky or compulsive sexual behavior, etc.), and, of course, empirical and survey methodologies. Research in this area continues to expand in numerous directions.

10.4 Data and Models

In this analysis we use a large nationally representative sample of young adults to analyze gambling behavior and its relationship to criminal behavior, binge drinking, drug use, and hiring prostitutes. The study represents an important contribution to the literature because our data and empirical analysis enable us to control for many factors that may affect the behaviors of interest, but that have not been considered in other published studies. In addition, since we have data on different types of gambling behavior, our empirical model allows us to evaluate how different types of gambling contribute to the propensity to commit crimes and engage in the other "vices" we are studying. To our knowledge, our data source has never been used to study these behaviors commonly associated with problem gambling behavior. The findings from our study complement previous research in this area. We utilize a large number of control variables and a large sample size, relative to many other studies, and we believe our results provide an interesting contribution to the literature.

The National Longitudinal Study of Adolescent Health (Add Health)[4] is a survey of a US nationally representative sample of adolescent students in grades seven

---

[4]This research uses data from Add Health, a program project designed by J. Richard Udry, Peter S. Bearman, and Kathleen Mullan Harris, and funded by a grant P01-HD31921 from the National Institute of Child Health and Human Development, with cooperative funding from 17 other agencies. Special acknowledgment is due Ronald R. Rindfuss and Barbara Entwisle for assistance in the original design. Persons interested in obtaining data files from Add Health should contact Add Health, Carolina Population Center, 123 W. Franklin Street, Chapel Hill, NC 27516–2524 (addhealth@unc.edu). Many of the studies that have used Add Health data are posted at http://www.cpc.unc.edu/projects/addhealth/publications. See Harris et al. (2003) for a detailed description of the Add Health design.

through twelve, from 134 schools. It includes a follow-up survey conducted when the individuals were between 18 and 27 years old. Our study relies mostly on the data from this last wave of the study, when the average age of respondents was 22.

The Add Health contains an initial in-school survey administered to 90,118 students for the 1994–1995 school year. Subsequently, there were three waves of in-home surveys administered to many of the same students in 1994–1995, 1996, and 2001–2002, as well as two school administrator questionnaires, and a parents' survey. The wave 1 in-home survey includes responses from 20,745 students and approximately 18,000 parents. The wave 2 in-home survey contains information on 14,738 adolescents. The wave 3 in-home survey contains information on 15,197 individuals. The in-school and wave 1 and 2 in-home surveys cover health-related behavior and life experiences, while the wave 3 in-home survey is targeted at evaluating academic, career, and personal outcomes for these individuals. Individuals who participated in the in-home surveys were surveyed twice during the ages of 12 through 19 (waves 1 and 2), and again when most of the respondents were 18–27 years old (wave 3). In order to ensure a complete data set, we eliminated any individuals from the wave 3 survey who were missing any survey data. This adjustment reduces our sample for the crime, drug use, and binge drinking analyses to 6,145 individuals—all of whom complete all three waves of the Add Health. For the prostitution analysis, an additional nine individuals were dropped, as they failed to answer that specific question, leaving us with a sample of 6,136. Means and standard deviations for other variables in the model do not vary across the two samples.

The Add Health survey is one of the most comprehensive sources of information on the US young adults available, and has been widely used in research. The study includes self-reported data on a number of variables, including academic performance, weight, relationships with parents, previous criminal behavior, sexual activity, drinking and drug use, and relationships with peers. Generally, interviewees answered questions asked by the interviewer who then recorded the answer on a laptop computer. For sensitive questions interviewees entered answers directly into the laptop. The primary benefits of using Add Health data for examining the relationship between gambling and crime, drug use, binge drinking, and hiring prostitutes are that the sample is very large, it examines young adult gambling behavior and other relevant risky behaviors, the survey does not focus only on problem or pathological gamblers, and it includes many questions other than gambling behavior that may help explain criminal activity, drug use, binge drinking, and hiring prostitutes.

10.4.1 Data

Among a variety of other questions in the Add Health, respondents to the third wave of the survey were asked about their gambling behavior, criminal behavior, any drug or alcohol use, as well as sexual behavior. The survey questions dealing with gambling are reproduced in Table 10.1. Also included in the table are similar questions

Table 10.1 Selected gambling-related questions from the Add Health, DSM-IV, and SOGS (similar questions are shown across rows)

Question ID (Used in Table 10.2)	Add Health	DSM-IV	SOGS
Lotto played	Have you ever bought lottery tickets, such as daily, scratch-offs, or lotto?		1. Please indicate which of the following types of gambling you have done in your lifetime. For each type, mark one answer: "Not at all," "less than once a week," or "once a week or more." Options include the following: played cards for money; bet on horses, dogs, or other animals; bet on sports; played dice games; went to casino; played the numbers or bet on lotteries; played bingo; played the stock and/or commodities market; played slot machines, or other gambling machines; bowled, shot pool, etc. for money
Casino games played	Have you ever played casino tables or video games for money—such games as craps, blackjack, roulette, slot machines, or video poker?		
Other games played	Have you ever played any other games, such as cards or bingo, for money, bet on horse races or sporting events, or taken part in any other kinds of gambling for money?		
Largest amount behind	In all the time since you first started any type of gambling, what would you say was the largest amount of money that you have ever been behind across an entire year of gambling? Options include the following: none/never gamble; loss<$100; $100–500; $501–1,000; $1,001–5,000; $5,001–10,000; loss>$10,000		2. What is the largest amount of money you have ever gambled with on any one day? Options include the following: never have gambled; $1 or less; up to $10; up to $100; up to $1,000; up to $10,000; more than $10,000

10.4 Data and Models

Thinking about gambling	Have there ever been periods lasting 2 weeks or longer when you spent a lot of time thinking about your gambling experiences or planning out future gambling ventures or bets?	1. Is preoccupied with gambling (e.g., preoccupied with reliving past gambling experiences, handicapping or planning the next venture, or thinking of ways to get money with which to gamble)	
Gamble to relieve feelings	Have you ever gambled to relieve uncomfortable feelings such as guilt, anxiety, helplessness, or depression?	5. Gambles as a way of escaping from problems or of relieving a dysphoric mood (e.g., feelings of helplessness, guilt, anxiety, depression)	
Gamble to get even	Has there ever been a period when, if you lost money gambling one day, you would return another day to get even?	6. After losing money gambling, often returns another day to get even ("chasing" one's losses)	4. When you gamble, how often do you go back another day to win back money you lost?
Relationship problems	Has your gambling ever caused serious or repeated problems in your relationships with any of your family members or friends?	9. Has jeopardized or lost a significant relationship, job, or educational or career opportunity because of gambling	12. Have you ever argued with people you live with over how you handle money?

Source: Clark and Walker (2009). Used with permission from Taylor & Francis

from two well-known diagnostic instruments, the DSM-IV (American Psychiatric Association 2000) and the South Oaks Gambling Screen (SOGS; Lesieur and Blume 1987).[5] Although the Add Health questions are not identically worded to the DSM and SOGS questions, there are interesting parallels among questions.

Below we explain how the different questions from the Add Health, DSM-IV, and SOGS were incorporated into our empirical model to help explain criminal behavior, drug use, drinking, and hiring prostitutes by young adult gamblers.

One important issue to keep in mind is that the DSM-IV-TR and SOGS, among the other more recently developed diagnostic instruments, are often administered to individuals presumed to or suspected of having a gambling problem. The Add Health survey, on the other hand, was administered to a nationally representative sample, and was not aimed at individuals who were suspected of having a gambling problem. The Problem Gambling Severity Index (PGSI), for example, is designed for use with the general public. However, its questions are formatted as "how much" rather than "yes/no." For this reason we do not compare Add Health questions to the PGSI criteria.

For this study we are using data primarily from the third wave of the Add Health survey, with some demographic variables pulled from the earlier waves. There are thousands of questions asked to participants in the Add Health survey. We have collected response data on those questions which we believe most closely relate to problem gambling behavior and our dependent variables, *Serious crime*, *Binge drinking*, *Hard drug use*, and *Pay for sex*, which are defined in Table 10.2. The explanatory variables used in our study, along with their descriptions and summary statistics, are also presented in Table 10.2. The table also indicates the Add Health wave from which the survey questions were taken. For the sake of brevity, Table 10.2 excludes a series of state- and county-level variables that are included in the regressions.

Although the table describes each of the variables, several are worth highlighting. First, note that roughly 15 % (927 of 6,145 individuals) of the sample admits to having committed a crime over the past year (*Serious crime*, one of our dependent variables). In addition, 7 % of the sample (430 individuals) admits to having used cocaine, crystal meth, or another illegal drug over the past 30 days (*Hard drug use*). Roughly a third of the sample (35 % or 2,151 individuals) reports binge drinking more than twice in the last year. This number is perhaps not as large as it might seem, as the threshold for *Binge drinking* is rather low—drinking five or more drinks in a row more than twice in the past year. Only 2.4 % of the individuals in the sample (147) report having paid someone to have sex with them in the last 12 months.

A large proportion of the survey respondents has gambled at some point in their lifetime: 63 % (3,865 individuals) have played the lotto, about 50 % (3,048 individuals) have played casino games, and 43 % (2,612 individuals) have gambled in some other form. When asked how much is the largest amount of money they have been down from gambling over the course of a year, the average response was "less than $100."

---

[5] Other instruments are available, such as the DSM-IV-J and SOGS-RA, designed for juveniles and adolescents. However, none of these instruments more closely parallels the Add Health questions than the DSM-IV or the SOGS.

10.4 Data and Models

Table 10.2 Variable definitions and summary statistics ($n=6{,}145$)

Variable	Definition	Wave	Mean	(SD)
Dependent variables				
Serious crime	=1 if steal, break and enter, assault, sell drugs, or fight, during past year; =0 otherwise	Third	0.151	(0.358)
Binge drinking	During the past 12 months, on how many days did you drink five or more drinks in a row?	Third	0.347	(0.476)
	=1 if the individual reported binge drinking more than twice; =0 otherwise			
Pay for sex	During the past 12 months, how many times have you paid for sex?	Third	0.024	(0.154)
(Sample size=6,136)	=1 if individual reports paying for sex in the last 12 months; =0 otherwise			
Hard drug use	=1 if cocaine=1, crystal=1, or other drugs=1 (see below); =0 otherwise	Third	0.069	(0.253)
Cocaine	During the past 30 days, how many times have you used any kind of cocaine?	Third	0.031	(0.174)
	=1 if individual reports using cocaine at all over the last 30 days; =0 otherwise			
Crystal meth	During the past 30 days, how many times have you used crystal meth?	Third	0.015	(0.121)
	=1 if individual reports using crystal meth at all over the last 30 days; =0 otherwise			
Other drugs	During the past 30 days, how many times have you used any of these types of illegal drugs (LSD, PCP, ecstasy, mushrooms, inhalants, ice, heroin, or prescription medicines not prescribed for you)?	Third	0.048	(0.213)
	=1 if individual reports using any of these illegal drugs at all over the last 30 days; =0 otherwise			
Add health gambling questions				
DSM	=1 if yes to at least one of the four: Thinking about gambling, Gamble to relieve feelings, Gamble to get even, Relationship problems; =0 otherwise	n/a	0.022	(0.148)
SOGS	=1 if yes to "Down over $500", or if "yes" to more than four of the following: Lotto played, Casino games played, Other games played, Thinking about gambling, Gamble to relieve feelings, Gamble to get even, Relationship problems; =0 otherwise	n/a	0.021	(0.142)

(continued)

Table 10.2 (continued)

Variable	Definition	Wave	Mean	(SD)
Down $501–1,000	=1 if down $501–1,000 across 1 year of gambling; =0 otherwise	Third	0.020	(0.139)
Down $1,001–5,000	=1 if down $1,001–5,000 across 1 year of gambling; =0 otherwise	Third	0.014	(0.117)
Down $5,001–10,000	=1 if down $5,001–10,000 across 1 year of gambling; =0 otherwise	Third	0.002	(0.040)
Down $10,001 or more	=1 if down $10,001 or more across 1 year of gambling; =0 otherwise	Third	0.001	(0.029)
Lotto played	=1 if yes; =0 if no (see Table 10.1 for definition)	Third	0.629	(0.483)
Casino games played	=1 if yes; =0 if no (see Table 10.1 for definition)	Third	0.496	(0.500)
Other games played	=1 if yes; =0 if no (see Table 10.1 for definition)	Third	0.425	(0.494)
Largest amount behind	=0 if none/never gamble; =1 if down<$100; =2 if $100–500; =3 if $501–1,000; =4 if $1,001–5,000; =5 if $5,001–10,000; =6 if>$10,000 (see Table 10.1 for definition)	n/a	0.758	(0.850)
Thinking about gambling	=1 if yes; =0 if no (see Table 10.1 for definition)	Third	0.013	(0.114)
Gamble to relieve feelings	=1 if yes; =0 if no (see Table 10.1 for definition)	Third	0.005	(0.069)
Gamble to get even	=1 if yes; =0 if no (see Table 10.1 for definition)	Third	0.020	(0.138)
Relationship problems	=1 if yes; =0 if no (see Table 10.1 for definition)	Third	0.004	(0.066)
Demographic				
Male	=1 if the individual is male; =0 otherwise	n/a	0.483	(0.500)
White	=1 if the individual reports being Caucasian and reports that he/she is not Hispanic; =0 otherwise	n/a	0.613	(0.487)
GPA	Math and English GPA	First	2.697	(0.942)
Vocab	Add Health Picture—Vocabulary Test Score	First	102.89	(14.03)
South	=1 if individual lives in southern region of the United States; =0 otherwise	Third	0.259	(0.438)
West	=1 if individual lives in western region of the United States; =0 otherwise	Third	0.274	(0.446)
Midwest	=1 if individual lives in midwestern region of the United States; =0 otherwise	Third	0.313	(0.464)
Age	Individual's current age	Third	21.770	(1.665)
Education	Individual's current education level (years of school)	Third	13.415	(1.949)
Work	Individual's current work status, =1 if working; =0 otherwise	Third	0.720	(0.449)

(continued)

10.4 Data and Models

Table 10.2 (continued)

Variable	Definition	Wave	Mean	(SD)
Welfare	=1 if the individual currently received welfare; =0 otherwise	Third	0.036	(0.187)
Income	Individual's current annual income (in US dollars)	Third	13833.55	(16460.13)
Married	=1 if the individual is currently married; =0 otherwise	Third	0.147	(0.354)
Expelled	=1 if the individual has ever been expelled from school; =0 otherwise	Third	0.062	(0.240)
Parents and family				
Children 0–6	Number of children in the household under the age of 6	Third	0.306	(0.652)
Children 6–12	Number of children in the household aged between 6 and 12	Third	0.114	(0.412)
Disapprove college	=1 if strong parental disapproval if adolescent does not attend college; =0 otherwise	First	0.458	(0.498)
Neighborhood	=1 if parent moved to neighborhood because of school system; =0 otherwise	First	0.494	(0.500)
Brilliant	=1 if parent believes adolescent being brilliant is top priority; =0 otherwise	First	0.626	(0.484)
Project help	=1 if parent recently aided adolescent with school project; =0 otherwise	First	0.204	(0.403)
Grade talk	=1 if parent recently spoke with adolescent about grades; =0 otherwise	First	0.469	(0.499)
Single parent	=1 if single-parent household; =0 otherwise	First	0.267	(0.442)
Parent graduate	=1 if parent graduated from college; =0 otherwise	First	0.263	(0.440)
Parent works	=1 if parent is employed outside the home; =0 otherwise	First	0.764	(0.425)
Curfew	=1 if parent has strict weekend curfew for adolescent; =0 otherwise	First	0.665	(0.472)
Weekly dinners	Number of days per week adolescent has dinner with family	First	4.666	(2.451)
Religion	Measure of family attendance at religious services (0=no attendance, 1=weekly, 2=monthly, 3=yearly)	First	2.289	(1.202)
No monitor	=1 if parent does not monitor friends of adolescent; =0 otherwise	First	0.053	(0.224)
Older sibling	=1 if older sibling in household; =0 otherwise	First	0.383	(0.486)
Household income	Household income (in thousands of US dollars)	First	49.579	(54.219)

Source: Clark and Walker (2009). Used with permission from Taylor & Francis

Relatively few respondents gave a positive answer to any of the other gambling questions listed in Table 10.1: *Thinking about gambling* (1.3 % or 80 individuals), *Gambling to relieve feelings* (0.5 % or 31 individuals), *Gamble to get even* (2 % or 123 individuals), and *Relationship problems* (0.4 % or 25 individuals).

We created a series of dichotomous variables to partition the *Largest amount behind* variable from the Add Health. These resulting new variables provide more detailed information on the extent to which the Add Health respondents have lost money gambling. As noted above, relatively few respondents reported being down a significant amount of money. Approximately 3.7 % of survey respondents (227 individuals) indicated being down at least $501 during a particular year. About 1.4 % (86 individuals) indicated that they have been down a maximum of between $1,001 and $5,000 during a particular year. Only 0.1 % (six individuals) indicated being down more than $10,000 during a particular year.

Finally, we created variables to account for a positive response to the Add Health questions that were closely related to the DSM-IV and SOGS criteria listed in Table 10.1. The variable DSM is scored with a 1 if a respondent gives an affirmative response to at least one of the four Add Health questions of *Thinking about gambling, Gamble to relieve feelings, Gamble to get even*, and *Relationship problems*. If the respondent does not give a positive response to any of the four criteria, the DSM variable is scored with a 0 for that respondent. As shown in Table 10.2, 2.2 % (or 135) of the respondents gave an affirmative response to at least one of the four questions considered in DSM. The SOGS variable is recorded as a 1 if the Add Health respondent had a *Largest amount behind* response of 3, 4, 5, or 6 (that is, being behind by at least $501), or if he/she gave an affirmative response to more than four of these variables: *Lotto played, Casino games played, Other games played, Thinking about gambling, Gamble to relieve feelings, Gamble to get even*, and *Relationship problems*. Otherwise, the respondent gets a 0 for the SOGS variable. Approximately 2.1 % of Add Health respondents (129 people) received an affirmative score on the SOGS variable.

The DSM and SOGS variables are included in order to allow us to determine how Add Health respondents may compare to individuals if they were evaluated under the DSM-IV and SOGS instruments. Importantly, we are not claiming that the DSM and SOGS variables we created replicate the actual instruments. First, the Add Health items are not worded the same as items in the DSM or the SOGS. Second, the Add Health contains only four items similar to those in the DSM, and only four items similar to those in SOGS. Clearly, we are not suggesting that the Add Health is a substitute for either diagnostic tool. Rather, we are simply suggesting that there are some potentially interesting parallels with some of the survey items, and that a person who affirms our DSM or SOGS criteria may be more likely to be diagnosed as a problem gambler.

The other variables in the model, as shown in Table 10.2, are related to the individual's demographic information which may be expected to have an impact on the propensity to commit crimes, use drugs, binge drink, and, perhaps, to pay for sex. These include income, education, school performance, employment, and marital status. Additional variables accounting for aspects of the survey respondent's parental and family situation are also included in the model. For the sake of brevity I do not discuss the parental and familial variables here.

10.4.2 Models

In order to test whether gambling has a significant impact on criminal acts, drug use, binge drinking, or hiring prostitutes, we posit a series of linear probability models to explain these behaviors, measured as *Serious crime*, *Hard drug use*, *Binge drinking*, and *Pay for sex*:

$$\Pr(\text{Serious crime}_i = 1) = \beta_0 + \beta_1 \text{ Gambling}_i + \beta_2 X_i \\ + \beta_3 \text{ State / county controls} + \beta_i \quad (10.1)$$

$$\Pr(\text{Hard drug use}_i = 1) = \beta_0 + \beta_1 \text{ Gambling}_i + \beta_2 X_i \\ + \beta_3 \text{ State / county controls} + \beta_i \quad (10.2)$$

$$\Pr(\text{Binge drinking}_i = 1) = \beta_0 + \beta_1 \text{ Gambling}_i + \beta_2 X_i \\ + \beta_3 \text{ State / county controls} + \beta_i \quad (10.3)$$

$$\Pr(\text{Pay for sex}_i = 1) = \beta_0 + \beta_1 \text{ Gambling}_i + \beta_2 X_i \\ + \beta_3 \text{ State / county controls} + \beta_i \quad (10.4)$$

As listed in Table 10.2, *Serious crime* equals 1 if, during the year prior to taking the wave 3 survey, the individual says he/she committed any of these crimes: stealing, breaking and entering, assault, selling drugs, or fighting. *Hard drug use* equals 1 if, within the year prior to taking the survey, the individual used any of the following drugs: cocaine, crystal meth, LSD, PCP, ecstasy, mushrooms, inhalants, ice, heroin, or prescription medicines not prescribed for them. *Binge drinking* equals 1 if the individual reported binge drinking (drinking five or more drinks in a row) more than twice in the last 12 months. Finally, *Pay for sex* equals 1 if the individual reported paying for sex in the last 12 months.

A linear probability model is designed to explain and predict the likelihood that the event measured in the dependent variable will occur. In this case, we use the variety of right-side variables to explain and predict the likelihood than an individual will have committed a crime, used drugs, binge drank, or paid for sex, in the time period leading up to their wave 3 survey. We are particularly interested in the role that gambling behavior may have on the dependent variables. The linear probability model provides more reliable results than simple correlations, for example, as it attempts to control for many other factors that might explain the propensity to engage in the activities we test. Therefore, the specific effect of gambling on these behaviors is isolated in this type of model.

The explanatory variables in (10.1–10.4) are described in turn. The variables contained in X_i are listed in Table 10.2 under "Demographic" and "Parents and Family" headings. Some of these variables are "current," from wave 3 of the Add Health, while others are from the respondents' adolescence (wave 1). The X_i variables are intended to control for many factors or effects that may contribute to or reduce the likelihood of engaging in crime, drug use, binge drinking, and hiring prostitutes.[6]

The *State/County controls* variables include a variety of state- and county-level data on population demographics (e.g., income, unemployment, poverty rate), designed to control for state- and county-specific population characteristics. For the sake of brevity, I do not list these variables or their results. Of particular interest in our study, the *Gambling$_i$* variables are intended to measure the individuals' current gambling practices.

10.5 Results

The results are divided into two subsections. I first present the crime results, and then the results on drug use, binge drinking, and hiring prostitutes.

10.5.1 Results for Gambling and Crime

Our models highlight the extent to which Add Health survey respondents' gambling activities can explain their propensity to commit serious crimes as young adults. The results from the four different versions of (10.1) are presented in Table 10.3. I discuss each model in turn.

The first model includes all of the gambling-related questions from the Add Health survey in a linear probability model to explain criminal activity within the year prior to the wave 3 Add Health survey being administered. The results of model 1 indicate that when respondents report having lost larger amounts of money there is a significant positive impact on the propensity to commit serious crimes. In particular, moving up by one category in the *Largest amount behind* variable increases the probability a person will commit a crime by about 4.7 %. This result is strongly significant (1 % level). This finding is certainly consistent with previous studies, which report that problem gamblers who lose large amounts of money often turn to criminal behavior to support their gambling.

The other statistically significant variable in model 1 is *Other games played*, which includes all forms of gambling other than lottery and casino games. This result was positive at the 1 % level, indicating that individuals who have played other than lotto or casino games were almost 6.3 % more likely to commit crimes later in life. Taken together with the lack of significance of the *Lotto played* and

---

[6]The dependent variable *Serious crime* is included in X_i for (10.2–10.4). Similarly, drug use variables are included in X_i for (10.1).

10.5 Results

Table 10.3 The effects of gambling on crime (dependent variable is *Serious crime*)

Variable	Model 1	Model 2	Model 3	Model 4
Lotto played	−0.0101			
	(0.0115)			
Casino games played	−0.0043			
	(0.0123)			
Other games played	0.0632*			
	(0.0115)			
Largest amount behind	0.0474*			
	(0.0095)			
Thinking about gambling	−0.0851			
	(0.0752)			
Gamble to relieve feelings	0.0909			
	(0.1122)			
Gamble to get even	0.0535			
	(0.0607)			
Relationship problems	−0.0631			
	(0.1120)			
Down $501–1,000		0.1546*		
		(0.0441)		
Down $1,001–5,000		0.2753*		
		(0.0534)		
Down $5,001–10,000		0.2401		
		(0.1597)		
Down $10,001 or more		0.2573		
		(0.2043)		
DSM			0.1694*	
			(0.0419)	
SOGS				0.2167*
				(0.0438)
Sample size	6,145	6,145	6,145	6,145

Notes: Coefficients are listed with standard errors below in parentheses. All variables included in X_i and *State controls* are included in each model, but their results are omitted for brevity
Source: Clark and Walker (2009). Used with permission from Taylor & Francis
*Indicates statistically significant at the 1 % level

Casino games played variables, this result is interesting. Contrary to what is commonly believed, the Add Health survey data suggests that gamblers other than casino and lotto gamblers are more likely to commit crimes. Of course, these results are based on the general public and not on a sample limited to problem gamblers.

The other gambling variables in model 1 were statistically insignificant. Respondents who reported being preoccupied with gambling, who gambled to relieve "uncomfortable" feelings, who returned another day to get even, or whose gambling created problems with family members were *not* found to be more likely to commit crimes than individuals who did not report such gambling-related characteristics.

Model 2 includes dummy variables for the different ranges of money lost gambling, which were part of the *Largest amount behind* question from model 1.

These variables replace the Add Health gambling questions from the first model. Survey respondents who reported being down between $501 and $5,000 have a statistically significant higher propensity to commit crimes. Individuals indicating gambling losses of between $501 and $1,000 were about 15 % more likely than the average respondent to commit a serious crime. The effect is even larger for individuals who admitted being behind between $1,001 and $5,000 during a particular year. These people were 27.5 % more likely than the average respondent to commit a serious crime. Both results are statistically significant at the 1 % level. These results are interesting, and they make intuitive sense. Individuals who have lost more money are more likely to need to find an alternative source of funding, *ceteris paribus*. The magnitude of this effect remains high for losses above $5,000, but the coefficients are not statistically significant. This lack of significance is likely due to the fact that only 0.3 % of the sample (or 18 of 6,145 individuals) had losses that large.

In models 3 and 4 we are examining individuals who gave positive responses to Add Health questions that were similar to some of the criteria from the DSM-IV or the SOGS. That is, in these models, the explanatory gambling variables include a bundle of conditions. The DSM variable in model 3 counts individuals who affirm at least one of the last four conditions discussed for model 1 (*Thinking about gambling*, *Gamble to relieve feelings*, *Gamble to get even*, or *Relationship problems*). These people are about 17 % more likely than the average respondent to commit a serious crime. This result confirms that individuals who have at least one of these four of the DSM criteria—individuals who are perhaps more likely to be diagnosed as problem gamblers—are more likely to commit crimes.

Finally, the results of model 4 support the above results. Like the DSM variable, the SOGS variable in model 4 tests a combination of Add Health questions. These questions are similar to some of the questions found in the SOGS instrument. As shown in Table 10.2, the SOGS variable tracks individuals who were down at least $501, or if they gave affirmative responses to at least four of the remaining criteria (aside from *Largest amount behind*) from model 1. The result of model 4 indicates that these individuals are over 21 % more likely than the average survey respondent to engage in criminal activity. Considering all four models, our results strongly suggest that higher gambling losses increase the probability that an individual will commit a crime. Individuals who give affirmative responses to multiple questions similar to some of those found on the DSM-IV and SOGS diagnostic instruments are also statistically more likely to engage in crime than the average Add Health wave 3 survey respondent.

Next we ran each model separately for females and males in the sample to determine whether there were notable differences between them. These results are shown in Table 10.4.

There are several interesting differences between the sexes. In particular, model 1 for the females in the sample indicates a negative and significant impact of "thinking about gambling" and "relationship problems" on crime, as well as a significantly positive effect of "gambling to relieve feelings." None of these variables was significant in model 1 for males or in the full sample. In model 2, we also find some significant differences in the gambling loss variables, with females actually having negative signs on two of the categories (*Down $1,001–5,000* and *Down $10,001 or more*).

10.5 Results

Table 10.4 The effects of gambling on crime, female and male respondents (dependent variable is *Serious crime*)

Variable	Model 1 Female	Model 1 Male	Model 2 Female	Model 2 Male	Model 3 Female	Model 3 Male	Model 4 Female	Model 4 Male
Lotto played	−0.0016 (0.0116)	−0.0219 (0.0184)						
Casino games played	−0.0075 (0.0123)	−0.0051 (0.0194)						
Other games played	0.0262** (0.0121)	0.0817*** (0.0179)						
Largest amount behind	0.0154 (0.0106)	0.0538*** (0.0127)						
Thinking about gambling	−0.3418** (0.1358)	−0.0511 (0.0745)						
Gamble to relieve feelings	0.6303*** (0.1900)	0.0333 (0.1135)						
Gamble to get even	0.0499 (0.1321)	0.0106 (0.0668)						
Relationship problems	−0.4786* (0.2477)	−0.1121 (0.1025)						
Down $501–1,000			0.1722* (0.0938)	0.1560*** (0.0478)				
Down $1,001–5,000			−0.1222** (0.0486)	0.1838*** (0.0545)				
Down $5,001–10,000			0.3885 (0.3650)	0.1998 (0.1606)				

(continued)

Table 10.4 (continued)

Variable	Model 1 Female	Model 1 Male	Model 2 Female	Model 2 Male	Model 3 Female	Model 3 Male	Model 4 Female	Model 4 Male
Down $10,001 or more			−0.0664* (0.0357)	0.5064*** (0.1921)				
DSM					0.1533 (0.1130)	0.1403*** (0.0430)		
SOGS							0.0657 (0.1141)	0.1710*** (0.0450)
Sample size	3,174	2,971	3,174	2,971	3,174	2,971	3,174	2,971

Note: Coefficients are listed with standard errors below in parentheses
All variables included in X_i and *State controls* are included in each model, but their results are omitted for brevity
Source: Clark and Walker (2009). Used with permission from Taylor & Francis
*Indicates statistically significant at the 10 % level, **at the 5 % level, and ***at the 1 % level

10.5 Results 131

Again here, however, the positive and significant results for males have offset the results for females, and the full model results are consistent with the males' results. Finally, in models 3 and 4, the results for males are significant, while for females the DSM and SOGS variables are not. Again here, the results in the full model (Table 10.3) are due to the males in the sample. These gender differences vis-à-vis the full results suggest that gambling affects males' propensity to commit crimes more than females'. Only 8 % of our sample of females (259 of 3,174) admitted to committing a serious crime, while 22.5 % of the males (669 out of 2,971) did. This is consistent with the fact that males commit more crimes than females, in general, but the Add Health data do not provide a basis on which to further analyze the gender differences.

10.5.2 Results for Gambling and Binge Drinking, Drug Use, and Hiring Prostitutes

We test three additional specifications based on variations of the $Gambling_i$ variables. In model 5, gambling is measured using the variables *Lotto played*, *Casino games played*, and *Other games played*, as defined in Table 10.1. These variables take a value of 1 if the respondent indicated having played the relevant game(s). In models 6 and 7, gambling is measured using the DSM and SOGS variables, respectively, as explained above and in Table 10.2. The models highlight the extent to which Add Health survey respondents' gambling activities can explain their propensities to use drugs, binge drink, or pay for sex as young adults. The results from the three variations on (10.2–10.4) are presented in Table 10.5. We discuss the models of each dependent variable in turn.

10.5.2.1 Hard Drug Use

The first model on drug use (model 5) includes the three types of gambling questions (*Lotto played*, *Casino games played*, and *Other games played*) from the Add Health survey in a linear probability model to explain drug use within the month prior to the wave 3 Add Health survey being administered. The results of model 5 indicate that when respondents report having gambled on "other games" (i.e., not lotto or casino games) they are more likely to have used drugs in the last 30 days. The coefficient on the variable *Other games played* is 0.02 and is statistically significant at the 1 % level, indicating that if the individual engaged in gambling outside a casino the probability that they use drugs increases by 2 percentage points. The mean value for drug use is 0.069, so a 2 percentage point increase translates to a 30 % increase in the probability that an individual will use drugs. The other gambling variables in model 5 were statistically insignificant.

In models 6 and 7 we are examining individuals who gave positive responses to Add Health questions that were similar to some of the criteria from the DSM-IV or the SOGS. That is, in these models, the explanatory gambling variables include a bundle of conditions. The DSM variable in model 6 counts individuals who affirm at least one

Table 10.5 Effects of gambling on hard drug use, binge drinking, and payment for sex

	Dependent variable = hard drug use			Dependent variable = binge drinking			Dependent variable = pay for sex		
	Model 5	Model 6	Model 7	Model 5	Model 6	Model 7	Model 5	Model 6	Model 7
Lotto played	0.0051 (0.0069)	–	–	0.0146 (0.0131)	–	–	−0.0007 (0.0027)	–	–
Casino games played	0.0090 (0.0075)	–	–	0.0731*** (0.0137)	–	–	0.0041* (0.0025)	–	–
Other games played	0.0208*** (0.0073)	–	–	0.0920*** (0.0133)	–	–	0.0017 (0.0027)	–	–
DSM	–	0.0577* (0.0299)	–	–	0.1094*** (0.0390)	–	–	0.0636** (0.0270)	–
SOGS	–	–	0.0508* (0.0313)	–	–	0.0928** (0.0413)	–	–	0.0628** (0.0281)
Sample size	6,145	6,145	6,145	6,145	6,145	6,145	6,136	6,136	6,136

Note: Coefficients are listed with standard errors in parentheses
All variables included in X_i and *State/county controls* are included in each model, but their results are omitted for brevity.
Source: Walker, Clark, and Folk (2010). Used with permission from Digital Scholarship@UNLV
*Indicates statistically significant at the 10 % level, **at the 5 % level, and ***at the 1 % level

of the four variables: *Thinking about gambling, Gamble to relieve feelings, Gamble to get even*, and *Relationship problems*. In model 6, the coefficient on DSM is 0.058. Given the mean for Hard drug use is 0.069, the DSM coefficient implies that individuals to which the DSM variable applies are almost 84 % more likely than the average Add Health respondent to have used hard drugs. This result confirms that individuals who endorse at least one of the four DSM criteria—individuals who are perhaps more likely to be diagnosed as problem gamblers—are much more likely to use hard drugs.

Finally, the results of model 7 support the above results. Like the DSM variable, the SOGS variable in model 7 tests a combination of Add Health questions. These questions are similar to some of the questions found in the SOGS instrument. As shown in Table 10.2, the SOGS variable tracks individuals who were down at least $501, or if they gave affirmative responses to at least four of the following criteria: *Lotto played, Casino games played, Other games played, Thinking about gambling, Gamble to relieve feelings, Gamble to get even*, and *Relationship problems*. The coefficient on *SOGS* is 0.051; relative to the mean of 0.069, this indicates that SOGS respondents are 73 % more likely than the average respondent to use hard drugs.

10.5.2.2 Binge Drinking

When using *Binge drinking* as the dependent variable, the results of model 5 indicate that when respondents report having gambled inside *or* outside of a casino they are more likely to have binge drunk more than twice in the last year. The coefficient on the variable *Casino games played* is 0.07 and is statistically significant at the 1 % level, indicating that if the individual engaged in casino gambling the probability that they binge drink increases by 7 percentage points. The mean value for binge drinking is 35 %, so a 7 percentage point increase translates to a 20 % increase in the probability that an individual will binge drink. The coefficient on the variable *Other games played* is 0.09 and is also statistically significant at the 1 % level. This coefficient translates to a 26 % increase in the probability that the individual will binge drink.

Model 6 uses the DSM variable, as described above, to explain binge drinking. The coefficient of 0.11 indicates that individuals for whom our DSM criterion applies are about 31 % more likely than the average respondent to binge drink (the mean value of *Binge drink* is 0.35). The results of model 7 support the DSM results from model 6. The coefficient on SOGS is 0.09, a statistically significant result at the 1 % level. Since the mean value of *Binge drink* is 0.35, this coefficient implies that individuals who affirm the SOGS criterion are over 26 % more likely than the average respondent to binge drink.

10.5.2.3 Hiring Prostitutes

The last three columns of Table 10.5 contain the results of estimating models 5 through 7 with *Pay for sex* as the dependent variable. The results for model 5 indicate that individuals who gamble in casinos are significantly more likely to have

Table 10.6 Gambling and hiring prostitutes: Males only

	Dependent variable = pay for sex		
	Model 5	Model 6	Model 7
Lotto played	−0.0003 (0.0059)	–	–
Casino games played	0.0085* (0.0053)	–	–
Other games played	−0.0003 (0.0053)	–	–
DSM	–	0.0677** (0.0303)	–
SOGS	–	–	0.0654** (0.0305)
Sample size (# of individuals)	2,965	2,965	2,965

Notes: Coefficients are listed with standard errors in parentheses. All variables included in X_i and *State/county controls* are included in each model, but their results are omitted for brevity
Source: Walker, Clark, and Folk (2010). Used with permission from Digital Scholarship@UNLV
*Indicates statistically significant at the 10 % level, and **at the 5 % level

paid for sex. The coefficient on *Casino games played* is 0.004, which is statistically significant at the 10 % level. Given about 2.4 % of the Add Health respondents acknowledged that they had paid for sex in the past year, the coefficient indicates that casino patrons are almost 17 % more likely than the average survey respondent to have paid for sex in the past year.

As with drug use and binge drinking, model 6 for *Pay for sex* focuses on the DSM variable. The coefficient on DSM is 0.06, indicating that if an individual affirms the DSM criterion the probability that he/she has paid for sex increases by 6 percentage points. This result is statistically significant at the 5 % level. Given the mean value of the *Pay for sex* variable, 0.024, this implies that the individual to whom the DSM variable applies is over 2.6 times (260 %) as likely as the average survey respondent to hire a prostitute. Model 7 for *Pay for sex*, shown in the rightmost column of Table 10.5, shows a similar result as in model 6. The coefficient on SOGS is also roughly 0.06. As in model 6, this coefficient indicates that the SOGS-affirmative respondents are more than 2.6 times as likely as the average respondent to have paid for sex.

Since men are perhaps more likely than women to hire prostitutes, we also run the *Pay for sex* models using only the male respondents from Add Health. The sample size is 2,965. The results of these models are presented in Table 10.6.

The results in the male-only model are consistent with those found in the full model (Table 10.5). The magnitudes and significance for the DSM and SOGS models are not different from the full model. However, the magnitude of the coefficient on *Casino games played* in the male-only sample doubles to 0.0085, which is also significant at the 10 % level. This result indicates that men who gamble in casinos are 17 % more likely to pay for sex than those respondents who do not gamble at casinos. (The mean value for *Pay for sex* is 0.05 for the males in the sample.) This particular result is no different than the result in the full model. These results suggest that, as expected, men are driving the results for the full sample.

10.6 Conclusion

We have tested the effects of gambling behavior and indicators of problem gambling on the likelihood that Add Health respondents engage in crime, use hard drugs, binge drink, or pay money for sex. Our results suggest that individuals who gamble, and more significantly, those who are more likely to be diagnosed with gambling problems, are more likely to also engage in these other behaviors. These results are consistent with other published research. This may not be surprising, however. Individuals who gamble enjoy taking risks. So it may be perfectly consistent that they would be more likely than the non-gambling public to engage in other forms of risky behaviors.

The crime results are particularly interesting, since one of the most serious concerns in jurisdictions with casinos or considering legalizing them is the impact of casinos on crime. Although the results indicate that survey respondents who are more involved with gambling are more likely to engage in criminal acts, interestingly, our significant results are found for non-lottery and non-casino gamblers.

Considering all three models on *Hard drug use* (10.2), our results strongly suggest that individuals who give affirmative responses to multiple questions similar to some of those found on the DSM-IV and SOGS diagnostic instruments are also statistically more likely to engage in drug use than the average Add Health wave 3 survey respondent. Interestingly, the results from model 1 on drug use apply only "Other games played," not to casino or lotto players. One possible explanation of this is that the average age of wave 3 respondents is around 22; about 75 % of the respondents were at least 21 years old. Fully one-quarter of the survey respondents were not of legal age to gamble in a casino at the time they completed wave 3 of the Add Health.

Our results on (10.3) for *Binge drinking* imply that individuals who give affirmative responses to multiple questions similar to some of those found on the DSM-IV and SOGS diagnostic instruments are also statistically more likely to engage in binge drinking than the average wave 3 survey respondent.

The results on *Pay for sex* are perhaps most interesting, as this issue has rarely been addressed in the gambling literature. Taken as a group, the models for (10.4) suggest that individuals who gamble at casinos, and who may be more at risk to be diagnosed as problem gamblers, are significantly more likely than the average Add Health respondent to pay for sex. Perhaps casinos create an atmosphere where risky behavior is acceptable: alcohol is often consumed and it is sometimes provided free to casino patrons. Prostitutes may be more likely to congregate at casinos since casino patrons may have large amounts of cash with them. When we isolate the sex models to males only, we find that the effect of potential problem gambling, as indicated by our DSM and SOGS variables, is much stronger—by a factor of 2.6. This result is consistent with the risk-taking behavior exhibited by gambling.

Our results confirm what more focused studies on problem gamblers have found: links between problem gambling, crime, drug use, and other risky behaviors. Our results are based on a relatively large and representative sample of young adults in the United States. Thus, our analysis complements the literature by showing that comorbid behaviors are not confined to individuals diagnosed with or in treatment for problem gambling. I believe ours to be one of the largest samples used in a study of this type. This is also one of few studies to examine a link between gambling and hiring prostitutes.

Although our models test the effect of gambling behavior on criminal behavior, hard drug use, binge drinking, and hiring prostitutes, it must be emphasized that our analysis does not allow us to rule out these relationships running in the opposite direction as well. Indeed, the direction of causation among coexisting disorders continues to be an important, unresolved issue in the literature, as indicated by Stewart and Kushner (2005), among others. Our analysis here does not address the issue of *why* these behaviors are linked, but it does provide evidence that gambling behavior among the US young adults is often associated with criminal activity, drug use, binge drinking, and hiring prostitutes. But individuals with "problem" levels of these coexisting behaviors represent a miniscule percentage of the population. Rather than further analyzing prevalence issues, future research in this area should attempt to answer the "why" question and what types of treatments and policies could help alleviate such problems.

Chapter 11
Gambling and Attention Deficit Hyperactivity Disorder

11.1 Introduction

We continue the analysis of the Add Health data used in Chap. 10 to examine the relationship between gambling behaviors and attention deficit hyperactivity disorder (ADHD). ADHD is a neurobehavioral condition, affecting 3–10 % of youth and persisting into adulthood in 30–50 % of cases (Richters et al. 1995; Smalley et al. 2003). ADHD accounts for a third to a half of all referrals to child mental health services and is characterized by developmentally inappropriate behaviors, low frustration tolerance, impulsivity, poor organization, distractibility, and a lack of concentration (Richters et al. 1995).

The DSM-IV (American Psychiatric Association 2000) posits three subtypes of ADHD: (a) Inattentive type, marked by disorganization, distractability, and inability to sustain attention over time; (b) Hyperactive–Impulsive type, marked by psychomotor agitation and an inability to restrain speech or behavior; and (c) Combined type, marked by characteristics of both groups.

Individuals with ADHD, particularly the Hyperactive–Impulsive subtype, typically disregard future consequences and prefer small, immediate rewards to larger, delayed rewards (Crone, Vendel, and vanderMolen 2003; Ernst et al. 2003; Luman et al. 2005). Similar findings have been reported in studies of problem gamblers (Dixon, Jacobs, and Sanders 2006; Goudriaan et al. 2004; Petry 2001, 2003), who demonstrate preferences for immediate rewards that result in larger losses and for present experiences without regard for future and past events. In one study, higher scores on measures of impulsivity and disordered gambling severity proved the biggest predictors of the high levels of delay discounting, irrespective of age, gender,

---

The material in this chapter is based on Clark C, L Nower, and DM Walker. 2013. The relationship of ADHD symptoms to gambling behavior: Results from the National Longitudinal Study of Adolescent Health. *International Gambling Studies* 13(1): 37–51. Used with permission from Taylor & Francis.

years of education, substance abuse treatment, and/or cigarette smoking history (Alessi and Petry 2003). Notably, disordered gamblers with ADHD exhibit a significantly lower capacity to delay gratification than those without ADHD, despite similar levels of sustained attention (Rodriguez-Jiminez et al. 2006).

The literature suggests, therefore, that heightened impulsivity, which is a hallmark of both the Hyeractive–Impulsive subtype of ADHD and disordered gamblers, heightens the risk of youth developing gambling problems. Studies have reported that adolescents with gambling problems endorse higher numbers of ADHD symptoms (Derevensky et al. 2007), and those with Hyperactivity–Impulsivity type ADHD are more likely than those with Combined-type ADHD to have gambling problems (Faregh and Derevensky 2011). In addition, those who report childhood ADHD symptoms that persist into young adulthood experience greater gambling problem severity than those with no ADHD or nonpersistent ADHD (Breyer et al. 2009).

Blaszczynski and Nower (2002) have suggested that the combination of neurobiological vulnerabilities, impulse dysregulation, and ADHD symptoms are characteristic of one specific etiological subtype of problem gamblers. In support, a growing number of investigations highlight the relationship among these factors. For comprehensive reviews, see Goudriaan et al. (2004), Petry (2005), and Shah, Potenza, and Eisen (2004). Recent investigations regarding decision-making suggest that some gamblers have selective cognitive dysfunction, due to deficits in the orbitofrontolimbic circuitry, that predispose them to disorder before the advent of identifiable psychopathology (Grant et al. 2011). Such deficits in disordered gamblers are characterized not only by reward seeking but also by heightened levels of impulsivity and sensation-seeking, the use of maladaptive stress coping strategies (Blaszczynski and Nower 2002; Derevensky and Gupta 2004; MacLaren et al. 2012; Nower, Derevensky, and Gupta 2004) and impaired risk assessment and decreased reward sensitivity that may result in adverse consequences (Goudriaan et al. 2006). Similarly, hyperactive children suffer persistent problems of over-activity, poor school performance, defiant behavior, peer rejection, and discipline problems leading to impaired relationships and consequent low self-esteem (Diamantopoulou et al. 2007; Richman, Hope, and Mihalas 2010), factors that are also characteristic of a subset of problem gamblers (Nower and Blaszczynski 2003).

Despite these findings, few studies have investigated a potential relationship between ADHD and disordered gambling or the prevalence and characteristics of individuals with those co-occurring disorders in a large representative sample. This study uses a US longitudinal and nationally representative sample to examine the relationship among retrospectively reported childhood ADHD symptoms and young adult disordered gambling behaviors. It is hypothesized that youth who endorse Hyperactive–Impulsive subtype ADHD symptoms as children will endorse more symptoms of disordered gambling as young adults.

11.2 Data

In this chapter we analyze data from the National Longitudinal Study of Adolescent Health (Add Health), the data set used in Chap. 10. Unlike many general population surveys, wave 3 of the Add Health collected information on both ADHD and gambling-related behaviors in a large, nationally representative sample. During wave 3 interviews, participants were asked to answer eight questions related to lifetime disordered gambling severity. As shown in Table 10.1, the gambling questions loosely parallel some items in two widely used clinical diagnostic tools for disordered gambling: the DSM-IV (American Psychiatric Association 2000) and the South Oaks Gambling Screen (SOGS) (Lesieur and Blume 1987).

In addition, the survey also included a set of retrospective questions reflective of the diagnostic criteria for ADHD from the DSM-IV (American Psychiatric Association 2000). Participants were asked to think back to when they were 5–12 years of age and to indicate which statements best described their symptoms and behaviors during that time. Table 11.1 presents the list of relevant Add Health questions by ADHD subtype (hyperactivity, impulsivity or inattention).

Table 11.2 lists the gambling behavior indicator variables we created (DSM and SOGS, introduced and explained in Chap. 10) and the ADHD type variables we created (*Combined type*, *Hyperactive–Impulsive type*, and *Inattentive type*) from the Add Health survey data, which are explained in detail below. Table 11.2 also shows the relevant demographic control variables. Most of the variables included here were also shown in Table 10.2, but the analysis in this chapter uses subsamples of males and females. Therefore, Table 11.2 shows the mean values and standard deviations for the full sample and, separately, for males and females. For variables that take the value of 0 or 1 (dummy variables), the mean values can be interpreted as the probability that an individual respondent is identified with that characteristic. As in the previous chapter, to ensure a complete data set for analysis, we eliminated all participants who were missing any pertinent survey data. This adjustment reduced our sample to 6,145 participants. As indicated in Table 11.2, the wave 3 Add Health participants include 48.3 % ($n=2,971$) males, and 51.7 % ($n=3,174$) females. The average age of participants was 21.7 years.

Most of the individuals who are identified with gambling variables DSM or SOGS are men (around 4 % of the men in our sample); few are women (about 0.5 % of the women in our sample). Men are also more likely to be identified by our ADHD variables. Other demographic and socioeconomic variables are shown in the last section of Table 11.2. For the sake of brevity I do not discuss all of these variables here.

11.2.1 Gambling Behavior Variables

A large proportion of the survey participants indicated they had gambled at some point in their lifetimes: 62.9 % ($n=3,865$) played the lotto; 49.6 % ($n=3,048$) played casino games; and 42.5 % ($n=2,612$) reported gambling in some other form.

Table 11.1 Add health ADHD symptom questions

Question	ADHD type
You failed to pay close attention to details or made careless mistakes in your work.	Inattention
You had difficulty sustaining your attention in tasks or fun activities.	Inattention
You didn't listen when spoken to directly.	Inattention
You didn't follow through on instructions and failed to finish work.	Inattention
You had difficulty organizing tasks and activities.	Inattention
You avoided, disliked, or were reluctant to engage in work requiring sustained mental effort.	Inattention
You lost things that were necessary for tasks or activities.	Inattention
You were easily distracted.	Inattention
You were forgetful.	Inattention
You fidgeted with your hands or feet or squirmed in your seat.	Hyperactivity
You left your seat in the classroom or in other situations when being seated was expected.	Hyperactivity
You felt restless.	Hyperactivity
You had difficulty doing fun things quietly.	Hyperactivity
You felt "on the go" or "driven by a motor."	Hyperactivity
You talked too much.	Hyperactivity
You blurted out answers before the questions had been completed.	Impulsivity
You had difficulty awaiting your turn.	Impulsivity

Source: Clark, Nower, and Walker (2013). Used with permission from Taylor & Francis

About 43.5 % of those who gambled ($n = 2{,}642$) reported losing "less than \$100" over the course of a year. However, approximately 3.6 % ($n = 227$) reported being "down" at least \$501 during a particular year. Relatively few participants gave a positive answer to any of the other gambling questions: Thinking about gambling (1.3 %, $n = 80$); Gambling to relieve feelings (0.5 %, $n = 31$); Chasing gambling losses (2.0 %, $n = 123$); and relationship problems (0.4 %, $n = 25$).

In order to test the relationship of ADHD symptoms to potentially problematic gambling behaviors, we created two gambling indicators (DSM and SOGS, as discussed in Chap. 10 and above), which are the dependent variables in our empirical analysis. These indicators represent different combinations of the Add Health gambling questions discussed above and listed in Tables 10.1 and 11.2.

As explained in Chap. 10, DSM was scored with a "1" if a participant gave an affirmative response to at least one of the four Add Health questions of *Thinking about gambling*, *Gambling to relieve feelings*, *Chasing losses*, and *Relationship problems*. If the participant gave a negative response to all four criteria, the DSM variable was scored with a "0" for that participant. As shown in Table 11.2, about 2.2 % of the participants gave an affirmative response to at least one of the four questions included in DSM. (That is, the mean value for DSM denotes probability $p = 0.022$.)

In the case of the SOGS variable, it was recorded as a "1" if the Add Health participant indicated a *Largest amount behind* response of 3, 4, 5, or 6 (that is, being behind by at least \$501), or if s/he gave an affirmative response to more than four of

11.2 Data

Table 11.2 Variable definitions and summary statistics

Variable	Definition	Full sample Mean (SD)	Males Mean (SD)	Females Mean (SD)
Add Health gambling questions				
Down more than $500	=1 if down more than $500 across 1 year of gambling; 0 otherwise	0.036 (0.187)	0.065 (0.246)	0.009 (0.095)
Lotto played	=1 if yes; 0 if no (see Table 10.1 for definition)	0.629 (0.483)	0.650 (0.477)	0.610 (0.488)
Casino games played	=1 if yes; 0 if no (see Table 10.1 for definition)	0.496 (0.500)	0.552 (0.497)	0.442 (0.497)
Other games played	=1 if yes; 0 if no (see Table 10.1 for definition)	0.425 (0.494)	0.526 (0.499)	0.330 (0.470)
Largest amount behind	=0 if none/never gamble; =1 if down<$100; =2 if $100–500; =3 if $501–1,000; =4 if $1,001–5,000; =5 if $5,001–10,000; =6 if >$10,000 (see Table 10.1 for definition)	0.758 (0.850)	0.944 (0.979)	0.584 (0.662)
Thinking about gambling	=1 if yes; 0 if no (see Table 10.1 for definition)	0.013 (0.114)	0.025 (0.155)	0.003 (0.050)
Gamble to relieve feelings	=1 if yes; 0 if no (see Table 10.1 for definition)	0.005 (0.069)	0.007 (0.086)	0.002 (0.047)
Chasing losses	=1 if yes; 0 if no (see Table 10.1 for definition)	0.020 (0.138)	0.036 (0.186)	0.004 (0.066)
Relationship problems	=1 if yes; 0 if no (see Table 10.1 for definition)	0.004 (0.066)	0.008 (0.091)	0.001 (0.025)
Gambling indicator variables				
DSM	=1 if yes to at least one of the four: Thinking about gambling, Gamble to relieve feelings, Chasing losses, Relationship problems; =0 otherwise	0.022 (0.148)	0.041 (0.198)	0.005 (0.071)
SOGS	=1 if yes to "Down over $500", OR if "yes" to more than four of the following: Lotto played, Casino games played, Other games played, Thinking about gambling, Gamble to relieve feelings, Chasing losses, Relationship problems	0.021 (0.142)	0.039 (0.193)	0.004 (0.061)
ADHD variables				
Combined Type ADHD	=1 if the individual stated that six or more of the Inattention behaviors listed in Table 11.1 occurred often or very often between the ages of 5 and 12 years old AND that six or more of the Hyperactivity–Impulsivity behaviors listed in Table 11.1 occurred often or very often between the ages of 5 and 12 years old	0.258 (0.437)	0.326 (0.469)	0.193 (0.395)

(continued)

Table 11.2 (continued)

Variable	Definition	Full sample Mean	Full sample (SD)	Males Mean	Males (SD)	Females Mean	Females (SD)
Hyperactive–Impulsive Type ADHD	=1 if the individual stated that six or more of the Hyperactivity–Impulsivity behaviors listed in Table 11.1 occurred often or very often between the ages of 5 and 12 years old	0.095	(0.293)	0.099	(0.299)	0.090	(0.286)
Inattentive Type ADHD	=1 if the individual stated that six or more of the Inattention behaviors listed in Table 11.1 occurred often or very often between the ages of 5 and 12 years old	0.168	(0.374)	0.188	(0.391)	0.150	(0.357)
Demographic and socioeconomic variables							
Male	=1 if the individual is male	0.483	(0.500)	1	–	0	–
White	=1 if the individual reports being Caucasian and reports that he/she is not Hispanic	0.613	(0.487)	0.621	(0.485)	0.605	(0.489)
GPA	Math and English GPA	2.697	(0.942)	2.564	(0.958)	2.821	(0.911)
Vocab	Add Health Picture—Vocabulary Test Score	103	(14)	104	(14)	102	(14)
South	Individual lives in southern region of United States	0.259	(0.438)	0.255	(0.436)	0.262	(0.440)
West	Individual lives in western region of United States	0.274	(0.446)	0.273	(0.445)	0.274	(0.446)
Midwest	Individual lives in midwestern region of United States	0.313	(0.464)	0.316	(0.465)	0.311	(0.463)
Age	Individual's current age	21.770	(1.665)	21.892	(1.662)	21.655	(1.660)
Education	Individual's current education level	13.415	(1.949)	13.259	(1.917)	13.560	(1.968)
Work	Individual's current work status	0.720	(0.449)	0.744	(0.437)	0.697	(0.460)
Welfare	=1 if the individual currently received welfare	0.036	(0.187)	0.008	(0.090)	0.063	(0.242)
Income	Individual's current income	13,834	(16,460)	15,647	(16,822)	12,136	(15,930)
Married	=1 if the individual is currently married	0.147	(0.354)	0.121	(0.326)	0.172	(0.377)
Serious Crime	=1 if steal, break and enter, assault, sell drugs, or fight, during past year; 0 otherwise	0.151	(0.358)	0.225	(0.418)	0.082	(0.274)
Expelled	=1 if the individual has ever been expelled from school	0.062	(0.240)	0.091	(0.287)	0.034	(0.181)
Sample size (individuals)		6,145		2,971		3,174	

Source: Clark, Nower, and Walker (2013). Used with permission from Taylor & Francis

these variables: *Lotto played; Casino games played; Other games played; Thinking about gambling; Gamble to relieve feelings; Chasing losses; Relationship problems*. Otherwise, the participant was coded as "0" for the SOGS variable. Approximately 2.1 % of Add Health participants received an affirmative score to SOGS.

While the two indicator variables contain elements similar to the DSM or SOGS criteria, it should be emphasized (as it was in Chap. 10) that the Add Health survey did not ask specific DSM or SOGS questions. Our purpose in creating the indicators is to have multiple gambling-related criteria to highlight those participants from the Add Health survey who endorsed items similar to those on commonly administered measures of disordered gambling severity. We utilized all gambling-related Add Health questions to inform our analyses, but those indicators do not include all symptoms from the SOGS or DSM criteria required for diagnostic assessment.

11.2.2 ADHD Symptom Variables

We used the ADHD-related questions from the Add Health survey (refer to Tables 11.1 and 11.2) to create three variables: *Hyperactive–Impulsive type*, *Inattentive type*, and *Combined type*. These variables are created to be consistent with the Center for Disease Control's diagnostic criteria, which are taken from the DSM-IV (American Psychiatric Association 2000). The Add Health survey included questions that asked respondents whether they had experienced the various ADHD associated behaviors between the ages of 5 and 12 years. As per the DSM-IV, if a respondent endorsed six (6) or more symptoms of hyperactivity–impulsivity between the ages of 5 and 12 years, and indicated that the symptoms occurred either "often" or "very often," then the respondent is classified as exhibiting *Hyperactive–Impulsive type* symptoms. Similarly, to be classified as exhibiting *Inattentive type* symptoms, the respondent must endorse at least six (6) symptoms, indicating that they occurred often or very often when the person was between 5 and 12 years old. Finally, those who endorsed six (6) or more of *each* type (i.e., at least 12 symptoms total) are classified as exhibiting *Combined type* ADHD symptoms. If an individual is classified with Combined type, they are not classified in either of the other two categories. Table 11.2 defines these variables and presents their summary statistics.

Notably, the Add Health questions identify individuals who endorse symptoms of ADHD, but the data do not address whether or not these participants were ever actually diagnosed with or treated for an attentional disorder. About 25.8 % of the sample ($n=1,585$; 32.6 % of males and 19.3 % of females) reported symptoms consistent with Combined type ADHD. In contrast, 9.5 % ($n=584$; 9.9 % of males and 0.9 % of females) reported symptoms consistent with Hyperactive–Impulsive type ADHD only. That is, they endorsed at least six of the Hyperactive–Impulsive type symptoms, but did not endorse at least six of the Inattentive type symptoms. Finally, 16.8 % ($n=1,032$; 18.8 % of males and 15.0 % of females) reported at least six Inattentive type ADHD symptoms, but did not endorse at least six of the Hyperactive–Impulsive type symptoms.

In summary, 25.8 % of our sample reported Combined type symptoms; 9.5 % reported Hyperactive–Impulsive type symptoms; and 16.8 % of our sample reported Inattentive type ADHD symptoms.

11.3 Model

The analysis estimated the relationship of ADHD-type variables on the gambling behaviors, represented in the variables DSM and SOGS, controlling for the impact of a variety of demographic and socioeconomic variables (see Table 11.2). To test the relationship of ADHD symptoms to the gambling behaviors, we estimate the following linear probability model for each gambling indicator variable, similar to the models from the previous chapter:

$$\text{Prob.}(\text{Gambling Indicator}_i = 1) = \beta_0 + \beta_1 \text{ADHD Type}_i \\ + \beta_2 \text{Demographics}_i + \varepsilon_i \quad (11.1)$$

The dependent left-side variable is the probability that the survey participant affirmed the gambling indicator variable (DSM or SOGS). The β_0 represents a common term. The ADHD Type variable provides data on whether the participant is categorized into one of the three ADHD type categories. The *Demographics$_i$* variables we include are some from the Add Health survey that have been identified in previous studies as relevant to disordered gambling symptoms (National Research Council 1999; Petry 2005). These demographic and socioeconomic variables are listed and defined at the bottom of Table 11.2. In addition, as a robustness check we estimate logistic regression models with the same dependent and independent variables as those listed in (11.1), because a linear model is not necessarily the ideal model for estimating a probability in all contexts.

The models were tested with six different specifications for each model type (linear probability and logistic), three for each gambling Indicator variable, with each model including one of the ADHD type variables. Thus, we have 12 separate models. This empirical strategy helps us to isolate which ADHD types impact the gambling behaviors represented by the Indicator variables. (We also ran the model including all three ADHD categories in a single model; the results are similar to those reported here.) Of note, the models were run using our full sample; as shown in Table 11.2, although there are more females in the full sample, almost all of the participants with a positive response on the gambling indicator variables are males (4.1 % of men (=122) for DSM, and 3.9 % (=116) for SOGS; only 0.5 % (=16) and 0.4 % (=13) of women, respectively).

Table 11.3 The effects of adolescent ADHD symptoms on young adult gambling behaviors

	Dependent variable=DSM			Dependent variable=SOGS		
	Model 1	Model 2	Model 3	Model 1	Model 2	Model 3
Linear probability model						
Combined Type ADHD	0.0095 (0.0051)	–	–	0.0068 (0.0047)	–	–
Hyperactive–Impulsive Type ADHD	–	0.0169* (0.0081)	–	–	0.0222* (0.0042)	–
Inattentive Type ADHD	–	–	−0.0104* (0.0047)	–	–	−0.0014* (0.0043)
Logistic regression						
Combined Type ADHD	0.0031 (0.0019)	–	–	0.0020 (0.0015)	–	–
Hyperactive–Impulsive Type ADHD	–	0.0069* (0.0035)	–	–	0.0084* (0.0037)	–
Inattentive Type ADHD	–	–	−0.0037* (0.0016)	–	–	−0.0034* (0.0013)
Sample size	6,145	6,145	6,145	6,145	6,145	6,145

Notes: Coefficients (or marginal effects for logistic regressions) are listed with standard errors in parentheses. Other variables included in the models are omitted from the table for brevity
Source: Clark, Nower, and Walker (2013). Used with permission from Taylor & Francis
*Indicates statistical significance at the 0.05 level or better

11.4 Results

Our models estimate the relationship of ADHD-related symptoms in childhood and gambling behaviors later in young adulthood. The results from the 12 versions of (11.1) are presented in Table 11.3. The top panel shows the linear probability model and bottom panel shows the logistic regression results. The first column of Table 11.3 shows the estimated effect of a participant experiencing Combined type ADHD symptoms on their probability of later exhibiting the gambling behaviors represented by our DSM variable. In Columns 2 and 3 we report the effects for Hyperactive–Impulsive type ADHD and Inattentive type ADHD symptoms. The self-reported Combined-type ADHD symptoms proved insignificant in predicting future gambling behaviors. However, the Hyperactive–Impulsive type symptoms were statistically significant predictors of gambling behavior, with a coefficient of 0.0169. This indicates that the probability that that an individual will report the gambling behaviors associated with DSM is 1.69 percentage points higher for individuals who self-reported Hyperactive–Impulsive type ADHD symptoms in childhood than for the rest of the sample. This is a relatively large effect given that only 2.2 % of the sample reports the behaviors represented by DSM. The third row of the table shows the results for the Inattentive type ADHD symptoms. We find a negative, statistically significant effect, with a coefficient of −0.0104. This suggests that individuals who identify themselves with the Inattentive type ADHD symptoms are less likely than the rest of our sample to identify with the gambling behaviors captured by the DSM variable.

The results obtained from our logistic regressions for DSM reinforce the findings obtained from the linear probability model. Both the Hyperactive–Impulsive type and Inattentive type variables are statistically significant, and have the same signs as in the linear probability model. The marginal effect associated with Hyperactive–Impulsive type ADHD symptoms is 0.0069, which supports the conclusion that individuals who suffer from these symptoms are more likely to report the type of gambling behaviors represented by DSM. The marginal effect for the Inattentive type ADHD symptoms is −0.0037.

The three right-most columns of Table 11.3 contain the results of estimating the effect of self-reported ADHD symptoms on the probability of an individual reporting the gambling behaviors associated with the SOGS variable. The results for Hyperactive–Impulsive type ADHD in the linear probability model were very similar when using the SOGS measure of gambling behavior as the dependent variable. A coefficient of 0.0222 on Hyperactive–Impulsive type ADHD symptoms proved statistically significant. This coefficient indicates that individuals who self-report Hyperactive–Impulsive type ADHD symptoms were much more likely than the rest of the sample to exhibit the gambling behavior measured by SOGS. The Combined-type variable was again insignificant in predicting SOGS; as before, the Inattentive type variable is negative and significant (coefficient of −0.0014) in predicting SOGS. Once again, we find that the results of our logistic regressions support the findings of our linear probability model for SOGS. When using logistic regression, Hyperactive–Impulsive type ADHD symptoms were a statistically significant, positive predictor of SOGS gambling behaviors (coefficient of 0.0084). The logistic regression model for the Inattentive type variable was negative and significant, as with the linear probability model.

All four approaches (the two estimation techniques and the two measures of gambling behavior) indicate that individuals who have suffered from Hyperactive–Impulsive type ADHD symptoms are much more likely to exhibit gambling behaviors indicative of disordered gambling. Those individuals who indicated Inattentive type ADHD symptoms are statistically significantly less likely than the rest of the sample to exhibit the gambling behaviors captured by our indicators.

11.5 Discussion and Conclusion

The analysis in this chapter focuses on the relationship of retrospective reports of childhood ADHD symptoms to gambling behaviors in young adults. Analysis of the Add Health data provided evidence, indicating that youths who reported symptoms consistent with Hyperactive–Impulsive type ADHD from ages 5 to 12 years were significantly more likely than those without those ADHD symptoms to later report clinical characteristics of disordered gambling, large past-year losses and/or multiple

11.5 Discussion and Conclusion

forms of gambling as young adults (ages 18–27). However, those individuals who reported symptoms similar to those for Inattentive type ADHD were significantly less likely than those without those symptoms to later report symptoms associated with disordered gambling. We find no relationship between Combined type ADHD symptoms and the gambling behaviors we examined.

This study lends limited support to the relationship of the Hyperactive–Impulsive subtype of ADHD to gambling behavior. It is the first investigation of these relationships in a large, nationally representative sample of young adults, adding to the existing literature which is primarily derived from small samples and clinical populations of gamblers or youths with ADHD. These findings suggest that the impulsivity and hyperactivity characteristic of a subset of youths with ADHD symptoms may be related to the impulse dyscontrol characteristic of disordered gambling. Conceptually, the behavioral reinforcement schedule of gambling, combined with the sensory and mental stimulation of select games, should appeal to youth with hyperactive features. In addition, youths characterized by impulsivity should also be at increased risk for disordered gambling, because the inability to delay gratification and/or engage in reasoned decision-making in the face of mounting losses could lead to gambling problems. Similarly, there is a dissociative phenomenon that occurs with passive forms of gambling like video games that also require the ability to sit and attend to a machine over time. Those who are inattentive would likely lack the drive and/or the focus to engage in either form of gambling behavior for a significant period of time, becoming bored with passive forms of gambling and too distracted when playing action games that require focus and recall to play. These findings are consistent with prior studies that examined linkages among ADHD subtypes and disordered gambling, and highlight the need to uniformly examine comorbidity by subtypes to avoid misleading findings, e.g., see Breyer et al. (2009).

Replication studies with diverse samples are necessary to confirm findings due to three main limitations of this study. As discussed, the gambling indicators were identified based on their similarity to questions utilized in clinical diagnostic instruments. It is unknown whether results would differ had the Add Health questions included actual diagnostic criteria that would have provided a complete measure of gambling problem severity. In addition, the answers were not based on a diagnostic assessment of the participants but, rather, on respondent self-reporting which may not accurately reflect findings in a clinical assessment. Similarly, ADHD symptomatology was assessed retrospectively by asking participants to recall and identify symptoms and behavior from ages 5 to 12, the responses are limited by the potential effect of recall bias, combined with the subjective nature of symptom endorsement that fails to account for frequency and severity across participants.

The results of this study underscore the need for further investigation of the potential biological underpinnings of both disorders and for clinicians to screen for gambling as well as other high risk behaviors in youth who display impulsive and/or hyperactive symptoms consistent with ADHD and high levels of impulse dysregulation. Protocols used for treating hyperactivity and impulsivity in youths with ADHD should also include gambling education and evaluate for treatment needs. Future studies should include both longitudinal and diagnostic assessment, and, ideally, a neurobiological and/or genetic component to aid in better identifying the multifactorial etiology of gambling disorder in youths with ADHD symptomatology.

Chapter 12
Overview of Part II

In the previous three chapters, we have examined some problem behaviors that are often associated with casino gambling. Overall, the empirical analyses in these chapters suggest that individuals who engage in gambling are more likely than non-gamblers to engage in the other risky behaviors studied.

In Chap. 9 we examined county-level data on drunk-driving fatalities, and found that rural casinos tend to increase the level of alcohol-related traffic fatalities, while urban casinos actually have a negative impact on drunk-driving fatalities. The best explanation of this is that the rural casinos tend to increase the miles driven, so there is an increase in accidents. Since many casinos offer free alcohol to patrons, this result is perhaps not surprising. In urban areas, there are transportation options, such as taxis or buses, so casino patrons who have drank have other options for getting home.

Chapter 10 used a nationally representative survey of young adults to examine the relationship between gambling behaviors and other problematic behaviors, including crime, binge drinking, hard drug use, and hiring prostitutes. Perhaps unsurprisingly, we find that individuals who engage in gambling generally are more likely to engage in these other activities. However, one interesting finding is that the link between gamblers and criminal activity was for non-lottery, non-casino gamblers. The same group is more likely to use hard drugs. However, casino gamblers are more likely to binge drink and pay for sex, compared to individuals who engage in other forms of gambling.

In Chap. 11 we use the same survey of young adults to analyze the relationship between gambling behavior and ADHD symptoms. We found a statistically significant positive relationship between hyperactive–impulsive-type ADHD symptoms and the measured gambling behaviors. There was a small negative relationship between gambling and inattentive-type ADHD symptoms, and no relationship between gambling behaviors and the combined-type ADHD criteria.

Part II contains mainstream economic analyses of gambling and related behaviors. Interestingly and perhaps unsurprisingly, these results are fairly consistent with much of the psychology literature on the same relationships.

In Part III we move back to a more traditional economics discussion, focusing on the "social costs" often associated with legalized casinos and gambling. Over the past two decades these issues have been the subject of very interesting political and academic debate.

Part III
Negative Socioeconomic Impacts of Gambling

Chapter 13
The Social Costs of Gambling

Perhaps the most controversial issue surrounding the casino legalization debate is the "social costs" that accompany gambling. The casino industry maintains that its product is simply a form of entertainment like going to movies and football games, and consumers are willing to pay a price for entertainment.[1] But many researchers argue that gambling is fundamentally different from other forms of entertainment because gambling, unlike movies and football games, can lead to addiction. As noted in Chap. 10, the prevalence rate of disordered gambling has been estimated to be between 0.4 and 2.0 % of the general population.

Disordered gamblers are purported to inflict high costs on society.[2] These costs may offset the potential economic benefits that casinos may provide. Studies in which researchers estimate the "social costs" of pathological gambling have been important evidence in debates concerning the virtues of legalized gambling.[3] As would be expected, different investigators have arrived at different conclusions regarding the magnitude of these costs. As a consequence, the social cost issue has been hotly debated in the gambling literature. Recent academic conferences have been dedicated to the issue, illustrating its importance and controversy.[4]

The material in this chapter is based on Walker DM, and AH Barnett. 1999. The social costs of gambling: An economic perspective. *Journal of Gambling Studies* 15(3): 181–212. Used with permission from Springer.

[1] The development of gambling from "vice" to accepted entertainment is chronicled by McGowan (2001).

[2] The social costs usually discussed in the literature refer to those caused primarily by disordered gamblers. This is what is meant by "social costs" and the "social costs of gambling."

[3] It is important to keep in mind that social costs need not result only from *legal* gambling. The discussion here is not meant to be limited to government-sanctioned forms of gambling.

[4] Two such conferences were the Whistler Symposium (2000, Whistler, BC, Canada), the papers of which were published in *Journal of Gambling Studies*, 2003, and the 5th Annual Alberta Conference on Gambling Research (2006, Banff, Alberta, Canada), some papers from which were published in Smith, Hodgins, and Williams (2007).

The one fundamental problem that characterizes most social cost studies is the omission of a clear statement of what is being measured. No one clearly defines "social costs." Instead of starting with objective criteria for what constitutes a social cost, most authors have adopted an ad hoc approach asserting that some activities constitute costs to society and then quantifying the impact of those activities.

Goodman's work (1994a) was one of the most comprehensive at the time of its publication. In his estimate of the social costs of gambling, Goodman includes estimates for income lost by gamblers who lose their jobs, the costs of prosecuting and incarcerating those who commit crimes to support gambling habits, and contributions from family members and others who "bail out" gamblers. In addition to these, he lists other costs that are not as easily quantifiable:

> impaired judgment and efficiency on the job, lost productivity of spouses, unrecovered loans to pathological gamblers, divorces caused by gambling behavior, added administrative costs in programs like unemployment compensation, the costs of depression and physical illnesses related to stress, lower quality of family life and increased suicide attempts by gamblers and spouses of pathological gamblers. (Goodman 1994a, 63–64)

Other authors have lists of costs that vary slightly. Table 13.1 presents a partial list of the alleged social costs of gambling, along with some of the authors who have addressed the issue.

Importantly, *none* of the researchers listed has defined exactly what constitutes a "social cost." The failure of analysts to use a conceptually sound criterion for identifying social costs has led to a capricious classification of some behavioral consequences of gambling as social costs and the inappropriate omission of other consequences from social cost calculations. A clear and explicit definition of "social cost" must be a starting point for any attempt to quantify the negative effects of gambling.

13.1 Chapter Outline

The purpose of this chapter is to explain the economic perspective on social costs and to critique the gambling literature in light of this perspective. Using the economics paradigm, the measurement of social costs becomes more objective and less a function of researcher whims, preferences, emotional reactions, and political biases. The chapter is organized into five additional sections. Section 13.2 presents the economic definition of "social cost." In Sect. 13.3 basic economic tools are used to model social costs. Section 13.4 lists and describes many of the legitimate social costs identified in earlier studies. Section 13.5 is an explanation of why several potential effects of pathological gambling cannot be properly defined as social costs. Section 13.6 concludes the chapter.

13.2 The Economic Definition of "Social Cost"

Table 13.1 Alleged social costs of gambling, and relevant papers

Alleged social costs	Partial list of sources that address social costs
(1) Income lost from missed work	Anielski (2008)
(2) Decreased productivity on the job	Boreham, Dickerson, and Harley (1996)
(3) Depression and physical illness related to stress	Office of Planning (FL) (1995)
	Gazel (1998)
(4) Increased suicide attempts	Goodman (1994a, 1994b, 1995a, 1995b)
(5) Bailout costs	Grinols (1994a, 1994b, 2004)
(6) Unrecovered loans to pathological gamblers	Grinols and Mustard (2001)
(7) Unpaid debts and bankruptcies	Grinols and Omorov (1996)
(8) Higher insurance premiums resulting from pathological gambler-caused fraud	Gross (1998)
	Kindt (1994, 1995)[a]
(9) Corruption of public officials	LaFalce (1994)
(10) Strain on public services	Ladd (1995)
(11) Industry cannibalization	Lesieur (1995)
(12) Divorces caused by gambling	National Gambling Impact Study Commission (1999)
	National Opinion Research Center (1999)
	Nower (1998)
	Politzer, Morrow, and Leavey (1985)
	Tannenwald (1995)
	"Task Force" (1990)
	Thompson (1996, 1997)
	Thompson, Gazel, and Rickman (1997, 1999)
	US House (The National Impact of Casino Gambling Proliferation 1995)
	Zorn (1998)

Source: Walker and Barnett (1999). Used with permission from Springer
[a] Kindt's work should perhaps not even be listed here, as it lacks any hint of scientific rigor

13.2 The Economic Definition of "Social Cost"

There are a number of consequences of gambling that are viewed by some, if not most, individuals as undesirable; many of these are listed in Table 13.1. Unfortunately, many of the "obvious" or "common sense" social costs, upon closer examination, cannot legitimately be considered social costs. Indeed, common sense alone is not an adequate criterion for the determination of what constitutes a social cost. A more objective criterion is required if social cost studies are to be taken seriously.[5] The obvious question then is what criteria should be used for classifying the consequences of human behavior as social costs. Welfare economics provides one answer to this question.

---

[5] Just as objective criteria are useful in estimating the prevalence of pathological gambling, objective criteria are important for the measurement of social costs. Harberger (1971, 785) makes this point in the context of welfare economics in general and cost–benefit analyses in particular: "Just as the road-construction standards that a team of highway engineers must meet can be checked by other highway engineers, so the exercise in applied welfare economics carried out by one team of economists should be subject to check by others."

The definition of social cost is a reduction in social real wealth. The term "wealth" does not simply refer to money stock. Instead, it refers to whatever is valued by individuals. For example, suppose an action harms some members of society and benefits no one. The social cost of the action in this case is the sum of the amounts by which real wealth is reduced for those who are harmed. Suppose, on the other hand, that an action harms some members of society (say by taxing away part of their income) and benefits others (say by providing them with income transfers). Assume further that the collective harm to those made worse off is equal to the gains of the beneficiaries. Since the gains for some members of society are equal to the losses of others, the level of social real wealth is unchanged, and the action produces no social cost or benefit.

This definition of a social cost has not been arbitrarily chosen. It is rooted in the Pareto criterion.[6] The Pareto criterion states that a change in the state of the world improves social welfare (i.e., produces a social benefit) when that change makes at least one member of society better off while making no one else worse off (Layard and Walters 1978, 30). Obviously, this criterion does not provide a practical guide to welfare calculations since any conceivable policy change is likely to leave someone worse off. However, a variant of the Pareto criterion, first proposed by Kaldor (1939) and later by Hicks (1940), can provide guidance in such calculations.

The Kaldor–Hicks criterion states that a change in the state of the world improves social welfare if the change "would enable the gainers to compensate the losers while continuing to gain themselves. The compensation need only be hypothetical, and a Kaldor–Hicks improvement offers only a potential Pareto improvement" (Layard and Walters 1978, 32). On the other hand, a given change in the state of the world reduces welfare (i.e., produces a social cost) when those who gain from the change do not have gains sufficient to fully compensate those who lose. In other words, if a change in the state of the world reduces the wealth of some members of society more than it increases the wealth of others, then the aggregate wealth of society is reduced and a social cost (in the amount of the difference) is produced by the change.

A change in the state of the world that simply redistributes wealth from some persons to others without changing the sum of wealth for all individuals taken together would produce neither a social cost nor a social benefit. Such redistributions would make some individuals better off and others worse off, but society would be no worse off.[7] This neutrality of wealth transfers in welfare applies even when the transfers are involuntary.[8]

---

[6]The concept is named for Vilfredo Pareto, an early twentieth-century economist. The Pareto criterion is the central concept in welfare economics. A full understanding of the meaning of social costs, as economists use the term, requires an understanding of this concept.

[7]To be strictly correct, interpersonal utility comparisons are problematic. In applied welfare studies, economists nevertheless typically assume that all individuals have approximately identical utility functions. Given this assumption, it is possible to draw unambiguous welfare implications (i.e., measures of social benefits and costs) by aggregating individuals' willingness to pay for policy changes.

[8]For related discussions, see Baumol and Oates (1988), Bhagwati (1983), Bhagwati, Brecher, and Srinivasan (1984), Johnson (1991), Krueger (1974), Mueller (1989), Posner (1975), Tollison (1982), and Tullock (1967).

13.3 Modeling Social Costs

The definition of social cost as a reduction in social real wealth can be illustrated using the basic tools of microeconomics.[9] Using this framework, the social costs of gambling become clearer, which may help lead researchers toward a consensus. Using the production possibilities frontier (PPF) and indifference curve (IC) framework explained in the Appendix, we can represent optimality as the point of tangency between the PPF and highest possible IC. A "social cost" can be represented as an inefficient situation in which production and consumption occur under the initial PPF or on a lower PPF–IC.

13.3.1 The Definition Applied

Tullock (1967) used the now famous example of theft to illustrate the concept of social cost. Theft is a transfer of wealth that does not represent a social cost with no net change in the value of resources. Landsburg offers a succinct explanation of Tullock's point:

> stolen property does not cease to exist. When a television set is moved from one house to another, it remains as reliable a source of entertainment as it ever was. This is true even when the new recipient of those services is a thief or a dealer in stolen property. (Landsburg 1993, 97–98)

The transfer of wealth from victim to thief may be unfortunate and is certainly inequitable from the perspective of most members of society. Nevertheless, the value of the stolen property is simply a transfer between thief and victim that does not change aggregate social real wealth.[10]

However, there *are* two social costs associated with theft. First, crime may impose "psychic costs" on the victim that are unrelated to the pecuniary value of the lost property. For example, the victim may feel violated and fearful after a theft.[11] Second, the existence of theft creates behavior geared toward preventing involuntary wealth transfers.[12] Because some people engage in theft, others in

---

[9] This type of exposition is used by Dixit and Grossman (1984). A slightly more technical presentation would include a discussion of relative prices, input coefficients, and preferences. See any intermediate microeconomics text for more details on the foundations of these models.

[10] Grinols (2007) develops a model using two individuals' utility functions that shows that, under his assumptions, one person stealing from another does lead to a reduction in aggregate utility. Thompson, Gazel, and Rickman (1999) make a similar argument.

[11] Psychic costs are discussed in Sect. 13.4.3.

[12] Behavior that involves attempts to obtain or prevent wealth transfers is generally referred to as "rent seeking" discussed in more detail in Chap. 15. Also see Johnson (1991) and Mueller (1989) for extensive discussions.

society use scarce resources to prevent theft, e.g., buying locks and burglar alarms.[13] As a result, society must forego other "useful" goods and services and this opportunity cost is a social cost. As Tullock (1967, 231) explains, "the existence of theft as a potential activity results in very substantial diversion of resources to fields where they essentially offset each other, and produce no positive product." Note that it is the *existence of theft* not the value of goods stolen which is the source of the social cost.

Excise taxes (i.e., taxes on specific products) provide another useful example. Although these taxes represent wealth transfers and the value of a tax does not belong in cost–benefit analyses (Landsburg 1993, 96), the taxes do cause social costs. An excise tax causes a reduction in the number of mutually beneficial voluntary transactions, which reduces consumer and producer surplus. This is called a deadweight loss (described in the Appendix). In addition, the collection of taxes requires the use of resources that could be used to produce goods and services are instead used by governments in tax collection efforts. At the same time, taxpayers change consumption patterns and use resources in an attempt to reduce or avoid their tax burdens by hiring accountants and lawyers. These uses of resources represent the "excess burden" of taxes, and are social costs.

With an understanding of involuntary wealth transfers in theft or taxes, it is clear that voluntary wealth transfers themselves do not generally result in social costs. In the gambling literature, however, the monetary amount of voluntary wealth transfers is usually counted as part of the social cost of gambling. An example is the alleged "bailout costs" (see Sect. 13.5.3) that pathological gamblers impose on society. These bailouts neither create nor destroy wealth, but they simply redistribute it.

Redistributions of wealth, especially when they are arbitrary and involuntary, can produce social costs. The social costs produced by such transfers are the value of the psychic, collection, and avoidance costs caused by the transfer that is over and above the value of the transfer itself. In other words, the amount of bad debt, unemployment compensation, or other wealth redistribution is not a measure or a meaningful proxy of social costs.

This provides enough background so that we can use the example of theft to illustrate the economic definition of social cost.

13.3.2 Theft as an Illustration of Social Cost

Let us suppose that society is initially producing at point a on PPF_1 and IC_1 in Fig. 13.1 in a world absent of theft. When we introduce theft, thieves begin using resources to commit crimes creating an incentive for individuals to use resources in

---

[13] Becker argues that, in the case of a *competitive* crime market, the value of the resources used in producing locks and paying police can be assumed to approximate the social cost of the crime (1968, 171, note 3; italics added).

Fig. 13.1 Social cost of theft

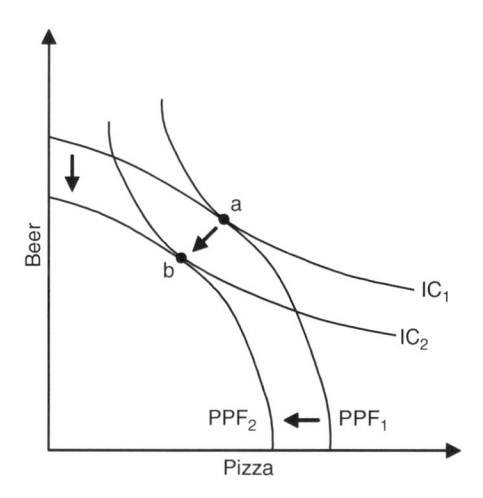

an effort to prevent theft. In the model this would mean that real resources are diverted from the production of beer and pizza into producing crowbars, locks, and alarm systems. This change can be represented by a contraction of the PPF (to PPF$_2$) and movement from *a* to some point like point *b*.[14]

The existence of theft means that we have fewer resources with which to produce other things society wants moving the intercept points of the PPF closer to the origin. This causes an inefficiency (at point *b*) compared to the theft-absent case (at point *a*). The social cost is the beer and pizza that are now not produced because some resources are used in executing and preventing thefts.[15] Note that the value of the goods or money stolen is *not* the social cost of theft, as the theft is merely a transfer of wealth.

Redistribution itself does not entail a social cost since the costs to one individual are offset by benefits to another.[16]

13.3.3 *Externalities and Social Costs*

"Externality" is a concept closely related to social cost that also leads to confusion in the gambling literature. Specifically, some investigators equate externalities and

---

[14] Dixit and Grossman (1984) use a similar example but do not show a contraction of the PPF. Carbaugh (2004, Chap. 2) explains that the axes in the PPF model give a scale for output *per unit of input resource*. Social costs effectively reduce productive capacity (given input endowments) since production is diverted to some other use, which would be unnecessary in the absence of theft.

[15] In this discussion, we are ignoring any psychic costs to the victims of theft.

[16] McGowan (1999) notes that this is a utilitarian interpretation of wealth transfers.

social costs[17] while others appear to think that any third-party effect qualifies as a social cost. Both views are misguided.

Externalities occur when the actions of one person impact the welfare of another. Without doubt, pathological gamblers often engage in behavior that has negative effects on others. However, not all negative externalities represent social costs.

Since the 1930s, welfare economists have taken care to distinguish between "technological externalities" and "pecuniary externalities."[18] Technological externalities are defined as those for which the external effect impacts real (i.e., nonmonetary) arguments in utility or production functions. In other words, technological externalities impact the ability of an economic actor to transform a given amount of inputs into outputs (utility). A technological externality occurs, for example, when a polluter discharges pollutants into a stream so that a downstream water user must clean the water before it can be used. As a result of the pollution, the amount of real resources required for the downstream producer to produce a given amount of output has increased. The important point is that more resources are required to produce the same amount of the externality-affected output. Hence, fewer resources are available to produce other goods, and real wealth is reduced as a result of the pollution.[19]

Pecuniary externalities, on the other hand, impact prices and wealth distribution but they do not affect aggregate social real wealth. A pecuniary externality may impact the price of a product and hence the money cost of producing a given amount of that product, but it would not affect the amount of real resources required to produce a given amount of the product. As a consequence, pecuniary externalities may redistribute wealth among members of society, but they do not reduce the aggregate amount of real wealth. For example, when a gambler loses the money that would otherwise have been used to buy groceries for his family, the family is worse off. Because the gambler's actions reduce their wealth, he imposes an externality on his family. However, since the gambler's actions do not generally impact real arguments in utility functions, the externality is pecuniary. Put another way, the losses of the gambler and his family are equal to the winnings of others[20] and there is no loss in aggregate social wealth.

In a nutshell, negative technological externalities are externalities that cause inefficiency in the use of resources and produce social costs as well as costs for the person harmed. These typically occur outside markets through resources for which property rights do not exist. Negative pecuniary externalities, on the other hand, cause harm to the affected individual but do *not* produce inefficiencies or social costs. They are simply wealth transfers, usually occurring within markets, e.g., through price changes.

---

[17] For example, see Grinols and Omorov (1996), Grinols and Mustard (2001, 2006), LaFalce (1994), and Thompson (1997).

[18] Seminal work in this area was by Jacob Viner (1931).

[19] The issue is a bit more complicated than the discussion here implies. Whether society's wealth is reduced by the pollution depends upon whether the pollution is marginally relevant. For a discussion of the importance of marginally relevant externalities, see Barnett and Kaserman (1998).

[20] The winners are a combination of other gamblers who win and the gaming industry involved.

An example of the latter occurs when a new employer enters a labor market and drives up wage rates for existing employers.[21] The former occurs when a factory discharges waste into the air that harms the health of those downwind from the polluter.[22]

In the context of the PPF–IC model introduced in the previous example of theft, a technological externality means that the same inputs result in less output. Put differently, it takes more inputs to yield the same output as in the absence of the externality. This suggests a contraction of the PPF, since it represents the amount of production per unit of input resource available.

The distinction between pecuniary and technological externalities, though extremely important in welfare economics, is generally confused or ignored by those who write on the social costs of gambling. As a result, it is common for gambling researchers to aggregate real technological and pecuniary effects[23] to produce sums characterized as social costs.

For example, Grinols and Omorov (1996, 52) note, "gambling is associated with significant negative externalities ..." They cite as examples "crime-related apprehensions, adjudication, and incarceration costs, as well as social service costs for themselves and their families" (p. 53). Here Grinols and Omorov confuse the issue by their failure to note that crime-related apprehensions, adjudication, and incarceration costs represent technological externalities. These are legitimate social costs. However, the social service costs for the gamblers and costs to the gamblers' families are generally pecuniary externalities that do not represent direct social costs.

13.3.4 Alleged Social Costs of Gambling[24]

Most gambling studies do not perform original estimates of social costs. Instead, studies usually simply repeat previous monetary estimates without explaining what costs are included in the estimates, or they present a range of cost figures and call the lower end of the range "conservative." Few studies explain the underlying methodologies. Table 13.2 summarizes some of the social cost studies.[25]

---

[21] This applies even when, for example, the now higher labor costs drive some existing firms out of business.

[22] For more detailed discussions of externalities, particularly the distinction between pecuniary and technological externalities, see Barnett (1978, 1980), Barnett and Bradley (1981), Barnett and Kaserman (1998), and Baumol and Oates (1988, Chap. 3, especially p. 30).

[23] Baumol and Oates (1988, 30) write, "the price effects that constitute pecuniary externalities are merely the normal competitive mechanism for the reallocation of resources in response to changes in demand or factor supplies."

[24] McCormick's (1998) discussion of "uncompensated social costs" is a useful complement to this section. The private consequences issue is dealt with in more detail by Eadington (2003).

[25] In addition, see "Casinos in Florida" (1995), Tannenwald (1995), and US House (The National Impact of Casino Gambling Proliferation 1995).

Table 13.2 Examples of social cost studies

Study	Summary
Goodman (1995a)	Goodman explains that the "costs to government and the private economy" are estimated at $13,200 per year per pathological gambler (p. 56). This is the same number used in his 1994 study. He does not explain the criteria by which items are included but does list some of the "costs" included. Much of Goodman's research is based on newspaper articles.
Grinols (1995)	Grinols has one of the most alarmist and deceptive discussions. He suggests that the social costs of gambling are like destruction of wealth amounting to "losses equal to the lost output of an additional 1990:III–1991:II recession every eight to fifteen years, or an additional hurricane Andrew (the most costly natural disaster in American history) every year, or two 1993-level Midwest floods (the largest floods on record for the area) annually." (p. 7)
Grinols (2004)	Grinols simply takes the average of many of the social cost estimates performed during the 1990s to arrive at an estimate of $10,330. Surprisingly, he does not even analyze the different cost estimates to determine whether or not they are all measuring the same things or whether they use appropriate methodologies.
Grinols and Omorov (1996)	In this paper the costs are called externalities. The authors use estimates from previous studies: "Focusing only on social costs that can be measured—primarily apprehension, adjudication, incarceration, direct regulatory costs, and lost productivity costs—leads to annual costs per pathological gambler between $15,000 and $33,500." (p. 56)
Kindt (1994, 1995)	Kindt simply discusses previous estimates. He cites a relatively high cost estimate: "The social, business, economic and governmental costs of [pathological gamblers] are potentially catastrophic. The average socio-economic cost per [pathological] gambler per year has been calculated at $53,000" (1995, 582). Kindt's work, usually published in law journals, is remarkably unscientific and biased.
Maryland (1990)	The social cost of pathological gambling in Maryland is estimated at $30,000 per gambler per year, in 1988 dollars (p. 59). "Abused dollars" are the basis for these costs.
Thompson, Gazel, and Rickman (1997)	This paper contains an original social cost estimate, $9,469 per pathological gambler per year, and is regarded by its authors and other researchers as "conservative." This is a frequently cited study.

Source: Walker and Barnett (1999). Used with permission from Springer

Each of these studies discusses the high level of costs associated with gambling but none explains what conditions must be satisfied for a consequence of gambling to be considered a social cost. In many cases, they combine technological with pecuniary externalities, ignore certain social costs, and wrongly include other "effects" in their social cost estimates. One further complication is that there appears to be little consistency among researchers for what is or is not included in the estimates.

Generally, costs to individuals do not qualify as social costs unless they are coupled with negative technological externalities. In an early draft, McCormick (1998) provided a useful example: "Suppose I break my leg riding a horse. Is there a social cost? No. The pain, suffering, and loss of income are mine. Jobs, income, taxes, crime, and divorce are not benefits or costs, they are markers and indicators."

There are numerous potentially negative effects of pathological gambling that do not qualify as social costs in the economic paradigm.[26]

Among the studies that offer estimates of the social costs of pathological gamblers, the work by Thompson, Gazel, and Rickman (1996, 1997, 1999) is among the most complete and most carefully done. They note the shortcomings of previous researchers:

> Several studies have offered evidence about the societal cost of problem gambling. However, for the most part, we have seen only attempts to either list all the cost factors without analysis and without totaling up the effects, or to offer numbers without any indication of how the numbers were determined. (Thompson, Gazel, and Rickman 1997, 82–83)

In their study, Thompson, Gazel, and Rickman (1996, 16–21) give an explanation of each of the "social costs" ("employment costs, bad debts and civil-court costs, thefts and criminal-justice costs, the costs of therapy, and welfare costs") and their estimation but as in their 1997 study the authors fail to disclose the specific criteria used for determining just what constitutes a social cost.[27] Nevertheless, Thompson, Gazel, and Rickman (1997) are to be commended for being transparent in their estimation procedure. Indeed, their paper is often cited as being one of the most respectable, thorough, and conservative social cost studies.[28] Therefore, where researchers typically provide empirical estimates, I give as an example the estimates from Thompson, Gazel, and Rickman (1997). Table 13.3 is a reproduction of their social cost estimate.

13.4 Legitimate Social Costs

According to the social cost definition in Sect. 13.2 there are several legitimate social costs that have been identified by previous researchers. In the following subsections, the alleged social costs of gambling, including those listed in Tables 13.1 and 13.3, are evaluated within the context of the economic tools developed in the Appendix.

13.4.1 Legal Costs

Some individuals face legal problems as a result of their disordered gambling. For example, a person may steal in order to get money for a gambling habit. This activity can lead to social costs because the resources expended on police, courts, and incarceration could have been spent on other goods or services.[29] Importantly,

---

[26] See Baumol and Oates (1988) for a complete discussion of externalities.

[27] More recent comprehensive studies by NORC (1999) and the NGISC (1999) are similar in this respect.

[28] It is for this reason that I have scrutinized their work.

[29] Expenditures on police may also result in positive externalities. For example, an increased police presence on the streets may discourage some amount of crime.

Table 13.3 Annual societal cost per compulsive gambler ($)

Cost type	Component cost	Total
Employment		2,941
Lost work hours	1,328	
Unemployment compensation	214	
Lost productivity/unemployment	1,398	
Bad debts		1,487
Civil court		848
Bankruptcy court	334	
Other civil court	514	
Criminal justice		3,498
Thefts	1,733	
Arrests	48	
Trials	369	
Probation	186	
Incarceration	1,162	
Therapy		361
Welfare		334
Aid to dependent children	233	
Food stamps	101	
Total		9,469

Data source: Thompson, Gazel, and Rickman (1997, 87)
Source: Walker and Barnett (1999). Used with permission from Springer

the money stolen or any awards in civil court decisions are not social costs because they represent wealth transfers.

For legal costs of police, courts, and incarceration to be fully attributed to pathological gambling, there are two requirements. First, the costs must be borne by others, not the pathological gambler.[30] Second, pathological gambling must be the sole cause of the behavior (that is, the primary disorder). In reality, many cases are characterized by comorbidity with more than one disorder. This issue is addressed in Chap. 14.

With these *caveats*, we can reconsider the Thompson, Gazel, and Rickman (1997) estimates for costs associated with "civil court" and "criminal justice." To the extent that pathological gambling is the primary disorder, the estimate of $848 is properly classified as a social cost if it excludes cash awards. However, from the $3,498 estimate of criminal justice costs, we must subtract the $1,733 for theft since it is merely a wealth transfer. This leaves $1,765 that can potentially be considered a social cost related to criminal justice.

These legal costs are illustrated in Fig. 13.2. When casinos are legalized and open, movement from *a* to *b* might occur. Assuming consumers like casino gambling, this represents an improvement in welfare, as indicated by the movement from IC_1 to IC_2.

---

[30]This does not, however, imply that all government expenditures are social costs. (In many cases, such expenditures represent wealth transfers.)

13.4 Legitimate Social Costs

However, disordered gamblers that may exhibit criminal behavior create a need for society's resources to be expended on police, courts, and incarceration. This diversion of resources from other modes of production can be represented by a contraction of the PPF, and a reduction in consumption, say from point *b* to point *c*.

Recall that a social cost is a decrease in social wealth, compared to *what it otherwise would have been*. In the context of the PPF–IC model, this is illustrated by movement to a lower PPF–IC. Though the model is not conducive to precise empirical estimates, it does offer a useful way to conceptualize social costs. Not all negative effects of gambling cause a reduction of real social wealth. It is interesting to note that the model suggests that society might be better off at point *c* with gambling and its social costs than at the original point *a* with neither gambling nor its social costs.[31] Of course, if the social costs of casinos are so great as to move us to point *d* on IC_4 then we would be better off prohibiting gambling, assuming that the social costs would also largely disappear.

13.4.2 Treatment Costs

Assume that those who seek therapy for their gambling problem would not require treatment in the absence of their gambling problem. Assume further that when a person decides to gamble he believes that he will not pay the therapy costs even if he becomes addicted. Under these questionable assumptions, the $361 attributed by Thompson, Gazel, and Rickman (1997) to therapy cost could be considered a social cost. Again, Fig. 13.2 could be used as a representation of this type of social cost. As with legal costs, we can consider this a social cost only if someone other than the treated individual pays for treatment.

13.4.3 Psychic Costs[32]

From an economic perspective, not only have researchers inappropriately classified numerous consequences of pathological gambling as "social costs" as discussed below, but they have also omitted several legitimate social costs from their studies. Some of the neglected costs amount to the negative psychological impact on individuals caused by pathological gamblers, while others are associated with government restrictions and the legalization process. Discussion of the latter type is found in Chap. 14 while the focus of the present chapter is more on the costs caused by individual gamblers.

---

[31] There is an assumption here that pathological gambling occurs only when gambling is legal. Of course, this is not always the case. Society would likely have some of the social costs whether or not gambling was legal, since people could gamble online, in other jurisdictions, or illegally.

[32] At the Whistler Symposium (2000) several psychologists informally told me that the term "psychic cost" is "offensive." No offense is intended.

Fig. 13.2 Social costs of pathological gambling

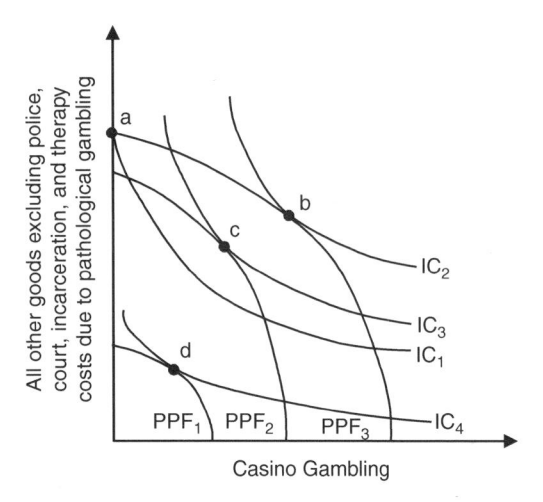

Problem gambling behavior may harm family members, no doubt. But some researchers have argued that these costs are "internalized" and do not belong in social cost measures (Manning et al. 1991; Walker and Barnett 1999). Others are less sure how to deal with the issue but suggest that the costs are probably not internalized (Sloan et al. 2004, 220–221). Even if harm to family members is a social cost, it is unclear how to measure it in money terms. There are other examples of harms from gambling that are not easily measured. For example, how should we measure the cost of a divorce caused by problem gambling? Rather than focusing on money measures, perhaps simply noting that family problems are a likely side effect of pathological gambling would be a better way to acknowledge this issue.

Walker and Barnett (1999) discuss the emotional "costs" that may be imposed by pathological gamblers on their friends and family. Emotional harm, to the extent it is caused by the pathological affliction, is a social cost because it can be considered a negative technological externality when relevant arguments are included in a utility function. For example, an interdependent utility function might be $U_a = U(C, U_f, U_r, Z)$, where C is consumption, U_f is the utility of friends, U_r is the utility of relatives, and Z represents all other arguments. If $\delta U_a/\delta U_f$ and $\delta U_a/\delta U_r > 0$ then a psychic cost is imposed on person a when harm occurs to either a friend or a relative. The result is lower utility for person a.

Psychic costs are not easily modeled in the context of a PPF–IC model because although some people are less happy they are not necessarily less productive or consuming less. One important question to debate is whether or not this type of psychic cost should be under consideration for policy intervention. After all, people are affected daily by countless psychic costs and benefits.[33] In addition, one could

---

[33] The value of psychic costs could be measured by asking individuals how much they would be willing to pay to avoid them. Surveys asking such questions would need to be very carefully constructed in order to be valid. This particular issue is beyond the scope of this book.

argue that psychic costs imposed on family members or friends are "internalized." Since the individuals have close relationships, they understand and accept that there will be both benefits and costs of such relationships.[34]

13.5 Items Improperly Defined as Social Costs

The underlying key to the development of methodologically sound social cost estimates is an appropriate definition of social cost. Earlier the Walker and Barnett (1999) definition was stated and explained in detail. In this section, many of previously alleged social costs are examined through the lens of that definition. Although many or all of these effects of pathological gambling behavior are unfortunate, this is not sufficient for them to qualify as social costs, decreases in real social wealth. Most of these effects are incorrectly included in social cost estimates. Refer to Tables 13.1 and 13.3 for examples. Simple examples are offered in many cases to illustrate why the classification of some of these effects as social costs is inappropriate. At the end of the discussion, the various effects that are not true social costs are summarized with succinct explanations.

13.5.1 Wealth Transfers

Some researchers have argued that wealth transfers do not change the overall level of societal wealth and do not belong in cost–benefit calculations (Clement 2003; Collins and Lapsley 2003; Eadington 2003; National Research Council 1999; Single 2003; Walker and Barnett 1999). Others argue that transfers such as bankruptcies, thefts, "bailouts," and "abused dollars" belong in the equation (Grinols 2004; Grinols and Mustard 2001; Markandya and Pearce 1989; Thompson, Gazel, and Rickman 1997), because a transfer is a cost to *someone*. This is an important issue because how transfers are treated will have perhaps the largest impact on the magnitude of social cost estimates.

Some researchers base their argument that "transfers are costs" on an extremely vague concept coined "abused dollars" by Politzer, Morrow, and Leavey (1985, 133):

> [the] amount [of money] obtained legally and/or illegally by the pathological gambler which otherwise would have been used by the pathological gambler, his family, or his victims for other essential purposes. These abused dollars include earned income put at risk in gambling, borrowed, and/or illegally obtained dollars spent on basic needs and/or provided to the family which otherwise would have been "covered" by that fraction of earned income which was used for gambling, and borrowed and/or illegally obtained dollars for the partial payment of gambling related debts.

---

[34] See ACIL (1999) on this issue.

Researchers who cite "abused dollars" are typically staunch antigambling advocates (e.g., Grinols 2004; Grinols and Mustard 2001; Kindt 2001). Kindt (2001, 31) suggests that the abused dollar cost concept "was given the actual or implied imprimatur of the *Journal* [*of Gambling Behavior*]." However, the editor of the *Journal* at the time, Henry Lesieur, has indicated that he regrets publishing the article and that it has been "justifiably criticized" (Lesieur 2003).[35]

On the surface "abused dollars" might appear to be a reasonable way to measure the negative effects of gambling since it seems to measure the waste or damage associated with gambling. Upon closer examination the concept is too vague to be useful. For example, measuring the amount of dollars spent gambling that "could have been used for other essential purposes" does not provide much information. First, what is an "essential purpose"? The concept loses its meaning once we consider gambler income levels. Is an "essential purpose" for a millionaire the same as for a person with average income? Furthermore, a generous interpretation of "abused dollars" would imply that the sum of all money bet (i.e., handle) represents abused dollars. This is likely to be significantly higher than the actual amount lost by a casino gambler.[36] The concept also treats borrowed money as abused dollars. Many later authors attempt to make a similar measurement but call it by another name (e.g., "bailout cost" or "social cost").[37] In any case, the "abused dollars" concept is far too vague to serve as a useful classification mechanism in social cost estimates.

The issue of wealth transfers, say from bad debts and bankruptcies, is important. Most noneconomists are not satisfied with the "transfer of wealth" argument. But treating transfers as social costs has its own problems explained by Walker (2003, 165–166). In any case, measuring transfers is relatively simple, once it is determined how they should be handled in cost–benefit studies.

13.5.2 Bad Debts

Researchers typically classify "bad debts," money borrowed but not paid back, as a social cost of pathological gambling if the borrowed funds are used to finance gambling activities. Thompson, Gazel, and Rickman (1997) estimate that a pathological gambler will have $1,487 in bad debts annually.

---

[35] Lesieur writes that he regrets publishing the article because he believes that many of the costs of problem gambling are not measurable.

[36] Walker (2004) gives the example that a gambler bets an average of $1,000 in order to lose $100 at slot machines with a 90 % payout.

[37] Grinols and Mustard (2001) resurrect the "abused dollars" concept, but define it differently than Politzer, Morrow, and Leavey (1985).

Certainly bad debts are costly to the creditors but the result of these bad debts is simply to transfer wealth from creditors to debtors. Since transfers are not considered social costs, the inclusion of bad debts in the estimate of social costs is inappropriate.[38]

Bad debts are simply wealth transfers that cannot be considered a social cost because they do not reduce social wealth, but the cost of resources used in the collection of bad debts can be characterized as a social cost. To the extent that bad debts accumulated by gamblers exceed those that would occur in efficient capital markets, social wealth is reduced when resources that would have been used to produce goods and services are instead used in efforts to collect or avoid paying bad debts. Previous researchers have not identified this as a potential social cost of pathological gambling behavior.

13.5.3 Bailout Costs

Frequently pathological gamblers find themselves in dire financial situations. When they turn to family members or friends for financial help, it is often labeled "bailout costs." Numerous researchers provide estimates of this type of "cost."[39] Transfers of wealth, whether voluntary or not, cannot be considered social costs since the overall wealth does not decline and an inefficiency is not created.[40] The NRC (1999, 163) notes, "One of the biggest stumbling blocks in economic impact analysis is determining which effects are real and which are merely transfers." The PPF model helps to shed light on whether an effect is real or pecuniary.

If one considers bailouts as social costs, then perhaps *every* exchange of money should be one. The argument quickly runs into problems. If I give someone 50¢ to buy a soft drink, should it represent a social cost analogous to a bailout cost? Call this a social cost of thirst, or an "abused 50¢" due to thirst. When the university pays me my monthly salary, is that a social cost analogous to any other government

---

[38] The argument that defaults on bad debts will lead to higher prices (interest rates, for example) and that this is a social cost is the result of misunderstanding the distinction between pecuniary and technological externalities. Any externalities that merely alter relative prices are pecuniary, not technological.

[39] See "Casinos in Florida" (1995), Goodman (1995b), Kindt (1994), Politzer, Morrow, and Leavey (1985), and Thompson, Gazel, and Rickman (1997).

[40] Consider a schoolboy who loses his money pitching pennies at recess. Rather than see him go without food, his mother may deliver a stiff lecture and replacement lunch money. The mother would certainly be displeased with his behavior but her "gift" is a voluntary transfer of wealth that does not constitute a decrease in social wealth and is not a social cost. Similarly, if her adult son is a pathological gambler and loses his own income gambling, she may choose to provide funds for his food and shelter. The wealth transfer would not constitute a social cost because her gift is purely a transfer and there is no loss in wealth for the community.

expenditure? Call this a social cost of education. These examples show that the whole concept of social cost quickly loses its meaning when it is defined to be so general. This is one reason why the definition of social cost is critical.

13.5.4 Government Welfare Expenditures

Some researchers have been confused about how government spending relates to social costs. In economics, a social cost is a decrease in the wealth of society. However, Thompson, Gazel, and Rickman (1997) attribute social costs of $334 to welfare expenditures. From the previous discussion, it should be clear that mere wealth transfers, from taxing Sam to pay Joe, do not represent social costs because the level of wealth remains constant. However, a related social cost would be any excess burden incurred raising the tax revenue used for transfers.

What about non-transfer government spending? Do these constitute social costs? This question was raised, for example, by one of Walker and Barnett's referees (1999, 187, note 10): "[The authors] even deny that thefts are costs to society. They deny that the costs of welfare are social costs. If not, they would not have to be included in the state budgets, so how can they not be social costs?"

Even when particular government-paid costs of gambling are agreed to be "social costs" their measurement may be tricky. Most researchers count government expenditures relating to the treatment of problem gambling as social costs (Collins and Lapsley 2003; Eadington 2003; Single 2003; Walker and Barnett 1999). The magnitude of these social costs in a country depends critically on the level of treatment-related expenditures by government. This makes the comparison of social costs across countries difficult. If one country increases its expenditures on problem gambling treatment the social costs of gambling in that country increase, according to most studies, even if the number of problem gamblers or the severity of their problematic behavior decreases. A country whose government spends nothing to deal with problem gambling may have a significantly lower social cost, *ceteris paribus*.[41]

Social cost studies that simply use government spending as measure of social costs are problematic. Yet, there is no obviously better way to handle these costs. One could argue that government spending should be handled in a fundamentally different way since they may be tied more directly to politics than to the level of problem gambling. Even so, the level of government spending can provide useful information to researchers interested in studying the cost-effectiveness of different treatment options.

This is a critical point. Simply because the government spends money on something does *not* necessarily imply that the expenditure represents a social cost or a

---

[41] Alternatively, suppose one country compensates pathological gamblers 150 % of their treatment costs. Then the social costs of gambling in this country would be overestimated.

decrease in social wealth, though it *may*. Members of society must give money to government in taxes, and so in a sense it is a cost to society members. However, the benefits also go to society members. For example, education, research, police, and unemployment benefits would all be social costs if government expenditures are sufficient to qualify as social costs. These things are fundamentally different from the social costs associated with pathological gambling. We seek to minimize the social costs of gambling, but we do not seek to minimize education, research, police protection, or many other forms of government spending. If government spending implied social costs, the social cost problem would be easily solved by eliminating government spending! This point hopefully illustrates why social cost must be something other than mere expenditures by a person, or negative consequences to an individual.

Browning (1999) discusses government expenditures as externalities. His discussion is in the context of smoking and the related health care costs that are borne by government. He calls these "fiscal externalities." They are not technological externalities because spending by government results in taxes on citizens and tax rates are not arguments in utility functions (Browning 1999, 7). In discussing cigarette smoking and medical care subsidies, Browning (pp. 12–13) explains,

> If the fiscal externality in the cigarette market is associated with excessive cigarette smoking and there is a welfare cost, it is simply a reflection of the welfare cost produced by the medical care subsidy. There is no "new" inefficiency produced by the fiscal externality. Fiscal externalities, therefore, do not necessarily imply any inefficiency. If there is inefficiency associated with the fiscal externality, it reflects the distorting effect of the policy (here, the medical care subsidy) that creates the fiscal externality. Fiscal externalities themselves do not cause any new inefficiency in resource allocation.

This is an important perspective that must be considered and addressed by gambling researchers, especially as researchers call for more government support of pathological gambling treatment and prevention expenditures.

13.5.5 Modeling Transfers

We can illustrate the analysis of transfers in bad debts, bailouts, or government expenditures by using people's wealth on the axes of a PPF model as in Fig. 13.3.[42] The PPF represents the possible distributions of wealth of $100.[43] As before, all points on the PPF are efficient though both members of society might not consider them all equitable or "fair." Bailout costs, bad debts, and government welfare costs are all transfers of wealth, from concerned family members, the bank, and taxpayers to the pathological gambler in question. In each case the person losing money is

---

[42] Alternatively, one could simply point out that if tax revenues, political contributions, etc. are not social costs, then certainly abused dollars, bad debts, and bailout costs cannot be.

[43] The straight line PPF indicates that the "good," i.e., money, is perfectly shiftable between individuals. In production cases, PPFs are bowed, as explained in the Appendix.

Fig. 13.3 Wealth transfer

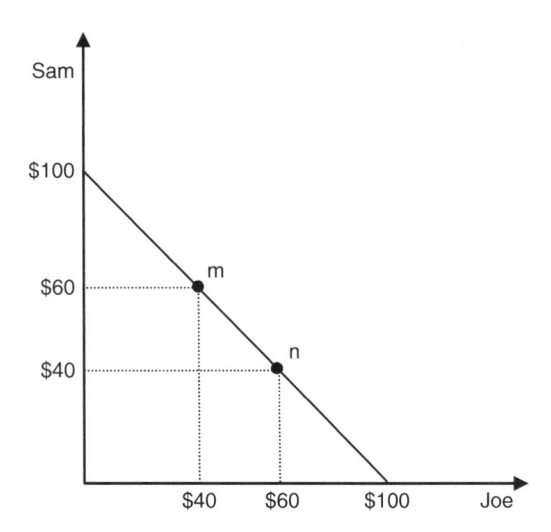

likely to be unhappy with the transaction but it is also a net benefit to the recipient whether or not he suffers from pathological behavior.[44]

Assume we are initially at point *m* in Fig. 13.3. Now suppose Joe is a pathological gambler and that he (1) receives a $20 "bailout" from his father Sam, (2) defaults on a $20 loan from Sam the banker, (3) receives a $20 check from the government financed by Sam's taxes, or (4) steals $20 from Sam's wallet. Each case can be represented by movement from point *m* to *n*. None of the cases is a decrease in social wealth. Rather, they are transfers from Sam to Joe.

An important *caveat* must be reiterated. There might be social costs associated with the above transfers that are unrelated to the size of the transfer. An example is the psychic cost of having to provide a bailout to a relative. A bailout, one might argue, is made under duress. A person might face a prison term if owed money is not paid to a lender. Consider a case where individual *g* is a pathological gambler who will receive either a bailout or a prison sentence, and individual *b* is the concerned family member who has the choice of bailing out *g* or letting him go to prison. Let the individuals' utility functions be $U_g = U(C, G, P, U_b, B, Z)$ and $U_b = U(C, U_g, B, Z)$, where *C* represents consumption, *G* is gambling, *P* is prison time, *B* is a bailout, and *Z* is other arguments affecting utility. We might legitimately expect the following: $\delta U_g/\delta G > 0$, and $\delta U_g/\delta P$, $\delta U_g/\delta B$, $\delta U_b/\delta B < 0$. Both the prison term and bailout have a negative psychic effect on both individuals. If the prison sentence has a greater total negative effect than the bailout, then *b* will bailout *g*. This *is* a choice.

Giving a birthday gift, on the other hand, is usually a choice not made under duress. We might expect both giving and receiving a birthday gift to increase utility

---

[44]This discussion ignores a potential social cost associated with administering wealth transfers. With government transfer payments, for example, there is often a cost to collecting (and avoiding) the taxes. These are social costs of taxation.

though it need not. The recipient might feel that now he or she owes the giver. The giver might feel that he or she was somehow compelled or obligated to give in the first place. Such a transfer might have either positive or negative psychic connotations. The same is true of any wealth transfer.

It should be noted that the redistribution of wealth caused by gambling is often very important in policy deliberations. The suffering of the families of pathological gamblers is cause for serious concern, but it is important to recognize that neither the gambler's losses nor the transfers of wealth that they prompt are social costs. More importantly, using the amount of wealth transferred as a result of pathological gambling as a measure of social costs, and the addition of these amounts to "real" social costs, is adding apples and oranges. The resulting sum is meaningless.

13.5.6 Industry Cannibalization

"Industry cannibalization" is the term used by many researchers to describe the negative effects gambling establishments have on neighboring businesses. When casinos open in a particular town, sales at nearby restaurants and other entertainment firms may fall. This consequence of casino introduction is considered by many to be a social cost. Adherents to this view argue that any positive economic effects of casinos are offset by losses to other industries, so net economic growth is unlikely. Refer to Sect. 4.1 for a complete discussion of this issue. Generally, we can view "cannibalization" as a normal activity within market economies.

13.5.7 Money Outflow

Somewhat less common than the other alleged social costs is the argument that monetary outflows represent social costs. Political arguments and common sense seem to dictate that the introduction of gambling into a region or a state can be economically beneficial only if the introduction brings about a net inflow of money. The complementary argument is that money outflow from a region reduces the wealth in the region. As with "industry cannibalization" this issue was discussed in Chap. 4 in the context of economic development. The concern of money outflow can be discounted because consumers do not pay for something unless they expect the value of what they receive to be higher than the price they pay.

13.5.8 Productivity Losses

Most researchers allege that pathological gamblers create social losses because their gambling affects their jobs. They may become less productive on the job, miss work, or become unemployed as a result of their gambling problem. Thompson, Gazel, and Rickman (1997) estimate costs of lost work hours, unemployment compensation, and lost productivity from unemployment at $2,941 (see Table 13.3). Grinols and Mustard (2001), Grinols (2004), and Single et al. (2003, Sect. 4.4), also count productivity losses as social costs. Other authors have argued that such costs are internalized because the costs fall upon one of the parties of the labor contract (e.g., Eadington 2003; Walker 2003; Walker and Barnett 1999). If a worker's productivity falls or if he fails to show up to work, either the employer or the employee is the residual claimant to the loss, the "stolen wages" to which Thompson, Gazel, and Rickman (1999) refer. There is no "social" aspect to this. If the employer chooses, he or she may reduce the wages paid to the worker in the proportion of missed hours. Alternatively, he or she may fire the worker and replace him or her with someone else who offers a higher marginal product. If the employer chooses not to take action against the worker, the employer incurs the cost of the worker shirking. In either case, there is no externality to outside parties. McCormick (1998, 8) provides a useful explanation:

> Imagine a person spends considerable time playing video poker, so much so that this person loses his or her job and has to seek a lower paying, less demanding position. Emphatically, the lost wages are not an uncompensated social cost. The individual directly bears these costs and still plays the games, then the individual feels all the consequences of his or her actions. In this case, there can be no welfare improvement from limiting this person's access to video poker games. This is true even if other people were depending on the gambler to supply them with income. While indeed it might be sad and a deep personal tragedy, it was a decision made by the individual and one for which, in classical economics, there is no gain from government intervention.

13.5.9 Theft

From the discussion above, theft is a transfer of wealth, and therefore does not qualify as a social cost.

13.6 Conclusion

Although there are bound to be new claims of negative effects as social costs, most of these effects appear to be easy to classify given a definition of social cost. Using the economics definition described in Sect. 13.2 we can concisely explain why many of the alleged social costs are "bad effects" that may be associated with pathological gambling but not true social costs or reductions in societal wealth. Table 13.4 summarizes this information.

Items (4) and (12) in Table 13.4 require additional comments. Suicide and divorce are obviously serious personal tragedies that affect other people. These can technically be considered to be "internalized" to the people involved. In the case of divorce, it is possible that it improves the situation for the couple. But it could be the case that the marriage may not have turned bad in the absence of the gambling

13.6 Conclusion

Table 13.4 Alleged "social costs" of gambling

Alleged social cost	Economic perspective
(1) Income lost from missed work	Costs borne by gambler
(2) Decreased productivity on the job	("internalized")
(3) Depression and physical illness related to stress	
(4) Increased suicide attempts	
(5) Bailout costs	Transfers or pecuniary externalities
(6) Unrecovered loans to pathological gamblers	
(7) Unpaid debts and bankruptcies	
(8) Higher insurance premiums resulting from pathological gambler-caused fraud	
(9) Corruption of public officials	
(10) Strain on public services	
(11) Industry cannibalization	
(12) Divorces caused by gambling	Value judgment

Source: Walker and Barnett (1999). Used with permission from Springer

problem. Nevertheless, both of these unfortunate actions may be associated with disordered gambling. However, it would be extremely difficult to estimate monetary values for them.

Using the economics paradigm for defining social costs, it is likely that the typical social cost estimate grossly overestimates the true social costs of pathological gambling. For example, the Thompson, Gazel, and Rickman (1997) estimate of social costs (per pathological gambler per year) must be reduced from $9,469 to $2,974 (Walker and Barnett 1999). However, even if researchers were to accept the economic perspective on social cost, there are remaining complications in performing social cost estimates. Some of these issues are addressed in the next chapter.

Even after defining "social costs," we are still left with the question, "Why does this matter?" Experience has shown that in the absence of an explicit definition of social cost researchers use ad hoc methodologies in estimating costs. Many such estimates have been arbitrary and meaningless. Although a welfare economics methodology is not the only one, it has precedence and provides a framework by which existing and forthcoming cost–benefit analyses may be compared. This perspective may give researchers a different, valuable perspective on the varieties of negative consequences from pathological gambling.

Chapter 14
Issues in Social Cost Analysis

14.1 Introduction

In the previous chapter, I explained a mainstream economics definition of "social cost" and how it could be applied in cost–benefit analyses of gambling. Throughout the chapter, potential pitfalls of cost–benefit analyses are indicated by way of specific examples from previous studies. Cost–benefit analyses have garnered a significant amount of attention from media, industry, government, and researchers. Yet, aside from the fundamental problem of defining social cost, performing such studies in any meaningful and useful way is surprisingly difficult to do. In this chapter, we examine different issues that complicate social cost analysis. This chapter complements the previous one, as it raises some new issues or emphasizes issues only mentioned in Chap. 13.

There are several possible explanations of the low quality and rather confused nature of social cost research. First and perhaps foremost, this is a new area of research. As a result, one should not expect complete agreement among researchers. Second, contributors to the literature have a surprisingly wide array of academic backgrounds in economics, law, medicine, political science, psychology/psychiatry, public administration, sociology, and even architecture. We would expect different researchers to approach the social cost issue in different ways. This variety is important because gambling research is by its nature interdisciplinary. But problems can develop when people step outside their areas of expertise. Aside from this, with so many different backgrounds, agreement on any particular issue is unlikely.

Finally, a possible indicator or perhaps source of confusion in the literature is the type of redundant jargon one finds in the social cost literature. The terminology just to

---

The material in this chapter is based on Walker DM. 2003. Methodological issues in the social cost of gambling studies. *Journal of Gambling Studies* 19(2): 149–184. Used with permission from Springer. Walker DM. 2007. Problems with quantifying the social costs and benefits of gambling. *American Journal of Economics and Sociology* 66(3): 609–645. Used with permission from John Wiley & Sons.

describe "costs" is surprisingly vast including terms like private and social, internal and external, direct and indirect, harms and costs, intangible and tangible, external costs and externalities, and pecuniary and technological externalities. Do we really need so many different terms to describe the negative effects of pathological gambling?[1] In addition to confusion surrounding costs, the psychology literature has evolving terminology to describe gambling problems. The terms used to describe such behavior include disordered gambling, problem gambling, pathological gambling, probable pathological gambling, compulsive gambling, and addictive gambling. While these terms all refer to problematic gambling behavior, there are different levels of the affliction. This disagreement on the nomenclature, coupled with different levels of problem gambling, makes the estimation of social costs even more difficult.

All of the above issues will abate as the research matures. The remainder of this chapter examines some longer term, more substantive concerns related to social cost research. Section 14.2 discusses some of the problems in attributing costs to gambling behavior and measuring the costs. In Sect. 14.3, I discuss different methodological perspectives on social costs. Then in Sect. 14.4 I discuss several potential social costs of gambling that have not been identified or measured in previous research. Section 14.5 concludes the chapter.

14.2 Problems Estimating Social Cost Values

Despite numerous attempts to estimate the social costs from casino gambling in different countries, there are serious problems in this line of research that have not been adequately addressed. In some cases, these problems are so serious as to completely invalidate the results of many social cost studies. Although there may not be immediate solutions to these problems, researchers should at least recognize these hurdles in their studies so that policymakers and voters can be better informed. In recent years, I believe that the quality of research has increased in these regards, mainly because we see fewer attempts at estimating a monetary value of social costs of gambling. Fewer studies of this type is actually an improvement because, I believe, developing a legitimate monetary estimate of social costs is not possible.[2]

14.2.1 Counterfactual Scenario

When considering the costs (or benefits) associated with gambling and gambling behavior, it is important to consider the counterfactual scenario. That is, we must be

---

[1] Part of the explanation for this, of course, is that few authors define "cost."
[2] The recent comprehensive Canadian study by Humphreys et al. (2011) also takes this view. The study examines negative social impacts from gambling, but does not attempt to provide monetary estimates for the unmeasurable.

mindful of what otherwise would have happened.[3] In the social costs case, we must consider the magnitude of such costs if casinos were not legal. Gamblers can travel to casinos outside their city, state, region, or country. Illegal and Internet gambling may be available. In any case, legalizing casinos in the home area may not significantly affect the social costs that accrue to that region.

Even if we accept this argument, measuring the social costs in the counterfactual may be difficult. One way to do this would be to identify similar regions that do not have casino gambling. Of course, such a comparison must be done carefully to control for as many societal factors as possible.

As an example, consider casinos and crime. A variety of studies have found results that link casinos to increases in the crime rates. (This issue will be discussed in Chap. 16.) For the increased crime rate to be appropriately attributable to casinos, it is not enough to just show that the crime rate went up near casinos. A researcher would need to show that the crime rate went up relative to what it would have had some other tourist business been introduced instead of the casino. This difference would correctly isolate the *casino tourism* effect on crime from a *general tourism* effect on crime.

As another example of the counterfactual problem, consider the casino industry's impacts on employment. The American Gaming Association's *State of the States* is an annual report that details each state's casino industry, taxes paid to state government, revenues, and employment. In Missouri in 2011, for example, the AGA reported that there were 10,435 people employed at Missouri casinos. But this does not mean that the industry created that many net jobs. It is possible that the industry has expanded at the expense of other industries, so the net number of jobs created is lower. On the other hand, it is also possible that the industry increases economic growth, and perhaps the number of jobs the casino industry has created relative to the counterfactual is *more than* 10,435. The counterfactual may be difficult to determine but it is the relevant baseline by which to analyze the benefits and costs of casinos.

14.2.2 Comorbidity

Even after reconsidering existing social cost estimates, it is important to consider the matter of the net or marginal contribution of pathological gambling to socially undesirable behavior. Investigators usually observe that pathological gamblers have legal problems, often require public assistance in the form of various kinds of welfare payments, and may require more medical services than other individuals.[4]

---

[3] See Collins and Lapsley (2003), Eadington (2003), Grinols (2004), and Walker (2007).
[4] For example, see Grinols (2004), Grinols and Omorov (1996), and Thompson, Gazel, and Rickman (1997).

These observations are easily verified but prove little. As most authors would acknowledge, simply observing that gambling is correlated with such problems does not imply that gambling causes them. If gambling were not an option, a person who is predisposed to a pathological disorder may manifest his disorder in other destructive ways. More importantly, if pathological gambling is simply a symptom of some more basic disorder, it is the more basic disorder rather than gambling itself that is the underlying cause of the adverse consequences and social costs of the pathological gambling. Most researchers (e.g., Grinols 2004; Grinols and Mustard 2001; Thompson, Gazel, and Rickman 1997) simply attribute all of the costs to gambling. A mechanism is needed to allocate the harm among coexisting disorders, yet most authors ignore this issue.

In comorbidity cases pathological gambling may make little or no marginal contribution to the legal problems, bankruptcy, need for public assistance, or high medical care costs that often characterize pathological gamblers. Since social cost calculations should include only the marginal contribution that pathological gambling makes to destructive behavior, a determination of whether such behavior is caused by, rather than simply correlated with, pathological gambling is crucial to correctly estimating the social cost of gambling.

In large part, this issue revolves around whether pathological gambling is a primary or a secondary disorder. Shaffer, Hall, and Bilt (1997) have addressed this issue. They note that the DSM-IV (American Psychiatric Association 1994) indicates that "a person meeting all of the criteria for pathological gambling is *not* considered a pathological gambler if he or she also meets the criteria for a Manic Episode, and the Manic Episode is responsible for excessive gambling" (Shaffer, Hall, and Vander Bilt 1997, 72). The authors explain that pathological gambling may be independent of other afflictions or it may be only a reflection of other problems (p. 73).[5] Obviously, if the conditions for pathological gambling are a subset of another affliction or of a combination of other afflictions, then we cannot legitimately attribute all the social costs of pathological gambling to the gambling per se. On the other hand, Ross et al. (2008, Chap. 6) argue that gambling is the "basic" form of addiction.

The study by Petry, Stinson, and Grant (2005) indicates the extent to which pathological gamblers exhibit other behavioral problems. They estimate that 73.2 % of the US pathological gamblers have an alcohol use disorder. The lifetime prevalence rate for drug use disorders among pathological gamblers is 38.1 % and for nicotine dependence it is 48.9 %. Other comorbid conditions include mood disorders (49.6 %), anxiety disorders (41.3 %), and obsessive-compulsive personality disorder (28.5 %)

---

[5] Briggs, Goodin, and Nelson (1996) report results suggesting that alcoholism and pathological gambling are independent addictions. However, as Shaffer, Hall, and Vander Bilt (1997, 72–73) note, "the Briggs et al. study employed a unique subject sample that likely represents the tails of two special self-selected distributions; they also employ a small sample size. Taken collectively, these factors encourage us to view their results as tentative and their conclusions as uncertain."

(Petry, Stinson, and Grant 2005, 569).[6] The study by Westphal and Johnson (2007) provides supporting evidence. Among their study subjects, 77 % with a gambling problem had co-occurring behavioral problems, and 56 % had multiple problems.

Given many pathological gamblers exhibit other disorders, it is difficult if not impossible to accurately estimate the social costs attributable specifically to pathological gambling. As an example, consider a pathological gambler who is also a drug addict and engages in behavior resulting in social costs of $5,000. What proportion of the cost should be attributed to the gambling disorder and to drug use? Although it is critical to deal with this issue *no* social cost study of which I am aware has taken account for comorbid disorders. Instead, researches have simply attributed all the costs to disordered gambling. This results in overestimates of the social costs of disordered gambling.

The counterfactual scenario further complicates this issue. Again consider a drug-addicted pathological gambler. If the person was not a pathological gambler, his behavior from drug use might result in social costs higher or lower than in the case with both disorders. It is theoretically possible that with comorbid disorders a particular disorder might actually decrease social costs compared to the counterfactual. This issue has not been considered in the literature.

The important implication to be drawn from these studies of multiple disorders is that observing a correlation between social problems or socially costly behavior and pathological gambling is not adequate to attribute the social problems to gambling. Both pathological gambling and the probability that one will run afoul of the law may be symptoms of a more basic ("primary") disorder. While this point is obvious to most observers, it is typically (and inappropriately) ignored in estimating the social cost of gambling. Studies which fail to address the causality and marginal contribution issues are likely to overstate the actual social costs of gambling. Social cost estimates for gambling that do not address these issues should be viewed with skepticism, or not be viewed at all.

14.2.3 Surveys on Gambling Losses

Diagnostic/screening instruments like DSM-IV and SOGS typically ask how the person financed his/her gambling and the maximum amount lost gambling in a single day. Blaszczynski et al. (2006, 124) explain that clinicians rely on estimates of gambling losses to identify at-risk gamblers. In addition, such measures can be used to measure the reduction in gambling activity post treatment. Examples of financial questions from the DSM-IV and SOGS are shown in Table 14.1.

Surveys including questions about sources of money and gambling losses have been used to make social cost estimates. Examples include Thompson, Gazel, and Rickman (1997), Thompson and Schwer (2005), and papers used by Grinols (2004) in deriving

---

[6]Thompson, Gazel, and Rickman (1997, 87–88) provide some anecdotal evidence from a survey of Gamblers Anonymous members.

Table 14.1 Financial questions from *DSM-IV* and SOGS screening instruments

Screening instrument	Instrument item
DSM-IV	8. "… has committed illegal acts such as forgery, fraud, theft, or embezzlement to finance gambling."
DSM-IV	10. "… relies on others to provide money to relieve a desperate financial situation caused by gambling."
SOGS	2. "What is the largest amount of money you have ever gambled with on any one day?" Possible responses include the following: I've never gambled; $1 or less; more than $1 but less than $10; more than $10 but less than $100; more than $100 but less than $1,000; more than $1,000 but less than $10,000; more than $10,000.
SOGS	14. "Have you ever borrowed from someone and not paid them back as a result of your gambling?"
SOGS	16a–k. "If you borrowed money to gamble or to pay gambling debts, who or where did you borrow from?" Possible responses include the following: household money; your spouse; other relatives or in-laws; banks, loan companies, or credit unions; credit cards; loan sharks; you cashed in stocks, bonds, or other securities; you sold personal or family property; you borrowed on your checking account (passed bad checks); you have (had) a credit line with a bookie; you have (had) a credit line with a casino.

Sources: American Psychiatric Association (1994, 618) and Lesieur and Blume (1987, 1187)

his social cost of gambling estimate.[7, 8] This practice is problematic for several reasons. First, it is unclear whether respondents understand how to calculate gambling losses. Blaszczynski et al. (2006, 127) explain "without specific instructions regarding how gambling expenditures are to be calculated, participants use different strategies." The obvious problem with this is "different strategies used lead to variations in the expenditures reported and, therefore, cast doubt on the validity of the data and raise questions that there may be potential serious biases regarding gambling expenditures currently reported in the gambling literature" (Blaszczynski et al. 2006, 128).

A second problem is asking survey respondents to accurately identify the source of their gambling money. Keep in mind that such surveys ask problem gamblers who admit to having or who are diagnosed with spending control problems to classify various sources of income used for specific types of expenditures. *Budgets are fungible.* It is difficult or impossible for an individual to unequivocally specify the source of money lost gambling from paycheck, credit card, and borrowing from friends or family. People have several sources of income or money and also many types of expenditure. Even financially responsible individuals may not typically link specific sources of income to specific expenditures.

---

[7] An additional problem with these studies is that they estimate "abused dollars," "bad debts," and "bailouts" and call these social costs.

[8] The survey questions are typically omitted from published papers, so it is difficult to know exactly what questions survey respondents were asked.

Third, any particular person's financial problems may be due to gambling but that is not easy to determine unequivocally.[9] Several examples can illustrate. Suppose a problem gambler buys a car beyond what his budget would allow even if he did not have a serious gambling problem. It is quite possible that in answering or using the DSM-IV or the SOGS criteria, the person will attribute his financial woes to gambling. But who can determine the extent to which the financial woes are due to gambling or a preference for expensive cars? Perhaps the person exhibits financial irresponsibility in many aspects of his life. The screening devices do not distinguish between gambling and other potential causes of financial problems. As a final example, how do the screening devices handle a situation in which a person secures a loan and *then* decides to gamble the money away? The person does not borrow to gamble, but gambles after he has borrowed. In either case the person might have a gambling problem, but these are different situations. How likely is it that the person or the clinician will correctly answer the financial related questions in these situations?

Finally, extrapolating from the experience of the most serious problem gamblers to the general population as is often done is inappropriate (Walker and Barnett 1999). Thompson, Gazel, and Rickman (1997), Thompson and Schwer (2005), and Grinols (2004) base their estimates in part on survey responses by Gamblers Anonymous members. These are arguably the most serious cases and are not representative of the general population of pathological gamblers.

The point here is that financial woes and problem gambling may be correlated, but that does not indicate a causal relationship that is implied in the diagnostic instruments or in social cost studies that rely on surveys of problem gamblers. This is a critical issue that has not yet been adequately addressed in the literature.

14.3 Different Approaches to Social Costs

The methodology in the previous chapter comes from a welfare economic perspective. This approach has garnered a significant amount of criticism. Particularly objectionable to many noneconomists is the argument that transfers, including theft, are not social costs. Generally the criticisms focus on the fact that the economic perspective fails to count as costs many of the negative effects that researchers and practitioners believe are important to include (Hayward and Colman 2004; Thompson, Gazel, and Rickman 1999). At the other extreme, however, Thompson, Gazel, and Rickman (1997) and Grinols (2004) count as a social cost almost anything negative that can be remotely linked to gambling. The differences in opinion on these issues are illustrated by Thompson, Gazel, and Rickman (1999) and Walker (2003).

One of the most interesting things about gambling research is that it is interdisciplinary. As a result one finds a variety of discipline-based approaches to the social cost problem. Several conferences have been dedicated to sorting out these social

---

[9]Obviously there will be cases where gambling is a clear problem. But it may doubtful that irresponsible gamblers are otherwise financially responsible.

cost issues, with a goal of developing a "gold standard" for social cost research. These conferences include the International Symposium on the Economic and Social Impacts of Gambling (Whistler, September 2000) and the Fifth Annual Alberta Conference on Gambling Research (Banff, April 2006).[10] At both conferences, researchers from a variety of disciplines and perspectives met to discuss the appropriate way to identify and measure the socioeconomic effects of gambling. Little progress seems to have been made, in terms of agreeing on the appropriate methodology. As Wynne and Shaffer (2003, 120) explain,

> While the ultimate goal of the Whistler Symposium was to derive "best practice guidelines" for conducting future gambling socioeconomic impact studies, participants rapidly realized this was an overly ambitious expectation that would not be achieved. Moreover, the Symposium experience showed that there was little consensus on (a) the most salient philosophical perspective, or conceptual framework, that should underpin research into the social and economic impacts of gambling; (b) definitions of private costs versus social costs attributable to gambling; (c) what costs and benefits should be counted in socioeconomic impact analyses; and (d) the best methods for measuring gambling benefits and costs.

It should be noted that one Canadian study attempted to develop a "gold standard" approach for analyzing social costs of gambling (Anielski Management Inc. 2008). Although the study examines the relevant issues in some depth, its attempt to move toward a single methodology creates at least as many new measurement problems as it solves.

The three major perspectives represented at Whistler and Banff were cost of illness (Single 2003), economic (Collins and Lapsley 2003; Eadington 2003; Walker 2003), and public health (Korn, Gibbins, and Azmier 2003). Each of these approaches is (briefly) described below.

14.3.1 Cost-of-Illness Approach

One popular mechanism for estimating the costs of problem gambling is based on COI studies that have previously been applied to alcohol and drug abuse. Single (2003) describes these generally while Single et al. (2003, vi) provide a detailed explanation of the approach:

> The impact of substance abuse on the material welfare of a society is estimated by examining the social costs of treatment, prevention, research, law enforcement, and lost productivity plus some measure of the quality of life years lost, relative to a counterfactual scenario in which there is no substance abuse.

As Harwood, Fountain, and Fountain (1999, 631) explain,

> Underlying ... COI [studies] is the premise that an illness or social problem imposes "costs" when resources are redirected as a result of that illness or problem from purposes to which they otherwise would have been devoted, including goods and services and productive time.

---

[10]Papers from both conferences are published. The Whistler papers are in the *Journal of Gambling Studies* (2003, vol. 19). Some papers from Banff were published in Smith, Hodgins, and Williams (2007).

There are other methodologies that are commonly associated with the COI approach. These include the "willingness to pay" and "demographic" approaches (Harwood, Fountain, and Fountain 1999).

The COI approach to problem gambling is useful because it has its foundation in alcohol and drug studies. The application to problem gambling does not require a reinvention of the wheel. In addition, this approach has much in common with the economic perspective. The issue of opportunity cost or the counterfactual scenario is important in both but they differ in how they treat worker productivity and some types of expenditures.

Like the other approaches described below, COI studies are not without criticism (e.g., Kleiman 1999; Reuter 1999). As the name suggests, COI studies are focused on costs, not benefits.

14.3.2 Economic Approach

The approach to social costs discussed in Chap. 13 is representative of the economic approach (also see Collins and Lapsley 2003; Eadington 2003; Walker 2003; Walker and Barnett 1999). This approach has much in common with COI studies. Many of the same "costs" appear in both but there are differences in how they view what should be included as a cost and how costs should be measured.

The economic perspective is concerned with the overall level of aggregate wealth in society. If an action decreases overall wealth, it is a social cost. "Wealth" refers to well-being, not simply material wealth. This approach has been criticized by McGowan (2009) and Thompson, Gazel, and Rickman (1999) among others. Researchers such as Hayward and Colman (2004, 4) have argued that the economic approach ignores certain negative effects of problem gambling. Many of the criticisms are unfounded because they are based on an assumption that "economic" implies "money measurement." This is more a description of accounting than economics.

14.3.3 Public Health Perspective

The public health perspective is perhaps the most general of the three approaches. It is based on the Ottawa Charter (1986) and focuses on prevention, treatment, harm reduction, and quality of life. In terms of gambling, it focuses on how gambling can affect individuals, families, and communities (Korn and Shaffer 1999, 306).

The public health approach does not primarily focus on how to measure costs and benefits but they are an important component of the public health perspective. There are quality-of-life components that defy measurement and it is important for these to be considered along with components that are easier to quantify. In this sense, the public health framework helps to show how the other approaches fit into the big picture.

While there are areas of agreement among the different perspectives, there are also some significant differences. Each approach has its merits and limitations, and each would imply a different approach to measuring the costs and benefits from gambling.

14.3.4 Can a Consensus Be Reached?

It is interesting to consider that even within a particular discipline's approach there can be very different perspectives. Consider the "economic approach," of which I am an advocate, and the similar COI approach. In Chap. 13 we defined social cost as something that reduces the overall wealth (generally defined) in society. Some researchers (e.g., APC 1999; Collins and Lapsley 2003; Single 2003; Single et al. 2003) have based their definition of social costs on that posited by Atkinson and Meade (1974) and Markandya and Pearce (1989). According to these researchers, for a cost to be "private" the actor must have *full knowledge* about the potential costs of consuming the good. For smoking, this definition implies that if the consumer is not "fully informed" about the harm from smoking, he underestimates the harms and chooses to smoke too much. The result, according to these authors, is a social cost, *even if the cost is borne by the smoker himself.*

The Markandya and Pearce (1989) social cost definition ignores the fact that consumers are never fully informed about any of their decisions. For example, when I decide to get into my car and drive to work, I am not fully informed about the chances of being in an accident or my probability of surviving a particular accident. Furthermore, consumers may be likely to overestimate as they are to underestimate the dangers from smoking or gambling.[11] For example, Viscusi and Hakes (2008) find that people tend to *overestimate* the risks of lung cancer and life expectancy losses from smoking. Following the logic of Markandya and Pearce, if a consumer *over*estimates the costs of smoking, he will smoke too *little*. The result is less smoking than is socially optimal. Yet, this possibility is not acknowledged by Markandya and Pearce (1989) or researchers who cite them. The view that unknown or unexpected costs are necessarily social is fraught with potential problems. A careful analysis of the Markandya and Pearce social cost definition should be undertaken since the use of this methodology likely results in a significant overestimate of the social costs of gambling.[12]

---

[11] One could argue that to the extent gamblers are uninformed about the odds of the games they play, they are more likely to overestimate their chances of winning. The majority of lottery players arguably overestimate the chances of winning. After all, 1 in 100 million is hardly distinguishable from zero, yet lottery players relish imagining what they will do with their winnings if theirs is the lucky ticket.

[12] Walker and Kelly (2011) examine the issue in a bit more depth.

14.3 Different Approaches to Social Costs

Unless I misunderstand the Markandya and Pearce approach to social cost, it is very difficult for me to believe that all economists who study gambling could come to an agreement as to the correct way to deal with social costs. But even if that did happen, there are still major differences among the different disciplines that address the social cost issue in their gambling research. Perhaps the best example of this is the economic concept of "rational addiction."

While the treatment of addictions and studies of their prevalence have primarily received attention by psychologists, economists have investigated the rationality of choice over a wide range of human behavior, including that influenced by addictions. Nobel Prize winning economist Gary Becker is largely responsible for the development of economic theory in this area. The framework of the rational addiction model is explained most succinctly in Becker, Grossman, and Murphy (1994, 85). The model considers

> the interaction of past and current consumption in a model with utility-maximizing consumers. The main feature of these models is that past consumption of some goods influences their current consumption by affecting the marginal utility of current and future consumption. Greater past consumption of harmfully addictive goods such as cigarettes stimulates current consumption by increasing the marginal utility of current consumption more than the present value of the marginal harm from future consumption. Therefore, past consumption is reinforcing for addictive goods.

Empirical tests confirm that the models have substantial predictive power.[13]

A central implication of this literature is that prior to becoming addicted to gambling, the decision of whether or not to gamble is a rational choice. This simply means that the person weighs the expected costs and benefits of an action before acting. Then even pathological gambling is a condition that results from rational behavior. Consider that there is a risk element in many decisions that we face daily. When deciding to drive a car, a person may consider that there is a slight risk of death from unforeseen accidents. Likewise, the choice of whether to play casino games includes a slight risk of developing an addiction. But risking addiction is not inconsistent with rationality. The initial choice of whether or not to consume a potentially addictive good is generally a rational decision, as Orphanides and Zervos (1995, 741) explain:

> Addiction results from a time-consistent expected utility maximizing plan. Addiction is voluntary, yet it is not intentional. It is the unintended occasional outcome of experimenting with an addictive good known to provide certain instant pleasure and only probabilistic future harm. Despite the rationality of their decisions, addicts regret their past consumption decisions and are not "happy." Had they correctly assessed their addictive potential, addicts would have acted differently. Had they known, they would never have chosen to become addicted.

---

[13] For a comprehensive discussion of the rational addiction model, see Becker (1996), a collection of his previous papers, including Becker (1992), Becker and Murphy (1988), and Stigler and Becker (1977). Empirical tests of the model can be found in Chaloupka (1991) and Becker, Grossman, and Murphy (1991, 1994). Mobilia (1992a) applies the model to gambling behavior. Smith and Tasnádi (2007) claim to provide a biological foundation for the model, showing that there are conditions under which it is optimal to form a habit (p. 316).

This work alleviates criticisms of earlier rational addiction models that had not accounted for unknown probabilities of developing an addiction. Becker (1992, 121) anticipated the need for such a model:

> Nothing in the analysis of forward-looking utility-maximizing behavior presumes that people know for sure whether they will become habituated or addicted to a substance or activity, although that is sometimes claimed by the critics of this approach. An individual may have considerable uncertainty about whether she would become an alcoholic if she begins to drink regularly. A troubled teenager who begins to experiment with drugs may expect, but not be certain, that his life will begin to straighten out, perhaps because of a good job or marriage, before he becomes addicted. Since these and other choices are made under considerable uncertainty, some persons become addicted simply because events turn out to be less favorable than was reasonable to anticipate—the good job never rescued the drug user. Persons who become addicted because of bad luck may regret their addictions, but that is no more a sign of irrational behavior than is any regret voiced by big losers at a race track that they bet so heavily.

Landsburg (1993, 100–101) supports this view, arguing that medical costs resulting from illegal drug use cannot be considered a social cost. He argues, "an increase in consumer surplus is already net of health costs and lost income. Any such losses would have been reflected in people's willingness to pay for drugs so would have been implicitly accounted for in the original [cost-benefit] calculation." The same argument applies to gambling.

To reiterate, whether or not a person has pathological or compulsive tendencies prior to placing a bet at a casino, the decision to gamble *is* rational prior to developing an addiction. If a person becomes an addict his quality of life may fall in a variety of ways. However, the development of an addiction does not imply that the initial decision to gamble was irrational even if the person regrets the original decision. Since the adverse consequences experienced by a person as a result of his own rational actions cannot be considered a social cost, the reduced quality of life experienced by a gambler who becomes addicted cannot be considered to be a social cost. In the words of Orphanides and Zervos (1995, 752), "when forward-looking expected utility maximizing individuals possess the correct information regarding the distribution of [addictive tendencies], a ban or any other restriction on consumption is never Pareto optimal." Further, to argue that the original decision to gamble was irrational is an example of the "bad-outcome-implies-bad-decision" fallacy discussed by Frank (1988, 72–75).

This perspective on addictive behaviors, especially as it relates to disordered gamblers, is not particularly popular with noneconomists. The economic perspective on addiction is more of a technical argument, whereas most noneconomist researchers who deal with gambling are more interested in the human aspect of disordered gambling—people have real problems, and researchers should try to understand and treat those problems. Aside from definitional and measurement issues, the different disciplines have different goals when they study gambling. This may be one key reason why there is unlikely to be an interdisciplinary consensus on how to deal with social costs.

14.4 Unidentified and Unmeasured Social Costs

Even if one takes a liberal or "inclusive" definition of social costs, most studies have overlooked what are surely quite sizable social costs associated with casinos. In particular, these costs result from the political process by which casinos are legalized and regulated, which may explain why they have been ignored. They do not deal with gamblers and their behavior. Yet, from an economic perspective, these costs are no less real. Since gambling is regulated by government, there are potentially very high social costs associated with the regulation of the industry. Two specific issues are addressed below.

14.4.1 Restriction Effects

A significant social cost can occur as a result of government restriction of casino gambling. The fact that gambling is not universally available means that the government prevents mutually beneficial voluntary transactions from occurring. Even though gamblers face negative expected values from their activity, it must be the case that they expect to benefit with increased utility if they decide to place bets. When individuals are prevented from making what they see as mutually beneficial, voluntary transactions, they are harmed. Producers are also harmed by a restriction of their potential transactions because their profits are lower than they otherwise would have been without the restrictions.

Wright (1995, 52) explains the benefits of moving away from a total ban on casino gambling. It removes economic distortions, including "dead-weight losses, enforcement costs, and incentives to lobby and bribe." Eadington (1996, 6) is another of the researchers who has identified the benefits to consumers of gambling legalization and implicitly the cost to consumers of restrictions on legalized gambling.

Simply put, the restriction of gambling (or any other good or service demanded by consumers) causes a reduction in mutually beneficial voluntary transactions that would have otherwise occurred except for the government restriction. This welfare loss can also be illustrated in the PPF–IC framework developed earlier. In Fig. 14.1, suppose the number and size of casinos in a jurisdiction are restricted from the market equilibrium of q_e to level q_2. As a result, the mix of goods changes from point *a* to *b* and welfare decreases from that represented on IC_1 to that associated with IC_2.

We can also see that the level of casino gambling expenditures would not normally remain above level q_e. If the current mix of consumption was at point *c*, society would be better off shifting expenditures away from casino gambling toward other goods and services. As a result the society would move to a higher IC.[14]

---

[14] At point *c* the level of casino output has a marginal cost of production that exceeds the marginal benefit of consumption. In this case, the market is oversaturated, and we may expect some casinos to go out of business until spending at casinos falls to point *a*.

Fig. 14.1 Welfare loss from restricting casino gambling

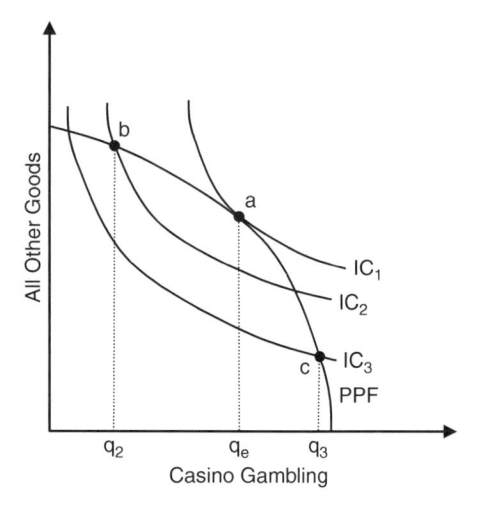

Fig. 14.2 Deadweight loss from a quantity restriction

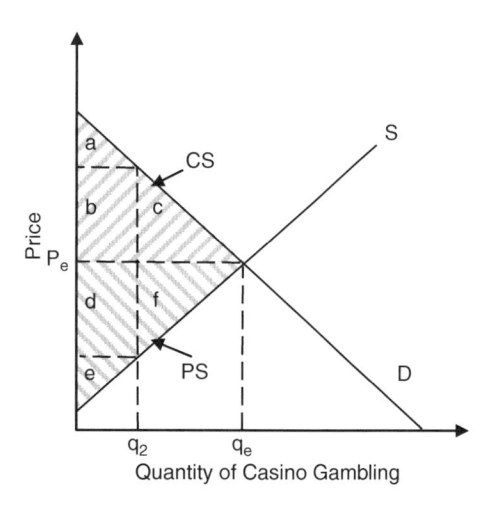

Alternatively, we can show the harm caused by artificial restrictions on markets by considering the CS and PS lost as a result of the restrictions on casinos.[15] For each transaction or bet that does not occur as a result of government restrictions, the CS and PS lost represents the social cost of the government restriction. Figure 14.2 illustrates CS and PS and an artificial restriction on quantity in the casino market.

---

[15] The Australian Productivity Commission report (1999, Appendix C) provides a detailed discussion of the CS derived from gambling.

14.4 Unidentified and Unmeasured Social Costs

As before, CS and PS are indicated by the shaded areas. CS is labeled $a+b+c$ and PS is labeled $d+e+f$. If government restricts the quantity of casino gambling from q_e to q_2, then the CS and PS areas become smaller. Specifically, CS falls by $b+c$ and PS falls by $d+f$. The social cost from the lost transactions is the difference between the social surplus at q_e and q_2 or area $c+f$. This is called a "deadweight loss" by economists. It represents a loss to one or more parties that is not offset by gains to some other party.

In the case of the casino industry and in the context of Fig. 14.2, areas $b+d$ will likely go to the casino industry. Since the quantity of casinos is typically restricted, the firms in the industry can expect economic profits or a rate of profit above the average level. Because the supply of casinos is restricted, there is less competition in the market than would occur otherwise. As a result, casinos can charge above market prices. These higher prices may be manifested in higher hotel rates, more expensive restaurants, or even worse odds/payouts in casino games. These profits are represented by areas $b+d$, the difference between what consumers pay and the sellers' cost of production. The point is that there will be a transfer of CS to producers in the amount b so that total PS will be $b+d+e$ when a government restriction is imposed.[16]

Although the restriction on casinos causes a welfare loss to society in PS and CS lost, casino suppliers may actually prefer the limitation on the number of casinos to a free market. They receive a transfer from consumers (b). If $b>f$ then the casinos actually benefit from the restriction.[17] Governments may prefer the regulated quantity as well since they have the power to tax. They may charge the casinos fees and taxes, reducing the benefits to casinos. Obviously if taxes and permit fees are too high (greater than $b-f$ in Fig. 14.2) the casinos would prefer a free market to regulation.

One possible reason that gambling researchers have ignored the cost of restricting gambling is that authors rarely acknowledge the benefits of gambling to consumers. Consumer transactions are ignored. The basic point here is that the competitive market absent of artificial government limitations would bring about the social welfare maximizing level of casino gambling capacity. To some extent, this topic speaks to the counterfactual scenario issue. In the absence of *casino bans*, consumers and producers may be better off. We must consider the social costs of banning products that consumers would like to consume. When these are considered they will balance, to some extent, the marginal social costs associated with casino legalization.

Another type of social cost related to banning casinos is that it may result in individuals seeking illegal gambling venues. It is well known that the illegal status of certain drugs pushes consumers to the black market. When markets are illegal,

---

[16] The discussion here is limited because what happens with the lost surplus depends on the specifics of the market.

[17] One way of thinking about this is that area f represents profit lost from consumers who now do not gamble; area b represents the higher prices that can be charged to the remaining customers.

consumers cannot be as certain of the quality of goods and have no legal recourse if the product is faulty or if they are cheated. Similarly, if casinos are illegal and as a result individuals engage in illegal forms of gambling, the consumers are worse off relative to having legal gambling options. Since the vendors are unregulated, consumers have less assurance that the games are being operated properly. Obviously it is difficult to know the volume of illegal gambling, but despite attempts by the federal government to prohibit online gambling, many people still do it.

14.4.2 Lobbying

Another significant cost related to casino gambling and legalized gambling in general has to do with the legalization process itself. There is an incentive for wasteful lobbying in two related cases. First, lobbying will occur by both casino advocates and opponents over the legalization of casinos in new jurisdictions. Second, lobbying can be expected by prospective casino operators vying for permits where casinos are legal.

The mere facts that there is a government ban on gambling and that government policy can be influenced create incentives to engage in socially wasteful behavior. Specifically, the effort by opponents and proponents of legalized gambling to influence government policy constitutes a social cost because resources would have been used to produce goods and services. This social cost is the result of "rent-seeking behavior" and is expected given the legal framework within which gambling is controlled. Tollison describes rent-seeking behavior and provides a useful example illustrating why it is the *institutional framework* in which gambling is legalized that is the source of this social cost:

> Consider a simple example in which the king wishes to grant a monopoly right in the production of playing cards. In this case artificial scarcity is created by the state, and as a consequence, monopoly rents are present to be captured by monopolists who seek the king's favor. Normally, these rents are thought of as transfers from playing card consumers to the card monopolist. Yet in the example, this can only be the case if the aspiring monopolists employ no real resources to compete for the monopoly rents. To the extent that real resources are spent to capture monopoly rents in such ways as lobbying, these expenditures create no value from a social point of view. *It is this activity of wasting resources in competing for artificially contrived transfers that is called rent seeking. If an incipient monopolist hires a lawyer to lobby the king for the monopoly right, the opportunity cost of this lawyer (e.g., the contracts that he does not write while engaged in lobbying) is a social cost of the monopolization process.* (Tollison 1982, 577–578; italics added)

Johnson (1991, 336) stresses the government role in rent-seeking behavior:

> The most serious rent seeking is caused by government, because only government has the power to create and enforce monopoly powers and to create and finance a system of special privileges without the possibility of competition eroding the values of these monopoly powers or special privileges.

14.4 Unidentified and Unmeasured Social Costs

Since the casino industry is typically not perfectly competitive due to government restrictions, a particular casino may expect a level of profits above the normal level.[18] Based on Tullock's discussion (1967, 231) the maximum rent-seeking expenditures by a prospective casino owner would be the subjective risk-adjusted net present value of the future stream of profits for that casino.[19] The total rent-seeking expenditures of all potential gaming industry firms could be very large.

The opponents of casinos may also use resources in attempts to prevent legalization. Opponents may include other gambling or entertainment industries, restaurants, hotels, and other firms even in other jurisdictions. Firms that fear being "cannibalized" by casinos would be willing to sacrifice up to the risk-adjusted present value of their expected losses from having nearby casinos in an effort to prevent legalization.[20] As with the gambling proponents, the sum of these expenditures could be quite sizable.

The rent-seeking lobbying for a particular legislative proposal is a sunk cost that cannot be retrieved. We would expect a sizable amount of rent-seeking expenditures each time a legalization proposal is considered. The social costs caused simply as the result of the gambling legalization process could be large. Tullock (1967, 230) explains,

> Transfers themselves cost society nothing, but for the people engaging in them they are just like any other activity, and this means that large amounts of resources may be invested in attempting to make or prevent transfers. These largely offsetting commitments of resources are totally wasted from the standpoint of society as a whole.

Both Tullock (1967, 228) and Krueger (1974, 291) suggest that measurement of these social costs would be complicated. Tullock explains, "the potential returns are large, and it would be quite surprising if the investment was not also sizable."

It is critical to understand that any money paid directly to politicians in lobbying efforts is simply a transfer.[21] The social cost of lobbying comes from the hired lobbyists and lawyers whose efforts are aimed at promoting or fighting gambling legislation. These activities are socially costly because these individuals could be working in some productive capacity, not just in attempting to secure the government's favor.

It is useful to consider the level of political contributions by the gaming industry shown in Table 14.2. Although the contributions themselves are transfers and do not represent social costs, it is likely that there is a positive relationship between the level of contributions and the social costs associated with lobbying.

Even after casinos are legalized, local governments may regulate the number, size, types, location, and ownership of potential gambling establishments. This regulation creates an incentive for the potential owners to compete for the

---

[18] This "normal level" of profit, as well as the difference between economic and accounting profit, is explained in any intermediate microeconomics text.

[19] The prospective gaming firm adjusts its willingness to lobby based on its perception of the likelihood of legalization or securing an operation permit.

[20] As in the case of the proponents, this ignores the expenditures by parties whose gains or losses are not measured in terms of expected profit changes. An example of such an opponent might be a religious organization.

[21] See Mueller (1989, 231) or Johnson (1991, 336–338) for an explanation of this.

Table 14.2 Casino/gambling industry political contributions in the United States

Election cycle	Industry rank	Total contributions (millions)[a]
2012	13	$47.8
2010	33	$14.5
2008	34	$19.0
2006	30	$14.0
2004	38	$14.0
2002	27	$19.1
2000	36	$17.2
1998	38	$9.2
1996	40	$10.4
1994	50	$5.0
1992	71	$2.3
1990	75	$0.9
Total	30	$173.4

[a]Figures are adjusted for inflation, reported in 2012 dollars
Data source: Center for Responsible Politics (opensecrets.org)

limited number of permits. The rent seeking at this stage could potentially exceed that described above since many more firms may be interested in competing for gambling permits once gambling has been legalized. This situation is analogous to Kreuger's (1974, 301) case of import permits in which "an import prohibition might be preferable to a non-prohibitive quota if there is competition for licenses under the quota." Applied to the restriction on the availability of casino gambling, a complete (nonnegotiable) ban on gambling may be preferable to the current process of campaigns and votes on legalization and subsequent competition for casino permits.[22]

Another socially wasteful behavior related to the legalization process is the effort of government bureaucrats and others attempting to be on the receiving side of the contributions and lobbying by the parties discussed above. Krueger (1974, 293) explains this behavior by bureaucrats:

> Successful competitors for government jobs might experience large windfall gains even at their official salaries. However, if the possibility of those gains induces others to expend time, energy, and resources in seeking entry into government services, the activity is competitive for present purposes.

This cost would be difficult to estimate but it could be significant, especially considering how generous the gaming industry is in its contributions to politicians.

14.4.3 Summary of Political Costs

Although previous studies typically focus on the social costs related to pathological gambling, the costs associated with government restrictions, legalization,

---

[22]This depends on the specific legal framework being considered.

regulation, and lobbying are potentially larger than the social costs associated with pathological gambling. Perhaps the focus has been on pathological gambling because the afflicted individuals and their loved ones suffer. On the other hand, costs in the political process seem to be much less "personal" or obvious. Still, researchers wishing to give a complete picture of the economic effects of casino gambling must not ignore the potentially significant social costs due to related political processes.

14.5 Conclusion

In this chapter I discuss three general problems with social cost research. The first is that there are some methodological problems with defining and measuring costs. Comorbidity, in particular, is problematic for developing legitimate cost estimates. Second, since gambling research is interdisciplinary, it will be very unlikely that researchers will ever agree on a "gold standard" for analyzing social costs. Third, most social cost studies have overlooked some potentially large social costs, mainly dealing with politics and regulation of the casino industry.

Together, I think these problems make it very unlikely that the quality of social cost studies will increase dramatically in the near future. However, there have been some key improvements. For example, a recent study in Alberta (Humphreys et al. 2011) seemed to treat costs appropriately, measuring those that could be measured, but just identifying those that could not be measured. Although this may not be as convenient for policymakers, my view is that it better represents what we do and do not understand about social costs.

If researchers continue to offer social cost estimates, they should estimate costs that are measurable (police, court, incarceration, and therapy costs). But for other costs such as psychic costs that cannot be reasonably measured, or for negative effects that are not social costs such as pecuniary externalities, let us identify them without providing spurious empirical estimates. Offering methodologically flawed cost estimates does not improve our understanding nor does it promote sound policy.

At Banff in 2006 I was advocating for trying to adopt a single social cost methodology, consistent with that presented in Chap. 13, initially explained in Walker and Barnett (1999). Since Banff, I am more convinced that it is simply not possible to effectively estimate the social costs associated with disordered gambling. There are too many complications and too many arbitrary assumptions necessary to provide such estimates.

Policymakers and the press are still interested in gambling research, especially related to the social costs and benefits of gambling. Simple measures, like money values for social costs or benefits, or prevalence estimates for disordered gambling are easily misinterpreted. When researchers provide these data, readers of the data are not likely to be aware of the controversies involved in creating the data. In areas where research is still quite primitive, perhaps *no* data would be better than flawed data. For researchers such estimates are important to replicate and debate. This is part of the process of scientific development. If policymakers wish to utilize whatever data are available, researchers should do a better job at highlighting the potential flaws or controversies in their research.

Moving forward, I expect the interest in social cost of gambling studies to decrease. After all, the political debate over land-based casinos is largely over. With over 1,000 casinos in the United States, the monetary value of the social costs of gambling may not be relevant for policy decisions anymore. If researchers do continue to examine these issues, the most fruitful research focus may be on incremental changes to gambling regulation. Since casinos are widely legal, policy changes could now be focused on harm reduction. A cost–benefit analysis of such policy changes could be valuable. If so, the ongoing debate of social costs will be informative and valuable.

Chapter 15
Is Gambling an "Unproductive" Activity?

15.1 Introduction

Among the criticisms of gambling and the casino industry is the claim that gambling is a waste of time, or worse a "directly unproductive profit-seeking" (DUP) activity. Clearly, gambling is a form of entertainment, like golf, tennis, snow skiing, or watching television and movies. Some gamblers may develop a gambling problem, and we should be concerned with that. But it is inappropriate to classify gambling by professionals, for example, as a wasteful activity.

In this brief chapter we examine the claim that some gambling is unproductive, focusing on the relevant economics literature.

15.2 The Claims

The "gambling is a wasteful activity" argument has been made by Grinols (1994a, 2004), Grinols and Mustard (2000), Grinols and Omorov (1996), Kindt (1994), and Thompson and Schwer (2005). For example, Thompson and Schwer (2005, 64) demonstrate a questionable understanding of why people gamble:

> Some economists will argue that there is no economic gain from gambling activity as it represents only a neutral exercise in exchanging money from one set of hands to another. Indeed, as no product is created to add wealth to society, the costs of the exchange (time and energy of players, dealers, and other casino employees) represent a net economic loss for society.

The authors do not claim to hold this view but suggest that "some economists" do. But Thompson and Schwer do not criticize the statement. They could have

---

The material in this chapter is based on Walker DM. 2001. Is professional gambling a directly unproductive profit-seeking (DUP) activity? *International Gambling Studies* 1: 177–183. Used with permission from Taylor & Francis.

pointed out, for example, that this is the same thing that happens when someone pays to attend a football game or to enter a movie theater. They could have explained that no one would voluntarily "redistribute" his or her income to someone else if there was not *some* benefit to giving up the money. This is true even in the case of donating money to a church or other charity. The fact that Thompson and Schwer (2005) present this view without questioning it suggests that they are sympathetic to the argument. They attribute the "gambling is unproductive" perspective to Paul Samuelson (1976). Indeed, their paper is named after Samuelson's words "beyond the limits of recreation."

There are numerous other examples of this perspective in the literature, although they are all due to a small number of researchers who seem to consistently argue that casino gambling is unambiguously harmful. For example, Grinols and Omorov (1996, 50) write, "Economists have long known that for many gamblers and those who provide them gambling services, gambling is in a class of activities called [DUP activities]." Yet they provide no citations to support this "long known" view. Grinols and Omorov do quote Bhagwati, Brecher, and Srinivasan (1984, 292) who define DUP activities as

> ways of making a profit (i.e., income) by undertaking activities which are directly unproductive; that is, they yield pecuniary returns but produce neither goods nor services that enter a conventional utility function directly nor intermediate inputs into such goods and services.

From this definition Grinols and Omorov (1996, 50) argue, "an individual who does not gamble for utility value, but to acquire money engages in income-reducing directly unproductive activity."[1] Grinols and Mustard (2000, 224) make the same argument and give an example of when an individual "quits his job to earn a living as a professional blackjack or poker player, gambling for money and not for enjoyment, [and] reduces national income by his lost production."

Although the professional gambler represents a very small proportion of all gamblers, it is informative to analyze these claims in detail because the conclusions can be more generally applied to the claims about nonprofessional disordered gamblers and their reduced work productivity.

15.3 Samuelson's *Economics* Text

The apparent source of the idea that professional gambling may be a DUP activity is an economics principles textbook. Many antigambling activists selectively quote from a 1976 edition of Samuelson's famous *Economics*. The specific passage describes an economic case against gambling: it "creates no new money or goods," and "when pursued beyond the limits of recreation ... gambling subtracts from the

---

[1] Marfels (1998, 416) provides a valid but brief attack on Grinols and Omorov's interpretation of DUP activities.

national income" (Samuelson 1976, 425).[2] In a nutshell, the argument is that some people quit their widget-production jobs to become professional gamblers. If they do not enjoy gambling, then from society's perspective, they are producing nothing of value. The net cost of this to society is the value of the widgets not produced, and gross domestic product (GDP) is lower.[3] Grinols and Kindt consistently use this DUP argument in arguing that casino gambling is harmful to society.

It is unclear why researchers who quote this passage do not report other relevant material. For example, in the paragraph immediately preceding that quoted by Kindt, Grinols et al., Samuelson writes:

> Why is gambling considered such a bad thing? Part of the reason, *perhaps the most important part*, lies in the field of morals, ethics, and religion; upon these the economist as such is not qualified to pass final judgment. (1976, 425, emphasis added)

On the very next page, as a footnote to his discussion, Samuelson explains:

> The astute reader will note ... the case for prohibiting gambling must rest on extraneous ethical or religious grounds; or must be withdrawn; or must be based on the notion that society knows better than individuals what is truly good for them; or must be based on the notion that we are all imperfect beings who wish in the long run that we were not free to yield to short-run temptations. Some political economists feel that moderate gambling might be converted into socially useful channels. (1976, 426, note 7)

After reading more of the context of the popular quotation, one wonders why researchers resort to making a selective reference to an old principles textbook in an attempt to convince readers that gambling is "bad." Perhaps it is an attempt to appeal to authority, as Samuelson is a Nobel Laureate.

Later editions of Samuelson's *Economics* have a coauthor. The discussion on gambling in the 17th edition, for example (Samuelson and Nordhaus 2001, 208–209), retains a negative flavor, arguing that the activity produces nothing tangible and is "irrational." When I asked Nordhaus about the negative tone about gambling in *Economics* and I suggested that consumers actually do get utility from gambling, he replied, "You make several valid points." However, he argues that there are fundamental differences between "cocaine and compulsive gambling and ice cream and tennis shoes" (Nordhaus 2002).

In any case, Samuelson is not the only famous economist to have written about gambling. For example, Gary Becker (1992 Nobel Laureate) published a *Business Week* magazine article titled, "Gambling's Advocates are Right—But for the Wrong Reasons," in which he writes, "I support this trend toward legalizing gambling, although my reasoning has little to do with revenues .... It would enable the many people who wish to place a bet to do so without patronizing illegal establishments and facilities controlled by criminals" (Becker and Becker 1997, 45).

---

[2]This passage has been cited or quoted by Grinols (1994b, 8; 1995, 8), Grinols and Mustard (2000, 224), Grinols and Omorov (1996, 50), Kindt (1995, 567; 2001, 19), and Thompson and Schwer (2005, 64).

[3]GDP refers to the value of goods and services produced in the economy.

15.4 Why Gambling Is Not a DUP Activity

There are numerous problems with the idea that gambling may constitute a DUP activity. One can sympathize with Ignatin and Smith (1976, 75), who write, "it is difficult to understand why economists, who believe that gamblers must lose, do not infer that the act of gambling must, therefore, provide utility." Microeconomic theory suggests that most gamblers probably receive some level of consumer surplus (CS) from the activity as discussed in Chap. 3.[4]

Grinols and Omorov (1996) and Grinols (1997) do admit that gambling provides utility for many gamblers but say "professional" gambling may constitute a DUP activity. This is an unbelievable claim, especially considering that televised professional poker tournaments have become wildly popular in recent years. Even if the players do not enjoy the games, apparently many television viewers do. It is difficult to understand how poker players, any more than professional athletes or Hollywood actresses, are engaging in DUP.

If we did accept the argument that professional gamblers reduce GDP, then certainly professional boxers and football players would be engaged in DUP, as they physically harm each other in their sports.[5] The whole idea of applying DUP to gambling (even professional gambling) seems silly. People often make choices for which, under an alternative choice, national income might have been higher. Are all such choices "bad" because they decrease national income from some potential maximum?

In terms of the gambler himself, even if he does not "enjoy" gambling, we must assume that all things considered he decides how to best spend his time. Even though he may not enjoy it, his gambling career including the expected return must be preferred to any alternative career path, no matter how much utility he might have received. If he is successful, his income and purchases rise, which would lead to increased utility. If, on the other hand, the professional gambler fails to earn an adequate living, we expect him to turn to some other method of earning a living.[6]

Scitovsky (1986, 192) writes, "the active participants' satisfactions from engaging in sex, social and competitive sports, social games, gambling, etc., depend on the availability of equally active participants as partners; and that kind of interdependence ... is symmetrical." Further, he notes,

> in social activities, like bridge, chess, tennis, football, or gambling, each active participant both needs partners and provides one. In other words, he creates both demand and supply, which complement each other and are mutually offsetting. That explains why most such activities do not go through the market, which, in these cases, only performs the ancillary services of providing the tools, the premises, the training, the bringing together of partners, and occasionally provides a standby professional partner when amateur partners are not available. (p. 192)

---

[4]For more detailed discussions, see ACIL (1999, 60–61) and Crane (2006).
[5]I thank Russell Sobel for these examples.
[6]Consider, as another example, an entrepreneur who starts his own business. If the business fails, of course, the investor is not likely to "enjoy" the experience. Is failed entrepreneurship therefore a DUP activity?

Thus, even in cases when the professional gambler does not enjoy his "career" others may benefit from his choice, thus creating wealth.

15.5 DUP and Rent Seeking

Aside from these problems, a review of the DUP literature from the early 1980s makes it clear that gambling cannot technically be considered a DUP activity. Bhagwati (1982, 1983) and Bhagwati, Brecher, and Srinivasan (1984) reveal that DUP is the general class of activities that includes "rent seeking." Bhagwati (1983, 635) writes, "I call DUP activities the set of phenomena that Tollison et al. call rent seeking."[7] (Rent seeking was explained in Sect. 14.4.2.) In the case of a government-created monopoly, rents are available to a potential monopolist, and interested parties compete to win government favor. This lobbying for the monopoly privilege is rent seeking or DUP. Gambling lacks the characteristics required to classify it as rent seeking, since there is no artificially contrived transfer by government.

Bhagwati (1982, 989, 991) christens the term DUP and explains that while most DUP activities are related to attempts to influence government policies, they "can in principle be government free or exclusively private.[8] Thus, effort and resources may be (legally) expended in getting a share of the 'going' transfer by an economic agent, what may be described as 'altruism seeking'." Given that Bhagwati leaves the door open for the possibility of private DUP activities, does gambling by a professional qualify?

Consider an example that follows directly from Bhagwati's discussion. Suppose a church has announced that it will contribute $1,000 to local charities. The administrators of soup kitchens and shelters might spend time and other resources "lobbying" the church for contributions. This lobbying constitutes DUP, and potential recipients use scarce resources to compete for the transfer.

Is a casino bet by a professional gambler a DUP? No. Casino patrons are not vying for a fixed transfer of wealth. Their transactions with the casinos are bets placed—putting some money at risk on an uncertain event. Even if it is not entertaining for the professional gambler, still it is a private transaction that is mutually beneficial. Each player that walks into the casino has the potential to win, regardless of other players' performance.[9]

---

[7]Tullock (1981, 391, note 2) explains, "Bhagwati is attempting to get the term 'rent-seeking' shifted to 'directly unproductive profit seeking, DUP (pronounced dupe)'. I do not like rent-seeking as a term and would agree that this revision of the language would be an improvement, but I suspect that it is too late to make the change now."

[8]Bhagwati and Srinivasan (1982, 34) also make this point. Bhagwati (1982, 994) and Bhagwati and Srinivasan (1982) explain that in some cases DUP activities may be welfare enhancing.

[9]An exception to this would be playing poker at a casino, where players compete against each other rather than against the casino. In some games (e.g., blackjack) one player's actions can affect other players' performance. A final exception might be a case in which the casino is filled to capacity so that a given player is unable to place bets.

DUP activities are wasteful behavior that is geared at receiving a transfer that is, by nature, *rival*. If one firm receives government consent to become a monopolist, other firms are necessarily excluded from the privilege. If soup kitchen A receives the $1,000 church donation, kitchen B does not. In contrast, my placing a bet at a casino and winning does not preclude other players from also playing, or even making the same bets. Put slightly more formally, in a standard rent seeking/DUP case where n individuals compete for a monopoly right, $n-1$ of the individuals will be unsuccessful. In contrast, if there are n professional gamblers trying to make a living, it is *not* the case that $n-1$ or n minus some number >1 must be unsuccessful. All n gamblers may earn a positive return. Of course, in the long run casinos have the advantage.

A bet in a casino is a voluntary private market transaction between casino and player. There exists no *rivalrous* "artificially contrived" public transfer, nor a "going" private transfer that is up for grabs, so gambling is not a DUP activity.

15.6 Conclusion

It is difficult to understand how professional economists could argue that gambling—even professional gambling—is a DUP activity. It could be simply following Samuelson's argument (again, in a principles text), without giving it much thought. But I think the more likely explanation for this is that some researchers simply look for any argument they can to inflate the costs of gambling. Examining the writings of Grinols and Kindt, for example, one is hard-pressed to find any acknowledgement that gambling could be on net beneficial to society. Indeed claims were being made about the catastrophic damages caused by gambling in the early–mid 1990s—before there was any empirical evidence on the matter.

Certainly disordered gambling causes social costs, and it is not a trivial problem. But most casino patrons simply enjoy the activity. Individuals who choose to become professional gamblers may not be producing tangible products for other people, but each individual has the right to choose their own pursuits as long as they do not harm others.

I view the argument that gambling can be a DUP activity as one of the most fallacious ideas in the literature. Fortunately, it is becoming less common. The application of the concept of DUP to gambling seems to me to be a stretch; even in the case of professional gambling, it is not rent seeking. For most people, gambling is a form of entertainment, and professional gamblers create entertainment for many people too.

Chapter 16
Casinos and Crime: A Review of the Literature

16.1 Introduction

One part of the analysis in Chap. 10 focused on gambling behavior and criminal behavior among adolescents. The findings were that individuals who are more likely to gamble are also more likely to engage in criminal activity. However, the results showed that the type of gambling was important; this effect did not occur among lottery or casino gamblers; rather, it was individuals who engage in other types of gambling who were significantly more likely to engage in crime. These results confirm that there is a link between gambling behavior and criminal behavior. But there is no indication from our evidence that casino players engage in crime any more than other individuals do. Of course, our sample was limited to adolescents, so there may still be a general link between casino gambling and crime.

Disordered gamblers are thought to be the key source of the link between casinos in crime. As discussed earlier, these are individuals who gamble to such an extent that it creates financial turmoil and disrupts their personal and/or professional lives. These individuals may eventually turn to crime for the money needed to continue gambling or to pay off debts. It is beyond the scope of an economics book to analyze disordered gambling in any detail. Rather, in this chapter we only examine a statistical link between casino activity and crime, rather than a narrow link between disordered gamblers and crime. The chapter provides a brief review of the literature, with a focus on how the crime rate is calculated.

The material in this chapter is based on Walker DM. 2008. Evaluating crime attributable to casinos in the U.S.: A closer look at Grinols and Mustard's "Casinos, crime, and community costs." *Journal of Gambling Business and Economics* 2(3): 23–52. Used with permission from the University of Buckingham Press. Walker DM. 2008. Do casinos really cause crime? *Econ Journal Watch* 5(1): 4–20. Used with permission from *Econ Journal Watch*. Walker DM. 2010. Casinos and crime in the USA. In B. Benson and P. Zimmerman, eds., *Handbook on the economics of crime*, pp. 488–517. Used with permission from Edward Elgar.

Casinos have long been assumed to be linked to crime, particularly organized crime ("the mob"). Indeed, even as recently as 1996, a majority of Americans "agreed with the statement that legalized gambling 'opens the door to organized crime'" (Giacopassi, Stitt, and Nichols 2001, 152). Yet, most casinos are now corporate owned and managed. I believe that the stereotype of casinos as a mob money laundering operation has mostly faded. Still, crime associated with casinos is a major concern in jurisdictions with casinos and those contemplating legalizing them. In this chapter I review much of the literature on the alleged link between casinos and crime. I then focus on one study which has been particularly influential in the literature and in political debate. Overall, it is my opinion that there is not enough empirical evidence to be confident about a link between casinos and crime. I suspect that the relationship between casinos and crime is market specific.

16.2 Theoretical Background

Most of the studies in the literature focus on how casinos affect local crime rates. In most cases, the studies examine some or all Index I crimes reported in the FBI's *Uniform Crime Reports* (UCR). These include aggravated assault, rape, robbery, murder, larceny, burglary, and auto theft. Although most studies examine the impact of casinos on individual crime types, the emphasis is usually on the aggregate crime rate. Researchers have posited several different theories for how casinos may be related to crime. We review these different theories and then summarize some of the empirical results from the literature.

16.2.1 Economic Theory of Crime

An economic theory of crime based on rational choice suggests that criminals are rational utility maximizers, and that they calculate the risk of being caught and the potential penalties, and weigh those against the potential benefits of engaging in crime. Elements of the well-known economic approach to crime developed by Becker (1968) can certainly be applied to the issue of casinos and crime. However, most of the research on casino crime is framed in the context of more specific theories of crime. In particular, the "routine activities theory" and "hot spot" theories of crime have often been used as frameworks for analyzing the relationship between casinos and crime. However, these frameworks are consistent with an economic approach to crime.

16.2.2 Routine Activities Theory

The "routine activities approach" by Cohen and Felson (1979) can be applied to increasing crime activity following the introduction of casinos. The routine activities theory holds that criminal activity increases when three conditions hold simultaneously: likely offenders, suitable targets, and a lack of enforcement against crime. Obviously, these conditions may characterize a new casino development in a previously undeveloped area, or an area into which now there will be a large influx of tourists. Sherman, Gartin, and Buerger (1989) emphasize that a critical contribution of this theory is noting that not only are the numbers of offenders and targets important but also "the factors affecting the frequency of their convergence in time and space."

Jarrell and Howsen (1990) examine the specific effect of tourists or "strangers" in an area on crime. In analyzing 120 counties in Kentucky, they conclude, "tourism, which represents a group of highly transient individuals, has a positive impact on the crimes of burglary, larceny, and robbery" (p. 490). However, they find little connection between visitors and assault, murder, and rape. A casino would represent a clear example of the routine activities theory of crime, as potential criminals and victims may be attracted to casinos. It becomes more interesting once one distinguishes between "casino-based" and "community-based" crimes. This distinction was raised initially by Curran and Scarpitti (1991). Casino-based crimes may not conform as well to the routine activities explanation of crime, as the security technology and enforcement on casino premises are extremely effective and permeate the entire location. However, community-based crimes (i.e., those criminal acts that do not occur on casino properties) may better conform to the routine activities conditions described above. Although policing in communities usually increases with the introduction of casinos, it is unclear whether police per capita increases proportionally to the number of casino tourists. If it does not, then per capita policing actually falls. This may contribute to ripe conditions for community-based crimes as suggested by the routine activities theory.

16.2.3 Hot Spot Theory

Sherman, Gartin, and Buerger (1989) explain a related theory of crime incidence, the "hot spot" theory of crime. This is the idea that the majority of crimes occur in very small geographic areas. As an extension of routine activities theory, Sherman et al. found empirical evidence in Minneapolis that over 50 % of calls to police were attributed to only 3 % of places (addresses) in the city. Even more interesting is that calls reporting predatory crimes were extremely concentrated, with all robberies, rapes, and auto thefts reported in less than 3 % of places in the city.

When a casino is introduced into a small town, for example, it is possible that the casino grounds would act as a hot spot for crime. This could be because of the large number of tourists, or the fact that people often carry large amounts of cash in casinos, for example.

16.2.4 Economic Development

The above theories have explained why casinos may contribute to increased crime. However, it is also possible that casino development might decrease crime, on net.

This may occur, for example, if the introduction and operation of casinos create increased demand for labor, on net, and lead to higher wages and lower unemployment. Similarly, if the casino acts as a catalyst for economic growth, the resulting increase in standard of living might decrease the propensity to engage in criminal activities. Grinols and Mustard (2006, 31–32) discuss some other mechanisms through which casinos may affect crime.

16.3 Measurement Issues

As noted earlier, most of the studies on casinos and crime use the Index I reported crimes data found in the FBI's UCR.[1] In some studies the types of offenses are aggregated; in others they are considered separately. Most studies examine the crime rate, i.e., the number of reported offenses divided by the population. Studies have examined the crime rate at the state level, county level, or city level. Two important questions to be considered at the outset of any study are the following: What is the researcher trying to measure? And what is the appropriate way to calculate the crime rate? Presumably, the purpose of using a crime rate is to understand how dangerous an area is, or the risk to an individual of being victimized by crime.

Virtually *all* studies of casino communities find that the raw number of reported crimes and arrests increase following the introduction of casinos. This is hardly surprising, as the large influx of tourists means more potential criminals and more potential victims. It would be rather shocking if such an increase in population did not correspond to an increase in criminal activity. As is clear from the discussion of the routine activities and hot spot theories of crime, whenever a large tourist attraction is introduced, there is likely to be an increase in the number of crimes committed in the area.

There is one key issue that seems to determine whether or not a particular study will find a link between casinos and crime: how the visiting population is treated in the crime rate. The standard crime rate is simply measured as the number of crime incidents (c) divided by the population (p), or $\frac{c}{p}$. Thus, we have a measure of the likelihood that a particular person will be victimized by crime. If we distinguish between "residents" (r) and "visitors" (v), for both the crimes committed (i.e., crimes committed either by residents, c_r, or by visitors c_v) and the population targeted by criminals (i.e., members of either the resident population, p_r, or the visiting population, p_v, can be victimized by crime), then we get a better picture of how different crime rate calculations would be interpreted.[2]

---

[1] It is beyond the scope of this review to discuss the issues surrounding the choice of crime variable, e.g., reported offenses versus arrests. Those issues have been extensively discussed in the crime literature.

[2] The term "visitors" follows Grinols and Mustard (2006). Alternatively, this has been termed "strangers" (Jarrell and Howsen 1990), or more commonly, simply "tourists."

16.3 Measurement Issues

The traditional crime rate measure counts all crimes committed in an area (e.g., nation, state, or county), divided by the population in that area, $\frac{c}{p}$, or using the resident/visitor notation it would be $\frac{c_r + c_v}{p_r}$. However, if there is a large amount of tourism to the area, some researchers argue that this crime rate will overstate the actual risk of being victimized by crime. To correct this, the visiting population should be added to the denominator so that it accurately reflects the "population at risk" of being victimized. The crime rate thus becomes $\frac{c_r + c_v}{p_r + p_v}$.

On the other hand, if we are simply interested in calculating the raw number of crimes, relative to the resident population, regardless of the volume of tourism to the area, then the standard crime rate can be used. But this will overstate the risk of being a crime victim, the more so the larger the visiting population. In the case of casinos, which are often located in less populated areas, the tourism they draw can represent a significant change in the population. Thus, the distinction between "population" and "population at risk" vis-à-vis the crime rate is an important one.

Several authors have discussed how visitors or tourists should be handled when analyzing the crime rate. Nettler (1984, 48) explains, "*The rationale for the computation of* [crime] *rates is a predictive one* ... To increase the accuracy of forecasts, a rate should be 'refined' so that it includes in its denominator *all those persons and only those persons who are at risk* of whatever kind of event is being tallied in the numerator." Nettler describes rates that do not correctly represent the population at risk as "crude" (p. 48). Boggs (1965) gives the example of central business districts, which attract large number of daily visitors. She explains that ignoring the visitors will produce spuriously high crime rates (p. 900). Giacopassi (1995, 7) offers an example:

> It would be possible to have a casino and to have a vast amount of crime in a jurisdiction where there were no residents. This presents a dilemma: with no residents, there would be no denominator in the crime equation, so there could be no "official" crime rate. Clearly, calculating crime and crime rates without taking into account the population at risk can lead to wildly inappropriate conclusions.

Albanese (1985, 41) also provides a simple numerical example to illustrate the point:

> A city with a population of 100 citizens might experience 10 reported Index crimes in a year. Therefore, the probability that any one citizen will be the victim of one of these crimes is 1 in 10. If the population of this city suddenly doubles [after a casino opens] to, say, 200 citizens, it is likely that the number of crimes that occur there will also rise—simply because there are more people to be offenders and victims. If the number of crimes also doubled to 20, it would appear as if crime increased 100 %. However, this is not the case. If 200 people are now at risk and 20 crimes are committed, the probability of being a victim is *still* 1 in 10 (i.e., 20 in 200). Therefore, the risk of being victimized by crime can remain the same when *both* the population and crime increase together.

Curran and Scarpitti (1991) explain, "it is problematic to accept a rate based exclusively on the resident population. In fact, the FBI [the source of the GM crime data] shares this concern" and warns,

The Uniform Crime Reports give a nationwide view of crime based on statistics contributed by state and local law enforcement agencies. Population size is the only correlate of crime utilized in this publication. While other factors listed above are of equal concern [this list includes stability of population with respect to commuting patterns and transient factors], no attempt is made to relate them to the data presented. *The reader is, therefore, cautioned against comparing statistical data of individual reporting units from cities, counties, states, or colleges and universities solely on the basis of their population.* (Quoted from Curran and Scarpitti 1991, p. 438)

Miller and Schwartz (1998) also discuss this issue in detail. They are critical of a variety of studies that have ignored the effect of tourism on the population at risk when calculating crime rates.

Another important factor worth emphasizing is the *location* at which the crimes are committed. Whether the crimes are being perpetrated on the casino premises or in the outside community will have a real effect on who is being victimized: residents or visitors. Finally, it would be ideal for analyzing risk to potential victims if data were available on who is victimized by crime and who the criminals are (i.e., residents or visitors).

16.4 Empirical Evidence

I now summarize the findings of some of the published studies on the relationship between casinos and crime. What is very interesting—but perhaps not surprising—is that how tourists are accounted for in the crime rate appears to be a key determinant of the relationship between casinos and crime. Of course, there are other important variables, and each study takes a different approach to their analysis. The focus here is on the visitors issue because, as is discussed below, the most influential studies have focused on that issue.

16.4.1 "Early" Studies

The "early" studies on casinos and crime date from 1985 to 2000. This cutoff is arbitrary, but I think the quality of empirical analysis began to improve markedly after 2000. In general, these studies suggest that casinos cause crime if the visitors are not included in the population component of the crime rate.

When crime rates are calculated without factoring the number of tourists or visitors, almost all studies show that casinos lead to higher crime rates. This is consistent with common sense, which suggests that if there is a large increase in the number of people in an area, there is likely to be an increase in the number of crime incidents. Table 16.1 summarizes the findings of selected studies that examine crime rates in casino communities. The table lists information on the casino market studied, general findings, and whether visitors were considered in calculating the crime rates.

16.4 Empirical Evidence

Table 16.1 Casino–crime rate studies, 1985–2000

Study	State/region studied	Years analyzed	Year casinos opened	Casinos increase crime rate?	Population adjusted for visitors?
Albanese (1985)	Atlantic City	1978–1982	1978	No	Yes
Friedman et al. (1989)	Atlantic City	1974–1984	1978	Yes	No
Hakim and Buck (1989)	Atlantic City	1972–1984	1978	Yes	No
Curran and Scarpitti (1991)	Atlantic City	1985–1989	1978	No	Yes
Giacopassi and Stitt (1993)	Biloxi, MS	1991–1993	1992	Yes	No
Chang (1996)	Biloxi, MS	1986–1994	1992	No	Yes
Stokowski (1996)	Colorado	1989–1994	1991	No	Yes
General Accounting Office (2000)	Atlantic City	1977–1997	1978	No	Yes

Source: Walker (2010). Used with permission from Edward Elgar

The table suggests that whether a researcher finds an impact of casinos on crime correlates strongly to whether the visitors are accounted for in the population.

Some of these studies are methodologically or empirically weak. For example, the studies analyze data for only a very short time frame (in one case, as little as 2 years), do not control for other factors that may impact crime, and do not distinguish between crime attributable to casinos specifically and to tourism generally. Indeed, few of the studies listed in the table perform econometric analyses in which they control for relevant variables. Most of the shortcomings in these early studies may be attributed to the lack of available data. We cannot make any strong conclusions regarding the relationship between casinos and crime based on these studies because there simply were not many jurisdictions that offered casinos for a long period of time. What we can do is confirm that *how* the crime rate is measured will have a significant impact on the findings in casino jurisdictions. This result is consistent with the routine activities theory of crime.

16.4.2 "Recent" Studies

The trend toward commercial casino legalization slowed drastically in the late 1990s. Michigan legalized casinos in 1996, and Pennsylvania was the next state to legalize, in 2004. (Pennsylvania initially legalized casinos with slot machines only; they have since introduced table games.) Another wave of legalization began more recently. The maturation of the casino industry in states that legalized in the early 1990s has meant more data to study the crime issue. The more recent studies on casinos and crime are often more comprehensive, analyzing longer time periods and often more cross sections of states with casinos. Still, most of these later studies also suffer from some data limitations.

Table 16.2 summarizes the findings of the more recent studies on casinos and crime. As with the early studies, one thing that stands out is that how the researchers

Table 16.2 Casino–crime rate studies, 2001–2010

Study	State/region studied	Years analyzed	Year casinos opened	Casinos increase crime rate?	Population adjusted for visitors?
Gazel, Rickman, and Thompson (2001)	Wisconsin (tribal)	1981–1994	(various)	Yes	No
Wilson (2001)	Indiana	1992–1997	1995	No	No
Evans and Topoleski (2002)	National (tribal only)	1985–1989	(Various)	Yes	No
Stitt, Nichols, and Giacopassi (2003)	Various	1980s–1990s	(Various)	Mixed	Yes
Betsinger (2005)	144 counties in 33 states	1977–2001	(Various)	Mixed	No
Grinols and Mustard (2006)	National	1977–1996	(Various)	Yes	No
Barthe and Stitt (2007, 2009a, 2009b)	Reno, NV	2003	1937	No	Yes
Reece (2010)	Indiana	1994–2004	1995	No	Yes

Source: Walker (2010). Used with permission from Edward Elgar

account for tourists in the crime rate appears to have a considerable effect on the results. Often, when tourism is accounted for in the model, the crime effect of casinos is diminished or it disappears entirely.

16.5 Two Key Studies

Among all of the studies mentioned thus far, I believe two deserve closer attention because they highlight what I see as key methodological issues in casino–crime studies. The papers by Grinols and Mustard (2006) and Reece (2010) are examined in more detail here.

16.5.1 Grinols and Mustard (2006)

Grinols and Mustard (2006) represents the most comprehensive study of the link between casinos and crime to date. These authors examine county-level crime data in every US county from 1977 through 1996. Perhaps the only complaint one can have about the scope of this study is that it does not extend to later years. Nevertheless, this study improves upon the previous studies, covering more casino markets and a longer sample period.

The paper represents an important contribution because the authors utilize an econometric analysis of panel data, rather than simply calculating crime rates, or comparing crime rates before and after the introduction of casinos, as many predecessors did. Their analysis includes numerous control variables that account for potentially critical determinants of criminal activity; most of these have been ignored by previous researchers. The authors analyze the effect that the introduction of a casino has on the crime rate in the county between 2 years prior to casino introduction and 5 years after the introduction of casinos. Although the average crime rate was falling during the sample period in their study, their results indicate that crime rates fell less in casino counties than in non-casino counties. The casinos appear to increase crime beginning around 4 years after the introduction of casinos. This result is similar to that found by Evans and Topoleski (2002) in their study of tribal casinos. Grinols and Mustard conclude that approximately 8 % of casino county crime can be attributed to casinos. All Index I crimes (except murder) are found to be exacerbated by casinos. They estimate the costs of casino crime to be around $75 per adult per year in the United States (pp. 28, 41).

As with other studies, there are limitations to this study too.[3] Most importantly, Grinols and Mustard do not adjust their county crime rates by tourists (i.e., they use the population, rather than the population at risk). As other researchers have shown, ignoring the visiting population will tend to overstate the crime rate as an indication of the risk of being victimized. However, Grinols and Mustard explain that the risk of being victimized is not their concern in their paper. Instead, they are interested in the "costs to the host county associated with a change in crime from whatever source. We are therefore interested in the total effect of casinos on crime ..." (p. 35). If one interprets the "total effect of casinos" to mean the change in reported crimes, then they clearly show that the number of reported crimes increases after casinos are introduced. One can question the importance of this finding, however, since an increase in crime would be correlated with any large influx of tourists, casino related or not. Unfortunately, their analysis does not allow them to truly distinguish between a "casino" and "tourism" effect on crime.[4]

Despite these issues, the Grinols and Mustard (2006) study is likely to be the benchmark for future studies. It does represent a significant improvement over previous studies, mainly due to the scope of their study. In addition, their attempt to control for other factors that might affect crime is commendable. Other researchers have already begun using the Grinols and Mustard framework for subsequent analyses.

---

[3] These issues and several others are debated in an exchange between the author and Grinols and Mustard, published in *Econ Journal Watch* in 2008. See Walker (2008a, 2008b) and Grinols and Mustard (2008a, 2008b).

[4] In a follow-up study Grinols, Mustard, and Staha (2011) find that National Park visitors have no effect on local crime rates. Such visitors are likely quite different from casino visitors, and they suggest that the type of visitor is important for determining the crime effect of casino visitors. One would expect, for example, that National Park visitors may include a relatively large proportion of children relative to casino visitors.

16.5.2 Reece (2010)

The paper by Reece (2010) represents perhaps the most carefully crafted study on casinos and crime to date. Reece improves upon the Grinols and Mustard (2006) study and previous studies by accounting for several factors that had been neglected. This study is limited because it examines casinos and crime only in Indiana. However, it provides a good blueprint for future researchers to study other casino markets.

The major contribution of the Reece (2010) study is that it introduces control variables that have not been utilized in previous studies, usually because of data limitations. First, Reece controls for tourism by using the number of hotel rooms in the county as an explanatory variable in his model. Since hotels often follow new casinos, the number of hotel rooms in a county can proxy for tourism in the county. It may be the case that "hotels" cause crime, rather than casinos causing crime. This variable will help to isolate the casino effect from a tourism effect. Second, Reece is one of few researchers to account for casino volume (using turnstile count) in studying the effects of casinos on crime. Most previous studies utilize only a dummy variable to indicate the presence of one or more casinos. But if casinos cause crime, then one would expect the volume of casino gambling to be an important explanation of the level of crime. Third, Reece includes a measure of enforcement in his analysis. This is critical because the economic model of crime (or the routine activities theory) suggests that if there is a greater degree of law enforcement, it will raise the cost of committing crimes. His variables for enforcement include the aggregate arrest rate for violent crimes.

Another important contribution of Reece's (2010) study is that it explains the potential problems with some previous studies because they apparently did not deal with various problems with the UCR data. Reece's care with the data makes it likely that his analysis avoids some of the potential problems in other papers that have also used the UCR data.

Reece begins with the basic model posited by Grinols and Mustard (2006). He improves on it by including measures of casino activity, tourism volume, and law enforcement. He first analyzes the growth of hotel rooms in casino counties. He finds that new hotel rooms follow the introduction of casinos into counties, and that these hotel rooms "seem to reduce the levels of larceny and motor vehicle theft" (p. 157). He continues, discussing casinos and crime,

> I find very limited support for the proposition that new casinos increase local crime rates. Opening new casinos appears to increase the number of burglaries in the county after a lag of a few years. Opening new casinos appears, however, to reduce the number of motor vehicle thefts and aggravated assaults. Increased casino activity, measured using turnstile count of casino patrons, seems to reduce rates of larceny, motor vehicle theft, aggravated assault, and robbery. These results do not match those of earlier studies that show large increases in a broad range of local crime rates after opening new casinos. (p. 157)

Reece points out that the significance of the turnstile count in his model suggests that "leaving out a measure of casino activity when estimating the effect of casinos on crime is a serious specification error" (pp. 157–158). The same argument applies to the hotel room variable. Finally, although Reece tests the effect of enforcement, his results are insignificant in explaining crime.

The results from this study emphasize the importance of accounting for tourism, casino volume, and law enforcement. Although previous researchers have discussed these issues, Reece is the first to effectively control for them all in an analysis of casinos and crime. As Reece notes, his results are based solely on Indiana data, and cannot be generalized. Of course, there are other potential problems in this analysis, but Reece's study does introduce a number of critical improvements to the analysis of casinos and crime.

16.6 Unresolved Issues

Even with the amount of research examining the relationship between casinos and crime, little is known. In this section I summarize some of the most important, yet unresolved, issues that cloud our understanding of the relationship between casinos and crime.

One thing is clear from the research. When casinos are introduced into a city or a region, they are going to attract tourists. And with a larger population of potential criminals and victims, there *will* be more crime incidents. This is a straightforward implication of routine activities theory, and every study has shown that. But what is more interesting is whether the introduction of a casino actually makes the area less safe. Hence, most authors have argued that using a crime rate where the population is measured as the "population at risk" (i.e., resident population plus tourists) is the relevant one. Unfortunately, visitor data are often difficult to acquire. But most studies that calculate the crime rate using both the resident population and the resident plus tourist population show the adjustment to make a significant difference in the results. Typically, when tourists are considered in the crime rate, any effect of casinos on crime diminishes or disappears. Still, more evidence is needed.

Tarlow (2006) provides an insightful discussion on casino tourism and crime, explaining

> it is hard or impossible to distinguish between crimes based on the social impacts of tourism versus those based on the social impact of casinos. The lack of clear definitions and imprecise data often means that the researcher can find almost any conclusion about which he/she is desirous. The tautological bias in most of these studies should be recognized (p. 102).

Indeed, Tarlow discusses the problems associated with determining who is being victimized (residents or tourists), how to distinguish where casino districts end, and what types of crimes can be attributed to the impacts of casinos.

Curran and Scarpitti (1991) raise the issue of casino-based versus community-based crimes, and Barthe and Stitt (2007, 2009a, 2009b) provide a related empirical analysis on the *location* of criminal offenses. However, no researcher has provided an in-depth analysis of how casinos may affect the distribution of crime offenses.

This question also plays into the "what are we trying to measure?" issue. Presumably, most researchers are interested in measuring how casinos affect safety. But if the concern is for the costs of enforcement, then other measures may be more relevant.

A third issue that deserves increased attention is the identity of the victims—resident or tourist. Just as the location of committed crimes can be useful for tailoring the analysis to the question at hand, the home addresses (city or zip code, not necessarily street address) of the criminals and victims may also be useful. Everyone agrees that the number of crimes will increase when casinos enter a market, simply because more people are coming into the area. But no one knows if the increase in criminal activity is due to new criminals coming in, new victims coming in, or mostly likely, a combination of changes among resident and visiting criminals and victims. Unfortunately, data on victim category (resident or tourist) as well as criminal category would be very difficult, if not impossible, to collect on any large scale.

A fourth issue to consider is the differentiation among types of casinos. In some markets riverboat casinos are the only type allowed; other states have both land-based and riverboat casinos. It is conceivable that these different types of casinos have different effects on crime. Similarly, there may be differences in how tribal and commercial casinos affect crime.

16.7 Conclusion

It seems clear that crimes in casino jurisdictions will increase, as tourists are drawn to casinos. Very little is understood as to whether it is the casino per se or tourism that is the cause of increased crime. Similarly, little is known whether casino jurisdictions are safer or less safe than non-casino or non-tourist jurisdictions. As more data from more jurisdictions become available, hopefully researchers will design better studies to take into consideration these issues. The study by Reece (2010) is a good step. Reece attempted to account for casino activity (through turnstile count), the increase in tourism (through hotel rooms), and law enforcement changes. The inclusion of these variables goes a long way in satisfying the necessary considerations for effectively measuring the effects of casinos on crime outlined by Albanese (1985). When these factors are considered, Reece found little evidence of a positive relationship between casinos and crime. However, his results are limited to casinos in Indiana, and there is no reason to expect that experience will necessarily be the same as in other casino markets.

The issues discussed in this chapter outline numerous opportunities for researchers to improve our understanding of whether and how casinos and crime are linked. More work is needed to understand both the general economic relationship between casinos and crime and the individual-level analysis of problem gamblers' propensities to commit crimes. Quality data are often not available. However, as more jurisdictions have longer term experiences with casinos, researchers should find it easier to come to some stronger conclusions on the relationship between casinos and crime.

16.7 Conclusion

Currently, the evidence is mixed. Some studies suggest that casinos cause crime, while others argue that it is more likely a tourism effect. More research is needed. A better understanding of these issues will have important economic, sociological, and political implications, as policymakers continue to eye legalized casinos as a way to deal with ongoing fiscal crises.

Chapter 17
Casinos and Commercial Real Estate Values: A Case Study of Detroit

As discussed in Chap. 4, casino industry observers, especially critics, have argued that the casino industry "cannibalizes" other industries or acts as a substitute to other industries. Although this is true of any new firm or industry, to an extent, this criticism of casinos has been particularly influential in political and public debate. Yet, there have been few empirical analyses of this issue. There is no paper of which I am aware that has addressed whether casinos cause a substitution effect with other businesses at the local level.[1] In this chapter we examine the substitution effect of casinos with other businesses using data from Detroit, Michigan.

Detroit is an ideal case study due to land-based commercial casinos that are located in the central business district of a major urban area. Detroit employment and population decline over the sample period while the revenues of the casino industry steadily increase. Using casino revenues as a measure of casino activity and retail property transaction data, we test the effect casinos have had on Detroit commercial property values. Our results indicate that casinos have a positive impact on commercial property prices, suggesting that casinos act as complements, rather than substitutes, to existing businesses. Although the results apply only to Detroit, the empirical approach used in this study can serve as an example for future market studies.

This chapter is organized as follows. The next section provides background on commercial casinos in Detroit, and Sect. 17.2 reviews literature on the influence of casino activity on real estate property values documented by previous research. The data and empirical approach are described in Sect. 17.3. In Sect. 17.4, the model is estimated and the empirical findings analyzed. The chapter concludes with a summary of the findings of the analysis.

The material in this chapter is based on Wiley JA, and DM Walker. 2011. Casino revenues and retail property values: The Detroit case. *Journal of Real Estate Finance and Economics* 42(1): 99–114. Used with permission from Springer.

[1] Some studies may get at the issue indirectly. For example, Cotti (2008) analyzes labor market effects of casinos.

17.1 Background

Michigan was the eleventh state to legalize casinos, in 1996. The first casino opened in Detroit in 1999. The three Detroit casinos are very close to each other—within a 1.4 mile drive of each other.[2] The only other casino in proximity is the Caesars Windsor, just across the Detroit River in Windsor, Ontario, Canada. Annual casino revenues in Detroit first topped $1.0 billion in 2001, and there has been a modest, steady increase in revenues since that year.[3] In 2010, gross gaming revenues were $1.38 billion, and the casinos paid $311 million in state and local taxes.

The academic literature contains a few studies that focus on casinos in Detroit. Wacker (2006) provides a thorough discussion of the political economy leading up to casino approval. The loss of manufacturing jobs in postindustrial Detroit and the economic decline of the central business district (CBD) are offered as key explanations. Wacker points out that there is a regional draw to the urban Detroit casinos where visitors emanate from adjacent states. In another descriptive paper, McCarthy (2002) discusses the "entertainment-led" strategy to revitalize Detroit's weakening economic base. Noted benefits include enhanced city marketing and tourism volume. Problems associated with the strategy are political in nature, related to governance, location, and isolation from potentially compatible land uses. The study by the Michigan Senate Fiscal Agency (2000) provides comprehensive information on the Detroit casino agreements, as well as expectations regarding revenues, employment, and tax payments. However, all three of these Detroit studies fail to provide any empirical analysis of the effects of the Detroit casinos on property values or on the performance of the local economy.[4]

Perhaps the most comprehensive study of the Detroit casino case is Moufakkir's (2002) study. This study is somewhat dated, but it addresses five specific issues influenced by casinos: tourism activity; gambling spending capture rates (relative to the nearby casino in Windsor, Canada); projections compared to actual results; crime in Detroit; and bankruptcy filings. Moufakkir provides evidence that crime and bankruptcy filings did not increase following casino openings in Detroit, and

---

[2] See Table 1.1 for 2010 data on Michigan's commercial casinos. Michigan also has 19 tribal casinos, as of 2008. The first of these opened in 1993. The nearest tribal casinos to Detroit are the Soaring Eagle Casino in Mt. Pleasant and the Saganing Eagles Landing Casino in Standish. Both are more than 140 miles from Detroit. Hereafter, when we refer to "casinos" we are referring only to the three commercial casinos in Detroit.

[3] For a more detailed discussion of Detroit's casino revenues, taxes, etc., see American Gaming Association (2008).

[4] There have been, of course, several other descriptive pieces such as policy reports and newspaper reports. These sources typically list a variety of statistics such as employment figures, tax receipts, and casino revenues, but generally fail to provide a valid econometric analysis of the casinos' effects. An example of this type of study is the American Gaming Association's annual *State of the States* report (2008).

the net impact of casinos is positive. Although the study examines a number of important social and economic issues, it does not address whether casinos create a local "substitution effect" that harms other businesses.

17.2 Casino Activity and Real Estate Property Values

Wenz (2007) develops a hedonic pricing model to estimate the net impact of casinos on residential property values, using national data from the Public Use Microdata Sample (PUMS) of the 2000 US Census. Wenz argues that the hedonic approach has advantages over other potential measures because it connects the value of public goods that are revealed in home values as a result of casino gambling. The study is general in nature, finding that casinos have a net positive impact on housing prices (about 2 %) in the same geographic area as a casino, while property values in bordering areas experience even greater positive spillover effects (about a 6 % increase in value).[5] Due to the national scope of the Wenz study, there is considerable heterogeneity across casinos, markets, and corresponding local economies; hence, some of these differences may be attributed to fundamental market differences or the timing of casino development. Most casinos in Wenz's sample are Native American casinos, while only two cities are identified with non-Native American legalized gambling: Atlantic City, NJ, and Deadwood, SD. Accordingly, Wenz finds that positive impacts of casino gambling decline as population density increases and that the number of gaming positions (i.e., casino industry size) has no effect on the local economy.

In another study specific to Atlantic City, Buck et al. (1991) examine 64 connecting localities to simultaneously estimate determinants for property crime and average housing values controlling for population, unemployment, government revenues, police expenditures, and distance from Atlantic City. They find that, although the development effect of casinos has a positive effect on property values, the crime attracted by the casinos has a negative effect on property values. Both effects diminish with the distance from a new casino.

The study by Phipps (2004) examined the effects of casino openings and closings on neighborhood crime and housing prices, using a time-series hedonic approach with MLS data in Windsor, Ontario. (Windsor is just across the river from Detroit.) Phipps finds that, although crime reports are higher and property values are lower in close proximity to casinos, crime and housing prices vary randomly around mean values after either the opening of a new casino or the closing of an existing one. According to this evidence, Phipps concludes that casinos have a benign effect on crime and housing prices in Windsor.

---

[5]Geographic area is defined as the US Census Public Use Microdata Area (PUMA), which contains at least 100,000 individuals.

There is no published evidence of the impact of casinos on commercial property values. In contrast to previous work, our study provides an original examination of the influence of casinos on retail property values. Property values should reflect the value of the business and should therefore help us determine the impact of casinos on other businesses. We focus on a single market, thus eliminating the bias introduced by casino and economic heterogeneity across the United States. The use of transaction-level data enables empirical methods that control for unique physical and locational differences across properties. Rather than using only an indicator variable to consider the fixed effect of casinos, the analysis is dynamic and features total casino revenues to account for time variation in industry performance. Finally, we consider the value impact on properties in close proximity to casinos. These methods elicit a more direct connection between consumer spending at casinos and changes in individual retail property values. The empirical tests are designed to answer the open question of whether casino performance causes a substitution effect away from other commercial land uses, or if certain property types exist as complements to casino gambling.[6]

17.3 Data and Methodology

Market selection is a key consideration for this analysis. A number of possible markets could be examined. The focus is on an urban location because of the interest in examining the impact on surrounding businesses. From the AGA (2008) list of the top 20 US casino markets, only four markets have population greater than 50,000 and greater than 50 retail sales observations in CoStar (our data source). These are Las Vegas, Detroit, St. Louis, and Kansas City. Las Vegas is problematic because the gaming industry contributes such a large share of the economic base. Multiple new casinos are built every year in Las Vegas, adding difficulty to isolating differences between the novelty effect of new casino development and the impact of existing industry trends. Casinos in Missouri are on rivers. The consequence of this is that gambling venues in Kansas City and St. Louis are relatively isolated from the core urban market and the opportunity to examine the impact on surrounding businesses is limited. Additionally, prior to 2008 the Missouri Gaming Commission enforced an unpopular $500 loss limit which largely restricted the drawing power for visitors in surrounding states.

Detroit is selected for this study due to the public disclosure of casino revenues combined with a steady gaming industry in a large metropolitan market. In addition, Detroit represents a convenient case study because its urban commercial casinos are

---

[6]Note that by "substitute" and "complement" we are not referring to the standard economic relationship between price of one good and demand for another. Rather, we are simply referring to a relationship among the revenues in different industries. Admittedly, this is somewhat of an indirect way to get at the substitution effect. The most direct way of analyzing it would be to look at revenues. But such firm-level data are not readily available.

17.3 Data and Methodology

Table 17.1 List of variables

Variable	Description
5mile	Equals 1 if property is within 5-mile radius of any Detroit casino
Age	Property age (in years)
Bldg_SF	Property size (in square feet)
Casino_rev	Total adjusted gross receipts from Detroit casino operations
Coverage	Lot coverage ratio
D_Type_i	Indicator variable for property type i
Distance	Average of measured distances from each casino (in miles)
Land_area	Land area for subject site (in square feet)
N_floors	Number of floors
Pop_Det	Estimated population for the Detroit-Livonia-Dearborn, MI area
Rel_days	Number of days since sale date (measured relative to August 14, 2008)
Sale_price	Recorded purchase price
$SubMkt_j$	Indicator variable for submarket j
Supply_RBA	Total existing inventory of retail space in the Detroit market (in square feet of rentable building area)

Source: Wiley and Walker (2011). Used with permission from Springer

distant from the tribal casinos in the state. Detroit has only three commercial casinos, all in close proximity to each other. This offers a relatively direct connection between casino performance and commercial property values. Finally, population and employment decline during the 2001–2008 period while casino revenues steadily rise. This divergence suggests that a connection to retail property values can more directly be attributed to casino performance than general urban growth. No other urban casino market in the United States offers this combination of characteristics along with adequate retail property transaction data to make this type of analysis possible.

We posit three separate models of commercial property prices in Detroit. The goal is to isolate the effect casinos in Detroit have had on commercial property prices. Data is collected on a number of variables that are expected to explain commercial property values. We utilize retail property sales data, along with property and locational characteristic data for Detroit provided by the CoStar Group. Data include a total of 1,135 observations (property transactions) over more than a 7-year period spanning from May 2001 to June 2008. The sample is limited to include the 488 observations where data are jointly available for the variables listed and described in Table 17.1. The sample is diverse in nature with property uses that range from service stations to day care centers. Table 17.2 provides descriptive statistics for the sample. The average property is almost 35 years old, and average selling price is just over $1.0 million.

In addition to property-specific information, data are collected on macroeconomic market factors that may influence the supply and demand of retail space. Retail supply data are extracted from a recent CoStar Retail Market Report for the Detroit market. Supply of rentable building area (RBA) is reported quarterly and ranges from a minimum of 194 million sq.ft. in the second quarter of 2001 to a

Table 17.2 Descriptive statistics

Panel A. Property information (n = 488)

Variable	Mean	Standard deviation	Mean (if 5mile = 1)	t-Test of difference
Age	34.7	25.4	30.4	(−0.68)
Bldg_SF	6,488	7,866	5,391	(−0.95)
Coverage	0.156	0.400	0.280	(1.18)
Distance	19.649	13.171	–	–
Land_area	69,161	280,565	16,116**	(−8.63)
N_floors	1.09	0.344	1.19	(0.96)
Rel_days	564	349	499	(−0.74)
Sale_price	$1,022,774	$1,196,730	$720,522*	(−2.67)

Panel B. Market information (Q2 2001 to Q2 2008)

Variable	Mean	Standard deviation	Minimum	Maximum
Casino_rev	$110,513,274	$6,219,181	$79,973,338	$123,755,238
Pop_Det	2,015,413	16,647	1,985,101	2,058,895
Supply_RBA	208,689,927	2,617,117	194,080,564	212,267,916

Source: Wiley and Walker (2011). Used with permission from Springer
** and * indicate significant difference from the mean of the control set at the 1 and 5 % levels, respectively

maximum of 212 million sq. ft. in the first quarter of 2008. Aggregate retail supply estimates are merged with property transaction data based on the quarter in which the transaction occurs to create the Supply_RBA variable.

Following the widely held belief that *retail follows residential growth*, population estimates are frequently the first line of even the most detailed demand models for retail market analysis. Annual population estimates from the Detroit-Livonia-Dearborn, MI Metropolitan Statistical Area (MSA), for years 2000 through 2007 were collected from the US Census Bureau. Population is lagged so that transaction sale dates are matched with population estimates from the previous year to create the Pop_Det variable. Consistent with publicized struggles of manufacturing industries in Detroit and resulting employment trends, population for the Detroit MSA is declining every year since the beginning of the decade—falling by as much as 1.36 % during our sample period. As shown in Table 17.2, population dropped from 2.06 million in 2001 to 1.99 million in 2008.

Detroit has only three casinos, MGM Grand Detroit, MotorCity Casino, and Greektown Casino, with openings in July 1999, December 1999, and November 2000, respectively. All casinos are within a maximum driving distance of 1.4 miles of each other and no new casino openings occur during the sample period.[7] Revenue from operations are made publicly available online from the Michigan Gaming Control Board. In March 2008, the three Detroit casinos reported their highest

---

[7] As noted earlier, tribal casinos are a significant distance away from the commercial casinos in Detroit; we therefore ignore their effect on the Detroit real estate market.

17.3 Data and Methodology

collective monthly revenue during our sample period, approaching $124 million. Monthly casino revenues are merged with property transaction data based on the month of sale to create the Casino_rev variable. This variable serves as a good proxy for the overall amount of consumer spending in Detroit that can be attributed to casino visitors.

If visitors only spend their money on an all-inclusive casino experience, then casino revenues should have little to no influence on retail property values. It is also possible that casinos oversupply the market with retail space and cannibalize competition so that casino revenues act as a substitute to other consumer spending, leading to a decrease in retail property values. On the other hand, if casino guests also spend disposable income outside the casino, then retail property values should be positively affected by the casino volume. Brueckner (1993) provides a formal model to argue that the successful performance of anchor tenants benefits in-line retail tenants by drawing customers for multipurpose shopping trips.[8] Although this earlier work is focused on enclosed shopping centers, it opens the question about possible customer spillovers in walkable urban locations when customers are drawn to the area by major retail or entertainment venues. Based on the economies of agglomeration principle, the influence of casinos is not expected to be constant and should vary by retail use and proximity to casinos.[9] According to this hypothesis, during periods where gaming spending is high, nearby complementary retail tenants should see improved sales revenue escalating the competition for their space. Retail is an income-producing property; therefore, higher rents for properties nearby casinos lead to higher valuations and sales prices. Chaing, Lai, and Ling (1986) demonstrate that base retail rents are positively related to expected tenant sales. Improved tenant performance increases the tenant's ability to pay more and intensifies competition for space. These economic influences are in turn capitalized into higher retail property values.

Latitude and longitude coordinates are used to measure the distance (in nautical miles, or "as the crow flies") from sold properties to the three casinos. With coordinates given as radians measured relative to 90°, the calculation of the variable Distance is made according to the spherical law of cosines.[10] Distance measures the distance between each retail observation and the midpoint of the casino triangle. The Distance variable is included in the hedonic model to control for the gradient of commercial values relative to the city center. In order to test whether the effects of casinos diminish further away from the casinos, we introduce a variable, 5mile, which identifies retail properties that are within 5 miles of any of the three Detroit casinos.

---

[8] This important retail concept is later supported by the findings of Gatzlaff, Sirmans, and Diskin (1994), Eppli and Shilling (1995), and Miceli and Sirmans (1995). Mejia and Eppli (2003) extend this analysis to find evidence of demand externalities between regional shopping centers.

[9] For theoretical discussion of economies of agglomeration, see Pascal and McCall (1980) and Goldstein and Gronberg (1984). Eppli and Benjamin (1994) provide a review of retail research that summarizes the literature linked to economies of agglomeration, along with other important retail concepts.

[10] Distance = $3{,}443.92 \times \arccos[\cos(lat1) \times \cos(lat2) + \sin(lat1) \times \sin(lat1) \times \cos(long1 - long2)]$, where 3,443.92 miles is the radius of the earth.

Panel A of Table 17.2 reports the means for selected variables describing properties within a 5-mile radius of any Detroit casino (if 5mile = 1). It is shown that properties within a 5-mile radius are similar in age, size, and sale date, yet lot sizes are smaller and the average selling price is significantly less than the overall market average. This preliminary observation would seem to suggest that the presence of Detroit casinos is a detriment to retail property values. However, the comparison of sample means is misleading since it fails to consider fundamental differences like property type, physical attributes, and location within an urban market. Regression analysis has the superior ability to directly link the influence of casino revenues to retail property values.

The starting point for the analysis is a traditional hedonic model using property characteristics to explain variation in selling prices. The model is log-linear where the dependent variable is ln(Sale_price).[11] The natural log of building size, ln(Bldg_SF), is included as an influential determinant of selling price because the dependent variable is not measured as price per unit of size. Property age, measured as ln(Age), is a key consideration due to functional obsolescence and continuous technological change in retail industry standards.[12] The Rel_days variable measures the number of days since the property sale relative to August 14, 2008, and is included to control for the time trend in retail prices relative to other market variables.[13] Since market locations range from urban to suburban and MSA periphery, lot size and building size are not highly correlated; hence, lot size is included as ln(Land_area) to measure the value of undeveloped land.[14] Coverage and ln(N_floors) measure density effects within the urban location according to the efficiency of land use and building height, respectively. The D_Type$_i$ indicator variables are included to identify properties according to 16 different types.[15]

Colwell and Munneke (2009) point out that the use of a constant gradient assumption to control for urban location and distance from the CBD may be inappropriate due to directional differences in many markets. To avoid this concern, the SubMkt$_j$ variables

---

[11] Colwell and Munneke (1997) verify concavity in property values with respect to lot size and point out the bias in using price per acre as a dependent variable in urban locations. The natural log of Sale_Price is used to alleviate this concern.

[12] An in-depth discussion of the interaction between age and retail depreciation is provided by Colwell and Ramsland (2003).

[13] The linear time trend assumption includes Rel_days as a dependent variable but is insignificant in all estimations. Instead, the nonlinear time trend is included as ln(Rel_days) and shows up as positive and statistically significant, improving the model fit for all estimations.

[14] The importance of including lot size when land values peak in urban locations is emphasized by Guntermann and Thomas (2005).

[15] Each of the following property types is included: auto dealership, auto repair, bank, bar, car wash, convenience store, day care center, drug store, fast food, general freestanding, restaurant, service station, storefront, storefront retail/office, storefront retail/residential, and supermarket. The variable for general freestanding is suppressed with 170 observations.

17.3 Data and Methodology

are used to control for differences across respective Detroit submarkets as distinguished by CoStar.[16] Additional market variables ln(Supply_RBA) and ln(Pop_Det) are included to control for macroeconomic influences on the supply and demand of retail space. Finally, the variable ln(Casino_rev) and the interaction term 5mile×ln(Casino_rev) are included to measure the scale and proximity effects of casino revenues on retail property values. Hence, the operational model to be estimated is

$$\ln(\text{Sale\_Price}) = \beta_0 + \sum_{i=1}^{15} \beta_i \times \text{D\_Type}_i + \sum_{i=16}^{36} \beta_i \times \text{SubMkt}_j$$
$$+ \beta_{37} \times \ln(\text{Age}) + \beta_{38} \times \ln(\text{Bldg\_SF}) + \beta_{39} \times \text{Coverage}$$
$$+ \beta_{40} \times \text{Distance} + \beta_{41} * \ln(\text{Land\_area}) + \beta_{42} \times \ln(\text{N\_floors})$$
$$+ \beta_{43} \times \ln(\text{Rel\_days}) + \beta_{44} \times \ln(\text{Pop\_Det}) + \beta_{45} \times \ln(\text{Supply\_RBA})$$
$$+ \beta_{46} \times \ln(\text{Casino\_rev}) + \beta_{47} \times 5\text{mile} \times \ln(\text{Casino\_rev}) + \varepsilon \qquad (17.1)$$

where ε is a normally distributed error term.

The second step of the empirical analysis is to examine whether there are specific property types driving the empirical results. In order to do this, (17.1) is modified so that the variables ln(Casino_rev) and 5mile×ln(Casino_rev) are omitted. Instead the ln(Casino_rev) variable is partitioned into interaction terms D_Type$_i$×ln(Casino_rev), measuring whether specific property types are influenced by casino revenues. The operational model to be estimated can be written as

$$\ln(\text{Sale\_Price}) = \beta_0 + \sum_{i=1}^{15} \beta_i \times \text{D\_Type}_i + \sum_{i=16}^{36} \beta_i \times \text{SubMkt}_j$$
$$+ \beta_{37} \times \ln(\text{Age}) + \beta_{38} \times \ln(\text{Bldg\_SF}) + \beta_{39} \times \text{Coverage}$$
$$+ \beta_{40} \times \text{Distance} + \beta_{41} \times \ln(\text{Land\_area}) + \beta_{42} \times \ln(\text{N\_floors})$$
$$+ \beta_{43} \times \ln(\text{Rel\_days}) + \beta_{44} \times \ln(\text{Pop\_Det}) + \beta_{45} \times \ln(\text{Supply\_RBA})$$
$$+ \beta_{46} \times \ln(\text{Casino\_rev}) + \beta_{47} \times 5\text{mile} \times \ln(\text{Casino\_rev})$$
$$+ \sum_{i=48}^{64} \beta_i \times \text{D\_Type}_i \times \ln(\text{Casino\_rev}) + \varepsilon \qquad (17.2)$$

The final step of the empirical analysis is to examine the partitioning of ln(Casino_rev) influences by property type for only those properties located within the 5-mile radius of the Detroit casinos. This is done because one might expect the effects of casinos to be more pronounced in closer proximity to the casinos, and to

---

[16]There are 31 submarkets in the sample, including Airport District, Auburn Hills, Birmingham Area, Bloomfield, Bloomfield West, CBD, Central I-96 Corridor, Dearborn, Detroit East of Woodward, Detroit West of Woodward, Detroit—New Center, Downriver North, Downriver South, Farmington/Farm Hills, Howell/Brighton Area, Lakes Area, Macomb East, Macomb West, Monroe County, Northern Outlying, Pontiac, Rochester, Royal Oak Vicinity, Southern I-275 Corridor, Southfield North of 10 Mile, Southfield South of 10 Mile, The Pointes/Harper Woods, Troy North, Troy South, Washtenaw East of 23, and Washtenaw West of 23. The variable for Northern Outlying is suppressed with 66 observations.

diminish as one moves further away. Hence, D_Type$_i$ × ln(Casino_rev) is multiplied by 5mile to create the following model:

$$\ln(\text{Sale\_Price}) = \beta_0 + \sum_{i=1}^{15} \beta_i \times \text{D\_Type}_i + \sum_{i=16}^{36} \beta_i \times \text{SubMkt}_j$$
$$+ \beta_{37} \times \ln(\text{Age}) + \beta_{38} \times \ln(\text{Bldg\_SF}) + \beta_{39} \times \text{Coverage}$$
$$+ \beta_{40} \times \text{Distance} + \beta_{41} \times \ln(\text{Land\_area}) + \beta_{42} \times \ln(\text{N\_floors})$$
$$+ \beta_{43} \times \ln(\text{Rel\_days}) + \beta_{44} \times \ln(\text{Pop\_Det}) + \beta_{45} \times \ln(\text{Supply\_RBA})$$
$$+ \beta_{46} \times \ln(\text{Casino\_rev}) + \beta_{47} \times 5\text{mile} \times \ln(\text{Casino\_rev})$$
$$+ \sum_{i=48}^{58} \beta_i \times 5\text{mile} \times \text{D\_Type}_i \times \ln(\text{Casino\_rev}) + \varepsilon \tag{17.3}$$

Equation (17.3) includes only eight interaction terms due to unavailable data for certain property types within the radius. The results from the empirical estimation of (17.1–17.3) are discussed in the next section.

17.4 Results

Table 17.3 provides the results from three estimations of (17.1).[17] The first model assumes β_{46} and β_{47} equal zero to ignore the influence of casino revenues. The model results suggest that property values are lower for older properties, which are more likely to be functionally obsolete or may have deferred maintenance. Property size and lot coverage both positively influence property values. Properties in urban locations are often associated with higher coverage ratios; hence, urban location is valuable for Detroit retail space. Properties with large land area *ceteris paribus* are linked to lower property values and often include substantial portions of undeveloped land. Speculative land holdings are risky and heavily discounted due to future cash flow uncertainty. In addition, unimproved land on a property can signal a lack of connection to surrounding land uses which is a very important attribute to retail tenants. Number of floors is not associated with any significant value differences. Retail tenants rarely succeed without street-level access and unlike office space, there is considerable homogeneity in the sample as most properties are characterized by a single floor. The time trend variable (Rel_days) reveals that retail property values are generally increasing throughout the sample period. This outcome is a result of urban trends in Detroit. New neighborhoods become popular and attract affluent homeowners. This is followed by new retail development. At the same time, continual efforts over the last decade lead to gentrification of aging neighborhoods and the eventual replacement of outdated, underperforming retail centers. Population in Detroit is decreasing while supply of existing space is generally increasing

---

[17] In the interest of brevity, the 15 D_Type$_i$ variable and the 30 SubMkt$_j$ variables included in the estimations are not reported.

17.4 Results

Table 17.3 Results for (17.1) [Dep. variable: ln(Sale_price)]

Variables	Equation (17.1) $\beta_{46}, \beta_{47}=0$ Coefficient (t-statistic)	Equation (17.1) $\beta_{47}=0$ Coefficient (t-statistic)	Equation (17.1) Full model Coefficient (t-statistic)
Constant	36.8 (0.18)	60.2 (0.30)	85.5 (0.43)
ln(Age)	−0.4098*** (−10.05)	−0.4148*** (−10.18)	−0.3997*** (−9.77)
ln(Bldg_SF)	0.5332*** (13.33)	0.5341*** (13.39)	0.5329*** (13.45)
Coverage	0.1823** (2.09)	0.2010** (2.29)	0.2020** (2.32)
Distance	−0.0074 (−1.40)	−0.0070 (−1.33)	−0.0055 (−1.04)
ln(Land_area)	−1.444** (−2.27)	−1.491** (−2.35)	−1.423** (−2.25)
ln(N_floors)	−0.1149 (−0.66)	−0.1322 (−0.76)	−0.1585 (−0.91)
ln(Rel_days)	0.2919** (2.50)	0.2786** (2.39)	0.3170*** (2.71)
ln(Pop_Det)	−13.59 (−1.43)	−12.38 (−1.30)	−14.49 (−1.53)
ln(Supply_RBA)	9.88 (1.43)	6.58 (0.93)	6.82 (0.97)
ln(Casino_rev)	–	1.236* (1.83)	1.213* (1.81)
ln(Casino_rev)×5mile	–	–	0.0281*** (2.58)
D_Type$_i$ variables	Included	Included	Included
SubMkt$_j$ variables	Included	Included	Included
R-square	64.2 %	64.5 %	65.0 %
Observations	488	488	488

Source: Wiley and Walker (2011). Used with permission from Springer
***, **, and * indicate significance at the 1, 5, and 10 % levels, respectively

throughout the sample, but neither appears to explain significant differences in property values.[18]

The second model in Table 17.3 adds the variable ln(Casino_rev) to consider the influence of casino revenues on retail property values. However, in this model we still ignore the 5-mile distance designation ($\beta_{47}=0$). The model is relatively stable,

---

[18]Eppli, Shilling, and Vandell (1998) analyze macroeconomic factors influencing retail returns at the metropolitan level for eight markets, including Detroit. They estimate six equations including retail construction starts, retail sales, mortgage rates, inflation, stock market returns, and stock market volatility. Using residuals from these estimations, they find that unexplained changes in retail supply and retail sales have no significant influence on retail returns.

showing only minimal differences in parameter estimates from the first model. The estimated coefficient for ln(Casino_rev) is positive and significant at the 5 % level, suggesting that casino revenues have a positive influence on retail property values. The coefficient can be interpreted to say that a 1 % increase in casino revenues is predicted to lead to an average 1.236 % increase in retail property values.

The final model in Table 17.3 includes the casino revenue interaction variable 5mile × ln(Casino_rev), so the influence of properties in close proximity to Detroit casinos can be directly examined. The coefficients for both 5mile × ln(Casino_rev) and ln(Casino_rev) variables are statistically significant in this estimation. Thus, retail properties within the 5-mile radius are influenced by casino revenues and more strongly so than those outside the 5-mile casino radius. This result is very interesting although not surprising; visitors considering Detroit as a casino destination are more likely to lodge, shop, dine, and find other entertainment venues in close proximity to casinos.

Retail properties and associated values vary widely by property type, making it inappropriate to assume that the influence of casino revenues will be identical across property type. The next step of the empirical analysis is to partition the effect of casino revenues to determine whether the results are driven by specific property types. Table 17.4 presents the results from the empirical estimation of (17.2). For the interactions of ln(Casino_rev) with the D_Type_i variables, only values for convenience stores and service stations are found to significantly increase with casino revenues. This result is fairly intuitive and suggests that the impact on the retail market as a whole may be attributed to out-of-town casino visitors who arrive via auto. It is interesting to note that none of the specific property types is significantly negatively affected by casino revenues.

Equation (17.3) provides a more direct test for the influence of casino revenues on specific property types within the immediate surrounding community (within the 5-mile radius). The interactions for general freestanding, restaurants, and service stations all have positive and significant coefficients, as shown in Table 17.5. General freestanding is by far the largest property type, represented with 170 observations, making up nearly 35 % of the sample. This includes many freestanding retail establishment not picked up by other indicators, such as apparel stores, restaurants, and theatres. Within the sample, general freestanding typically includes only a single tenant in a structure built around 1969 averaging roughly 10,000 sq. ft. The indicator for restaurants more commonly describes attached units that are smaller in size (averaging 5,500 sq. ft.) but newer (typically built around 1977). The significance of all three variables supports the hypothesis that the presence of casinos contributes to retail property values through the principle of cumulative attraction. Each category describes a retail use that is intuitively complementary to gaming, tourism, and entertainment. Interestingly, there are no significantly negative coefficients for property type interaction variables in Tables 17.4 and 17.5; hence, there is not a single property type identified where visitor spending in casinos significantly reduces retail property values.

17.4 Results

Table 17.4 Results for (17.2) by property type [Dep. variable: ln(Sale_price)]

Variables	Coefficient	SE	(t-Stat)
Constant	134.6	205.6	(0.65)
ln(Age)	−0.4185***	0.0414	(−10.10)
ln(Bldg_SF)	0.5302***	0.0406	(13.06)
Coverage	0.2181**	0.0960	(2.27)
Distance	−0.0066	0.0054	(−1.21)
ln(Land_area)	−1.684**	0.6576	(−2.56)
Ln(N_floors)	−0.1040	0.1802	(−0.58)
ln(Rel_days)	0.2477**	0.1205	(2.05)
Ln(Pop_Det)	−13.92	9.762	(−1.43)
ln(Supply_RBA)	5.110	7.352	(0.70)
ln(Casino_rev)×D_Auto dealership	−6.070	10.14	(−0.60)
ln(Casino_rev)×D_Auto repair	−1.434	2.655	(−0.54)
ln(Casino_rev)×D_Bank	4.776	4.982	(0.96)
ln(Casino_rev)×D_Bar	−2.744	4.833	(−0.57)
ln(Casino_rev)×D_Car wash	2.393	2.445	(0.98)
ln(Casino_rev)×D_Convenience store	5.508*	3.187	(1.73)
ln(Casino_rev)×D_Day care center	3.644	3.177	(1.15)
ln(Casino_rev)×D_Drug store	1.196	3.220	(0.37)
ln(Casino_rev)×D_Fast food	0.8200	1.992	(0.41)
ln(Casino_rev)×D_General freestanding	0.1007	0.9908	(0.10)
ln(Casino_rev)×D_Restaurant	2.010	1.862	(1.08)
ln(Casino_rev)×D_Service station	2.323**	1.111	(2.09)
ln(Casino_rev)×D_Storefront	3.336	5.657	(0.59)
ln(Casino_rev)×D_Storefront retail/Office	3.914	5.336	(0.73)
ln(Casino_rev)×D_Storefront retail/Resident	2.351	3.397	(0.69)
ln(Casino_rev)×D_Supermarket	3.740	15.59	(0.24)
D_Type$_i$ variables	Included	Included	Included
SubMkt$_j$ variables	Included	Included	Included
R-square	65.3 %		
Number of observations	488		

Source: Wiley and Walker (2011). Used with permission from Springer
***, **, and * indicate significance at the 1, 5, and 10 % levels, respectively

The results of this analysis provide empirical evidence that the commercial casinos in Detroit have had a positive impact on retail property values in the city. The effect is particularly strong within a 5-mile radius of the casinos, which suggests that the complementary effects of casinos on other businesses in our analysis diminish as the distance from casino increases.

Table 17.5 Results for (17.3) by property type: 5-mile radius [Dep. variable: ln(Sale_price)]

Variables	Coefficient	SE	(t-Stat)
Constant	70.2	195.8	(0.36)
ln(Age)	−0.3876***	0.0413	(−9.39)
ln(Bldg_SF)	0.5352***	0.0398	(13.45)
Coverage	0.1251	0.0868	(1.44)
Distance	−0.0054	0.0053	(−1.02)
ln(Land_area)	−1.501**	0.6251	(−2.40)
ln(N_Floors)	−0.1818	0.1737	(−1.05)
ln(Rel_days)	0.3656***	0.1173	(3.12)
ln(Pop_Det)	−18.10**	9.412	(−1.92)
ln(Supply_RBA)	11.56*	6.770	(1.71)
5mile × ln(Casino_rev) × D_Auto dealership	0.0164	0.0366	(0.45)
5mile × ln(Casino_rev) × D_Convenience store	−0.0041	0.0339	(−0.12)
5mile × ln(Casino_rev) × D_Fast food	−0.0041	0.0247	(−0.16)
5mile × ln(Casino_rev) × D_General freestanding	0.0993***	0.0256	(3.88)
5mile × ln(Casino_rev) × D_Restaurant	0.0827**	0.0344	(2.41)
5mile × ln(Casino_rev) × D_Service station	0.0621***	0.0195	(3.18)
5mile × ln(Casino_rev) × D_Storefront retail/Office	−0.0358	0.0264	(−1.36)
5mile × ln(Casino_rev) × D_Supermarket	−0.0042	0.0467	(−0.09)
D_Type$_i$ variables	Included	Included	Included
SubMkt$_j$ variables	Included	Included	Included
R-square	66.5 %		
Number of observations	488		

Source: Wiley and Walker (2011). Used with permission from Springer
***, **, and * indicate significance at the 1, 5, and 10 % levels, respectively

17.5 Conclusion

Few empirical analyses have examined the actual impact of casinos on property values. Detroit represents one of the first examples of "urban casinos" in the United States, making it an ideal case for this analysis. The analysis in this chapter examined the effect of Detroit's commercial casinos on commercial property values. Using retail property sales data, as well as property characteristics and casino volume, we empirically test the impact the Detroit casinos have had on commercial property values in the city.

The results indicate that casinos have a complementary effect on Detroit retail. An increase in casino revenues is associated with a statistically significant increase in retail property values. This effect is stronger in magnitude for properties within a 5-mile radius surrounding the commercial casinos. Restaurants, service stations, and general freestanding retail are each identified as property types that appreciate in value when nearby casinos generate higher revenue flows. Businesses who are either tenants or owners in these properties appear to significantly benefit from casino spillover effects. This is consistent with demand externalities on retail property that result from the drawing power of commercial casinos in an urban location.

17.5 Conclusion

This is some of the first rigorous empirical evidence of the impact of casinos on other commercial businesses. The findings suggest that casinos have a complementary effect on nearby businesses, as measured by commercial property prices. There is no evidence to support the hypothesis that a substitution effect exists whereby casinos merely absorb spending that might have taken place at other businesses. These results apply only to Detroit; however the model in this paper can provide a blueprint for subsequent empirical analyses. Understanding the influence of casinos on urban economies and real estate markets is of interest not only to policymakers and voters who may currently be considering casino legalization but also to academics and business owners who seek to better understand the full effects of casino development.

Several important caveats to this analysis should be emphasized. First, the casino–retail relationship in other markets may be markedly different than what we find for Detroit. Detroit is notably unique and strong conclusions about the general effects of casinos on surrounding businesses should not be drawn from this analysis. Current data availability makes it difficult to analyze all urban casino markets. Market heterogeneity alters expected outcomes from such efforts. Future research considering alternative markets and time periods is necessary to further the understanding of this relationship between casinos and retail property values.

Chapter 18
Relationships Among Gambling Industries

18.1 Introduction

In Part I of the book we examined the theoretical ways in which casinos could generate economic growth. We also found empirical evidence that suggests casinos do, in fact, have a positive growth effect at the state level. Also in Part I, however, we examined some of the criticisms of casinos. One key argument is that casinos expand at the expense of other industries. This is the so-called "substitution effect." In Chap. 17 we addressed this issue with respect to non-gambling industries. However, the analysis covered only one market (Detroit) and only for commercial real estate values. There have been several other studies in the literature to examine the impact of casinos on property values, as cited in Chap. 17.

It is also interesting to consider the impact of the casino industry on other gambling industries. In this chapter we focus very narrowly on the interindustry relationships among different sectors of the gambling industry. An understanding of these relationships is important as a matter of policy because tax revenues are often a goal of legalized gambling. (Yet, as discussed in Chap. 7, it is questionable whether there are significant positive tax impacts from legalized gambling.) If casinos and lotteries are complementary, for example, a lottery state can benefit by introducing casinos. If horse racing and casinos are substitutes for each other, a racing state may not want to introduce casinos.[1] The relationships between the various gambling industries have not received much attention in the literature.

In this chapter, seemingly unrelated regression (SUR) estimation is used to examine if and how the various gambling industries affect each other. The United States provides

---

The material in this chapter is based on Walker DM, JD Jackson. 2008. Do U.S. gambling industries cannibalize each other? *Public Finance Review* 36(3): 308–333. Used with permission from Sage.

[1] Here the terms "complementary" and "substitutes" are not referring to the relationship between the price of one good and the demand for another. Rather, it refers simply to whether two industries help each other, in terms of revenues, or harm each other.

an ideal case for analysis because data are publicly available and because it has well established gambling industries in a variety of states. Four industries are analyzed, from 1985 to 2000: casinos, greyhound racing, horse racing, and lotteries. The model uses industry volume as the dependent variable, with volume from the other industries, adjacent state industries, and a variety of demographic characteristics as explanatory variables. The results show that certain industries negatively impact each other (casinos and lotteries; horse and dog racing) while other industries help each other (casinos and horse racing; dog racing and lotteries; horse racing and lotteries).

This analysis is based on Walker and Jackson (2008a), which provides the first evidence on the general relationships between the different gambling industries in the United States.[2] No other studies, to my knowledge, have appeared for other countries. With information on the interindustry relationships, policymakers and voters can be more comfortable with their decisions regarding whether to expand gambling in their jurisdictions as well as the resulting economic and tax effects. This paper provides a critical foundation for studying these issues. Of course, the results here may not apply to other jurisdictions.

The chapter continues with a literature review in Sect. 18.2. The data used to test the relationships among gambling industries are described in Sect. 18.3. The model and results are described in Sect. 18.4; and Sect. 18.5 includes a discussion of the results and potential extensions.

18.2 Literature Review

Numerous studies have been published which focus on the demand for a particular type of gambling, the effect of one industry on another's revenues or on the state's tax revenue. In many cases, the papers have examined a single county or state, or a small group of states, and only during a short time frame.

As noted in Chap. 7, several papers focus on the effects of gambling industries on state tax revenues. (Refer to Sect. 7.2 for a more detailed review of the literature.) Anders, Siegel, and Yacoub (1998) examine the effect of Indian casinos on transactions tax revenue of one Arizona county. They find that tax losses from the retail, restaurant, bar, hotel, and amusement sectors were significant when casinos were introduced. Siegel and Anders (1999) examine Missouri sales tax revenues as a result of introducing riverboat casinos. Overall they find that aggregate taxes are not affected, but taxes from certain amusement industries fall. Popp and Stehwien (2002) examine county tax revenue in New Mexico and find that casinos have a

---

[2] Other published studies have focused more narrowly on estimating demand for individual gambling industries or have examined pairs of industries within single states.

negative effect on tax revenues within the county. But the effect of neighboring county casinos is somewhat odd in that the first casino has a negative effect while the second one has a positive effect on county tax revenues.

Other authors have focused more specifically on the interindustry relationships. Davis, Filer, and Moak (1992) test the factors that determine whether or not and when a state will adopt a lottery. Among other things, the authors find that state lottery revenue is higher the smaller the state's pari-mutuel industry and the smaller the percentage of bordering states that have lotteries. Mobilia (1992b) finds that a lottery dummy is negative and significant for pari-mutuel attendance but not for per attendee handle. Thalheimer and Ali (1995) find that lotteries reduce racetrack handle. However, the state that has both lotteries and racetracks benefits in terms of overall tax revenue. Ray (2001) finds that horse racing and casino dummies have significantly negative effects on total state greyhound handle. Siegel and Anders (2001) find the number of slot machines in Arizona Indian casinos has a significantly negative effect on lottery sales but horse and dog racing have no effect on the lottery. Elliott and Navin (2002) examine the probability of lottery adoption and the determinants of lottery sales. They find that casinos and pari-mutuels harm the lottery and that adjacent state lotteries have a small negative effect on lottery sales. The number of Indian casinos in a state and riverboat casinos in neighboring states do not significantly affect lottery sales. The note by Fink and Rork (2003) extends this work by taking into account that states self-select when legalizing casinos. Low-revenue lottery states are more likely to legalize casinos and this partly explains the negative relationship between casinos and lotteries. Kearney (2005) finds that spending on lottery tickets is financed completely by a reduction in non-gambling expenditures, implying that other forms of gambling are not harmed by a lottery.

Table 18.1 provides a summary of many of the studies which give information on the interindustry relationships. The table indicates the years examined, the scope of the study (e.g., one track or two states), whether the relationships were analyzed mainly with dummy variables, and key findings of the studies. The literature provides some important information about the relationships among gambling industries. The most common findings are that an industry either harms another industry or does not affect it. No study has found that different gambling industries help each other.

There are three important caveats regarding this area of research. First, the studies examine various often short time periods and tend to be limited to individual or small groups of states. It is difficult, if not impossible, to generalize from these studies to other regions or times. Second, most papers only provide a one-way test of the relationship between industries. For example, papers testing the effects of lotteries on pari-mutuels typically do not analyze the effect of pari-mutuels on lotteries. As a result, the literature lacks information on how some of the industries affect others. Third, many of the studies account for the existence of other gambling industries only through dummy variables. This ignores the volume of gambling in the industries.

Table 18.1 Review of literature on interindustry relationships

Paper	Years	States/counties	Primarily uses dummies?	Findings[a]
Anders, Siegel, and Yacoub (1998)	1990–1996	1 County (AZ)	Yes	Indian casinos harm other entertainment
Elliott and Navin (2002)	1989–1995	All states	No	Casinos and pari-mutuels harm lotteries
Kearney (2005)	1982–1998	All states	No	Lotteries do not harm other forms of gambling
Mobilia (1992b)	1972–1986	All racing states	Yes	Lotteries harm horse and dog racing
Popp and Stehwien (2002)	1990–1997	33 Counties (NM)	Yes	Indian casinos harm other entertainment
Ray (2001)	1991–1998	All dog racing states	Yes	Horse racing and casinos harm dog racing
Siegel and Anders (1999)	1994–1996	1 State (MO)	No	Casinos harm other entertainment
Siegel and Anders (2001)	1993–1998	1 State (AZ)	No	Slots harm the lottery; horse and dog racing do not affect the lottery
Thalheimer and Ali (1995)	1960–1987	3 Tracks (OH, KY)	No	Lottery harms horse racing

Source: Walker and Jackson (2008a). Used with permission from Sage
[a]"Other entertainment" refers to non-gambling industries, such as restaurants, hotels, and bars

To rectify these research issues, the present model covers all states and the District of Columbia during the 1985–2000 period. We examine how each of four industries (casinos, lotteries, dog racing, horse racing) affects the others. Finally, when analyzing the interindustry relationships, we rely on state-level industry volume, rather than using simple dummies to represent the industries' presence. This combination of features makes this analysis unique in the gambling literature.

18.3 Data

The main goal in this chapter is to determine the relationships among various gambling industries in the United States. A variety of demographic and industry volume data were collected for all states plus Washington, DC, for 1985–2000. There are a total of 816 observations for each of the variables, classified in three groups, discussed below.

18.3 Data

Table 18.2 Lottery availability in the United States, 1985–2000

State	First year	State	First year	State	First year	State	First year
AL		IL	*	MT	1988	RI	*
AK		IN	1990	NE	1994	SC	
AZ	*	IA	1986	NV		SD	1988
AR		KS	1988	NH	*	TN	
CA	1986	KY	1989	NJ	*	TX	1992
CO	*	LA	1992	NM	1996	UT	
CT	*	ME	*	NY	*	VT	*
DE	*	MD	*	NC		VA	1989
DC	*	MA	*	ND		WA	*
FL	1988	MI	*	OH	*	WV	1986
GA	1993	MN	1990	OK		WI	1989
HI		MS		OR	*	WY	
ID	1990	MO	1986	PA	*		

Notes: Unless otherwise indicated, data run through 2000. *Indicates lottery present from 1985 to 2000
Source: Walker and Jackson (2008a). Used with permission from Sage

18.3.1 Gambling Volume Variables

The gambling volume data for each industry in each state are summarized in Tables 18.2, 18.3, 18.4, 18.5, and 18.6.[3] The beginning year for the availability of each type of gambling in each state is indicated. An asterisk (*) indicates the availability of gambling in the state for the entire 1985–2000 period. In some states greyhound and horse racing were not available continuously. In these cases the

---

[3] The sources for the industry data follow. Lottery ticket sales come from *La Fleur's 2001 World Lottery Almanac*, 9th edition. TLF Publications, 2001. Casino revenues are from the American Gaming Association and various states' gaming commissions. Greyhound and horse racing handle are from the 1985–2000 issues of *Pari-Mutuel Racing*, published by the Association of Racing Commissioners International. The 1985–1990 dog and horse racing data and the 1995–2000 horse racing data were reported as handle. For horse and greyhound racing from 1991 to 1994, handle was calculated using the total pari-mutuel takeout and effective takeout rate (handle = total pari-mutuel takeout/effective takeout rate). The same process was used to calculate greyhound racing handle from 1995 to 2000. Thus all racing data are reported with a consistent measure. All of the above volume data are adjusted for inflation using the CPI from the Bureau of Labor Statistics (1982–1984 = 100). Annual state population estimates are from the Bureau of the Census. The states' annual Indian casino square footage was calculated using the casino listing at casinocity. com. At the time this was written, this source listed 126 Indian-owned casinos in the United States. Square footage and opening dates were collected from the casinos' Web pages or by phone calls to the casinos.

Table 18.3 Horse racing availability in the United States, 1985–2000

State	First year	State	First year	State	First year	State	First year
AL	1987, 1989–2000	IL	*	MT	*	RI	1991
AK		IN	1994	NE	*	SC	
AZ	*	IA	*	NV	1989	SD	*
AR	*	KS	1988	NH	*	TN	
CA	*	KY	*	NJ	*	TX	1989
CO	*	LA	*	NM	*	UT	
CT	*	ME	1985–1989, 1991–2000	NY	*	VT	1985–1997
DE	*	MD	*	NC		VA	
DC		MA	*	ND	1989	WA	*
FL	*	MI	*	OH	*	WV	*
GA		MN	1985–1992, 1994–2000	OK	*	WI	1996
HI		MS		OR	*	WY	*
ID	*	MO		PA	*		

Notes: Unless otherwise indicated, data run through 2000. *Indicates horse racing present from 1985 to 2000
Source: Walker and Jackson (2008a). Used with permission from Sage

Table 18.4 Greyhound racing availability in the United States, 1985–2000

State	First year	State	First year	State	First year	State	First year
AL	*	IL		MT		RI	*
AK		IN		NE		SC	
AZ	*	IA	*	NV		SD	*
AR	*	KS	1989	NH	*	TN	
CA		KY		NJ		TX	1990
CO	*	LA		NM		UT	
CT	*	ME		NY		VT	1985–1992
DE		MD		NC		VA	
DC		MA	*	ND		WA	
FL	*	MI		OH		WV	*
GA		MN		OK		WI	1990
HI		MS		OR	*	WY	
ID	1988	MO		PA			

Notes: Unless otherwise indicated, data run through 2000. *Indicates greyhound racing present from 1985 to 2000
Source: Walker and Jackson (2008a). Used with permission from Sage

years racing was available are listed. Some forms of gambling are exempt from the analysis (charity and private gambling, non-casino and racetrack video-poker or slot machines[4]).

---

[4] Slot machines and video poker at racetracks, called "racinos," are a relatively new phenomenon appearing in some states. Due to their relative newness and the inherent difficulties in classifying these non-racing bets (as racing handle or casino revenue?), this machine gambling is omitted from this analysis. For a discussion of racinos, see Eadington (1999, 176) and Thalheimer and Ali (2003, 908).

18.3 Data

Table 18.5 Casino availability in the United States, 1985–2000

State	First year	State	First year	State	First year	State	First year
AL		IL	1991	MT		RI	
AK		IN	1995	NE		SC	
AZ		IA	1992	NV	*	SD	1989
AR		KS		NH		TN	
CA		KY		NJ	*	TX	
CO	1991	LA	1993	NM		UT	
CT		ME		NY		VT	
DE		MD		NC		VA	
DC		MA		ND		WA	
FL		MI	1999	OH		WV	
GA		MN		OK		WI	
HI		MS	1992	OR		WY	
ID		MO	1994	PA			

Notes: Unless otherwise indicated, data run through 2000. *Indicates casinos present from 1985 to 2000
Source: Walker and Jackson (2008a). Used with permission from Sage

Table 18.6 Indian casino availability in the United States, 1985–2000

State	First year	State	First year	State	First year	State	First year
AL		IL		MT	1993	RI	
AK		IN		NE		SC	
AZ	*	IA	1992	NV		SD	*
AR		KS	1996	NH		TN	
CA	*	KY		NJ		TX	
CO	1992	LA	1988	NM	1987	UT	
CT	1992	ME		NY	*	VT	
DE		MD		NC		VA	
DC		MA		ND	1993	WA	*
FL	*	MI	1993	OH		WV	
GA		MN	*	OK	*	WI	*
HI		MS	1994	OR	1994	WY	
ID	1995	MO		PA			

Notes: Unless otherwise indicated, data run through 2000. *Indicates Indian casinos present from 1985 to 2000
Source: Walker and Jackson (2008a). Used with permission from Sage

As indicated above, we are interested in the volume of each type of gambling in each of the states. The data for greyhound racing, horse racing, and lotteries are "handle per capita," the total dollar value of bets placed divided by the state population.[5] The data for casino volume are "revenue per capita," the amount the casino

---

[5] In the case of lotteries, this is ticket sales per capita.

keeps after paying winning bets divided by state population.[6] Finally, for Indian casinos we use Indian-owned casino square footage as a proxy for gambling volume. Since Indian casinos are not required to report revenue or handle data, this is perhaps the best measure available.[7]

18.3.2 Adjacent-State Variables

Whether the various gaming activities act as substitutes or complements to each other, the presence of these activities in neighboring states can lead to border crossings by consumers that may cause potentially dramatic effects on the volume of a particular gaming activity in a given state. Certainly, failure to account for these effects in some way can lead to a serious misstatement of the effects of other in-state gaming activities on the volume of the activity in question. State border crossings by consumers have received considerable attention, especially in the bootlegging and tobacco tax literature.[8] They have also recently found their way into the literature on state lotteries by Garrett and Marsh (2002) and Tosun and Skidmore (2004).

There is no obvious "best" method for accounting for adjacent-state purchases of gambling services. The available measures include

1. Aggregate volume of adjacent state gambling
2. Aggregate per capita adjacent state gambling volume
3. Percentage of adjacent states to allow a particular type of gambling

The first measure is problematic because a higher level of adjacent state gambling volume may be the result of a larger population or a higher volume of tourists, or a combination of the two.

The second measure, per capita adjacent state gambling volume, is problematic because summing per capita measures across neighboring states results in a meaningless number. A higher sum may result from more gambling, more neighbors, or fewer residents. The interpretation of these two options is also difficult.[9]

---

[6] Revenue per capita is used rather than handle per capita because casino revenue cannot be reliably converted to handle. For example, suppose a person walks into a casino and buys $100 worth of chips and plays until she loses the $100. The total handle could range from $100 to any higher amount. It would be $100 if she lost a single $100 hand of black-jack. But suppose she plays and wins several thousand dollars, but later loses it all. The total handle in this case is in the thousands of dollars, even though she only lost $100 of her own money. This example illustrates why an estimate of casino handle would be unreliable. Even if it was possible to convert revenue to handle, say by using some multiple, this adjustment would not affect relative coefficient estimates in any meaningful way.

[7] I inquired with Caesars Entertainment, one of the largest US casino operators, who also manages numerous Indian-owned casinos. They confirmed that there is a general industry formula for the number of slot machines and table games as a function of square footage. For this reason, Indian casino square footage is a satisfactory, albeit imperfect, measure of Indian casino volume.

[8] For example, see Saba et al. (1995) and references therein.

[9] Other attempts to measure the intensity of adjacent-state gambling have similar difficulties. The primary concern here is the *availability* of gambling in nearby states.

18.3 Data

Table 18.7 States and their adjacent states

State	Adjacent states	State	Adjacent states
AL	MS, TN, GA, FL	NE	CO, WY, SD, IA, MO, KS
AZ	CA, NV, UT, CO, NM	NV	CA, OR, ID, UT, AZ
AR	TX, OK, MO, TN, MS, LA	NH	VT, ME, MA
CA	OR, NV, AZ	NJ	DE, MD, PA, NY, CT
CO	AZ, UT, WY, NE, KS, OK, NM	NM	AZ, UT, CO, OK, TX
CT	NY, MA, RI, NJ	NY	PA, VT, MA, CT, NJ
DE	MD, PA, NJ	NC	SC, TN, VA, GA
DC	VA, MD	ND	MT, MN, SD
FL	AL, GA	OH	IN, MI, PA, VW, KY
GA	AL, TN, NC, SC, FL	OK	NM, CO, KS, MO, AR, TX
ID	OR, WA, MT, WY, UT, NV	OR	WA, ID, NV, CA
IL	MO, IA, WI, IN, KY	PA	NY, NJ, MD, WV, OH, DE
IN	IL, MI, OH, KY	RI	CT, MA
IA	NE, SD, MN, WI, IL, MO	SC	GA, NC
KS	CO, NE, MO, OK	SD	WY, MT, ND, MN, IA, NE
KY	MO, IL, IN, OH, WV, VA, TN	TN	AR, MO, KY, VA, NC, GA, AL, MS
LA	TX, AR, MS	TX	NM, OK, AR, LA
ME	NH	UT	NV, ID, WY, CO, NM, AZ
MD	VA, WV, DC, PA, NJ, DE	VT	NY, NH, MA
MA	RI, CT, NY, VT, NH	VA	NC, TN, KY, WV, MD, DC
MI	WI, IN, OH	WA	OR, ID
MN	SD, ND, WI, IA	WV	KY, OH, PA, MD, VA
MS	LA, AR, TN, AL	WI	MN, MI, IA, IL
MO	KS, IA, IL, KY, TN, AR, NE, OK	WY	ID, MT, SD, NE, CO, UT
MT	ID, ND, SD, WY		

Note: Alaska and Hawaii are omitted
Source: Walker and Jackson (2008a). Used with permission from Sage

The third measure presents the fewest potential problems although it is the most general of the measures. To account for cross-border effects in this study, we follow Davis, Filer, and Moak's (1992) example and utilize the percentage of adjacent states with a particular form of gambling during each year.[10] While this measure will not perfectly reflect the amount of cross-border gambling, its interpretation is unambiguous and less problematic than other measures. What it does well is indicate the nearby gambling options of residents in a particular state. Its limitation, of course, is that it does not measure the intensity with which these options are offered by the surrounding states. Table 18.7 lists the states adjacent to each state.

---

[10] As an example, in 2000, Florida's adjacent state lottery observation would be 0.5, since Georgia had a lottery that year and Alabama did not.

18.3.3 Demographic Variables

Some studies have used surveys to get a general demographic picture of the typical gambler (American Gaming Association 2006a; Gazel and Thompson 1996; Harrah's Entertainment 1997). Variables on population and demographic characteristics, such as education, income level, age, and religious beliefs, may be helpful in explaining variations in gambling volume across states and industries.

There has been somewhat conflicting evidence on the level of education and the tendency to gamble. Obviously those with more education are more likely to understand the negative expected return from games of chance. However, Harrah's (1997) and the AGA (2006a) find that casino players tend to have an above average level of education. Clotfelter and Cook (1990) find that lottery play falls as education level rises. As a proxy for education levels, we include as a variable in the models the percentage of citizens over 25 years old holding bachelor degrees. This variable may be related to the income variable as income and education levels tend to move together.

Eadington (1976) suggests that gambling may be perceived by lower-income people as a means of achieving a higher level of income. Evidence on lotteries has suggested that lotteries amount to a regressive tax (Oster 2004). In an effort to test this proposition, the estimated percentage of people in the states living in poverty is included as a variable. While it may be true that the poor will tend to spend a larger proportion of their income on gambling, that does not imply that more in this group will lead to higher total gambling revenues for a state. Clotfelter and Cook (1990) find no clear relationship between income level and lottery play. The AGA (2006a) reports that the median income of casino players is slightly higher than that of the overall population. State real per capita income is included in the models to determine and account for the effect of average income on the tendency to gamble.

Another important demographic variable may be the age of the population. Retirees may be of particular interest, as Gazel and Thompson (1996) report that older people make up a high proportion of casino gamblers. Harrah's (1997) and the AGA (2006a) on the other hand find that the median age of casino players is about the average for the US population. The estimated percentage of people in the states over 65 years old is included as a variable in the model. Although previous evidence seems mixed, the variable may provide information as to who gambles.

Jackson, Saurman, and Shughart (1994) and Elliott and Navin (2002) use a variable for the number of Baptists in a state to help predict the probability of lottery adoption. Baptists are a large and well-organized interest group opposed to gambling and may have a negative effect on gambling revenues. Following these authors, we include the estimated percentage of Baptists in the states as an explanatory variable.

Finally, the number of hotel employees in each state is used as a rough measure of the volume of tourism in the states during each year.

State per capita income and hotel workers are reported annually.[11] For the data on Baptists, degree holders, older people, and poverty, 2 years' data are used to derive linear annual estimates for the 1985–2000 period for each state.[12]

18.4 Model and Results[13]

We are attempting to explain the relationships among gambling industries by modeling the gambling volume in each industry as a function of the volume in the other industries, adjacent state gambling activity, and demographic factors. A panel data model has the advantage of increasing the size of the data set, especially helpful for industries like gambling, which are rather young in some states. The econometric model is chosen based on the fact that the dependent variable (industry volume) in the model is left-censored. Left censoring is more prevalent for the casino and horse racing industries than it is for dog racing and lotteries.[14] Still, it is a problem for all industries. States self-select into legalizing a certain form of gambling. Those that do not elect to allow gambling get "0"s for the revenue variable leading to the censored data. We must account for this censoring in the parameter estimates. This is done with a probit model to explain the probability of legalizing each gambling industry. Following Heckman (1979) we obtain the inverse Mills ratio (IMR) from the probits and include it in the model as an additional explanatory variable for gambling revenue. This should correct for censoring bias. The probit models are presented in Table 18.8.[15]

In the panel model we use a time trend to account for intertemporal variation within a state and include regional dummies to pick up unexplained heterogeneity across regions as in fixed effect models. These regional dummies turn out to be significant to varying degrees across industries but they do not affect the coefficient estimates or the alternative gambling revenue coefficients appreciably, and the results are reported without these dummies.

A system of four equations is estimated where each equation is intended to explain the volume of one type of gambling as a function of volumes of other types of

---

[11] The hotel employee information and per capita income data come from the Bureau of Economic Analysis. The per capita income data are adjusted for inflation using the Bureau of Labor Statistics CPI data.

[12] Annual estimates for these are not available. The years used to derive the estimates vary due to data availability: Baptists (1980 and 1990); degree holders (1990 and 2001); older people (1990 and 2001); and poverty (1992 and 2001). The data come from the Bureau of the Census, with the exception of Baptists, from the *New Book of American Rankings*.

[13] Readers who are not interested in the technical details of the model can safely skip to Sect. 18.5.

[14] No model is posited for Indian casino gambling since the volume measure for this industry (square footage) is rather crude.

[15] Although the probit models are intended only to correct for left-censoring of the data, they do give some insight into the probabilities of adopting the various forms of gambling. Obviously their usefulness in this regard is limited because the specification of the models has a different goal.

Table 18.8 Sample selection probits

Variable	Casino	Dog racing	Horse racing	Lottery
Constant	−3.565***	−0.677*	1.343***	−6.266***
	(−6.572)	(−1.70)	(3.24)	(−10.69)
Casino dummy	–	−0.211	0.505**	2.303***
		(−1.31)	(2.39)	(4.77)
Dog racing dummy	−0.207	–	1.075***	0.897***
	(−1.41)		(7.04)	(5.66)
Horse racing dummy	0.434**	1.094***	–	1.060***
	(2.08)	(6.98)		(6.55)
Lottery dummy	1.202***	0.779***	0.881***	–
	(5.10)	(5.21)	(6.04)	
Indian casino dummy	0.529***	0.114	0.897***	−0.323**
	(3.74)	(1.04)	(6.09)	(−2.05)
Hotel workers	40.112***	−10.58	−0.189	−83.355***
	(7.19)	(−1.24)	(−0.05)	(−6.96)
Baptists	0.030***	0.004	−0.030***	−0.037***
	(4.68)	(0.76)	(−6.92)	(−7.46)
Degree holders	0.019	0.010	0.005	0.046***
	(1.21)	(0.81)	(0.38)	(3.01)
Income per capita	−0.695e−5	−0.920e−4***	−0.956e−4***	0.0004***
	(−0.19)	(−3.10)	(−2.66)	(10.38)

Notes: The z-statistic is indicated in parentheses below each coefficient. Significance: *0.10 level; **0.05 level; ***0.01 level
Source: Walker and Jackson (2008a). Used with permission from Sage

gambling, the presence of various types of adjacent state gaming, and state specific demographic factors. The system attempts to explain spending on casinos, dog racing, horse racing, and lotteries. Even after accounting for problems arising from left censoring of the spending measures and the panel nature of the data, we face the problem of a potential relationship among the errors of the four equations. Such a relationship could arise from neglected macroeconomic variables affecting the different equations via their errors in a given year or from differing general attitudes and preferences regarding gambling across states in a given time period. To the extent that this system of equations is a variant of a demand system, the theoretically implied adding up constraints require the sum of the disturbances across equations be zero so there must be some correlation between the disturbances in the different equations (Phlips 1983, 198–199). These types of problems are typically lumped under the heading of "contemporaneous correlation" of the disturbances across equations that can be handled by seemingly unrelated regression (SUR) estimation techniques. This empirical procedure allows us to estimate our four equation model jointly as a system of equations rather than applying OLS to each equation independently, thereby assuring us of more efficient parameter estimates and facilitating the imposition of cross equation parameter restrictions.

The system is similar to, but not identical to, a demand equation system, such as Stone's linear expenditure system or Theil's Rotterdam model. Demand systems

18.4 Model and Results

typically estimate a system of equations in which some measure of quantities demanded are functions of relative prices and real income, so that the estimated coefficients can be interpreted as (Hicksian) compensated own- and cross-price elasticities and income elasticities.[16] This system, on the other hand, involves expenditures (prices times quantities) rather than prices or quantities alone. Gambling, like most service industries, encounters measurement difficulties in attempting to separate prices from quantities, or more particularly, in attempting to measure quantities purchased. While we would like to exploit the similarity to demand systems as much as possible, the analogy is tenuous in at least two areas.

First, in demand systems estimates substitute commodities are typically indicated by positive coefficient estimates on the prices of related goods and complementarity by negative coefficient estimates. In the expenditure system, substitutable (or cannibalizing or competing) gaming activities are defined as ones in which increases in consumer expenditures on one activity result in decreased consumer expenditures on the related activity, or a negative coefficient estimate when the latter is a function of the former. Similarly, a complementary relationship among gaming activities arises when increased consumer spending on one activity results in increased expenditures on the related activity as well, a positive coefficient estimate when the latter is a function of the former. Our definition is consistent with the more traditional one only under some fairly restrictive assumptions concerning magnitudes of the price elasticities involved. However, our definition is heuristically valid and it is also perhaps more meaningful if the primary interest is in the tax-revenue-maximizing bundle of games of chance.

Second, in demand systems estimation, the compensated cross-price elasticity estimates are constrained to be symmetric across equations. That is, the compensated cross-price elasticity of demand for good A with respect to the price of good B must be identical to the compensated cross-price elasticity of demand for good B with respect to the price of good A. Imposing such restrictions is not only implied by demand theory, it also results in more efficient parameter estimates. Unfortunately, it is not at all clear that this type of symmetry restriction is appropriate when the equations are expressed in expenditure form. It is reasonable to expect that if a rise in expenditure on casino gambling results in a decreased expenditure on the lottery, then a rise in expenditure on the lottery should also result in a decreased expenditure on casino gambling, i.e., symmetry of signs on the corresponding expenditure variables across the relevant equations. However, there is no reason to suspect that the magnitudes involved would be the same. While there is an empirical rationale to impose symmetry constraints across equations, namely smaller standard errors, there is not the theoretical rationale that is present in demand theory. To gain some insight into how sensitive the estimates are to the imposition of cross equation symmetry restrictions, the equation system is estimated with them imposed and again without them. Tables 18.9 and 18.10 present the respective SUR results.

---

[16] These demand systems are often estimated by SUR. For example, see Wooldridge (2002, 144–145) or Greene (2003, 341 and 362–369).

Table 18.9 SUR model with cross-industry constraints

Variable	Casino	Dog racing	Horse racing	Lottery
Casino	–	−0.020***	0.277***	−0.104***
		(−2.89)	(14.18)	(−4.93)
Dog racing	−0.020***	–	−0.062***	0.136***
	(−2.89)		(−6.10)	(17.26)
Horse racing	0.277***	−0.062***	–	0.844***
	(14.18)	(−6.10)		(67.43)
Lottery	−0.104***	0.136***	0.844***	–
	(−4.93)	(17.26)	(67.43)	
Indian square footage	151.19***	11.289	154.05***	−86.08*
	(3.07)	(0.90)	(3.68)	(−1.75)
Adjacent casino	−0.035***	0.0006	0.087***	−0.065***
	(−3.71)	(0.24)	(11.27)	(−7.09)
Adjacent dog racing	−0.040	0.060***	0.085	−0.022
	(−0.61)	(3.55)	(1.53)	(−0.33)
Adjacent horse racing	0.136***	−0.02***	−0.269***	0.227***
	(6.603)	(−3.59)	(−15.87)	(11.36)
Adjacent lottery	0.007	−0.009**	0.128***	−0.118***
	(0.45)	(−2.21)	(10.00)	(−7.76)
Age >65	−0.297e7	0.176e8***	−0.541e7	0.319e7
	(−0.50)	(11.29)	(−1.08)	(0.54)
Baptists	0.489e7***	484,006.51*	−239,954.20	−0.126e7
	(4.79)	(1.88)	(−0.28)	(−1.23)
Degree holders	−0.102e8*	−0.240e7	0.326e7	−0.104e8*
	(−1.722)	(−1.59)	(0.65)	(−1.76)
Hotel workers	0.336e11***	0.144e10***	−0.350e10***	−0.377e10***
	(42.95)	(4.79)	(−3.87)	(−3.69)
Income per capita	6,643.48	1,016.18	−16,661.41**	47,573.32***
	(0.83)	(0.48)	(−2.48)	(6.04)
Constant	−0.366e11***	0.305e10	0.853e11***	−0.838e11***
	(−2.78)	(0.92)	(7.79)	(−6.51)
Year	0.182e8***	−0.162e7	−0.428e8***	0.419e8***
	(2.75)	(−0.97)	(−7.74)	(6.46)
Inverse mills ratio (IMR)	0.402e9***	0.730e8***	0.487e8***	0.655e8***
	(20.15)	(17.54)	(4.18)	(4.12)

Notes: The *t*-statistic is indicated in parentheses below each coefficient. Significance: *0.10 level; **0.05 level; ***0.01 level
Source: Walker and Jackson (2008a). Used with permission from Sage

18.4.1 Discussion of Results

Let us briefly consider the results presented in Table 18.9 where the corresponding cross equation industry volume coefficients have been constrained to equality, and Table 18.10 incorporating no cross equation constraints. In comparing the industry volume coefficient estimates, the most important result to note is that there are no sign or significance discrepancies between corresponding coefficient estimates

18.4 Model and Results

Table 18.10 SUR model, unconstrained

Variable	Casino	Dog racing	Horse racing	Lottery
Casino	–	−0.019***	0.234***	−0.115***
		(−2.64)	(10.04)	(−4.06)
Dog racing	−0.165	–	−0.956***	1.642***
	(−1.38)		(−9.63)	(14.46)
Horse racing	0.355***	−0.062***	–	1.042***
	(9.08)	(−6.01)		(38.42)
Lottery	−0.079**	0.122***	0.726***	–
	(−2.33)	(15.19)	(37.36)	
Indian square footage	113.04**	12.47	180.76***	−151.26***
	(2.25)	(0.99)	(4.30)	(−3.03)
Adjacent casino	−0.042***	0.001	0.087***	−0.083***
	(−4.26)	(0.46)	(11.23)	(−8.79)
Adjacent dog racing	−0.046	0.067***	0.213***	−0.244***
	(−0.68)	(3.96)	(3.74)	(−3.63)
Adjacent horse racing	0.148***	−0.018***	−0.241***	0.242***
	(6.78)	(−3.20)	(−14.07)	(11.61)
Adjacent lottery	−0.007	−0.010**	0.098***	−0.096***
	(−0.40)	(−2.54)	(7.44)	(−6.07)
Age >65	0.669e6	0.185e8***	0.200e8***	−0.391e8***
	(0.10)	(11.85)	(3.51)	(−5.83)
Baptists	0.516e7***	444,286.82*	−256,651.01	−0.126e7
	(5.04)	(1.73)	(−0.30)	(−1.23)
Degree holders	−0.687e7	−0.277e7*	−0.515e7	318,567.45
	(−1.14)	(−1.83)	(−1.01)	(0.05)
Hotel workers	0.339e11***	0.128e10***	−0.320e10***	−0.299e10**
	(42.06)	(4.23)	(−3.17)	(−2.50)
Income per capita	−1,796.71	2,844.01	9,334.11	12,761.11
	(−0.21)	(1.34)	(1.36)	(1.54)
Constant	−0.359e11***	0.218e10	0.693e11***	−0.793e11***
	(−2.70)	(0.66)	(6.26)	(−6.11)
Year	0.179e8***	−0.120e7	−0.349e8***	0.401e8***
	(2.667)	(−0.72)	(−6.27)	(6.12)
Inverse mills ratio (IMR)	0.395e9***	0.667e8***	0.481e8***	0.833***
	(19.55)	(15.88)	(4.12)	(5.18)

Notes: The *t*-statistic is indicated in parentheses below each coefficient. Significance: *0.10 level; **0.05 level; ***0.01 level
Source: Walker and Jackson (2008a). Used with permission from Sage

across the two tables, and there is only one notable discrepancy in terms of magnitude. The dog racing coefficient in the lottery equation is roughly ten times as large in the unconstrained estimate as in the constrained case. Even though the cross equation restrictions are of questionable theoretical validity, their imposition appears to have no appreciable impact on the industry volume coefficient estimates. In general, the corresponding coefficient estimates across tables are very similar in terms of sign, significance, and magnitude. For this reason we confine the interpretation of the results to the unconstrained case presented in Table 18.10.

The results for the casino revenue model indicate that increases in horse racing handle and Indian casino gambling and decreases in lottery sales in the state tend to significantly increase state licensed casino gambling revenues. The presence of casino gambling in adjacent states significantly decreases and the presence of horse racing in adjacent states significantly increases casino revenues. Only two of the demographic variables affected casino revenues, Baptists and tourism ("Hotel workers") and both affect it positively. While the tourism result was expected, the Baptist result was a surprise and may simply be the result of Baptists proxying a significant regional (southeast) effect. There is a significant positive trend ("Year") in casino revenues over the period of the sample. Finally, the significance of the IMR clearly indicates the importance of correcting for left censoring of casino revenues. All other parameters in the model are insignificant.

The results for the dog racing model indicate that increases in lottery sales and decreases in horse racing handle and casino revenues in the state in question statistically increase dog racing handle. Apparently, horse racing and lotteries in adjacent states compete with in-state dog racing since these variables have significant and negative coefficient estimates. There may be agglomeration economies in dog racing since the presence of dog racing in adjacent states appears to significantly increase dog racing handle. Increases in population over 65 and tourism significantly increase dog racing handle at the 1 % level while increases in Baptists and decreases in degree holders increase it at the 10 % level. The significance of the IMR indicates the importance of correcting for left censoring. All other parameters in the model are insignificant.

The results for the horse racing model indicate that increases in casinos, Indian casinos, and lotteries and decreases in dog racing handle increase horse racing handle. In addition, the presence of casino gambling, dog racing and lotteries in adjacent states increases horse racing handle while the presence of horse racing in adjacent states competes by significantly decreasing horse racing handle. Increases in population over 65 and decreases in tourism significantly increase horse racing handle. The tourism result is surprising but with the possible exception of major races (Triple Crown, Breeder's Cup, etc.) horse racing does not attract overnight type tourists. Finally, there is a significant downward trend in horse racing revenues, and the IMR is again significant. All other parameters in the horse racing equation are insignificant.

Results of the lottery model indicate increases in dog and horse racing handle and decreases in Indian casinos and casino revenues increase lottery sales. The presence in adjacent states of casino gambling, dog racing, and lotteries decreases in-state lottery sales, while the presence in adjacent states of horse racing increases them. Further, decreases in population over 65 and tourism significantly increase lottery revenues. In this case, the tourism result is not so odd. Few states *do not* have some form of state-run lottery. While tourists may indeed buy lottery tickets, it is unlikely that they go to a neighboring state and stay overnight solely to do so. Finally, there is an upward trend in lottery sales over the sample period, and the IMR is again significant. All other parameters in the lottery equation are insignificant.

18.4.2 Effects of Cross-Equation Constraints

Before turning to a detailed discussion of the substitution question, we should address a seemingly puzzling anomaly that is obviated by a careful comparison of the constrained and unconstrained results in Tables 18.9 and 18.10. First note that we only constrain the corresponding industry volume coefficients across equations. No constraints are directly applied to the adjacent state, demographic, and "other" variables' coefficients. Second, recall that the imposition of these industry volume constraints did not appear to appreciably alter the constrained estimates from their unconstrained counterparts. The constrained coefficients themselves are not the only estimates affected by the imposition of constraints. The unconstrained coefficient estimates can also be affected.

As an example, consider the coefficient estimates for the variable "Age > 65" in the constrained and unconstrained casino revenue models. In the constrained model, "Age > 65" has a coefficient estimate of -0.297×10^7 and in the unconstrained casino revenue model its estimate is 0.669×10^6. Neither coefficient is statistically significant. Indeed, with the exception of a few cases for a couple of the demographic variables, the pattern of signs and significance is amazingly uniform across the constrained and unconstrained results. Nevertheless, a point estimate discrepancy of this magnitude is worth noting, and is almost certainly attributable solely to the imposition of the cross equation constraints on the parameter estimates in Table 18.9.

As an illustration, consider the dropping of an important variable from a hypothetical regression. This is nothing more than imposing a constraint to equal zero on the coefficient. Econometric theory tells us that omitting a variable can lead to biased estimates of the remaining variables and that the extent of the bias depends in part on the correlation between the excluded and included variables. In the casino revenue case "Age > 65" was apparently highly correlated with one of the constrained variables. This is not always the case. Consider the constrained and unconstrained estimates of the "Baptists" variable in the lottery equation. They are almost identical (almost, due to rounding) and they are both insignificant. We can infer from this result that "Baptists" is uncorrelated with any of the constrained variables in the lottery equation of Table 18.9. These types of anomalous results in comparing constrained and unconstrained estimates are not unusual. They are replete throughout the empirical literature on demand system estimation.

In summary, there are no major point estimate discrepancies between corresponding constrained and unconstrained models in any of the statistically significant coefficients in any of the gambling models. Since there is no apparent gain from imposing the cross equation constraints, and since there is a potential for biased estimation if the constraints are not justified, our attention is confined in subsequent discussion to the unconstrained estimates of Table 18.10. A summary of the interindustry effects from the unconstrained model are presented in Table 18.11.

Table 18.11 Summary of intrastate industry relationships in the United States (unconstrained model)

Model variable	Casino	Dog racing	Horse racing	Lottery
Casino		−	+	−
Dog racing	(−)		−	+
Horse racing	+	−		+
Lottery	−	+	+	
Indian square footage	+	(+)	+	−

Note: ( ) indicates statistically insignificant at normal levels
Source: Walker and Jackson (2008a). Used with permission from Sage

18.5 Policy Issues

Our main interest is in discovering whether there are general intrastate relationships among the various gambling industries. It is for this reason that we focus our discussion of the results on the "industry volume" variables summarized in Table 18.11. The results suggest that horse and dog racing are substitutes. They are similar types of venues, and this result is reasonable. Lotteries and casinos are negatively related. This is consistent with findings by Elliott and Navin (2002) and Fink and Rork (2003). However, lotteries do *not* appear to cannibalize the racing industries. This is somewhat consistent with Kearney's (2005) finding that spending on lotteries comes at the expense of spending on non-gambling goods and services, but is contrary to the evidence by Gulley and Scott (1989), Mobilia (1992b), and Thalheimer and Ali (1995).

The availability of a type of gambling in adjacent states will harm that industry in the state (except for dog racing). Although many studies have not considered adjacent state effects, these results are consistent with those of Davis, Filer, and Moak (1992), Elliott and Navin (2002), Garrett and Marsh (2002) and Tosun and Skidmore (2004).

The differences in these findings and those of previous studies can be explained by differences in the industries and states considered, time periods, and econometric methodology. Of course a specific state or industry might behave differently than the aggregates studied here. Some of the results are not intuitive. For example, casinos and horse racing help each other, but casinos and dog racing harm each other. Indian casinos tend to complement casinos and horse racing, but harm lotteries. These results may be due to the peculiarities in certain states that exert significant influence.

Despite its aging data, this study is still one of the only attempts to examine all the industries in all states in an effort to provide a comprehensive understanding of the relationships among all the various gambling industries. The findings here may be used as a starting point for analyzing the expected effects of introducing or expanding gambling industries in a state, region, or country. Although this study is nation-wide, the relationship between two industries in a particular jurisdiction may be different than that indicated here. One *caveat*, however, is that our analysis does not include the effects of the recent expansion of the casino industry. We cannot generalize beyond our analysis period, which ended in 2000.

The fact that the analysis did not find a clear and consistent cannibalization effect among the different industries suggests that legislators should be careful to study their specific cases prior to acting to introduce or expand gambling in their jurisdiction. Legalizing additional forms of gambling may have either a positive or a negative impact on tax revenue and the economy. These issues call for further empirical study.

18.5.1 Tax Revenues

Tax policy has a lengthy history in the public economics literature. Various authors have examined "optimal taxes," including Ramsey (1927), Mirrlees (1971), Slemrod (1990), Sobel (1997), and Holcombe (1998). This literature typically deals with setting tax rates in an effort to minimize distortions or maximize welfare or efficiency. However, it would seem that governments are not so much interested in efficiency as they are in revenue maximization, at least when it comes to gambling legalization.[17] This seems especially relevant as record budget deficits become more commonplace. Consider the fact that the legal restrictions on gambling are extremely inefficient causing enormous deadweight losses. And since the jurisdictions rarely allow a competitive market in gambling when they do decide to legalize, it is unlikely that their primary concern is efficiency.[18] A much more likely goal or motivation is maximizing tax revenues given regulated gambling industries.

There are a few papers that examine revenue maximization from excise taxes, and some papers that examine legalized gambling specifically. These papers were discussed in Chap. 7, where we analyzed the impacts of the different gambling industries on state tax revenues.

What we did not address in that chapter was how the relationships among the industries could affect tax revenues. To illustrate the problem, consider a lottery state that is contemplating legalizing casinos. State revenue from a lottery is about 50 % of each dollar bet (Garrett 2001) while the taxes on casino revenues are typically a lower percentage. Our results indicate that casinos and lotteries negatively affect each other. The magnitude of this relationship among other variables will determine the extent to which tax revenue will change if casinos are introduced in a lottery state.[19]

---

[17] See Alm, McKee, and Skidmore (1993) and Madhusudhan (1996) on using legalized gambling to ease fiscal constraints.

[18] There is a variety of potential social concerns that may accompany legalized gambling, but these are not the subject of this chapter.

[19] Mason and Stranahan (1996) look more generally at the effects of casinos on state tax revenues, but not particularly at revenues from other forms of gambling.

If lotteries and casinos were perfect substitutes so that people who lose $X at newly opened casinos spend $X less on lottery tickets, then the introduction of casinos would lead to a *decrease* in state tax revenue from gambling. In New Jersey, for example, the revenue from the lottery is 50 % per ticket. The state tax on gross casino gambling revenues is 8 %. If lotteries and casinos were perfect substitutes, and New Jersey already had a lottery, and if all casino revenue were from lost lottery ticket sales, then we would expect the state's total gambling tax revenues to fall after casinos were introduced. In reality, most states have more complicated mechanisms for casino taxes, it is unlikely that any two industries are perfect substitutes, and the introduction of a new good (casino gambling) to a consumption menu is likely to draw in additional consumers. The example is purely hypothetical.

In any case, the empirical results do not provide the necessary data to confidently predict the net tax effect of introducing another type of gambling. This is because the coefficient estimates in Tables 18.9 and 18.10 are not standard elasticities, as explained in Sect. 18.4. What the results do provide that is important is information on the signs of the various gambling volume coefficients and their statistical significance, which in turn provides information on whether the gambling industries tend to be substitutes or complements.

18.6 Conclusion

The analysis in this chapter extends the analysis in Chap. 17, by considering the interindustry relationships among different gambling industries. It is thus, fundamentally, a study of the "substitution effect" among gambling industries. An understanding of these relationships may be very important for policymakers who are considering introducing a new form of gambling, but with a concern that it does not negatively affect other industries. In Kentucky, for example, they have been debating the introduction of casinos for several years. A major concern is the extent to which casinos might harm the well-established horse racing industry there.[20] Our results in this chapter suggest that the two industries are, in fact, complementary. Nevertheless, the racing industry's concern is an example of the general concern that many business owners have, regardless of industry, with casinos entering a regional economy.

Governments are in a unique situation when contemplating gambling legalization as they control not only the tax rates but also the quantity of gambling supplied. The revenue maximization problem depends on the size and types of existing gambling industries within the state or region, the intensity of their substitutability or complementarity, the prospective size of new industries, and the tax rates applied to the various industries. These issues require additional study, and the analysis here provides a good foundation for it.

---

[20] For example, see Hall and Loftus (2013).

Chapter 19
Overview of Part III

In the chapters in this part of the book we have focused on some of the social cost issues related to casinos. In Chaps. 13 and 14, we present the economic perspective on social costs. Importantly, many social cost studies do not define what they mean by "social cost." This has led to a wide variety of social cost estimates in the literature. Most of these likely overestimate the true social costs of gambling. Because of the inherent problems in defining and measuring social costs, it may be beneficial for researchers to stop trying to estimate a monetary value for costs, and instead identify the types of problems that disordered gamblers experience. Psychologists have been working on this issue for several decades.

The remaining chapters in Part III are more focused on specific types of costs that are often associated with casinos and gambling. In Chap. 15, I examine the claim that some types of gambling (especially professional gambling) qualify as wealth-reducing "directly unproductive profit-seeking" activities. However, I have tried to show why this is an incorrect characterization of gambling, even professional gambling. Indeed, for most people, gambling is like any other form of entertainment, and is in this sense productive.

One of the major concerns about legalizing casinos is that doing so will result in crime rate increases in areas surrounding casinos. In Chap. 16 I review some of this literature. Based on the empirical evidence from the literature, there is not a clear link between casinos and crime.

Another concern many people have about the introduction of casinos is that they will "cannibalize" other industries, either gambling- or non-gambling industries. In Chap. 17 we examine how casinos have affected commercial real estate values in Detroit. If casinos did, in fact, harm other businesses, one would expect to see a decrease in the price of commercial real estate surrounding the casinos. We actually found that casinos have a positive effect on certain types of retail property, especially those traditionally associated with tourism.

In Chap. 18, we examine the relationship among different gambling industries. We found that casinos have a negative impact on greyhound racing and lotteries, but that casinos are actually complementary to the horse racing industry. This evidence suggests that states looking to legalize casinos should carefully consider the impact on other gambling industries in their state. The net impact of casinos may be more or less than expected, depending on what other gambling industries are present.

Overall, the material in Part III provides a comprehensive overview of the different negative social and economic impacts that may be associated with casinos. However, when we examine specific types of social costs, we find that often the literature has overstated the magnitude of these costs. And in some cases, the casinos actually have a positive impact.

Part IV
Conclusion

Chapter 20
Past and Future

20.1 Introduction

In this concluding chapter I have two purposes. First, I wish to give a brief overview of the development of the "economics of gambling" research field. Second, I discuss important new areas of research and explain the direction in which I expect gambling research to move in the near future.

20.2 Development of the Gambling Research Field

Modern economic research on the casino industry and gambling began in the early 1970s. William Eadington was the first economist to focus exclusively on the economics of gambling. Going back to 1975, Bill has authored, coauthored, or edited over 100 articles, book chapters, and conference proceedings. More than any other economist, Eadington is responsible for the development of gambling research as a field.[1] His conference series, which began in 1974, has for decades brought together researchers from a wide variety of disciplines. This conference series has been extremely important in the development of gambling research and the subfield of the economics of gambling. This is because virtually everyone doing research in this area attends Eadington's conference.[2] The network that has been created by the conference series has been the major catalyst for gambling research development.[3]

---

[1] For more detail on Eadington's contributions and his developing the field of gambling research, see Philander and Walker (2012). The field of gambling studies suffered an enormous loss with Bill Eadington's passing in February 2013.

[2] A series of tributes to the International Conference on Gambling and Risk Taking was published in the *UNLV Gaming Research & Review Journal* 16(2), fall 2012.

[3] It is worth noting that the psychology/medicine branch of the field has developed much more quickly than the economics. This is largely due to the relatively large amount of research funding available for those topics. There is little research funding available, at least in the United States, for economics research on gambling and casinos.

The other major catalyst for the development of gambling research as a field in itself is the enormous expansion of the casino industry. Had casinos not expanded in the United States outside of Nevada and Atlantic City, it is doubtful that gambling research, either the psychology or economics branch, would have expanded as it has. As casinos have expanded, so has the interest in research on gambling.

When I began doing research on gambling and the casino industry in 1996, it was very difficult to get papers on gambling or the casino industry published in mainstream economics journals. The *Journal of Gambling Studies* was one of the only outlets for economists working on gambling. It could have been that the limited availability of data really limited the quality of research that could be produced, and that research did not reach the bar set by mainstream economic journals. Much of the research that was published in the early–mid 1990s was by (mostly anti-casino) advocates, such as Kindt, Goodman, and Grinols. However, these early papers usually did not appear in very influential journals. Eadington (2004) provides an interesting account of the development of some of this advocacy literature.

As the casino industry spread across the United States, the availability of data improved dramatically. I believe this is a key reason why one begins to see the quantity and quality of empirical research picking up toward the end of the 1990s. Of course, another reason is that over time there becomes more published research on which to build. Undoubtedly, research published during the past decade is generally of much higher quality than the research of the 1990s.

The areas that have garnered the most attention recently from economists are casino taxes and social costs. The impact of casinos on tax revenues from other industries has been studied by several different authors. Economists have also published papers on bankruptcy, crime, and other negative social and economic impacts of gambling. Economic journals and referees now seem much more open to papers on gambling and casinos than they did in the 1990s. Several journals now regularly publish papers related to casinos or gambling. These include *Contemporary Economic Policy*, *Public Finance Review*, *Public Choice*, *National Tax Journal*, and *Applied Economics*. In addition to these economic journals, there are now several journals dedicated entirely to gambling. In addition to the *Journal of Gambling Studies*, there are the *Journal of Gambling Business and Economics*, *International Gambling Studies*, and *Gaming Law Review and Economics*. I believe the economics of gambling research field is going to continue expanding at a good rate into the near future.

20.3 The Future of Research on the Economics of Gambling

In this book I have examined a few facets of the US casinos and their economic impacts. However, there are many other issues that deserve attention from economists. For example, little is known about the relationship between casino tax rates and the development of the industry. Few studies have examined the effects of casinos on the local and regional labor markets. The effects of smoking bans on casinos have not been fully explored. Finally, as casinos continue to spread, the question of a "market saturation point" becomes important. Although some of the "low hanging fruit" is gone, there are still countless topics that deserve economists' attention. As the casino industry matures, the quality of available data has improved dramatically.

As casinos spread around the world, there are obviously many new opportunities to explore topics that have already been examined in the United States. Evidence from different jurisdictions in the United States suggests that many of the economic and social impacts of casinos are specific to the particular geographic market. Therefore, the findings of the US studies are not generalizable to other countries.

It is difficult to predict the direction in which gambling research will go. The industry changes quickly with changes in regulation, the state of the economy, and technology. I would expect that researchers will and should continue to develop models of the various economic impacts of casinos on state economies, especially labor markets, economic growth, and tax revenues. These impacts will likely change as the casino industry continues to expand; one would expect that their positive marginal impacts on a particular state should decline as the industry grows. As I mentioned earlier, as more and more countries legalize casinos or expand their casino industries, research opportunities around the world will continue to grow. If the economics of gambling field continues to expand on a path similar to the sister branch of the psychology of gambling, then eventually, I believe some of these topics will become obsolete. With enough research on a wide variety of markets, it is likely that we will begin to see some general economic impacts of casinos that seem consistent across markets.

Other areas of research will certainly arise because of new availability of data or creative research strategies. One area that may not improve, in terms of research opportunities, is tribal casinos. As sovereign nations, Indian tribes do not publicize their casino revenue data, making it very difficult to do empirical analyses that include this segment of the industry. But other sectors of legalized gambling continue to produce usable data. With more data comes more research possibilities.

Of course, the most important changes to the casino industry are likely to be the result of changes in technology. The reader probably noticed that Internet gambling received virtually no attention in this book (except for a mention in Chap. 1). This is because online gambling data are not easily available, and this sector of the gambling industry is changing quickly. Two recent studies are Philander (2011) and Philander and Fiedler (2012). They provide evidence on how online gambling affects traditional casinos and gambling. But this is an area of which all gambling researchers will need to be familiar. Currently I see no more important aspect of gambling that will affect the existing industry. Indeed, Gainsbury (2012) notes that worldwide online gambling revenues were estimated to be US $33 billion in 2011—about the size of the entire US commercial casino industry. Online gambling will almost certainly expand at a pace greater than traditional casinos and lotteries, as technology continues to develop.

States have been working on regulatory frameworks for allowing online gambling, to include lottery, poker, and traditional casino games. This development could have a very significant impact on the "brick and mortar" casino industry. Concern on the part of the casino industry was evident in its lobbying efforts late in 2012. The American Gaming Association has been pushing for federal regulations of online gambling, rather than allowing states to regulate online gambling for their own citizens (Sieroty 2012). The casino industry wants online poker to be federally regulated, and other forms of online gambling (such as casino games) to be banned. Obviously this is an attempt by the industry to restrict its competition. Minton (2012) provides a good argument to leave the federal government out of the issue and let states regulate online gambling. As federal regulation was not implemented in 2012, many observers expect that it is more likely to be left up to states to regulate online gambling. Whatever regulatory framework develops, the expansion of online gambling opportunities and its effects on offline gambling will be an important topic for future research. Finally, changes in the regulatory environment will always provide topic for public choice-oriented research.

The other key area in which I expect research to continue to develop is the overlap between the economic and psychological and physiological aspects of gambling. How the brain functions with respect to gambling behavior and "addiction" is perhaps the key topic of focus for psychologists and medical researchers. The overlap of this with economics—which broadly studies decision making—is perhaps best illustrated by the work of Don Ross and his colleagues (Ross et al. 2008). Over the past decade I have noticed a significant shift at conferences from a purely psychological focus on the diagnosis and treatment of gambling problems to more of a focus on the brain and the analysis of gambling behavior. Neuroeconomics is a developing field that examines decision making in the brain, and is likely to become more crucial in our understanding of gambling behaviors.

Certainly other issues may move to the forefront in gambling research. These are difficult to predict. What researchers do in the future obviously depends on the past research, data availability, research technology, how gambling changes, interest on the part of policymakers, and the availability for research funding. However this field develops, I believe gambling research has a solid foundation. The past two decades have seen enormous development in the understanding of the psychology and economics of gambling.

20.4 Conclusion

The US casino industry has grown dramatically over the past two decades, and it is now one of the fastest growing entertainment industries in the United States. The industry grows at an even faster rate in other parts of the world. This ensures that this field of research will continue to be fruitful.

Since *The Economics of Casino Gambling* was published in 2007, the industry has changed fairly dramatically. One striking change is that the casino industry outside the United States has dwarfed the growth rate of the US casino industry. Recent changes in the federal government's interpretation of the Wire Act have set

20.4 Conclusion

the stage for dramatic changes to online gambling—poker, lotteries, and casino games. How these changes will affect online and offline gambling cannot be predicted reliably. But it seems clear that the potential expansion of online gambling, resulting from advancing technology and regulatory changes, will significantly affect the gambling industry landscape.

Since 2007, economic research on the casino industry has become more refined in several areas. Perhaps the most important change is that now researchers and politicians are less interested in producing monetary estimates of the social costs of gambling. This is not because social costs are not important. Rather, I believe there is more widespread understanding of the complexity of the social cost issue and serious researchers and politicians recognize that meaningful social cost estimates are simply not possible. Instead, there is more of a focus on acknowledging the different negative social impacts and their prevalence. This is much more informative, rather than focusing on meaningless and arbitrary monetary estimates.

Although there still has not been an enormous amount of research measuring the economic growth, tax, or labor market impacts of the casino industry, I believe there has become more of a consensus that casinos create net benefits for their host communities. The catastrophic harms predicted by authors like Kindt and Grinols were not realized. Citizens and politicians seem to have recognized that the casino industry can be beneficial. The continued expansion of the industry seems to confirm this.

Of course, as the casino industry continues to develop, it is possible that markets could become saturated and the relationship between casinos and their host communities could change. For this reason, research on the casino industry should continue to be useful for the future. It is still a relatively young industry, and despite the research advances that have been made, there are still many interesting questions about the economic and social impacts of casinos.

My hope is that this book has provided readers with a good overview of some key areas of research on the casino industry and that it will promote more interest in studying the industry.

Appendix: Primer on Microeconomics

This appendix provides an introduction to some of the economic tools used in this book. It is written for noneconomists. There are three basic tools explained: the production possibilities frontier, the indifference curve, and producer and consumer surplus. An introduction to supply and demand is also provided. These tools are explained in the appendix using general examples and are applied to casino gambling throughout the book.

A.1 The Production Possibilities Frontier

Economists use the production possibilities frontier (PPF) to model production by an individual, group of people, or economy. For simplicity, we begin by considering an economy in which only two goods are produced: beer and pizza.[1] The PPF (Fig. A.1) illustrates the production choices faced. Using all available input resources efficiently, the PPF shows all of the possible maximum combinations of beer and pizza that can be produced. The shape of the PPF—concave to the origin—implies an increasing opportunity cost of production as the quantity of production rises. That is, the cost of producing pizza in terms of beer sacrificed increases as the economy produces more pizza.[2] The reason is that input resources are not equally well suited for production of the different goods. So as the production of a particular good or service increases, the additional inputs are less suited to the production of that good. The result is increasing marginal (or incremental) production costs.

The slope of the PPF represents the opportunity cost of production. The steeper the PPF, the higher the opportunity cost of pizza (on the horizontal axis), since more

---

[1] The simplification of a two-good economy is not a serious problem. We could instead use beer and "all other goods," which would be a perfectly realistic, though a more general, example.
[2] This PPF shape corresponds to the standard positive-sloped supply curve, discussed below.

Fig. A.1 Production possibilities frontier

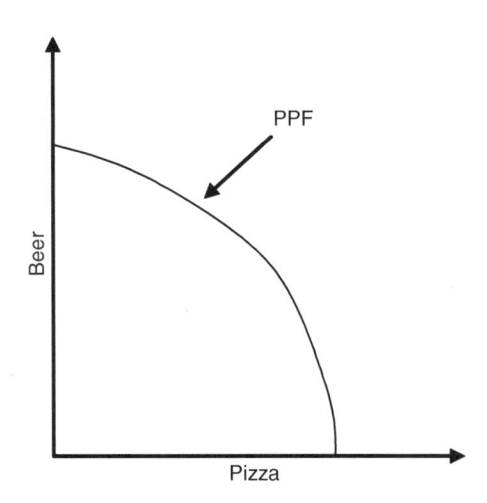

beer must be sacrificed to incrementally increase pizza production. The flatter the PPF, the higher the opportunity cost of beer in terms of pizza. The slope of the PPF is called the marginal rate of transformation (MRT).

A technological advance in pizza production (if, for example, an automatic dough machine is introduced) would cause the PPF to rotate out along the pizza axis (Fig. A.2,). Note that an increase in pizza technology may allow society to produce and consume more pizza *and beer* by moving from point *a* to point *b*.[3]

Without knowing something about the preferences of the individuals in society (discussed below) we cannot say that one point on the frontier is better than any other. For example, in Fig. A.3, we cannot say that point *b* is better than *c* or vice versa. We do know, however, that each point on the frontier is, by definition, efficient. This type of efficiency is "technological" referring to the situation in which output is maximized given inputs, technology, etc. Stated differently, technological efficiency occurs when a given level of output is produced with the least possible amount of resources. If production occurs on the PPF then input resources are not being wasted. Point *a*, on the other hand, exhibits waste, unemployment, or inefficiency because with the level of technology and inputs, the economy could produce more (say at point *b*). However, it is not possible to produce at point *d* or any other point outside the PPF because of input and/or technological limitations.

From the consumer perspective, we can compare the points on the frontier with many of the points off the frontier. For example, in Fig. A.3, *d* is preferred to *a*, *b*, and *c*, since the former includes more of both goods than the other three points. But *d* is unattainable. We can also say that *b* is preferred to *a*. However, we cannot necessarily say that *c* is preferred to *b* since it has more pizza but less beer.[4]

The ranking of various points can be summarized as in Fig. A.4. All points in quadrant *I* are preferred to point *e* and point *e* is preferred to all points in quadrant

---

[3] This is because pizza production has become more efficient. The same amount of pizza can now be produced in less time or with less labor or other input resources.
[4] "Allocative" efficiency refers to the situation in which the market is producing the optimal mix of goods considering preferences.

Fig. A.2 Technological advance in the pizza industry

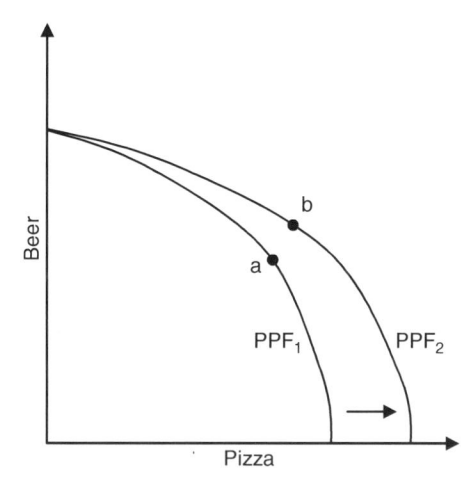

Fig. A.3 Efficient, inefficient, and unattainable production points

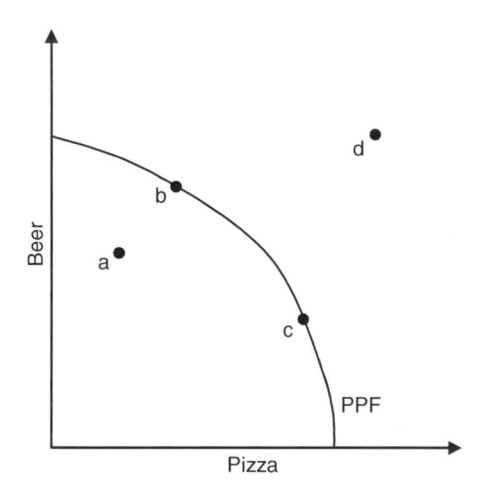

III. This is because each point in quadrant *I* has more beer, more pizza, or more of both goods compared to point *e*. Similarly, bundle *e* contains either more pizza or beer or more of both goods, compared to all the combinations in quadrant III.

We cannot legitimately rank the points in quadrants II or IV relative to point *e*. For example, all combinations represented in quadrant II have more beer than point *e* but less pizza. So unless we know something about preferences, we cannot compare points in II with point *e*. Similarly, combinations of goods represented in quadrant IV have more pizza but less beer than point *e* making a ranking of the points impossible without more information on the consumers' preferences.

Fig. A.4 Ranking consumption points

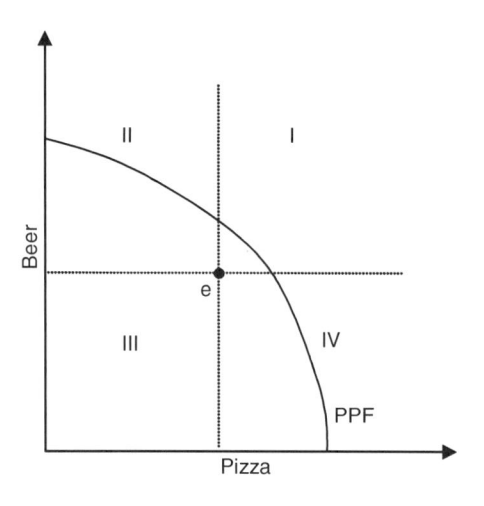

A.2 The Indifference Curve

An indifference curve (IC) for an individual or a society is the collection of points that represent indifferent combinations of two goods. We can develop an IC using the information in Fig. A.4. Any point in quadrant *I* is preferred to *e* and *e* is preferred to any point in quadrant III. More is always better than less. If society is initially producing and consuming at point *e* then we would be better off given more pizza. For us to be indifferent between this new situation and the original one at *e*, we must give up some beer which would reduce well-being. So the IC must have a negative slope.

The specific shape of the IC results from the law of decreasing marginal utility, the idea that each additional unit of consumption tends to provide less and less additional (marginal) benefit. With pizza and beer, the IC would appear as indicated in Fig. A.5.

Four example points are shown. Since they all lie on the same IC, the consumer is indifferent among them. The law of decreasing marginal utility can be illustrated by considering how much beer the consumer would be willing to give up for another slice of pizza and remain as well off. Consider two cases: movement from point *a* to *b* and from point *c* to *d*; each move represents a one-unit increase in the amount of pizza. Recall that a person must remain as happy as before getting the additional slice of pizza in order to remain on a given IC. When a person has little pizza and a lot of beer, the marginal utility of beer is low and for pizza it is high. This suggests the willingness to give up a lot of beer for another slice of pizza. But if a person has more pizza, say at point *c*, his willingness to sacrifice additional beer for another slice of pizza is lower. The result is a convex shape for an IC between the two goods.[5]

---

[5]The slope of the IC is referred to as the marginal rate of substitution (MRS). The MRS of pizza for beer, i.e., the willingness to sacrifice beer for pizza, falls as one moves down and right along the IC. If one of the products on the axes is a "bad" then the slope of the IC will be positive. This is a special case that we need not deal with here.

Fig. A.5 Indifference curve for beer and pizza

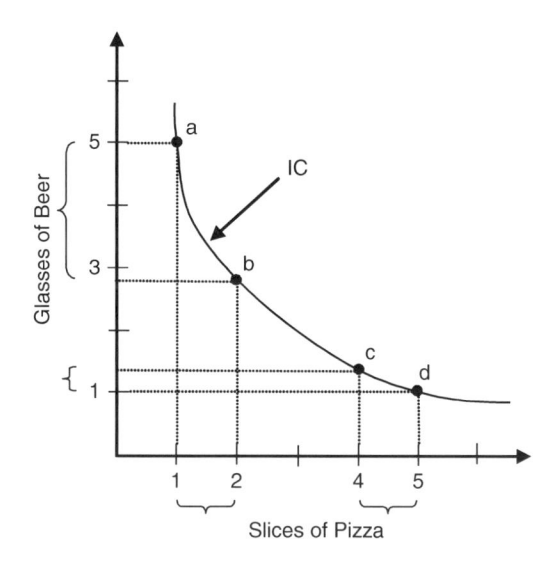

Since the gambling issue is social in nature (i.e., whether or not to legalize it is not an individual decision), it will be useful to think of a "community indifference curve" rather than an individual IC.[6]

Now that the shape of the IC has been explained, there are several important characteristics to keep in mind. As Ferguson (1966) explains, every point in commodity space lies on one (and only one) IC, and there are an infinite number of ICs for any two goods. Furthermore, ICs cannot intersect. The proof is simple. In Fig. A.6, note that point *a* lies on both IC$_1$ and IC$_2$. Ignore for a moment that this violates the condition that each point lies on a single IC. Then *a* must be indifferent to *c*, and *a* must be indifferent to *b*. This implies that *b* is indifferent to *c*. But *b* must be preferred to *c* since *b* has more beer and no less pizza than *c*, and more is always better. Hence, ICs cannot intersect.

One final point is that higher ICs indicate higher utility or satisfaction. In Fig. A.7, every point on IC$_2$ is preferred to every point on IC$_1$ and every point on IC$_3$ is preferred to all points on IC$_1$ and IC$_2$. This is because *a* is preferred to *b*, and *b* is preferred to *c*, and all points on a particular IC are valued equally. So consumers prefer to be on higher, rather than lower, ICs.

Using ICs we can now rank all possible combinations of the goods represented in the graph. This will be a useful tool for demonstrating economic growth and the social costs of gambling. It is important to understand that this is the standard tool used in economics for the analysis of individual welfare related to consumption choices.

---

[6]For more detail on community indifference curves, see Henderson and Quandt (1980, 310–319).

Fig. A.6 Proof that ICs cannot intersect

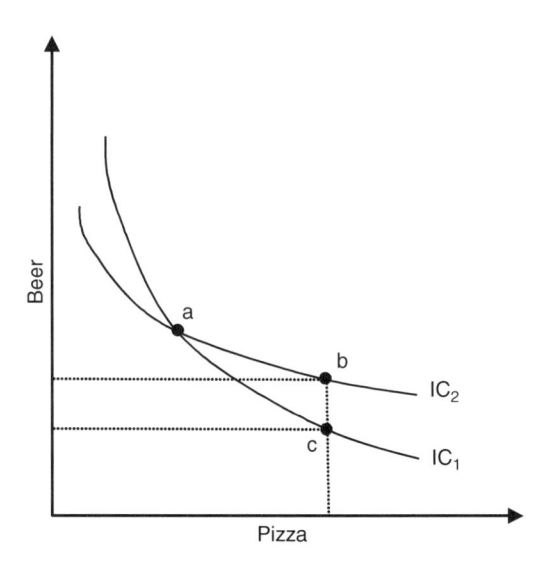

Fig. A.7 Indifference map

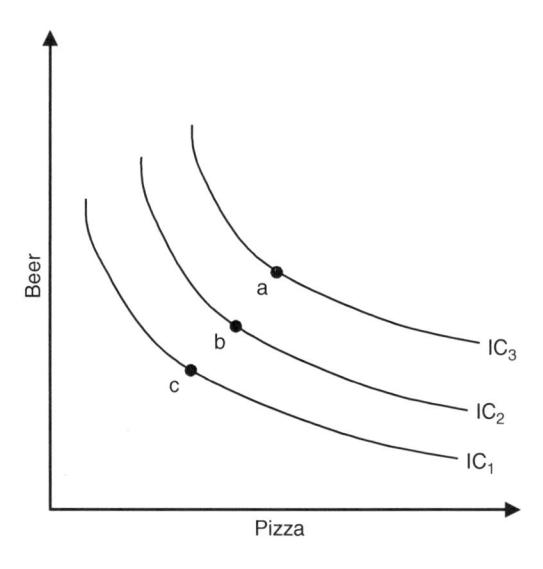

A.3 Allocative Efficiency

Technological efficiency occurs when production takes place on the PPF so that no input resources are wasted or unemployed and production is maximized given technology and input quantities. Once we consider preferences given by the IC, we can describe allocative efficiency.

Fig. A.8 Technological and allocative efficiency

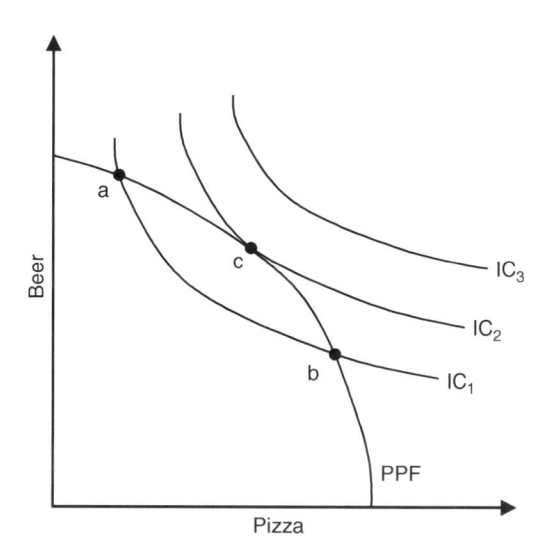

It is important that what is produced is what people want to consume. Now that we have considered the supply side of the market (or costs represented by the PPF) and the demand side (or preferences represented by the IC) we can put the two sides of the market together and illustrate economic efficiency, technological and allocative.

In Fig. A.8 each point on the PPF is technologically efficient (e.g., points a, b, and c). However, only point c is allocatively efficient. That is, only at point c is the optimal *mix* of goods produced. From a social perspective, we want consumers to be on the highest possible IC. This is done by producing at the point on the PPF that allows us to be on the best possible IC, in this case IC_2. That point represents the optimal combination of beer and pizza given preferences.[7] Points a and b are inferior to point c because they are on a lower IC. Using ICs and PPFs together, we can rank different points on the PPF.

Consumer preferences will affect the production that takes place in society. If consumers have a relatively strong preference for pizza, the ICs would appear steep, indicating a willingness to sacrifice more beer for an additional unit of pizza. The resulting tangency between the IC and PPF would then be closer to the pizza axis (more pizza and less beer). On the other hand, a relatively strong preference for beer would be represented by flat ICs and the resulting tangency with the PPF would be nearer to the beer axis with more beer and less pizza production and consumption.

---

[7] A complete treatment of consumer choice would require consideration of relative prices of the goods, preferences, and a budget constraint.

Fig. A.9 Supply and demand curves

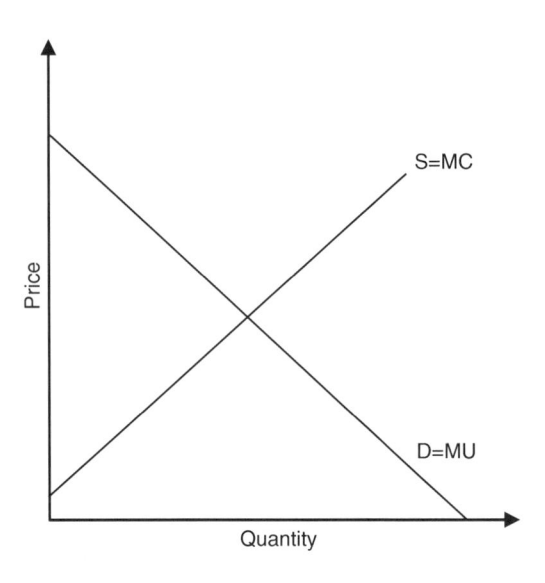

A.4 Supply, Demand, and Markets

The previous sections of this appendix explain production based on opportunity cost and consumption based on preferences. These concepts are the basis for the supply and demand curves, the two major components of market models.[8]

The supply curve represents the marginal opportunity cost of production. Recall that the PPF has a concave shape that represents an increasing opportunity cost of production. That is, as production of one of the goods increases, its marginal opportunity cost (MC) rises in terms of the other good. If we graph the positive relationship between cost of production and quantity, the result is a supply curve as illustrated in Fig. A.9. A more simple explanation for the positive slope of the supply curve is that as price rises sellers wish to sell greater quantities. This is because the increase in price makes each sale more profitable.

The demand curve represents the marginal utility (benefit) from consumption. Recall the law of decreasing marginal utility which says that each additional unit of consumption (of a good or a service) yields less and less marginal utility (MU). If each additional unit of consumption provides less utility, then each additional unit will be valued less than the previous one. A rational person's willingness to pay for additional units would therefore be expected to decline. This negative relationship between quantity and willingness to pay is illustrated in the demand curve of Fig. A.9.

When the two sides of the market, supply and demand, are put together, the result is a market model (Fig. A.10). The equilibrium price (P_e) is the only price at which

---
[8] The discussion of supply and demand here is very brief. For a complete treatment consult a principles of microeconomics text.

Fig. A.10 Prices and quantities in the market model

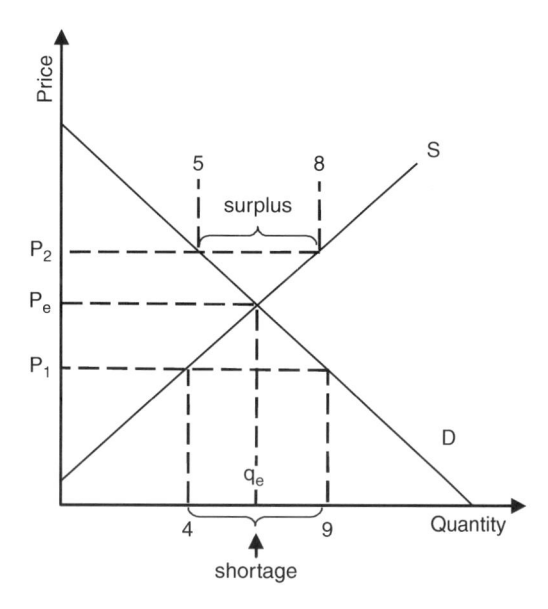

the quantity demanded is equal to the quantity supplied (called the equilibrium quantity q_e). If the current price in the market is *not* the equilibrium price, the self-interested motivations of buyers and sellers in the market push the price toward this equilibrium price.

Consider a price such as P_1 in Fig. A.10. At a price below P_e the quantity demanded in the market exceeds the quantity supplied. This situation is called a shortage. In the example there is a shortage of five units. With a shortage, buyers and sellers in the market will bid the price up toward P_e and the shortage disappears. Alternatively, at P_2 or any price above P_e a surplus exists. That is, quantity supplied exceeds quantity demanded. In Fig. A.10 there is a surplus of three units at P_2. In this case, the buyers and sellers act in their self-interest and bid the price down. Hence, when $P \neq P_e$, market forces push the price toward the equilibrium level. In this way, prices are determined in markets.[9]

The degree to which, and speed at which, prices adjust depend on the number of buyers and sellers in the market, the extent to which the products are homogeneous, and other market conditions. In any case, economists generally point to freely functioning markets as the most efficient mechanism for allocating scarce resources and producing what consumers want.[10]

---

[9]This is true in competitive markets. For a discussion of the assumptions underlying this model, see Mankiw (2007).

[10]There are exceptions, however. They include externalities, public goods, and monopolies. These are typically considered to be cases in which government intervention can improve the efficiency of the free market. However, sometimes the government "solutions" to market failures are worse than the original problem (State and market 1996).

Fig. A.11 Producer and consumer surplus

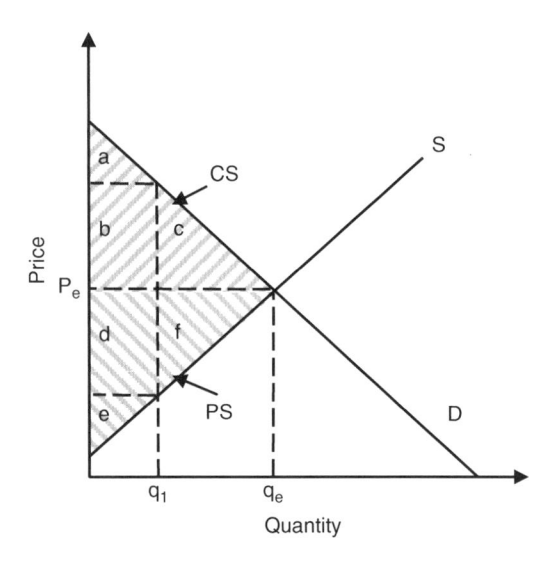

A.5 Producer and Consumer Surplus

Economists gauge welfare or well-being using producer surplus (PS) and consumer surplus (CS). Obviously, firms benefit from selling their products for prices in excess of their cost of production. This is typically referred to as "profit" conceptually similar to PS. This is simply the difference between the price they receive for producing and selling (the market price) and the minimum price they would be willing to accept (the cost of production, represented by the supply curve). So for all the transactions that occur in the market at the market equilibrium price, the PS is represented by the value of the triangle lying above the supply curve and below the horizontal line indicating the price. This is area $(d+e+f)$ in Fig. A.11.

Consumers benefit when they engage in market transactions. Indeed, in order to willingly make a purchase, the consumer must expect the benefits from consumption to exceed the market price they pay. The difference between what a consumer is willing to pay (the expected benefit from consumption, represented by the demand curve) and what must be paid (the market price) is the CS. In other words, CS represents the value of the product to the consumer in excess of its price. For all consumers who make purchases at the market price, total CS is represented by the value of the triangle lying below the demand curve and above the market price line. This is shown as area $(a+b+c)$ in Fig. A.11.

The sum of the PS and CS areas is called the "social" or "total" surplus. It is a measure of the net benefits to consumers and producers who are engaging in transactions in the market. It is important to recognize that both parties—consumer and producer—benefit from these transactions. As a result, the maximization of market transactions tends to maximize welfare in society. (This assumes that transactions do not harm other parties not involved in the transactions. Such third-party harms are called "externalities" and are discussed in Chap. 13.) So any restriction on the number of transactions leads to a reduction in the size of the social surplus. This is important in considering legal restrictions on gambling, for example. When the quantity of transactions, q_e in Fig. A.11, is artificially restricted to q_1 the amounts of CS and PS are reduced. The social surplus that remains at the restricted quantity of q_1 is $(a+e)$. The difference between initial levels (their sum) and the resulting sum represents the social cost of the quantity restriction.[11] Some of the benefits that would have occurred in a free market are now lost. (Social costs are discussed in detail in Chap. 13.)

A.6 Summary

The PPF, IC, CS, and PS are standard tools of economic analysis described in this appendix. We can analyze many of the economic and social costs and benefits of casino gambling using these tools. However, for more details on these and other important economic concepts, readers should consult an economics text such as Ferguson (1966).

---

[11] This statement is somewhat simplistic. There is no doubt that the social surplus and overall well-being are lower than in an unrestricted market, but some of the benefits probably go to the sellers or the government from restricting quantity.

References

ACIL Consulting. 1999. Australia's gambling industries: A submission to the Productivity Commission's inquiry into Australia's gambling industry. Canberra, Australia

Adams, S., and C.D. Cotti. 2008. Drunk driving after the passage of smoking bans in bars. *Journal of Public Economics* 92(5–6): 1288–1305.

Albanese, J. 1985. The effect of casino gambling on crime. *Federal Probation* 48: 39–44.

Alessi, S.M., and N.M. Petry. 2003. Pathological gambling is associated with impulsivity in a delay discounting procedure. *Behavioural Processes* 64: 345–354.

Allison, P.D., and R.P. Waterman. 2002. Fixed-effects negative binomial regression models. *Sociological Methodology* 32(1): 247–265.

Alm, J.M., M. McKee, and M. Skidmore. 1993. Fiscal pressure, tax competition, and the introduction of state lotteries. *National Tax Journal* 46: 463–476.

American Gaming Association. 2005. *State of the states, 2005: The AGA survey of casino entertainment*. Washington, DC: Author.

American Gaming Association. 2006a. *State of the states, 2006: The AGA survey of casino entertainment*. Washington, DC: Author.

American Gaming Association. 2006b. *Summary of gaming industry Katrina relief efforts*. Washington, DC: Author.

American Gaming Association. 2008. *State of the states, 2008: The AGA survey of casino entertainment*. Washington, DC: Author.

American Gaming Association. 2010. *State of the states, 2010: The AGA survey of casino entertainment*. Washington, DC: Author.

American Gaming Association. 2011. *State of the states, 2011: The AGA survey of casino entertainment*. Washington, DC: Author.

American Psychiatric Association. 1994. *Diagnostic and statistical manual of mental disorders (DSM-IV)*. Washington, DC: Author.

American Psychiatric Association. 2000. *Diagnostic and statistical manual of mental disorders (DSM-IV-TR)*. Washington, DC: Author.

Anders, G.C., D. Siegel, and M. Yacoub. 1998. Does Indian casino gambling reduce state revenues? Evidence from Arizona. *Contemporary Economic Policy* 16: 347–355.

Anielski Management Inc. 2008. The socio-economic impact of gambling (SEIG) framework: An assessment framework for Canada: In search of the gold standard. Inter-provincial consortium for the development of methodology to assess the social and economic impact of gambling.

Arellano, M. 1987. Computing robust standard errors for within-groups estimators. *Oxford Bulletin of Economics and Statistics* 49(4): 431–434.

Asplund, M., R. Friberg, and F. Wilander. 2007. Demand and distance: Evidence on cross-border shopping. *Journal of Public Economics* 91(1–2): 141–157.

Atkinson, A.B., and T.W. Meade. 1974. Methods and preliminary findings in assessing the economic health services consequences of smoking, with particular reference to lung cancer. *Journal of the Royal Statistical Society.* Series A (General) 137: 297–312.

Australian Productivity Commission. 1999. *Australia's gambling industries.* Canberra, Australia: AusInfo.

Balassa, B. 1978. Exports and economic growth: Further evidence. *Journal of Development Economics* 5: 181–189.

Barnett, A.H. 1978. Taxation for the control of environmental externalities. Ph.D. dissertation, University of Virginia, Charlottesville, VA.

Barnett, A.H. 1980. The Pigouvian tax rule under monopoly. *American Economic Review* 70: 1037–1041.

Barnett, A.H., and J. Bradley. 1981. An extension of the Dolbear triangle. *Southern Economic Journal* 47: 792–798.

Barnett, A.H., and D.L. Kaserman. 1998. The simple welfare economics of network externalities and the uneasy case for subscribership subsidies. *Journal of Regulatory Economics* 13: 245–254.

Barron, J.M., M.E. Staten, and S.M. Wilshusen. 2002. The Impact of casino gambling on personal bankruptcy filing rates. *Contemporary Economic Policy* 20(4): 440–455.

Barthe, E., and B.G. Stitt. 2007. Casinos as "hot spots" and the generation of crime. *Journal of Crime & Justice* 30(2): 115–140.

Barthe, E., and B.G. Stitt. 2009a. Impact of casinos on criminogenic patterns. *Police Practice and Research* 10(3): 255–269.

Barthe, E., and B.G. Stitt. 2009b. Temporal distributions of crime and disorder in casino and non-casino zones. *Journal of Gambling Studies* 25(2): 139–152.

Baughman, R., M. Conlin, S. Dickert-Conlin, and J. Pepper. 2001. Slippery when wet: The effects of local alcohol access laws on highway safety. *Journal of Health Economics* 20(6): 1089–1096.

Baumol, W.J., and W.E. Oates. 1988. *The theory of environmental policy*, 2nd ed. New York, NY: Cambridge University Press.

Becker, G.S. 1968. Crime and punishment: An economic approach. *Journal of Political Economy* 76: 169–217.

Becker, G.S. 1992. Habits, addictions, and traditions. *Kyklos* 45(3): 327–345.

Becker, G.S. 1996. *Accounting for tastes.* Cambridge, MA: Harvard University Press.

Becker, G.S., and G.N. Becker. 1997. Gambling's advocates are right—but for the wrong reasons. In *The economics of life.* New York, NY: McGraw-Hill.

Becker, G.S., M. Grossman, and K. Murphy. 1994. An empirical analysis of cigarette addiction. *American Economic Review* 84(3): 396–418.

Becker, G.S., M. Grossman, and K.M. Murphy. 1991. Rational addiction and the effect of price on consumption. *American Economic Review* 81(2): 237–241.

Becker, G.S., and K.M. Murphy. 1988. A theory of rational addiction. *Journal of Political Economy* 96(4): 675–700.

Berry, B.J., and F.E. Horton. 1970. *Geographic perspectives on urban systems.* Englewood Cliffs, NJ: Prentice-Hall.

Bertrand, M., E. Duflo, and S. Mullainathan. 2004. How much should we trust differences-in-differences estimates? *Quarterly Journal of Economics* 119(1): 249–275.

Betsinger, S. 2005. The relationship between gambling and county-level crime. M.A. thesis, University of Maryland, College Park, MD.

Bhagwati, J.N. 1958. Immiserizing growth: A geometrical note. *The Review of Economic Studies* 25: 201–205.

Bhagwati, J.N. 1982. Directly unproductive, profit-seeking (DUP) activities. *Journal of Political Economy* 90: 988–1002.

Bhagwati, J.N. 1983. DUP activities and rent seeking. *Kyklos* 36: 634–637.

Bhagwati, J.N., R.A. Brecher, and T.N. Srinivasan. 1984. DUP activities and economic theory. *European Economic Review* 24: 291–307.

References

Bhagwati, J.N., and T.N. Srinivasan. 1982. The welfare consequences of directly-un productive profit-seeking (DUP) lobbying activities: Price versus quantity distortions. *Journal of International Economics* 13: 33–44.

Blaszczynski, A.P., R. Ladouceur, A. Goulet, and C. Savard. 2006. "How much do you spend gambling?": Ambiguities in questionnaire items assessing expenditure. *International Gambling Studies* 6(2): 123–128.

Blaszczynski, A.P., and N. McConaghy. 1994. Criminal offenses in Gamblers Anonymous and hospital treated pathological gamblers. *Journal of Gambling Studies* 10(2): 99–127.

Blaszczynski, A.P., and L. Nower. 2002. A pathways model to problem and pathological gambling. *Addiction* 97: 487–499.

Blaug, M. 1978. *Economic theory in retrospect*. New York, NY: Cambridge University Press.

Boggs, S.L. 1965. Urban crime patterns. *American Sociological Review* 30: 899–908.

Boreham, P., M. Dickerson, and B. Harley. 1996. What are the social costs of gambling?: The case of the Queensland machine gaming industry. *Australian Journal of Social Issues* 31(4): 425–442.

Borg, M.O., P.M. Mason, and S.L. Shapiro. 1991. *The Economic consequences of state lotteries*. New York, NY: Praeger.

Borg, M.O., P.M. Mason, and S.L. Shapiro. 1993. The cross effects of lottery taxes on alternative state tax revenue. *Public Finance Quarterly* 21: 123–140.

Breitung, J., and W. Meyer. 1994. Testing for unit roots in panel data: Are wages on different bargaining levels cointegrated? *Applied Economics* 26: 353–361.

Breyer, J.L., A.M. Botzet, K.C. Winters, R.D. Stinchfield, G. August, and G. Realmuto. 2009. Young adult gambling behaviors and their relationship with the persistence of ADHD. *Journal of Gambling Studies* 25: 227–238.

Briggs, J.R., B.J. Goodin, and T. Nelson. 1996. Pathological gamblers and alcoholics: Do they share the same addictions? *Addictive Behaviors* 21: 515–519.

Browning, E.K. 1999. The myth of fiscal externalities. *Public Finance Review* 27: 3–18.

Brueckner, J.K. 1993. Inter-store externalities and space allocation in retail shopping centers. *Journal of Real Estate Finance and Economics* 7: 5–16.

Buck, A.J., J. Deutsch, S. Hakim, U. Spiegel, and J. Weinblatt. 1991. A Von Thünen model of crime, casinos and property values in New Jersey. *Urban Studies* 28: 673–683.

Bureau of Economic Analysis. 2005. *Estimated damage and insurance settlements effects from Hurricanes Katrina, Rita, and Wilma on quarterly and annual estimates of personal income*. Washington, DC: Author.

Calcagno, P.T., D.M. Walker, and J.D. Jackson. 2010. Determinants of the probability and timing of commercial casino legalization in the United States. *Public Choice* 142: 69–90.

Campbell, C.S., and D. Marshall. 2007. Gambling and crime. In *Research and measurement issues in gambling studies*, ed. G. Smith, D.C. Hodgins, and R.J. Williams. New York, NY: Academic Press.

Caputo, M.R., and B.J. Ostrom. 1996. Optimal government policy regarding a previously illegal commodity. *Southern Economic Journal* 62: 690–709.

Carbaugh, R.J. 2004. *International economics*, 9th ed. Mason, OH: South-Western.

Carpenter, C. 2004. How do zero tolerance drunk driving laws work? *Journal of Health Economics* 23: 61–83.

Chaing, R., T.-Y. Lai, and D.C. Ling. 1986. Retail leasehold interests: A contingent claims analysis. *Real Estate Economics* 14: 216–229.

Chaloupka, F.J. 1991. Rational addictive behavior and cigarette smoking. *Journal of Political Economy* 99: 722–742.

Chaloupka, F.J., M. Grossman, and H. Saffer. 2002. The effects of price on alcohol consumption and alcohol-related problems. *Alcohol Research and Health* 26: 22–34.

Chang, S. 1996. The impact of casinos on crime: The case of Biloxi, Mississippi. *Journal of Criminal Justice* 24(5): 431–436.

Clark, C., L. Nower, and D.M. Walker. 2013. The relationship of ADHD symptoms to gambling behavior. Results from the National Longitudinal Study of Adolescent Health. *International Gambling Studies* 13(1): 37–51.

Clark, C., and D.M. Walker. 2009. Are gamblers more likely to commit crimes? An empirical analysis of a nationally representative survey of U.S. young adults. *International Gambling Studies* 9(2): 119–134.

Clement, D. 2003. Gambling: A sure thing? In *Fedgazette*. Minneapolis, MN: Federal Reserve Bank of Minneapolis.

Clotfelter, C.T., and P.J. Cook. 1990. On the economics of state lotteries. *Journal of Economic Perspectives* 4: 105–119.

Clotfelter, C.T., and P.J. Cook. 1991. *Selling hope: State lotteries in America*. Cambridge, MA: Harvard University Press.

Cohen, L.E., and M. Felson. 1979. Social change and crime rate trends: A routine activity approach. *American Sociological Review* 44: 588–608.

Collins, D., and H. Lapsley. 2003. The social costs and benefits of gambling: An introduction to the economic issues. *Journal of Gambling Studies* 19: 123–148.

Collins, P.C. 2003. *Gambling and the public interest*. Westport, CT: Praeger.

Colwell, P.F., J. Maxwell, and O. Ramsland. 2003. Coping with technological change: The case of retail. *Journal of Real Estate Finance and Economics* 26(1): 47–63.

Colwell, P.F., and H.J. Munneke. 1997. The structure of urban land prices. *Journal of Urban Economics* 41: 321–336.

Colwell, P.F., and H.J. Munneke. 2009. Directional land value gradients. *Journal of Real Estate Finance and Economics* 39(1): 1–23.

Conte, M.A., and A.F. Darrat. 1988. Economic growth and the expanding public sector. *The Review of Economics and Statistics* 70: 322–330.

Cornfield, J. 2009. Many arrested for DUI said last drink served at Tulalip Casino. *HeraldNet*, 5 January.

Cotti, C.D. 2008. The effect of casinos on local labor markets: A county level analysis. *Journal of Gambling Business and Economics* 2(2): 17–41.

Cotti, C.D., and D.M. Walker. 2010. The impact of casinos on fatal alcohol-related traffic accidents in the United States. *Journal of Health Economics* 29(6): 788–796.

Crane, Y. 2006. New casinos in the United Kingdom: Costs, benefits and other considerations. Ph.D. Dissertation, Salford Business School, Salford, UK.

Crone, E.A., I. Vendel, and M.W. vanderMolen. 2003. Decision-making in disinhibited adolescents and adults: Insensitivity to future consequences or driven by immediate reward? *Personality & Individual Differences* 35: 1625–1641.

Cummings, P., F.P. Rivara, C.M. Olson, and K. Smith. 2006. Changes in traffic crash mortality rates attributed to use of alcohol, or lack of a seatbelt, air bag, motorcycle helmet, or bicycle helmet, United States, 1982–2001. *Injury Prevention* 12: 148–154.

Curran, D., and F. Scarpitti. 1991. Crime in Atlantic City: Do casinos make a difference? *Deviant Behavior* 12(4): 431–449.

Davis, J.R., J.E. Filer, and D.L. Moak. 1992. The lottery as an alternative source of state revenue. *Atlantic Economic Journal* 20(2): 1–10.

Dee, T.S. 1999. State alcohol policies, teen drinking and traffic fatalities. *Journal of Public Economics* 72: 289–315.

Dee, T.S. 2001. Does setting limits save lives? The case of 0.08 BAC laws. *Journal of Policy Analysis and Management* 20(1): 111–128.

Derevensky, J.L., and R. Gupta. 2004. *Gambling problems in youth: Theoretical and applied perspectives*. New York, NY: Plenum Publishers.

Derevensky, J.L., L.M. Pratt, K.K. Hardoon, and R. Gupta. 2007. Gambling problems and features of attention deficit hyperactivity disorder among children and adolescents. *Journal of Addiction Medicine* 1: 165–172.

Detlefsen, R. 1996. *Anti-gambling politics—Time to reshuffle the deck*. Washington, DC: Competitive Enterprise Institute.

Diamantopoulou, S., A.-M. Rydell, L.B. Thorell, and G. Bohlin. 2007. Impact of executive functioning and symptoms of attention deficit hyperactivity disorder on children's peer relations and school performance. *Developmental Neuropsychology* 32: 521–542.

References

Dixit, A., and G.M. Grossman. 1984. Directly unproductive prophet-seeking activities. *American Economic Review* 74: 1087–1088.

Dixon, M.R., E.A. Jacobs, and S. Sanders. 2006. Contextual control of delay discounting by pathological gamblers. *Journal of Applied Behavioral Analysis* 39: 413–422.

Eadington, W.R. 1976. Some observations on legalized gambling. In *Gambling and society: Interdisciplinary studies on the subject of gambling*, ed. W.R. Eadington. Springfield, IL: Charles C. Thomas.

Eadington, W.R. 1993. *The emergence of casino gaming as a major factor in tourism markets: Policy issues and considerations*. Reno, NV: Institute for the Study of Gambling & Commercial Gaming.

Eadington, W.R. 1995. Economic development and the introduction of casinos: Myths and realities. *Economic Development Review* 13: 51–54.

Eadington, W.R. 1996. The legalization of casinos: Policy objectives, regulatory alternatives, and cost/benefit considerations. *Journal of Travel Research* 34: 3–8.

Eadington, W.R. 1999. The economics of casino gambling. *Journal of Economic Perspectives* 13: 173–192.

Eadington, W.R. 2003. Measuring costs from permitted gaming: Concepts and categories in evaluating gambling's consequences. *Journal of Gambling Studies* 19: 185–213.

Eadington, W.R. 2004. Comment on Kindt's paper. *Managerial and Decision Economics* 25: 191–196.

Eadington, W.R. 2011. After the Great Recession: the future of casino gaming in America and Europe. *Economic Affairs* 31(1): 27–33.

Eisenberg, D. 2003. Evaluating the effectiveness of policies related to drunk driving. *Journal of Policy Analysis and Management* 22(2): 249–274.

Ekelund, R.B., and R.F. Hébert. 1997. *History of economic theory and method*, 4th ed. New York, NY: McGraw-Hill.

Ekelund, R.B., J.D. Jackson, R.W. Ressler, and R.D. Tollison. 2006. Marginal deterrence and multiple murders. *Southern Economic Journal* 72: 521–541.

el-Guebaly, N., S.B. Patten, S. Currie, J.V.A. Williams, C.A. Beck, C.J. Maxwell, and J.L. Wang. 2006. Epidemiological associations between gambling behavior, substance use & mood and anxiety disorders. *Journal of Gambling Studies* 22(3): 275–287.

Elliott, D.S., and J.C. Navin. 2002. Has riverboat gambling reduced state lottery revenue? *Public Finance Review* 30(3): 235–247.

Emerson, M.J., and F.C. Lamphear. 1975. *Urban and regional economics: Structure and change*. Boston, MA: Allyn and Bacon.

Eppli, M.J., and J.D. Benjamin. 1994. The evolution of shopping center research: A review and analysis. *Journal of Real Estate Research* 9: 5–28.

Eppli, M.J., and J.D. Shilling. 1995. Large-scale shopping center development opportunities. *Land Economics* 71: 35–41.

Eppli, M.J., J.D. Shilling, and K.D. Vandell. 1998. What moves retail property returns at the metropolitan level? *Journal of Real Estate Finance and Economics* 16: 317–342.

Ernst, M., S.J. Grant, E.D. London, C.S. Contoreggi, A.S. Kimes, and L. Spurgeon. 2003. Decision making in adolescents with behaviour disorders and adults with substance abuse. *American Journal of Psychiatry* 160: 33–40.

Evans, W.N., and J.H. Topoleski. 2002. The social and economic impact of Native American casinos. In *NBER working paper series*. Cambridge, MA: National Bureau of Economic Research.

Evart, C. 1995. *Presentation at the sports and entertainment conference, session on "Gambling and Gaming"*. Atlanta, GA: Federal Reserve Bank of Atlanta.

Faregh, N., and J.L. Derevensky. 2011. Gambling behavior among adolescents with attention deficit/hyperactivity disorder. *Journal of Gambling Studies* 27: 243–256.

Feigelman, W., P.H. Kleinman, H.R. Lesieur, R.B. Millman, and M.L. Lesser. 1995. Pathological gambling among methadone patients. *Drug and Alcohol Dependence* 39: 75–81.

Ferguson, C.E. 1966. *Microeconomic theory*. Homewood, IL: Richard D. Irwin.

Ferris, J.S. 2000. The determinants of cross border shopping: Implication for tax revenues and institutional change. *National Tax Journal* 53(4): 801–824.

Fink, S.C., A.C. Marco, and J.C. Rork. 2004. Lotto nothing? The budgetary impact of state lotteries. *Applied Economics* 36: 2357–2367.

Fink, S.C., and J.C. Rork. 2003. The importance of self-selection in casino cannibalization of state lotteries. *Economics Bulletin* 8: 1–8.

Fischer, S., and G.T. Smith. 2008. Binge eating, problem drinking, and pathological gambling: Linking behavior to shared traits and social learning. *Personality and Individual Differences* 44(4): 789–800.

Frances, P.H., and B. Hobijn. 1997. Critical values for unit root tests in seasonal time series. *Journal of Applied Statistics* 24(1): 25–48.

Frank, R.H. 1988. *Passions within reason: The strategic role of the emotions*. New York, NY: WW Norton.

Franklin, W. 1994. Testimony and prepared statement. In U.S. House (1995), "The national impact of casino gambling proliferation," pp. 18–32 and 50–55.

Friedman, J., S. Hakim, and J. Weinblatt. 1989. Casino gambling as a "growth pole" strategy and its effects on crime. *Journal of Regional Science* 29(4): 415–623.

Gainsbury, S. 2012. *Internet gambling: Current research findings and implications*. New York, NY: Springer.

Garrett, T.A. 2001. The Leviathan lottery: Testing the revenue maximization objective of state lotteries as evidence for Leviathan. *Public Choice* 109: 101–117.

Garrett, T.A., and T.L. Marsh. 2002. Revenue impacts of cross-border lottery shopping. *Regional Science and Urban Economics* 32: 501–519.

Garrett, T.A., and M.W. Nichols. 2008. Do casinos export bankruptcy? *The Journal of Socio-Economics* 37: 1481–1494.

Gatzlaff, D.H., G.S. Sirmans, and B.A. Diskin. 1994. The effect of anchor tenant loss on shopping center rents. *Journal of Real Estate Research* 9: 99–110.

Gazel, R.C. 1998. The economic impacts of casino gambling at the state and local levels. *Annals of Economic and Social Measurement* 556: 66–84.

Gazel, R.C., D. Rickman, and W.N. Thompson. 2001. Casino gambling and crime: A panel study of Wisconsin counties. *Managerial and Decision Economics* 22(1–3): 65–75.

Gazel, R.C., and W.N. Thompson. 1996. *Casino gamblers in Illinois: Who are they?* Las Vegas, NV: UNLV.

General Accounting Office. 2000. *Impact of gambling: Economic effects more measurable than social effects*. Washington, DC: Author.

Giacopassi, D. 1995. *An analysis of the Maryland Report, "The House Never Loses and Maryland Cannot Win..."*. Memphis, TN: University of Memphis.

Giacopassi, D., and B.G. Stitt. 1993. Assessing the impact of casino gambling on crime in Mississippi. *American Journal of Criminal Justice* 18(1): 117–131.

Giacopassi, D., B.G. Stitt, and M.W. Nichols. 2001. Community perception of casino gambling's effect on crime in new gambling jurisdictions. *The Justice Professional* 14: 151–170.

Goldstein, G.S., and T.J. Gronberg. 1984. Economics of scope and economies of agglomeration. *Journal of Urban Economics* 16: 91–104.

Goodman, R. 1979. *The last entrepreneurs: America's regional wars for jobs and dollars*. New York, NY: Simon and Schuster.

Goodman, R. 1994a. *Legalized gambling as a strategy for economic development*. Northampton, MA: United States Gambling Study.

Goodman, R. 1994b. Testimony and prepared statement. In U.S. House (1995), "The national impact of casino gambling proliferation," pp. 4–8 and 56–70.

Goodman, R. 1995a. Legalized gambling: Public policy and economic development issues. *Economic Development Review* 13: 55–57.

Goodman, R. 1995b. *The luck business: The devastating consequences and broken promises of America's gambling explosion*. New York, NY: The Free Press.

References

Goudriaan, A.E., J. Oosterlaan, E. deBeurs, and W. vandenBrink. 2004. Pathological gambling: A comprehensive review of biobehavioral findings. *Neuroscience & Biobehavioral Reviews* 28: 123–141.

Goudriaan, A.E., J. Oosterlaan, E. deBeurs, and W. vandenBrink. 2006. Psychophysiological determinants and concomitants of deficient decision making in pathological gamblers. *Drug & Alcohol Dependence* 84: 231–239.

Granderson, G., and C. Linvill. 2002. Regulation, efficiency, and Granger causality. *International Journal of Industrial Organization* 20: 1225–1245.

Granger, C.W. 1969. Investigating causal relationships by econometric methods and cross spectral methods. *Econometrica* 37: 424–438.

Granger, C.W. 1980. *Forecasting in business and economics*. New York, NY: Academic Press.

Grant, J.E., S.R. Chamberlain, L.R.N. Schreiber, B.L. Odlaug, and S.W. Kim. 2011. Selective decision-making deficits in at-risk gamblers. *Psychiatry Research* 189: 115–120.

Grant, J.E., M.G. Kushner, and S.W. Kim. 2002. Pathological gambling and alcohol use disorder. *Alcohol Research & Health* 26: 143–150.

Grant, J.E., and M.A. Steinberg. 2005. Compulsive sexual behavior and pathological gambling. *Sexual Addiction & Compulsivity* 12: 235–244.

Greene, W.H. 2000. *Econometric analysis*, 4th ed. Upper Saddle River, NJ: Prentice Hall.

Greene, W.H. 2003. *Econometric analysis*, 5th ed. Upper Saddle River, NJ: Prentice Hall.

Grinols, E.L. 1994a. Bluff or winning hand? Riverboat gambling and regional employment and unemployment. *Illinois Business Review* 51: 8–11.

Grinols, E.L. 1994b. Testimony and prepared statement. In U.S. House (1995), "The national impact of casino gambling proliferation," pp. 8–11 and 71–76.

Grinols, E.L. 1995. Gambling as economic policy: Enumerating why losses exceed gains. *Illinois Business Review* 52: 6–12.

Grinols 1997 is a personal email from E. Grinols to D. Walker and A. Barnett. Dated 16 June.

Grinols, E.L. 2004. *Gambling in America: Costs and benefits*. New York: Cambridge University Press.

Grinols, E.L. 2007. Social and economic impacts of gambling. In Smith, G., D. Hodgins, and R. Williams, eds. *Research and measurement issues in gambling studies*, pp. 515–540. New York, NY: Academic Press.

Grinols, E.L., and D.B. Mustard. 2000. Correspondence: Casino gambling. *Journal of Economic Perspectives* 14: 223–225.

Grinols, E.L., and D.B. Mustard. 2001. Business profitability versus social profitability: Evaluating industries with externalities, the case of casinos. *Managerial and Decision Economics* 22: 143–162.

Grinols, E.L., and D.B. Mustard. 2006. Casinos, crime, and community costs. *The Review of Economics and Statistics* 88(1): 28–45.

Grinols, E.L., and D.B. Mustard. 2008a. Correctly critiquing casino-crime causality. *Econ Journal Watch* 5(1): 21–31.

Grinols, E.L., and D.B. Mustard. 2008b. Connecting casinos and crime: More corrections of Walker. *Econ Journal Watch* 5(2): 156–162.

Grinols, E.L., D.B. Mustard, and M. Staha. 2011. How do visitors affect crime? *Journal of Quantitative Criminology* 27(3): 363–378.

Grinols, E.L., and J.D. Omorov. 1996. Development or dreamfield delusions? Assessing casino gambling's costs and benefits. *Journal of Law and Commerce* 16: 49–87.

Gross, M. 1998. Legal gambling as a strategy for economic development. *Economic Development Quarterly* 12: 203–213.

Grote, K.R., and V.A. Matheson. 2006. Dueling jackpots: Are competing Lotto games complements or substitutes? *Atlantic Economic Journal* 34: 85–100.

Gulley, O.D., and F.A. Scott. 1989. Lottery effects on pari-mutuel tax revenues. *National Tax Journal* 42: 89–93.

Guntermann, K.L., and G. Thomas. 2005. Parcel size, location and commercial land values. *Journal of Real Estate Research* 27: 343–354.

Hakim, S., and A.J. Buck. 1989. Do casinos enhance crime? *Journal of Criminal Justice* 17(5): 409–416.

Hall, G.A., and T. Loftus. 2013. Kentucky Gov. Steve Beshear may push for casino gambling without ties to racetracks. *Courier-Journal*, 5 January.

Hannum, R.C., and A.N. Cabot. 2005. *Practical Casino Math*, 2nd ed. Las Vegas, NV: Trace Publications.

Harberger, A.C. 1971. Three basic postulates for applied welfare economics: An interpretive essay. *Journal of Economic Literature* 9: 785–797.

Harrah's Entertainment. 1996. *Analysis of "Casino gamblers in Illinois: who are they?" by Gazel and Thompson (1996)*. Memphis, TN: Author.

Harrah's Entertainment. 1997. *Harrah's survey of casino entertainment*. Memphis, TN: Author.

Harris, K., F. Florey, J. Tabor, P. Bearman, J. Jones, and J. Udry. 2003. The National Longitudinal Study of Adolescent Health: Research design. http://www.cpc.unc.edu/projects/addhealth/design

Harwood, H.J., D. Fountain, and G. Fountain. 1999. Economic cost of alcohol and drug abuse in the United States, 1992: A report. *Addiction* 94: 631–635.

Hausman, J.A. 1998. New products and price indexes. NBER Reporter.

Hausman, J.A., B.H. Hall, and Z. Griliches. 1984. Econometric models for count data with an application to the patents-R&D relationship. *Econometrica* 52: 909–938.

Hausman, J.A., and G.K. Leonard. 2002. The competitive effects of a new product introduction: A case study. *The Journal of Industrial Economics* 50: 237–263.

Hayward, K., and R. Colman. 2004. *The costs and benefits of gaming: A summary report from the literature review*. Glen Haven, Canada: GPI Atlantic.

Heckman, J.J. 1976. The common structure of statistical models of truncation, sample selection and limited dependent variables and a simple estimator for such models. *Annals of Economic and Social Measurement* 5: 475–492.

Heckman, J.J. 1979. Sample selection bias as a specification error. *Econometrica* 47(1): 364–369.

Henderson, J.M., and R.E. Quandt. 1980. *Microeconomic theory: A mathematical approach*, 3rd ed. New York, NY: McGraw-Hill.

Hicks, J.R. 1940. The valuation of the social income. *Economica* 7: 105–124.

Hingson, R., T. Heeren, M. Winter, and H. Wechsler. 2005. Magnitude of alcohol-related mortality and morbidity among U.S. college students ages 18–24: Changes from 1998 to 2001. *Annual Review of Public Health* 26: 259–279.

Holcombe, R.G. 1998. Tax policy from a public choice perspective. *National Tax Journal* 51: 359–371.

Holtz-Eakin, D., W. Newey, and H.S. Rosen. 1988. Estimating vector autoregressions with panel data. *Econometrica* 56: 1371–1395.

Hoover, E.M., and F. Giarratani. 1984. *An introduction to regional economics*, 3rd ed. New York, NY: Alfred Knopf.

Huang, J.-H., D.F. Jacobs, J.L. Derevensky, R. Gupta, and T.S. Paskus. 2007. Gambling and health risk behaviors among U.S. college student-athletes: Findings from a national study. *Journal of Adolescent Health* 40(5): 390–397.

Humphreys, B.R., B.P. Soebbing, H. Wynne, J. Turvey, and Y.S. Lee. 2011. *Final Report to the Alberta Gaming Research Institute on the Socio-Economic Impact of Gambling in Alberta*. Edmonton: Alberta Gambling Research Institute.

Ignatin, G., and R. Smith. 1976. The economics of gambling. In *Gambling and society: Interdiscplinary studies on the subject of gambling*, ed. W.R. Eadington. Springfield, IL: Charles C. Thomas.

Jackson, J.D., D.S. Saurman, and W.F. Shughart. 1994. Instant winners: Legal change in transition and the diffusion of state lotteries. *Public Choice* 80: 245–263.

Jarrell, S., and R.M. Howsen. 1990. Transient crowding and crime. *American Journal of Economics and Sociology* 49(4): 483–494.

Joerding, W. 1986. Economic growth and defense spending. *Journal of Economic Development* 21: 35–40.

Johansson, A., J.E. Grant, S.W. Kim, B.L. Odlaug, and K.G. Götestam. 2009. Risk factors for problematic gambling: A critical literature review. *Journal of Gambling Studies* 25(1): 67–92.

Johnson, D.B. 1991. *Public choice: An introduction to the new political economy.* Mountain View, CA: Bristlecone Books.

Johnson, J.E.V., R. O'Brien, and H.S. Shin. 1999. A violation of dominance and the consumption value of gambling. *Journal of Behavioral Decision Making* 12: 19–36.

Jung, W.S., and P.J. Marshall. 1985. Exports, growth, and causality in developing countries. *Journal of Economic Development* 18: 1–12.

Kaldor, N. 1939. Welfare propositions of economics and interpersonal comparisons of utility. *Economic Journal* 49: 549–551.

Kearney, M.S. 2005. State lotteries and consumer behavior. *Journal of Public Economics* 89: 2269–2299.

Kindt, J.W. 1994. The economic impacts of legalized gambling activities. *Drake Law Review* 43: 51–95.

Kindt, J.W. 1995. U.S. national security and the strategic economic base: The business/economic impacts of the legalization of gambling activities. *Saint Louis University Law Journal* 39: 567–584.

Kindt, J.W. 2001. The costs of addicted gamblers: should the states initiate mega-lawsuits similar to the tobacco cases? *Managerial and Decision Economics* 22: 17–63.

Kleiman, M.A. 1999. "Economic cost" measurements, damage minimization and drug abuse control policy. *Addiction* 94: 638–641.

Klein, T.M. 1986. A method for estimating posterior BAC distributions for persons involved in fatal traffic accidents. DOT HS 807094. Department of Transportation, National Highway Traffic Safety Administration.

Korn, D., R. Gibbins, and J. Azmier. 2003. Framing public policy towards a public health paradigm for gambling. *Journal of Gambling Studies* 19(2): 235–256.

Korn, D.A., and H.J. Shaffer. 1999. Gambling and the health of the public: Adopting a public health perspective. *Journal of Gambling Studies* 15: 289–365.

Krueger, A.O. 1974. The political economy of the rent-seeking society. *American Economic Review* 64(3): 291–303.

Krugman, P.R. 1996. *Pop internationalism.* Cambridge, MA: MIT Press.

Kusi, N.K. 1994. Economic growth and defense spending in developing countries. *Journal of Conflict Resolution* 38: 152–159.

Ladd, H.F. 1995. Introduction to Panel III: Social costs. In *Casino development: How would casinos affect New England's economy?* ed. R. Tannenwald. Boston, MA: Federal Reserve Bank of Boston.

Ladouceur, R., N. Boudreault, C. Jacques, and F. Vitaro. 1999. Pathological gambling and related problems among adolescents. *Journal of Child & Adolescent Substance Abuse* 8: 55–68.

LaFalce, J.J. 1994. Opening statement. In U.S. House (1995), "The national impact of casino gambling proliferation." pp. 1–4 and 37–41

Lancaster, K. 1990. The economics of product variety: A survey. *Marketing Science* 9: 189–206.

Landsburg, S.E. 1993. *The armchair economist.* New York, NY: Free Press.

Layard, P.R., and A.A. Walters. 1978. *Microeconomic theory.* New York, NY: McGraw-Hill.

Lee, L.W. 1997. The socioeconomics of drunk driving. *Journal of Socio-Economics* 26(1): 95–106.

Lesieur, H.R. 1987. Gambling, pathological gambling, and crime. In *The handbook of pathological gambling*, ed. T. Galski. Springfield, IL: Charles C. Thomas.

Lesieur, H. R. 1995. The social impacts of expanded gaming. Paper presented at the *Future of Gaming Conference*, Canadian Mental Health Association, Regina, Saskatchewan, Canada. 19 October.

Lesieur, H.R. 2003. Personal email from H.R. Lesieur to W. Eadington, dated 21 February.

Lesieur, H.R., and S.B. Blume. 1987. The South Oaks Gambling Screen (SOGS): A new instrument for the identification of pathological gamblers. *American Journal of Psychiatry* 144: 1184–1188.

Li, G., X. Gu, and R.C. Siu. 2010. The impacts of gaming expansion on economic growth: A theoretical reconsideration. *Journal of Gambling Studies* 26: 269–285.

Light, S., and K. Rand. 2005. *Indian gaming & tribal sovereignty: The casino compromise*. Lawrence, KS: University Press of Kansas.

Lösch, A. 1954. *The economics of location. Translated by WH Woglom and WF Stolper*. New Haven, CT: Yale University Press.

Lott, W.F., and S.M. Miller. 1973. A note on the optimality conditions for excise taxation. *Southern Economic Journal* 40: 122–123.

Lott, W.F., and S.M. Miller. 1974. Excise tax revenue maximization. *Southern Economic Journal* 40: 657–664.

Luman, M., J. Oosterlaan, K.A. Harrigan, and J.A. Sergeant. 2005. The impact of reinforcement contingencies on AD/HD: A review and theoretical appraisal. *Clinical Psychology Review* 25: 183–213.

MacDonald, R. 1996. Panel unit root tests and real exchange rates. *Economic Letters* 50: 7–11.

MacLaren, V.V., J.A. Fugelsang, K.A. Harrigan, and M.J. Dixon. 2012. Effects of impulsivity, reinforcement sensitivity, and cognitive style on pathological gambling symptoms among frequent slot machine players. *Personality and Individual Differences* 52: 390–394.

Madhusudhan, R.G. 1996. Betting on casino revenues: Lessons from state experiences. *National Tax Journal* 49: 401–412.

Mankiw, N.G. 2007. *Essentials of economics*, 4th ed. Mason, OH: South-Western.

Manning, W., E. Keeler, J.P. Newhouse, E. Sloss, and J. Wasserman. 1991. *The costs of poor health habits*. Cambridge, MA: Harvard University Press.

Marfels, C. 1998. Development or dreamfield delusions? Assessing casino gambling's costs and benefits—A comment on an article by Professors Grinols and Omorov. *Gaming Law Review* 2(4): 415–418.

Marfels, C. 2001. Is gambling rational? The utility aspect of gambling. *Gaming Law Review* 5(5): 459–466.

Markandya, A., and D.W. Pearce. 1989. The social costs of tobacco smoking. *British Journal of Addiction* 84: 1139–1150.

Mason, P.M., and H. Stranahan. 1996. The effects of casino gambling on state tax revenue. *Atlantic Economic Journal* 24(4): 336–348.

McCarthy, J. 2002. Entertainment-led regeneration: The case of Detroit. *Cities*, April, 105–111.

McCormick, R.E. 1998. The economic impact of the video poker industry in South Carolina. Report prepared for Collins Entertainment.

McGowan, R.A. 1999. A comment on Walker and Barnett's "The Social Costs of Gambling: An Economic Perspective". *Journal of Gambling Studies* 15: 213–215.

McGowan, R.A. 2001. *Government and the transformation of the gaming industry*. Northampton, MA: Edward Elgar.

McGowan, R.A. 2009. The competition for gambling revenue: Pennsylvania v. New Jersey. *Gaming Law Review and Economics* 13(2): 145–155.

Mejia, L.C., and M.J. Eppli. 2003. Inter-center retail externalities. *Journal of Real Estate Finance and Economics* 27: 321–333.

Meyer, G., and M.A. Stadler. 1999. Criminal behaviour associated with pathological gambling. *Journal of Gambling Studies* 15(1): 29–43.

Miceli, T.J., and C.F. Sirmans. 1995. Contracting with spatial externalities and agency problems: The case of retail leases. *Regional Science and Urban Economics* 25(3): 355–372.

Michigan Senate Fiscal Agency. 2000. *Detroit casinos and their fiscal impact on the State*. Lansing, MI: Author.

Miller, W.J., and M.D. Schwartz. 1998. Casino gambling and street crime. *Annals of the American Academy of Political & Social Science* 556: 124–137.

Minton, M. 2012. Let states regulate internet gambling. *Washington Examiner*, 18 March.

Mirrlees, J.A. 1971. An exploration in the theory of optimum income taxation. *The Review of Economic Studies* 38: 175–208.

Mobilia, P. 1992a. An economic analysis of gambling addiction. In *Gambling and commercial gaming: Essays in business, economics, philosophy, and science*, ed. W.R. Eadington and J.A. Cornelius. Reno, NV: Institute for the Study of Gambling and Commercial Gaming.

Mobilia, P. 1992b. Trends in gambling: The pari-mutuel racing industry and effect of state lotteries, a new market definition. *Journal of Cultural Economics* 16: 51–62.
Moufakkir, O. 2002. Changes in selected economic and social indicators associated with the establishment of casinos in the city of Detroit: A case study. Ph.D. dissertation, Michigan State University.
Mueller, D.C. 1989. *Public choice II*. New York, NY: Cambridge University Press.
National Gambling Impact Study Commission. 1999. *Final report*. Washington, DC: Author.
National Highway Traffic Safety Administration. 2002. *Transitioning to multiple imputation—A new method to impute missing blood alcohol concentration (BAC) values in FARS. DOT HS 809403*. Washington, DC: Author.
National Opinion Research Center. 1999. *Report to the National Gambling Impact Study Commission*. Chicago, IL: Author.
National Research Council. 1999. *Pathological gambling*. Washington, DC: National Academy Press.
Nettler, G. 1984. *Explaining crime*, 3rd ed. New York, NY: McGraw-Hill.
Noble, N.R., and T.W. Fields. 1983. Sunspots and cycles: Comment. *Southern Economic Journal* 50: 251–254.
Nordhaus, W. 2002. Personal email from W. Nordhaus to D. Walker, dated 11 February.
North, D.C. 1975. Location theory and regional economic growth. In *Regional policy: Readings in theory and application*, ed. J. Friedmann and W. Alonso. Cambridge, MA: MIT Press.
Nourse, H.O. 1968. *Regional economics*. New York: McGraw-Hill.
Nower, L. 1998. *Social impact on individuals, families, communities and society: An analysis of the empirical literature*. St. Louis, MO: Washington University.
Nower, L., and A.P. Blaszczynski. 2003. A pathways model for the treatment of youth gamblers. In *Gambling problems in youth: Theoretical and applied perspectives*, ed. J.L. Derevensky and R. Gupta. New York: Kluwer Academic.
Nower, L., J.L. Derevensky, and R. Gupta. 2004. The relationship of impulsivity, sensation seeking, coping, and substance use in youth gamblers. *Psychology of Addictive Behaviors* 18(1): 49–55.
Office of Planning and Budgeting. 1995. *Casinos in Florida*. Tallahassee, FL: Author.
Olivier, M.J. 1995. Casino gaming on the Mississippi gulf coast. *Economic Development Review* 13: 34–39.
Orphanides, A., and D. Zervos. 1995. Rational addiction with learning and regret. *Journal of Political Economy* 103: 739–758.
Oster, E. 2004. Are all lotteries regressive? Evidence from Powerball. *National Tax Journal* 57: 179–187.
Pascal, A.J., and J.J. McCall. 1980. Agglomeration economics, search costs, and industrial location. *Journal of Urban Economics* 8: 383–388.
Petry, N.M. 2000. Gambling problems in substance abusers are associated with increased sexual risk behaviors. *Addiction* 95: 1089–1100.
Petry, N.M. 2001. Substance abuse, pathological gambling, and impulsiveness. *Drug & Alcohol Dependence* 63: 29–38.
Petry, N.M. 2003. Pathological gamblers, with and without substance use disorders, discount delayed rewards at high rates. *Journal of Abnormal Psychology* 110: 482–487.
Petry, N.M. 2005. *Pathological gambling: Etiology, comorbidity & treatment*. Washington, DC: American Psychological Association.
Petry, N.M. 2010. Editorial: Pathological gambling and the DSM-V. *International Gambling Studies* 10(2): 113–115.
Petry, N.M., F.S. Stinson, and B.F. Grant. 2005. Comorbidity of DSM-IV pathological gambling and other psychiatric disorders: Results from the National Epidemiological Surveys on Alcohol and Related Conditions. *Journal of Clinical Psychiatry* 66(5): 564–574.
Philander, K.S. 2011. The effect of online gaming revenue on commercial casino revenue. *UNLV Gaming Research & Review Journal* 15(2): 23–34.

Philander, K.S., and I. Fiedler. 2012. Online poker in North America: Empirical evidence on its complementary effect on the offline gambling market. *Gaming Law Review and Economics* 16(7/8): 415–423.

Philander, K.S., and D.M. Walker. 2012. William R. Eadington and the economics of gambling. *UNLV Gaming Research & Review Journal* 16(2): 9–18.

Phipps, A.G. 2004. Crime and disorder, and house sales and prices around the Casino Sites in Windsor, Ontario, Canada. *The Canadian Geographer* 48(December): 403–432.

Phlips, L. 1983. *Applied consumption analysis*. Amsterdam, The Netherlands: North-Holland.

Politzer, R.M., J.S. Morrow, and S.B. Leavey. 1985. Report on the cost-benefit/effectiveness of treatment at the Johns Hopkins Center for Pathological Gambling. *Journal of Gambling Behavior* 1(2): 131–142.

Popp, A.V., and C. Stehwien. 2002. Indian casino gambling and state revenue: Some further evidence. *Public Finance Review* 30(4): 320–330.

Posner, R.A. 1975. The social costs of monopoly and regulation. *Journal of Political Economy* 83: 807–827.

PricewaterhouseCoopers. 2011. *Global gaming outlook: The casino and online gaming market to 2015*. Las Vegas, NV: Author.

Ramirez, M.D. 1994. Public and private investment in Mexico, 1950–90: An empirical analysis. *Southern Economic Journal* 61: 1–17.

Ramsey, F.P. 1927. A contribution to the theory of taxation. *The Economic Journal* 37: 47–61.

Ray, M.A. 2001. How much on that doggie at the window? An analysis of the decline in greyhound racing handle. *Review of Regional Studies* 31: 165–176.

Reece, W.S. 2010. Casinos, hotels, and crime. *Contemporary Economic Policy* 28(2): 145–161.

Reuter, P. 1997. The impact of casinos on crime and other social problems: An analysis of recent experiences. Report for the Greater Baltimore Committee.

Reuter, P. 1999. Are calculations of the economic costs of drug abuse either possible or useful? *Addiction* 94: 635–638.

Ricardo, D. [1817] 1992. *Principles of political economy and taxation*. Rutland, VT: Charles E. Tuttle Co.

Richman, G., T. Hope, and S. Mihalas. 2010. Assessment and treatment of self-esteem in adolescents with ADHD. In *Self-esteem across the lifespan: Issues and interventions*, ed. M.H. Guindon. New York: Routledge.

Richters, J.E., L.E. Arnold, P.S. Jensen, H. Abikoff, C.K. Conners, and L.L. Greenhill. 1995. NIH collaborative multisite multimodal treatment study of children with ADHD: I. Background and rationale. *Journal of the American Academy of Child & Adolescent Psychiatry* 34: 987–1000.

Riedel, J. 1994. Strategies of economic development. In *Economic development*, ed. E.R. Grilli and D. Salvatore. Westport, CT: Greenwood Press.

Roberts, R. 2001. *The choice: A fable of free trade and protectionism*, Revised ed. Upper Saddle River, NJ: Prentice Hall.

Rodriguez-Jiminez, R., C. Avila, M.A. Jiminez-Arriero, G. Ponce, R. Monasor, and M. Jiminez. 2006. Impulsivity and sustained attention in pathological gamblers: Influence of childhood ADHD history. *Journal of Gambling Studies* 22: 451–461.

Rose, I.N. 1995. Gambling and the law: Endless fields of dreams. In *Casino development: How would casinos affect New England's economy?* ed. R. Tannenwald. Boston, MA: Federal Reserve Bank of Boston.

Ross, D., C. Sharp, R.E. Vuchinich, and D. Spurrett. 2008. *Midbrain mutiny: The picoeconomics and neuroeconomics of disordered gambling*. Cambridge, MA: MIT Press.

Rubin, D.B., J.L. Shafer, and R. Subramanian. 1998. *Multiple imputation of missing blood alcohol concentration (BAC) values in FARS. DOT HS 808816*. Washington, DC: National Highway Traffic Safety Administration.

Ruhm, C.J. 1996. Alcohol policies and highway vehicle fatalities. *Journal of Health Economics* 15(4): 435–454.

Ruhm, C.J., and W.E. Black. 2002. Does drinking really decrease in bad times? *Journal of Health Economics* 21(4): 659–678.

Rush, B., S. Veldhuizen, and E. Adlaf. 2007. Mapping the prevalence of problem gambling and its association with treatment accessibility and proximity to gambling venues. *Journal of Gambling Issues* 20: 193–213.

Ryan, T.P., and J.F. Speyrer. 1999. The impact of gambling in Louisiana. Report prepared for the Louisiana Gaming Control Board. New Orleans, LA.

Saba, R.P., T. R. Beard, R.B. Ekelund, and R. Ressler. 1995. The demand for cigarette smuggling. *Economic Inquiry* 37: 189–202.

Samuelson, P.A. 1976. *Economics*, 10th ed. New York, NY: McGraw-Hill.

Samuelson, P.A., and W. Nordhaus. 2001. *Economics*, 17th ed. New York, NY: McGraw-Hill.

Scherer, F.M. 1979. The welfare economics of product variety: An application to the ready-to-eat cereals industry. *The Journal of Industrial Economics* 28: 113–134.

Schumpeter, J.A. 1950. *Capitalism, socialism, and democracy*, 3rd ed. New York, NY: Harper & Row.

Schumpeter, J.A. [1934] 1993. *The theory of economic development*. New Brunswick, NJ: Transaction Publishers.

Scitovsky, T. 1986. *Human desire and economic satisfaction*. Washington Square, NY: New York University Press.

Seitz, V.A. 2011. *Opinion: Whether proposals by Illinois and New York to use the internet and out-of-state transaction processors to sell lottery tickets to in-state adults violate the Wire Act*. Washington, DC: U.S. Department of Justice, Office of Legal Counsel.

Shaffer, H.J., M.N. Hall, and J. Vander Bilt. 1997. *Estimating the prevalence of disordered gambling behavior in the United States and Canada: A meta-analysis*. Kansas City, MO: National Center for Responsible Gaming.

Shah, K.R., M.N. Potenza, and S.A. Eisen. 2004. Biological basis for pathological gambling. In *Pathological gambling: A clinical guide to treatment*, ed. J.E. Grant and M.N. Potenza. Washington, DC: American Psychiatric Publishing.

Sheehan, R.G., and R. Grieves. 1982. Sunspots and cycles: A test of causation. *Southern Economic Journal* 49: 775–777.

Sherman, L.W., P.R. Gartin, and M.E. Buerger. 1989. Hot spots of predatory crime: Routine activities and the criminology of place. *Criminology* 27: 27–55.

Siegel, D., and G.C. Anders. 1999. Public policy and the displacement effects of casinos: A case study of riverboat gambling in Missouri. *Journal of Gambling Studies* 15: 105–121.

Siegel, D., and G.C. Anders. 2001. The impact of Indian casinos on state lotteries: A case study of Arizona. *Public Finance Review* 29: 139–147.

Sieroty, C. 2012. American Gaming Association lobbies for web poker legislation. *Las Vegas Review-Journal*, 3 December. http://www.reviewjournal.com

Single, E. 2003. Estimating the costs of substance abuse: Implications to the estimation of the costs and benefits of gambling. *Journal of Gambling Studies* 19: 215–233.

Single, E., D. Collins, B. Easton, H. Harwood, H. Lapsley, P. Kopp, and E. Wilson. 2003. *International guidelines for estimating the costs of substance abuse*. Geneva, Switzerland: World Health Organization.

Siu, R.C. 2011. A conceptual reconsideration of price issues with casino gambling. *Gaming Law Review and Economics* 15(5): 264–277.

Siu, T., and C. Lo. 2012. Macau gaming revenue surges 42 pct in 2011. *Reuters*, 3 January.

Skinner, S.J., R.B. Ekelund, and J.D. Jackson. 2009. Art museum attendance, public funding, and the business cycle. *American Journal of Economics and Sociology* 68(2): 491–516.

Slemrod, J. 1990. Optimal taxation and optimal tax systems. *Journal of Economic Perspectives* 4: 157–178.

Sloan, F.A., J. Ostermann, G. Picone, C. Conover, and D.H. Taylor. 2004. *The price of smoking*. Cambridge, MA: MIT Press.

Smalley, S.L., J.N. Bailey, C.G. Palmer, D.P. Cantwell, J.J. McGough, and M.A. Del'Homme. 2003. Evidence that the dopamine D4 receptor is susceptibility gene in attention deficit hyperactivity disorder. *Molecular Psychiatry* 3: 427–430.

Smith, A. [1776] 1981. *An inquiry into the nature and causes of the wealth of nations*. Indianapolis, IN: Liberty Classics.

Smith, G. 2010. Fatal crashes, DUI arrests up in Southeast during 2009. *Norwich Bulletin*, 3 February.

Smith, G., D. Hodgins, and R. Williams (eds.). 2007. *Research and measurement issues in gambling studies*. New York: Academic Press.

Smith, T.G., and A. Tasnádi. 2007. A theory of natural addiction. *Games and Economic Behavior* 59(2): 316–344.

Sobel, R.S. 1997. Optimal taxation in a federal system of governments. *Southern Economic Journal* 62: 468–485.

Sobel, R.S., and P.T. Leeson. 2006. Government's response to Hurricane Katrina: A public choice analysis. *Public Choice* 127: 55–73.

State and market. 1996. *The Economist*, 17 February.

Stewart, S.H., and M.C. Kushner. 2005. Introduction to the special issue on "Relations between gambling and alcohol use". *Journal of Gambling Studies* 21(3): 223–231.

Stigler, G.J., and G.S. Becker. 1977. De gustibus non est disputandum. *American Economic Review* 67(2): 76–90.

Stinchfield, R.D., M.G. Kushner, and K.C. Winters. 2005. Alcohol use and prior substance abuse treatment in relation to gambling problem severity and gambling treatment outcome. *Journal of Gambling Studies* 21(3): 273–297.

Stitt, B.G., M.W. Nichols, and D. Giacopassi. 2003. Does the presence of casinos increase crime? An examination of casino and control communities. *Crime & Delinquency* 49(2): 253–284.

Stokowski, P.A. 1996. Crime patterns and gaming development in rural Colorado. *Journal of Travel Research* 34: 63–69.

Strazicich, M.C. 1995. Are state and provincial governments tax smoothing? Evidence from panel data. *Southern Economic Journal* 62: 979–988.

Tannenwald, R. (ed.). 1995. *Casino development: How would casinos affect New England's economy?* Boston, MA: Federal Reserve Bank of Boston.

Tarlow, P.E. 2006. Crime and tourism. In *Tourism in turbulent times: Towards safe experiences for visitors*, ed. J. Wilks, D. Pendergast, and P. Leggat. Boston, MA: Elsevier.

Task Force on Gambling Addiction in Maryland. 1990. *Final report*. Baltimore, MD: Maryland Department of Health and Mental Hygiene.

Thalheimer, R., and M.M. Ali. 1995. The demand for parimutuel horse race wagering and attendance. *Management Science* 41: 129–143.

Thalheimer, R., and M.M. Ali. 2003. The demand for casino gaming. *Applied Economics* 34: 907–918.

Thalheimer, R., and M.M. Ali. 2004. The relationship of pari-mutuel wagering and casino gaming to personal bankruptcy. *Contemporary Economic Policy* 22: 420–432.

Thompson, W.N. 1996. *An economic analysis of a proposal to legalize casino gambling in Ohio: Sometimes the best defense is to NOT take the field*. Las Vegas, NV: UNLV working paper.

Thompson, W.N. 1997. Sorting out some fiscal policy matters regarding gambling. Paper presented at the Southern Economic Association meeting.

Thompson, W.N. 2001. *Gambling in America: An encyclopedia of history, issues, and society*. Santa Barbara, CA: ABC-CLIO.

Thompson, W.N., and R.C. Gazel. 1996. *The monetary impacts of riverboat casino gambling in Illinois*. Las Vegas, NV: UNLV working paper.

Thompson, W.N., R.C. Gazel, and D. Rickman. 1997. Social and legal costs of compulsive gambling. *Gaming Law Review* 1: 81–89.

Thompson, W.N., R.C. Gazel, and D. Rickman. 1999. The social costs of gambling: A comparative study of nutmeg and cheese state gamblers. *UNLV Gaming Research & Review Journal* 5: 1–15.

Thompson, W.N., R.C. Gazel, and D.S. Rickman. 1996. The social costs of gambling in Wisconsin. Policy Research Institute Report.

References

Thompson, W.N., and F.L. Quinn. 1999. The video gaming machines of South Carolina: Disappearing soon? Good riddance or bad news? A Socio-economic analysis. In *11th International conference on gambling and risk-taking*. Las Vegas, NV.

Thompson, W.N., and K. Schwer. 2005. Beyond the limits of recreation: Social costs of gambling in southern Nevada. *Journal of Public Budgeting, Accounting & Financial Management* 17: 62–93.

Thompson, W.R. 1968. Internal and external factors in the development of urban economies. In *Issues in urban economics*, ed. H.S. Perloff and L. Wingo. Baltimore, MD: Johns Hopkins Press.

Thornton, D.L., and D.S. Batten. 1985. Lag-length selection and tests of Granger causality between money and income. *Journal of Money, Credit, and Banking* 17(2): 164–178.

Tiebout, C.M. 1975. Exports and regional economic growth. In *Regional policy: Readings in theory and applications*, ed. J. Friedmann and W. Alonso. Cambridge, MA: MIT Press.

Tollison, R.D. 1982. Rent seeking: A survey. *Kyklos* 35: 575–602.

Tosun, M.S., and M.L. Skidmore. 2004. Interstate competition and state lottery revenues. *National Tax Journal* 57: 163–178.

Tullock, G. 1967. The welfare costs of tariffs, monopolies, and theft. *Western Economic Journal* 5: 224–232.

Tullock, G. 1981. Lobbying and welfare: A comment. *Journal of Public Economics* 16: 391–394.

U.S. House of Representatives. 1995. Committee on small business. *The National Impact of Casino Gambling Proliferation*. 2nd sess, 103rd Congress. 21 September 1994.

Vaughan, R.J. 1988. Economists and economic development. *Economic Development Quarterly* 2: 119–123.

Villaveces, A., P. Cummings, T.D. Koepsell, F.P. Rivara, T. Lumley, and J. Moffat. 2003. Association of alcohol-related laws with deaths due to motor vehicle and motorcycle crashes in the United States, 1980–1997. *American Journal of Epidemiology* 157(2): 131–140.

Viner, J. 1931. Cost curves and supply curves. *Zeitschrift für Nationalökonomie* 111: 23–46.

Viscusi, W.K., and J.K. Hakes. 2008. Risk beliefs and smoking behavior. *Economic Inquiry* 46(1): 45–59.

Vitaro, F., M. Brendgen, R. Ladouceur, and R.E. Tremblay. 2001. Gambling, delinquency, and drug use during adolescence: Mutual influences and common risk factors. *Journal of Gambling Studies* 17(3): 171–190.

Wacker, R.F. 2006. Michigan gambling: The interactions of Native American, Detroit, and Canadian casinos. *American Behavioral Scientist* 50(November):373–380.

Walker, D.M. 1998a. Comment on "Legal gambling as a strategy for economic development". *Economic Development Quarterly* 12(3): 214–216.

Walker, D.M. 1998b. Sin and growth: The effects of legalized gambling on state economic development. Ph.D. Dissertation, Auburn University, Auburn, AL.

Walker, D.M. 1999. Legalized casino gambling and the export base theory of economic growth. *Gaming Law Review* 3(2/3): 157–163.

Walker, D.M. 2003. Methodological issues in the social cost of gambling studies. *Journal of Gambling Studies* 19(2): 149–184.

Walker, D.M. 2004. Kindt's paper epitomizes the problems in gambling research. *Managerial and Decision Economics* 25(4): 197–200.

Walker, D.M. 2007. Problems with quantifying the social costs and benefits of gambling. *American Journal of Economics and Sociology* 66(3): 609–645.

Walker, D.M. 2008a. Do casinos really cause crime? *Econ Journal Watch* 5(1): 4–20.

Walker, D.M. 2008b. The diluted economics of casinos and crime: A rejoinder to Grinols and Mustard's reply. *Econ Journal Watch* 5(2): 148–155.

Walker, D.M. 2008c. Evaluating crime attributable to casinos in the U.S.: A closer look at Grinols and Mustard's "Casinos, crime, and community costs". *Journal of Gambling Business and Economics* 2(3): 23–52.

Walker, D.M. 2010. Casinos and crime in the USA. In *Handbook on the economics of crime*, ed. B.L. Benson and P.R. Zimmerman. Northampton, MA: Edward Elgar.

Walker, D.M., and A.H. Barnett. 1999. The social costs of gambling: An economic perspective. *Journal of Gambling Studies* 15(3): 181–212.
Walker, D.M., C. Clark, and J. Folk. 2010. The relationship between gambling behavior and binge drinking, hard drug use, and paying for sex. *UNLV Gaming Research & Review Journal* 14(1): 15–26.
Walker, D.M., and J.D. Jackson. 1998. New goods and economic growth: Evidence from legalized gambling. *Review of Regional Studies* 28(2): 47–69.
Walker, D.M., and J.D. Jackson. 2007. Do casinos cause economic growth? *American Journal of Economics and Sociology* 66(3): 593–607.
Walker, D.M., and J.D. Jackson. 2008a. Do U.S. gambling industries cannibalize each other? *Public Finance Review* 36(3): 308–333.
Walker, D.M., and J.D. Jackson. 2008b. Market-based "disaster relief": Katrina and the casino industry. *International Journal of Social Economics* 35(7): 521–530.
Walker, D.M., and J.D. Jackson. 2009. Katrina and the Gulf states casino industry. *Journal of Business Valuation and Economic Loss Analysis* 4(2):article 9.
Walker, D.M., and J.D. Jackson. 2011. The effect of legalized gambling on state government revenue. *Contemporary Economic Policy* 29(1): 101–114.
Walker, D.M., and S.M. Kelly. 2011. The roots of modern "social cost of gambling" estimates. *Economic Affairs* 31(1): 38–42.
Welte, J., G. Barnes, W. Wieczorek, M.-C. Tidwell, and J. Parker. 2001. Alcohol and gambling pathology among U.S. adults: Prevalence, demographic patterns and co-morbidity. *Journal of Studies on Alcohol* 62(5): 706–712.
Welte, J., G. Barnes, W. Wieczorek, M.-C. Tidwell, and J. Parker. 2004. Risk factors for pathological gambling. *Addictive Behaviors* 29: 323–335.
Wenz, M. 2007. The impact of casino gambling on housing markets: A hedonic approach. *The Journal of Gambling Business and Economics* 1: 101–120.
Westphal, J.R., and L.J. Johnson. 2007. Multiple co-occurring behaviours among gamblers in treatment: Implications and assessment. *International Gambling Studies* 7(1): 73–99.
WFSB Radio. 2009. *Mohegan Sun to battle drunken driving.* Hartford, CT.
Whaples, R. 2009. The policy views of American Economic Association members: The results of a new survey. *Econ Journal Watch* 6(3): 337–348.
Wiley, J.A., and D.M. Walker. 2011. Casino revenues and retail property values: The Detroit case. *Journal of Real Estate Finance and Economics* 42: 99–114.
Williams, R.J., J. Royston, and B.F. Hagen. 2005. Gambling and problem gambling within forensic populations: A review of the literature. *Criminal Justice and Behavior* 32: 665–689.
Williams, W.E. 1992. Trade deficit blather is nonsense. *Dallas Morning News*, 30 January.
Wilson, J.M. 2001. Riverboat gambling and crime in Indiana: An empirical investigation. *Crime & Delinquency* 47(4): 610–640.
Wooldridge, J.M. 2002. *Econometric analysis of cross section and panel data.* Cambridge, MA: MIT Press.
World Health Organization. 1986. Ottowa Charter for Health Promotion. Author.
Wright, A.W. 1995. High-stakes casinos and economic growth. In *Casino development: How would casinos affect New England's economy?* ed. R. Tannenwald. Boston, MA: Federal Reserve Bank of Boston.
Wu, Y. 1996. Are real exchange rates nonstationary? Evidence from a panel-data test. *Journal of Money, Credit, and Banking* 28: 54–63.
Wynne, H., and H.J. Shaffer. 2003. The socioeconomic impact of gambling: The Whistler Symposium. *Journal of Gambling Studies* 19(2): 111–121
Xu, Z. 1998. Export and income growth in Japan and Taiwan. *Review of International Economics* 6: 220–233.
Zorn, K. 1998. *The economic impact of pathological gambling: A review of the literature.* Bloomington, IN: Indiana University.

Index

A
ADHD. *See* Attention deficit hyperactivity disorder (ADHD)
Alcohol-related fatal accidents (ARFAs), 149
  county-level annual data, 98–99
  methodology
    BAC laws, 102
    beer taxes, 102
    casino population interaction, 100–101
    county unemployment rates, 101
    fixed effects regression model, 99–100
    legal drinking age laws, 102
    zero tolerance alcohol policy, 102
  results
    border county analysis, 108–109
    casino entry, effects of, 103–105
    robustness checks, 105–108
Alcohol use disorder, 97, 115, 180
American Gaming Association, 56, 179, 260
ARFAs. *See* Alcohol-related fatal accidents (ARFAs)
Atlantic City, 2, 10, 39, 209, 219
Attention deficit hyperactivity disorder (ADHD), 137–138, 149
  adolescent symptoms, effects of, 145
  data
    Add Health questions, 139–142
    combined type, 141, 143, 144
    gambling behavior variables, 139–143
    hyperactive–impulsive type, 142–144
    inattentive type, 142–144
    symptom variables, 143–140
  empirical strategy, 144
  linear probability model, 144
  results
    combined-type, 145, 146
    hyperactive–impulsive type, 145, 146
    inattentive type, 145, 146
Avoidable tax, 14

B
BAC. *See* Blood alcohol content (BAC)
Bailout costs, 169–170
Bankruptcy, 93, 94
Binge drinking, gambling behavior, 90, 149
  Add Health, DSM-IV, and SOGS questions, 116–120
  linear probability model, 125
  results, 132, 133
  variable definitions and summary statistics, 120–124
Binge eating, 115
Blood alcohol content (BAC), 98–99

C
California v. Cabazon Band of Mission Indians, 2
Cannibalization, 26–28, 173
Casino gambling
  and ADHD (*see* Attention deficit hyperactivity disorder (ADHD))
  availability in United States, 1985–2000, 239
  commercial casinos (*see* Commercial casino industry)
  commercial real estate values, Detroit (*see* Detroit commercial property values)
  consumer behavior and welfare
    consumer surplus, 22, 23
    immiserizing growth, 23–24

Casino gambling (*cont.*)
    mutually beneficial transactions, 19–22
    producer surplus, 22, 23
    variety benefits, 23
  and crime (*see* Crime)
  DUP activity (*see* Directly unproductive profit-seeking (DUP) activity)
  economic growth (*see* Economic growth, casino gambling)
  gambling research, economics of
    American Gaming Association, 260
    Eadington's conference, 257
    economics journals, 258
    online gambling, 259–260
  IC (*see* Indifference curve (IC))
  labor market, 89
  PPF (*see* Production possibilities frontier (PPF))
  social costs (*see* Social costs)
  state tax revenues
    Granger causality, 85–86
    multiplicative heteroscedasticity model, 78–80
    panel data analysis, 73–76
    politicians, 87
    results, 82–83
    SUR model, 246, 247
Central business district (CBD), 218, 224
Civil court costs, 164
Commercial casino industry
  California v. Cabazon Band of Mission Indians, 2
  economic growth (*see* Economic growth, casino gambling)
  IGRA, 2
  legalization and 2010 data, 2–3
  online gambling, 5, 259–260
  2007–2009 recession, 54
  revenues and projected revenues, 4–5
  state tax revenues (*see* State tax revenues, legalized gambling)
Comorbidity, 96, 115, 179–181
Consumers
  consumer surplus, 22, 23
  immiserizing growth, 23–24
  mutually beneficial transactions
    economic development, 21
    price of casino gambling, 20–21
    spending, welfare impact of, 21–22
  producer surplus, 22, 23
  utility maximizers, 19
  variety benefits, 23
Consumer surplus (CS), 22, 23, 272–273

  deadweight loss, 190, 191
  welfare loss, 191
Cost-of-illness (COI) approach, 184–185
Crime, 149, 253
  casino-based *vs.* community-based crimes, 205, 213
  casino–crime rate studies, 208–210
  county-level crime data, 210, 211
  criminals and victims, 213, 214
  econometric analysis, 211
  economic model of, 212
  and gambling behavior
    Add Health, DSM-IV, and SOGS questions, 116–120
    casino gambling, 114
    linear probability model, 125
    problem/pathological gamblers, 113–114
    results, 126–131
    variable definitions and summary statistics, 120–124
  hotel rooms, 212, 213
  law enforcement, 212
  measurement issues
    "population" and "population at risk," 207, 208, 213
    standard crime rate, 206, 207
    tourism, 207, 208
    traditional crime rate, 207
  organized crime, 204
  theoretical background
    economic development, 205–206
    economic theory, 204
    hot spot theory, 205
    routine activities theory, 204–205
  tourism effect, 211–213
  UCR data, 212
Criminal justice costs, 164

D

Destination resort model, 93
Detroit commercial property values, 253
  annual casino revenues, 218
  CBD, 218
  crime and bankruptcy filings, 218–219
  data and methodology
    annual population, 222
    casino revenues, 223
    CoStar Retail Market Report, 221
    density effects, 224
    descriptive statistics, 221, 222
    distance variable, 223

Index

empirical analysis, 225–226
list of variables, 221
macroeconomic market factors, 221
market locations, 224
MSA, 222
operational model, 225
population and employment decline, 221
property characteristics, 224
property transaction data, 222, 223
RBA, 221, 222
regression analysis, 224
retail property sales data, 221
urban commercial casinos, 220, 221
"entertainment-led" strategy, 218
hedonic pricing model, 219, 223, 224
results
   casino revenues, influence of, 227–228
   empirical estimation, 228, 229
   general freestanding, 228
   property size, 226
   property type, coefficients for, 229, 230
   time trend variable, 226
   urban location, 226
transaction-level data, 214
Diagnostic and Statistical Manual of Mental Disorders (DSM-IV)
ADHD
   adolescent symptoms, effects of, 145
   gambling indicator variables, 140, 141, 144
binge drinking and drug use, 118–120
crime, 118–120
financial questions, social cost, 181, 182
pathological gambling, 111–112
prostitution, 118–120
Directly unproductive profit-seeking (DUP) activity, 253
definition of, 198
GDP, 199, 200
professional gambling/gamblers, 200–202
and rent seeking, 201–202
Disordered gambling
and ADHD (*see* Attention deficit hyperactivity disorder (ADHD))
drunk driving (*see* Drunk driving, casinos)
Divorce, 94
Drug use, 90, 149
gambling behavior, effect of
   Add Health, DSM-IV, and SOGS questions, 116–120
   linear probability model, 125
   results, 131–133

variable definitions and summary statistics, 120–124
problem gambling, 115
social costs, 181, 188
Drunk driving, casinos, 149
alcohol-related fatal accidents (*see* Alcohol-related fatal accidents (ARFAs))
casino alcohol policies, 96
destination resort model, 93
drinking activities, location of, 95
DUI arrests, 93, 96
local population, 97
Löschian location model, 95
pathological gamblers, 97
problem gambler, 96–97
product differentiation effect, 95
public policies, changes in, 94–95
rural/urban area, 97
substitution effect, 95

E
Economic growth, casino gambling
advertisements, 39
capital inflow, 13–14
clustering, 39
consumer behavior and welfare (*see* Consumers)
defensive legalization, 38
employment, 12–13, 90
export base theory, 30–32
exports, 15–16
factory–restaurant dichotomy, 28–30, 38
Granger causality analysis
   goal of, 40
   panel data, 41–46
   results, 47–49, 53–56
import substitution, 15, 38
industry cannibalization, 26–28
mercantilism
   in Illinois, 32–33
   positive trade balance, 33
   self-sufficiency, 34–35
   South Carolina video gaming machines, 33, 34
   welfare, 35
   zero sum transactions, 34
production possibilities frontier (*see* Production possibilities frontier (PPF))
supply-driven model, 16
tax revenue, 14, 90

Economic growth, casino gambling (*cont.*)
    threshold and range, 39
    in United States, 9–10
    wage rates, 12–13, 90
Economics, 198–199
Economic theory of crime, 204
Equilibrium price (P_e), 270, 271
Equilibrium quantity (q_e), 271
Export base theory, 30–32
Externality, 159–161

F
Factory–restaurant dichotomy, 28–30, 38
Federal Emergency Management Agency (FEMA), 61, 62
Fiscal externality, 171

G
Gamblers Anonymous, 113, 115, 183
Gambling industries, 253–254
    data
        adjacent state gambling, 240–241
        casino availability, 239
        demographic variables, 242–243
        gambling volume variables, 237–240
        greyhound racing availability, 238
        horse racing availability, 238
        Indian casino availability, 239
        lottery availability, 237
    interindustry relationships, 235, 236
    model and results
        casino revenue model, 248
        constrained and unconstrained models, 249
        demand systems estimation, 245
        dog racing model, 248
        econometric model, 243
        econometric theory, 249
        horse racing model, 248
        lottery model, 248
        probit models, 243, 244
        SUR model, 244–247
    policy issues
        intrastate industry relationships, 250
        tax revenues, 251–252
    state tax revenues (*see* State tax revenues, legalized gambling)
    substitution effect, 233, 252
Government welfare expenditures, 170–171
Granger causality
    casino gambling and economic growth
        goal, 40
        panel data, 41–46
        results, 47–49, 53–56
    greyhound racing
        goal, 40
        panel data, 41–46
        results, 49–50
    state tax revenues and casinos, 85–86
Greyhound racing
    advertisements and clustering, 39
    availability in United States, 1985–2000, 238
    Granger causality analysis
        goal of, 40
        panel data, 41–46
        results, 49–50
    state tax revenues
        lotteries, impact of, 71
        multiplicative heteroscedasticity model, 78–80
        panel data analysis, 73–76
        results, 83
    SUR model, 246, 247
    threshold and range, 39
Grinols, E.L., 210–211
Gross domestic product (GDP), 199, 200

H
Horse racing
    availability in United States, 1985–2000, 238
    state tax revenues
        lotteries, impact of, 71
        multiplicative heteroscedasticity model, 78–80
        panel data analysis, 73–76
        results, 83
    SUR model, 246, 247
    UK horse racing industry, 23
Hot spot theory, 205
Hurricane Katrina, 10, 56–64
Hurricane Rita, 56–64

I
IGRA. *See* Indian Gaming Regulatory Act (IGRA)
Indian casinos
    availability in United States, 1985–2000, 239
    IGRA, 2

Index

state tax revenues
  lottery sales, effect on, 71
  multiplicative heteroscedasticity model, 78–80
  panel data analysis, 73–76
  results, 82–83
  transactions tax revenue, 72
Indian Gaming Regulatory Act (IGRA), 2
Indifference curve (IC)
  for beer and pizza, 266, 267
  higher utility/satisfaction, 267
  immiserizing growth, 23
  indifference map, 267, 268
  welfare loss, 189, 190
Industry cannibalization, 26–28, 173
International Conference on Gambling and Risk Taking, 257
Internet gambling, 5
Inverse mills ratio (IMR), 80, 243, 248

J

Journal of Gambling Studies, 115, 258

L

Lake Charles, Louisiana, 56, 59–60
Legal costs, 163–166
Linear probability model, 125–126
Local Area Unemployment Statistics (LAUS) program, 101
Löschian location model, 95
Lotteries, 235
  availability in United States, 1985–2000, 237
  state tax revenues
    Arizona Indian casinos, 71
    greyhound and horse racing, 71
    multiplicative heteroscedasticity model, 78–80
    multi-state lotteries, effect of, 70
    new lottery adoptions, effects of, 70
    optimal taxes, 70
    panel data analysis, 73–76
    results, 80, 82
    time series analysis, 72
  SUR model, 246, 247
Louisiana casino industry
  employees in, 56
  hurricanes Katrina/Rita
    casinos damaged by, 57–58
    Lake Charles area, nominal revenue of, 59–60

New Orleans area, nominal revenue of, 58–59
OLS model, 62
personal income and casino revenues data, 60–61
regression results, 63–64
riverboat casino revenues, 57
state tax revenue, 56
total gaming revenues in 2004, 56
Louisiana Gaming Control Board, 58

M

Macau, 3–5, 30
Marginal opportunity cost (MC), 270
Marginal rate of transformation (MRT)., 264
Market models
  prices and quantities, 270, 271
  supply and demand curves, 270–271
Metropolitan Statistical Area (MSA), 222, 224
Michigan Senate Fiscal Agency, 218
Mississippi casino industry, 10
  employees in, 56
  hurricanes Katrina/Rita
    casinos damaged by, 57–58
    OLS model, 62
    personal income and casino revenues data, 60–61
    regression results, 63–64
    slot machine positions, 58–59
    state tax revenue, 56
    total gaming revenues in 2004, 56
Mississippi Gaming Commission, 58
Mississippi River, 57
Missouri Gaming Commission, 220
Multiplicative heteroscedasticity model, 79
Mustard, D.B., 210–211

N

National Gambling Impact Study Commission (NGISC), 114
National Highway Traffic Safety Administration (NHTSA), 98
National Longitudinal Study of Adolescent Health (Add Health), 116–120

O

Online gambling
  regulatory frameworks, 259–260
  UIGEA, 5
  Wire Act, 5

P

Pathological gambling/gamblers
  comorbid behaviors, 115
  criminal behavior, 113–114
  drunk driving, 97
  DSM-IV diagnostic criteria, 111–112
  social costs, 163
    alcohol use disorder, 180–181
    bad debts, 168–169
    bailout costs, 158, 169
    comorbidity, 179–181
    drug addict, 181
    emotional costs, 166
    legal costs, 164
    productivity losses, 173–174
    treatment costs, 166
    wealth transfers, 167–168, 172
Pecuniary externality, 160, 161
PPF. *See* Production possibilities frontier (PPF)
Problem gambling/gamblers
  ADHD, 138, 147
  alcohol use, 115
  compulsive shopping, 115
  criminal behavior, 113–114
  drug use (*see* Drug use)
  drunk driving, 96–97
  methadone patients, 116
  sexual behavior (*see* Prostitution, gambling)
  social costs
    COI approach, 184–185
    government welfare expenditures, 170
    psychic costs, 166
    treatment costs, 165
Problem Gambling Severity Index (PGSI), 120
Producer surplus (PS), 22, 23, 272–273
  deadweight loss, 190, 191
  profit, 272
  welfare loss, 191
Production possibilities frontier (PPF), 263, 264
  economic growth, casino gambling
    employment, 16–17, 26–27
    exports and demand, 16
    and non-casino industries, 27–28
    opportunity cost, 11
    productive resources, inflow of, 13
    welfare effects, 26–27
  efficient, inefficient, and unattainable production points, 264, 265
  opportunity cost, 264
  ranking consumption points, 265, 266
  technological advance, pizza industry, 264, 265
  technological and allocative efficiency, 268–269
  wealth transfer, 171, 172
  welfare loss, 189, 190
Prostitution, gambling, 90, 149
  Add Health, DSM-IV, and SOGS questions, 116–120
  linear probability model, 125
  problem gambling/gamblers, 115
  results, 133–134
  variable definitions and summary statistics, 120–124
Psychic costs, 165–167

R

Rational addiction model, 187, 188
RBA. *See* Rentable building area (RBA)
Recession, 56
Reece, W.S., 212–213
Rentable building area (RBA), 221, 222
Retail property values. *See* Detroit commercial property values
Riverboat casinos, 55, 70, 72, 214, 234, 235
Routine activities theory, 204–205

S

Seemingly unrelated regression (SUR) model, 71, 227, 244–247
Sin goods, 14
Social costs, 90, 150, 253, 254
  abused dollars, 167, 168
  alleged social costs, 155, 161–164, 175
  approaches to
    COI approach, 184–185
    economic approach, 185
    full knowledge, 186
    public health perspective, 185–186
    rational addiction model, 187, 188
  bad debts, 168–169
  bailout costs, 169–170
  collection of taxes, 158
  comorbidity, 179–181
  counterfactual scenario, 178–179
  divorce, 166, 174, 175
  economic definition of
    Kaldor–Hicks criterion, 156
    Pareto criterion, 156
    welfare economics, 155, 156
  excise taxes, 158

externalities and, 159–160
  pecuniary, 160, 161
  technological, 160, 161
fiscal externalities, 171
gambling losses, surveys on
  budgets, 182
  DSM-IV and SOGS, 181–183
  financial problems, 183
  strategies, 182
government welfare expenditures, 170–171
industry cannibalization, 173
involuntary wealth transfers, 157, 158
legal costs, 163–166
lobbying
  political contributions, casino/gambling industry, 193, 194
  rent-seeking behavior, 192, 193
money outflow, 173
of pathological gambling, 166
political costs, 194–195
productivity losses, 173–174
psychic costs, 165–167
restriction effects
  deadweight losses, 189–191
  illegal status, 191–192
  welfare loss, 189–191
theft, 158–159, 174
treatment costs, 165, 166
voluntary wealth transfers, 158
wealth transfers, 167–168, 171–173
South Oaks Gambling Screen (SOGS)
ADHD
  adolescent symptoms, effects of, 145
  combined-type, 146
  gambling indicator variables, 140, 141
  hyperactive–impulsive type, 146
  inattentive type, 146
binge drinking and drug use, 118–120
crime, 118–120
gambling losses, social costs, 181, 182
prostitution, 118–120
State tax revenues, legalized gambling, 90
brute force two stage procedure, 79
fiscal pressure, 67
fixed-effects model, 79
gambling-related revenue, 67–69
Heckman's two step approach, 79–80
interindustry relationships, 70–73
Missouri sales tax revenues, 72

multiplicative heteroscedasticity model, 79
non-gambling industries, 70
optimal taxes, 69–70
panel data analysis
  cross-border spending, 74
  demographic data, 74–75
  gambling volume variables, 74
  total state government revenue, 73
  variables and summary statistics, 76–77
random-effects model, 79
results, 81–82
  casino revenues, 82–83, 85–87
  education, 84
  federal transfers, 83
  greyhound racing, 83
  horse racing, 83
  hotel employees, 83–84
  lottery, 80, 82
  per capita income, 83, 84
  population and population density, 84
  poverty, 83
  regional dummies, 84
  voluntary taxation, 85

T
Technological externality, 160, 161
The Last Entrepreneurs, 34
Treatment costs, 165, 166
Tribal gambling, 2

U
UK horse racing industry, 22
Uniform Crime Reports (UCR), 204, 206, 208, 212
Unlawful Internet Gambling Enforcement Act (UIGEA), 5

V
Video gaming machines, 33–34
Voluntary taxation, 85

W
Wire Act, 5, 260–261
Wold's theorem, 43